FAMINE DEMOGRAPHY

The International Union for the Scientific Study of Population Problems was set up in 1928, with Dr Raymond Pearl as President. At that time the Union's main purpose was to promote international scientific co-operation to study the various aspects of population problems, through national committees and through its members themselves. In 1947 the International Union for the Scientific Study of Population (IUSSP) was reconstituted into its present form.

It expanded its activities to:
- stimulate research on population
- develop interest in demographic matters among governments, national and international organizations, scientific bodies, and the general public
- foster relations between people involved in population studies
- disseminate scientific knowledge on population.

The principal ways through which the IUSSP currently achieves its aims are:
- organization of worldwide or regional conferences
- operations of Scientific Committees under the auspices of the Council
- organization of training courses
- publication of conference proceedings and committee reports.

Demography can be defined by its field of study and its analytical methods. Accordingly, it can be regarded as the scientific study of human populations primarily with respect to their size, their structure, and their development. For reasons which are related to the history of the discipline, the demographic method is essentially inductive: progress in knowledge results from the improvement of observation, the sophistication of measurement methods, and the search for regularities and stable factors leading to the formulation of explanatory models. In conclusion, the three objectives of demographic analysis are to describe, measure, and analyse.

International Studies in Demography is the outcome of an agreement concluded by the IUSSP and the Oxford University Press. The joint series reflects the broad range of the Union's activities; it is based on the seminars organized by the Union and important international meetings in the field of population and development. The Editorial Board of the series is comprised of:

> John Cleland, UK Henri Leridon, France
> John Hobcraft, UK Richard Smith, UK
> Georges Tapinos, France

Famine Demography

Perspectives from the Past and Present

Edited by
TIM DYSON
CORMAC Ó GRÁDA

OXFORD
UNIVERSITY PRESS

Great Clarendon Street, Oxford OX2 6DP
Oxford University Press is a department of the University of Oxford.
It furthers the University's objective of excellence in research, scholarship,
and education by publishing worldwide in
Oxford New York
Auckland Bangkok Buenos Aires Cape Town Chennai
Dar es Salaam Delhi Hong Kong Istanbul Karachi Kolkata
Kuala Lumpur Madrid Melbourne Mexico City Mumbai Nairobi
São Paulo Shanghai Singapore Taipei Tokyo Toronto
with an associated company in Berlin

Oxford is a registered trade mark of Oxford University Press
in the UK and in certain other countries

Published in the United States
by Oxford University Press Inc., New York

© IUSSP, 2002

The moral rights of the authors have been asserted
Database right Oxford University Press (maker)

First published 2002

All rights reserved. No part of this publication may be reproduced,
stored in a retrieval system, or transmitted, in any form or by any means,
without the prior permission in writing of Oxford University Press,
or as expressly permitted by law, or under terms agreed with the appropriate
reprographics rights organization. Enquiries concerning reproduction
outside the scope of the above should be sent to the Rights Department,
Oxford University Press, at the address above

You must not circulate this book in any other binding or cover
and you must impose this same condition on any acquirer

British Library Cataloguing in Publication Data
Data available

Library of Congress Cataloging in Publication Data
Famine demography : perspectives from the past and present / edited by Tim Dyson and
Cormac Ó Gráda
p. cm.
Papers originally presented at a conference held at Les Treilles in May 1999.
Includes bibliographical references.
1. Famines—History—Congresses. 2. Mortality—History—Congresses. I. Dyson, Tim.
II. Ó Gráda, Cormac.
HC79.F3 F363 2002   363.8'09—dc21   2001052060
ISBN 0-19-925191-6

1 3 5 7 9 10 8 6 4 2

Typeset by Newgen Imaging Systems (P) Ltd, Chennai, India
Printed in Great Britain
on acid-free paper by
Biddles Ltd., www.biddles.co.uk

Foreword

This book has its origins in a conference held at Les Treilles in the south of France in May 1999. We are truly grateful to the Fondation des Treilles for hosting the meeting in magnificent surroundings and to Catherine Bachy and Sylvia Melkoyan of the Fondation for all their help. We thank also the Irish Department of Education and Science for arranging contributory UNESCO funding for the conference. The papers published here are revised versions of those presented at Les Treilles. All have benefited from the informal and lively conference sessions. We are particularly thankful to Markos Ezra, Jacques du Guerny, Barbara Sands, John Seaman, and Stephen Wheatcroft for their contributions. Pierre Alderson at the IUSSP was very supportive throughout, and we would also like to thank the anonymous referees involved in the reviewing process.

Tim Dyson
Cormac Ó Gráda

Contents

List of Contributors	ix
List of Figures	xi
List of Tables	xiii

1. Introduction — 1
   Tim Dyson and Cormac Ó Gráda

2. Famine Disease and Famine Mortality: Lessons from the Irish Experience, 1845–50 — 19
   Joel Mokyr and Cormac Ó Gráda

3. The Workhouses and Irish Famine Mortality — 44
   Timothy W. Guinnane and Cormac Ó Gráda

4. Famine Mortality in Nineteenth-Century Finland: Is there a Sex Bias? — 65
   Kari J. Pitkänen

5. Famine in Berar, 1896–7 and 1899–1900: Echoes and Chain Reactions — 93
   Tim Dyson

6. Famines and Epidemics: An Indian Historical Perspective — 113
   Arup Maharatna

7. Famine Yesterday and Today in Burundi — 142
   Christian Thibon

8. Famine in Nineteenth- and Twentieth-Century Russia: Mortality by Age, Cause, and Gender — 158
   Serguei Adamets

9. 'Send Us either Food or Coffins': The 1941–2 Famine on the Aegean Island of Syros — 181
   Violetta Hionidou

10. The Demographic Impact of a Mild Famine in an African City: The Case of Antananarivo, 1985–7 — 204
    Michel Garenne, Dominique Waltisperger, Pierre Cantrelle, and Osée Ralijaona

11. The Frequency of Famines as Demographic Correctives in the   218
    Japanese Past
    Osamu Saito

12. Famine and the Female Mortality Advantage   240
    Kate Macintyre

Index   261

List of Contributors

Serguei Adamets, INED, Paris, France

Pierre Cantrelle, Institut de Recherche pour le Développement, Paris, France

Tim Dyson, London School of Economics, London, UK

Michel Garenne, Centre Français sur la Population et le Développement, Paris, France

Timothy W. Guinnane, Yale University, USA

Violetta Hionidou, University of Southampton, UK

Kate Macintyre, Tulane University, USA

Arup Maharatna, Gokhale Institute of Politics and Economics, Pune, India

Joel Mokyr, Northwestern University, Evanston, USA

Cormac Ó Gráda, University College, Dublin, Ireland

Kari J. Pitkänen, University of Helsinki, Finland

Osée Ralijaona, Ministère de la Santé, Antananarivo, Madagascar

Osamu Saito, Hitosubashi University, Japan

Christian Thibon, Université de Pau et des pays de l'Adour, Burundi

Dominique Waltisperger, Ministry of Social Affairs, Paris, France

List of Figures

1.1.	A simple model of famine sequences	13
3.1.	Maps on the Irish Famine	56
4.1.	Regions hit frequently by famines in the nineteenth century	70
4.2.	The monthly number of deaths (by sex) and births in 1831–4 in regions affected by the famine of 1832–3	71
4.3.	The monthly number of deaths (by sex) and births in 1855–9 in regions affected by the famine of 1857–8	73
4.4.	The monthly number of deaths (by sex) and births in 1865–9 in Finland	75
4.5.	Proportional increases in age-specific mortality during the 1808–9 war and the famines of the 1830s, 1850s, and 1860s, by sex	78
4.6.	Differences between the actual and standard age-specific mortality rates during the 1808–9 war and the famines of the 1830s, 1850s, and 1860s, by sex	80
4.7.	Proportional and absolute increases in age-specific mortality during the famine of 1773 in Sweden, by sex	82
5.1.	The age and sex distribution of the population of Berar, 1891 and 1901	102
5.2.	Excess deaths in Berar by age and sex (reference = 1891–5)	106
5.3.	Registered monthly deaths in Berar, total and by cause, 1895–1902	108
6.1.	The price of jower and MI by month, Bombay, 1875–80. Ranges of variation: MI, 94 (October 1880) to 261 (September 1877); jower price, 26.12 (January 1875) to 8.3 seers per rupee (September 1877)	120
6.2.	The monthly distribution of deaths by cause, Bombay, 1876–8	121
6.3.	The price of jower and the MI by month, Berar, 1895–1901. Ranges of variation: MI 43.9 (August 1898) to 423.5 (July 1900); jower price, 33 (April 1899) to 7 seers per rupee (July 1897)	123
6.4.	The monthly distribution of deaths by cause, Berar, 1896–1900	124
6.5.	The price of jower and the MI by month, United Provinces, 1906–10. Range of variation: MI, 84.5 (June 1909) to 244.5 (November 1908); jower price, 19.6 (April 1907) to 7 seers per rupee (December 1907)	127
6.6.	The monthly distribution of deaths by cause, United Provinces, 1907–8	128
7.1.	Monthly movements in births/baptisms and deaths/burials (infants and adults) in five rural missions (corrected raw data)	149
7.2.	Monthly fluctuations in burials in eight rural missions, 1942–80	150
7.3.	Monthly fluctuations in births/baptisms, burials, and marriages at Bukeye mission, 1980–5	151
8.1.	Changes in Orthodox population 1800–70: Annual numbers of births, deaths, and marriages	161
8.2.	Population change in the 50 provinces of European Russia: Annual number of births, deaths, and marriages	162
8.3.	Expectation of life from birth between 1865 and 1950 in the Russian Empire and in Russia	163
8.4.	Mortality multipliers for males by age group during the famines of the nineteenth century (ratio of the death rate during the crisis to that in the benchmark years)	170

8.5.	Male mortality multipliers by age group during the famines of the twentieth century (ratio of the death rate during the crisis to that in the benchmark years)	170
8.6.	The main causes of death in 1933–4 and in 1947–8	172
8.7.	Ratio of the number of deaths in 1933 and 1947 to the respective numbers in the years following the crises (1934 and 1948)	173
8.8.	Mortality multipliers (ratios) by age groups and by sex during the famines of the nineteenth and twentieth centuries	175
8.9.	Increase in the death rate during the crisis by the importance of the link between excess male mortality and famine severity (as measured by the value of the R-square)	176
9.1.	The monthly number of deaths on Syros, 1939–45	190
9.2.	The monthly number of deaths and births on Syros, 1939–45	192
9.3.	The monthly number of deaths and a two-month moving average of conceptions on Syros, 1939–44	193
9.4.	The monthly percentage of male deaths, Syros, September 1941–November 1942	195
9.5.	The ratio of male to female deaths by age group, Syros	196
10.1.	Trends in registered deaths attributed to malnutrition, Antananarivo, 1976–95	212
10.2.	Trends in deaths from malaria, Antananarivo, 1976–95	214
11.1.	Climatic change and famines, 1441–1881: (A) famine points and (B) warmness index	227
11.2.	Population change (A), famines and epidemics (B), 1721–1846	232
12.1.	A conceptual framework of the female mortality advantage in famine	251

List of Tables

1.1.	The demographic effects of famines: Some generalizations, comments, and qualifications	10
2.1.	Comparing pre-famine census data	25
2.2.	Estimates of underreporting coefficients (λ) by province	28
2.3.	Adjustments for weighting bias	29
2.4.	Correcting for underreporting	30
2.5.	Decomposition of famine mortality contribution to excess mortality by disease, 1846–50 (%)	30
2.6.	Estimated disease-specific mortality rates per thousand (1846–50)	32
2.7.	Reported deaths by age in Mayo and Clare 1846–51 as a ratio of 1841–5	33
2.8.	Death from famine-related causes by age in the 1840s (%)	33
2.9.	Causes of excess deaths in Ireland, Russia, and India	38
3.1.	Reported deaths by age 1841–51	46
3.2.	Deaths in Ennistymon workhouse: Median lag after admission (in days)	48
3.3.	Workhouse deaths in selected counties	51
3.4.	Workhouse deaths in selected unions	52
3.5.	Causes of reported deaths inside and outside the workhouse 1841–51	53
3.6.	Accounting for the variation in death rates	58
3.7.	Including 'policy' variables	58
3.8.	The probit estimates	60
4.1.	Maternal mortality (per 1,000 deliveries) in the administrative provinces of Finland, 1865–71 (95% confidence intervals)	85
4.A1.	Age- and sex-specific death rates in the 1830s according to a 'standard' and during the famine of 1832–3 in regions affected by the famine (per 1,000 population)	89
4.A2.	Age- and sex-specific death rates in the 1850s according to a 'standard' and during the famine of 1857–8 in regions affected by the famine (per 1,000 population)	90
5.1.	Annual rainfall and vital rates, Berar, 1891–1902	97
5.2.	The marital status of the female population of Berar, 1891 and 1901	103
5.3.	Annual demographic estimates, Berar, 1891–1902	105
6.1.	Cause-specific death rates in the pre-famine (baseline) and famine years, historical famine locations	118
6.2.	Estimated values of test-statistics and the corresponding numbers of lag for variable values, historical famine locations	130
6.3.	Hospital admissions by major cause during the 1899–1900 famine, Ajmer and Merwara districts, Ajmer–Merwara Province	134
7.1.	Crises in collective memory, in oral and written sources	143
7.2.	Agricultural calendar, agrarian systems and dietary regimes in central Burundi (highland region) in the nineteenth and twentieth centuries	144
7.3.	Deaths in 1929 (child and juvenile mortality, per 1,000)	148
7.4.	Annual variations in births/baptisms, conceptions, and deaths/burials (1938–40 = 100)	149

7.5. Indices of excess mortality by mission	149
7.6. Crises and negative local shocks at the missions	152
7.7. Annual indices of excess mortality by mission	154
7.8. Calorie availability by region	155
7.9. Index of poverty by province and calorific supply by region in 1990	156
8.1. Death rates in the 50 provinces of European Russia (per 1,000)	164
8.2. USSR: Normal and excess mortality, 1918–23	164
8.3. Populations enumerated and expected, demographic losses and under-registration of deaths	167
8.4. Deaths according to the civil register (ZAGS) and hypothetical non-crisis deaths 1927–38 (in thousands)	168
9.1. Crude death and birth rate measures for Syros	190
9.2. Ratios of male to female deaths during the Greek famine of 1941–2	197
9.3. The main causes of death during the famine and their percentage contribution to overall mortality, Syros, 1941–2	198
10.1. Comparison of death rates computed from vital registration data with estimates obtained from the DHS of 1992 and 1997, Antananarivo	208
10.2. Trends in demographic estimates obtained from vital registration data, Antananarivo, 1976–95	210
10.3. Estimates of the excess number of deaths caused by the 1985–7 crisis, Antananarivo	211
10.4. Relative increase in mortality and sex ratios of deaths during the 1985–7 crisis, Antananarivo	211
10.5. Causes of death responsible for the mortality increase in the 1985–7 crisis, Antananarivo	213
10.6. Causes of death responsible for the mortality increase in 1988, Antananarivo	214
11.1. Summary of famine records for Japan for the period from the seventh to the nineteenth century	223
11.2. The proportions of famines triggered by droughts and cold summers for the period from the seventh to the nineteenth century	225
11.3. Short rainfall, cool summers, and famines: Hirosaki and Ikeda weather records, 1714–1864	229
11.4. Population change, famines, and epidemics, 1721–1885	231
11.5. Accounting for varying rates of population change in Japan, 1721–1885: Regression results	234
12.1. Famines and the female mortality advantage: A summary of the literature	243

1

Introduction

TIM DYSON AND CORMAC Ó GRÁDA

Most dictionary definitions of 'famine' equate it with food scarcity and widespread hunger. They tend to remain silent on the demographic aspects, although the extra mortality caused by famines offers one easy and obvious gauge for ranking famines. By this reckoning, for example, the Great Irish Famine of the 1840s was the greatest in nineteenth-century Europe. By the same token some of the modern famines highlighted in media accounts are 'small' by historical standards. Excess mortality, however, is only one aspect of famine demography. Famines typically reduce births and marriages too, and the migrations that they often give rise to may either increase or reduce the death toll. There are differences also between *how* modern famines kill and how historical famines did so. Modern famines differ too in *who* they kill; they tend to be more class-specific and they seem even more likely to target males than females than famines in the past. Moreover, famines often have demographic causes as well as consequences; and their consequences may be long-term as well as short-term.

The human toll of famines is often difficult to measure. Part of the problem is conceptual. Famine deaths may be hard to separate entirely from deaths from epidemic diseases such as cholera and malaria. Moreover, the dividing line between deaths resulting from food crises and deaths resulting from a background of endemic malnutrition is often hard to establish. In addition, civil registration is frequently either lacking or the system placed under great strain at the height of a crisis. For example, in the absence of civil registration, estimates of famine deaths in Ireland in the late 1840s depend upon assumptions about population growth in the years preceding it and net emigration during it. Similarly our estimates of excess mortality in the Ukraine in the early 1930s or in China during the Great Leap Forward famine are sometimes built on poor data and debatable assumptions. In more recent times estimating excess mortality from famine in sub-Saharan Africa is often little more than educated speculation and is complicated by the coincidence of warfare and civil disruption. On the other hand, the demography of some famines is extremely well documented.

The range is well represented in this book, which offers ten case studies on the demography of famines, historical and modern. Some of the studies are in effect attempts to override the defects of the available sources, while others draw on the wealth and detail of primary source material available. Three of our case studies concern Asian (India and Japan), two African (Burundi and Madagascar), and four European famines (Ireland, Finland, Greece, and Russia). Only America is missing, but this is because famines have had a small impact on the history of that continent (however, on Brazil see Davis 2001: 7). A final chapter reviews the evidence on the gender bias of famine mortality.

REVIEW OF CHAPTERS

Our review is broadly chronological. We therefore begin with two chapters which address the Great Irish Famine of the 1840s. As in most of the famines analysed in this volume, the main cause of excess mortality was not literal starvation but infectious disease. The best-known data source on the human toll of the Irish famine remains the detailed 'tables of death' constructed by William Wilde for the 1851 Irish census commissioners. Wilde's data are seductive: his cross tabulations record deaths by age, sex, cause, location, and date. However, they are also notoriously defective. In their critique of Wilde's efforts here, Joel Mokyr and Cormac Ó Gráda propose a range of corrections to them, and produce a nosological profile of the famine by province based on their revision. Two plausible nosological points emerge. First, the worse-hit a region in this famine, the higher the incidence of starvation and dysentery-diarrhoea, and the more likely were these to be proximate causes of death. Second, the proportion of famine-related deaths due to 'fever' tended to be fairly constant across Ireland's provinces, although the *incidence* of fever of course increased sharply in the worst-hit provinces. The revised data also help to distinguish between excess mortality due to hunger-induced diseases such as dysentery, and that due to diseases such as typhoid fever, which are less the product of hunger than of the social disruption that usually accompanies famine. Mokyr and Ó Gráda reckon that up to half the mortality was due to diseases of the second kind.

They then turn to a brief comparative analysis of the causes of famine mortality, emphasizing the contrast between the Irish pattern which was replicated, broadly speaking, in nineteenth- and twentieth-century India and Russia, and that found in 'modern' environments such as the Warsaw ghetto or the Netherlands during World War II. Their results prompt some reflection on the role of medical science in influencing the causes of famine deaths (compare Johansson 1999). A main reason why more recent famines differ from those further back in time is that we now understand better the role that infectious diseases play during nutritional crises. Yet despite medical advances, in the twentieth century there have been famines where infectious disease were the main killers (e.g. in Bengal in 1943–4 or in Ethiopia in the 1970s and 1980s) and in famines where they killed few (e.g. in Greece in 1942–3 and in the western Netherlands in the 'Hunger Winter' of 1944–5). In the famine conditions obtaining in the Warsaw ghetto during 1941 and 1942, where medical practitioners kept count of the causes of the mounting death toll, only 2,503 of 82,624 deaths were attributed to typhus against 18,245 to starvation (Apfelbaum 1946: 12).

The implication seems to be that where infectious diseases are endemic in non-crisis times they also bulk large when crisis strikes. In such instances, something like the connection posited by Thomas McKeown between medicine and mortality rules in reverse. McKeown (1976) famously claimed that in nineteenth-century Europe the decline in mortality preceded major progress in medical technology. However, in the twentieth-century Third World, it is the diffusion of medical techniques that has lagged: contagious diseases such as typhoid and cholera often persist despite the existence of the medical knowledge required to deal with them.

A careful analysis of epidemics during past famines can therefore help us towards a better understanding of what precisely happened in the past. It is also quite obvious that such knowledge has limited relevance to famines we may be facing today or in the future. The understanding of the epidemiology and aetiology of infectious diseases and the physiology of the symptoms, and the knowledge of how to treat patients suffering from basic ailments such as fever and diarrhoea will remain with us, even if antibiotics lose some of their effectiveness with the proliferation of drug-resistant strains. Moreover, even in the presence of severe food scarcity, the complete collapse of hygiene and personal care can usually be prevented.

About one-in-four of those who perished during the Great Irish Famine died in workhouses and workhouse hospitals. The chapter by Timothy Guinnane and Cormac Ó Gráda aims to offer a better understanding of why workhouse mortality was as high as it was, how it varied across Ireland, and how it affected different groups such as women and children. Established under the Irish Poor Law of 1838, the workhouses were funded from local taxation and managed by staff chosen by the local board of guardians. Thus their operation offers a preliminary analysis of the role of local factors or 'agency' in determining variations in mortality across Irish regions during the famine. The chapter provides examples of both the case study and the comparative approach. Individual case studies yield examples of both good and bad workhouse management. Close analysis of workhouse registers and qualitative data offers insight into crucial factors such as the quality of health care in the workhouses and the competence of the guardians. Accounts of individual workhouses focus largely on how they were managed during the crisis. However, management quality is arguably endogenous, and the relative poverty of a poor law union clearly influenced the magnitude of the task faced by any local agent. This suggests the need for a comparative approach. So Guinnane and Ó Gráda also include a cross-sectional analysis of Ireland's 130 poor law unions in order to determine which unions under- or over-performed, controlling for the economic and locational conditions that confronted them. The authors employ econometric methods and cross-sectional information on poor law unions before and during the famine to examine which unions were most badly hit by the crisis and identify, after controlling for exogenous factors, those that did unexpectedly badly or well.

Kari Pitkänen's paper on Finland addresses the issue of sex bias. During the Great Finnish Famine of the 1860s, which killed more than one hundred thousand people out of a population of 1.8 million, and also during several other periods of excess mortality in Finland in the preceding decades, Pitkänen finds little evidence for consistent sex differentials in mortality. However, there is one significant exception. In 1868, the peak year of famine in a decade of famine or near-famine, men did suffer more than women. A closer examination of the data, however, reveals that even in 1868 sex differentials in mortality increases were limited to certain regions and age categories. Pitkänen's paper rightly draws attention to the important distinction between proportional and absolute mortality increases. He notes that higher baseline (i.e. standard) levels of female adult mortality can help account for lower proportional increases in female mortality compared to male. When absolute increases in famine mortality between the sexes were compared for most of these Finnish famines, the differentials largely disappeared. However, in 1868 males still show greater absolute mortality rises. Overall, Pitkänen's evidence suggests that neither sex had an inherent biological disadvantage in resistance to the particular infectious diseases mainly responsible for the mortality increases during these calamities. Only in 1868 were men in certain age categories and in certain regions more likely to succumb than women. Pitkänen argues that this outcome was most likely linked to famine-induced temporary migration, which also tended to be age- and sex-selective. Moreover he stresses that in 1868 many undernourished Finnish men worked in miserable conditions on government relief work sites, where death rates were high. This consideration too may help account for the excess male mortality of 1868.

Moving from Finland in the 1860s to India some three decades later, Tim Dyson's chapter examines two interrelated famines which occurred in the region of Berar during the 1890s. Dyson's emphasiz is on famine as a *process* and the knock-on effects and synergistic interactions which can occur. Because Berar had good vital registration data some firm conclusions can be drawn about the demographic consequences of these famines. The sequence of events in both disasters was similar. Poor monsoon rains around June–August threatened a crop failure around November–December. The death rate during the first year of famine was unexceptional. Rather, the major death peak occurred in the second year when the population was greatly weakened by prolonged starvation, and the returning rains triggered outbreaks of diseases like malaria and dysentery. Mortality rose tortuously during the second year of famine to peak in August during the monsoon, but it then subsided rapidly, presumably chiefly because, as in normal years, health conditions improved with the passing of the rains. The main decline in the birth rate occurred in the third year of the process, and in the fourth year there was a birth rate 'rebound'. Other things equal, the second of two close famines is likely to be an even worse event, and this was certainly the case in 1899–1900 compared to 1896–7. The famine of 1899–1900 reduced Berar's population by about 5 per cent. Dyson estimates that period life expectancy in 1900 fell to only 9 years, and the registered infant mortality rate was 415 per thousand. The poorest sections of society died the most. Deaths of Hindus increased more than those of Muslims. Male mortality seems to have increased slightly more than that of females, the differential being greater for adults. Consequently the population sex ratio after the famine was more feminine. Marriages were delayed and there were major rises in widowhood. Interestingly, distress migration produced a limited, temporary urbanization in Berar; and it also caused a significantly higher registered urban death rate compared to rural areas. In absolute terms the famines killed young children and old people most, causing a change in population age structure. Interestingly there was little change in the ratio of registered stillbirths to live births. Accidents and suicides increased noticeably. Without doubt, the existence of a relatively sound database (e.g. relating to monthly rainfall and vital events) gave Berar's sanitary commissioners a better understanding of the potential for dangerous cumulative chain reactions. However, because of a lack of preparation, the sheer scale of the crises, and the generally niggardly attitude of the colonial administration towards famine relief, the 1890s was a time of interlocking, cumulative disaster in Berar.

The next chapter, by Arup Maharatna, also deals with the demographic consequences of famines in India, but from a slightly wider temporal perspective. Using time series data on prices and deaths by cause, Maharatna explores the intimate relationship between famines and outbreaks of specific diseases during several famines which occurred between the 1870s and the first decade of the twentieth century. His prime purpose is to question those previous analyses of Indian famines which have seen the associated mortality as being primarily due to the occurrence of epidemics—analyses which may therefore have seemingly implied that the famine mortality was partly independent of the conditions of acute under-nutrition and mass starvation which prevailed. Maharatna is also sceptical of the suggestion that severe under-nutrition may have had a protective effect against diseases such as malaria. The paper shows that there is a fairly clear, although somewhat lagged, correspondence between the development of famine distress (as reflected by rising food prices) and the occurrence of famine mortality. During the prime period of famine almost all major causes of death showed a rising trend, indicative of mounting under-nutrition among the population. That said, as Maharatna indicates, the precise timing of peak mortality from specific diseases was also partly shaped by climatic and environmental factors (e.g. the timing of the rains in the case of malaria, and shortages of drinking water in the case of cholera) and by patterns of migration and crowding (e.g. in relief camps) that themselves were due to the famine conditions. The data show clearly that the seasonal distribution of famine mortality fairly closely reflected the usual seasonal distribution of deaths in these populations. But, as Maharatna emphasizes, what was different in these crises was the occurrence of widespread hunger and starvation which, therefore, must be seen as ultimately responsible for the greatly elevated scale of deaths. Very much, this chapter refocuses attention squarely upon mass starvation as the principal underlying cause of famine mortality in India in the past.

The connection between prices, scarcity, and excess mortality addressed by Maharatna is a traditional one. In the cases of the famines he addresses high prices probably did reflect increased scarcity. However, this does not rule out the possibility, highlighted by Amartya Sen and others, that famines can occur without increases in food prices: a reduction in the purchasing power of some group may suffice. Moreover, high prices could reflect bubbles due to speculative hoarding or panic buying, rather than genuine supply shortfalls, but in that case too they could result in starvation and increased mortality. How markets function during famines remains an under-researched field (Ravallion 1997; Sen 1981).

In the next chapter, Christian Thibon offers an analysis of famines in the central African country of Burundi over the past century or so. The outcome, based on a combination of oral and written sources, is a complex one, in which shifting economic and epidemiological conditions played an important role. Neither conventional documentary sources nor communal memory alone reveals the full story, but a good deal can be extracted from the analysis of mission records. In demographic terms the broad outline of the history of Burundian food crises is severe famines in the late pre-colonial era, followed by severe local dearths in the 1920s, and the last major famine, referred to as 'Manori' in popular memory, in 1943–4. Thereafter there was a hiatus, brutally broken by the inter-tribal conflagration in 1972 which resulted in huge mortality (perhaps one in ten of the entire population). Since then famine-induced mortality crises have largely given way to localized but sometimes endemic hunger or malnutrition.

In the next chapter, Serguei Adamets contrasts the histories of famines in pre- and post-revolutionary Russia and the Soviet Union. He shows that from the mid-nineteenth century the geography and intensity of famine began to change, and it seemed as if Russia might be experiencing its final famines. However, the three massive crises of the early Soviet era killed far more people than any of the famines of the previous century. Adamets offers a critique of earlier estimates of excess mortality during the early 1920s and 1932–3. These estimates have been constrained by poor data, and influenced successively by Stalinist censorship and Cold War politics. Consequently he proposes his own alternative estimates, and exploits detailed Soviet civil registration data from the 1930s in order to offer new insights into the age and sex characteristics of excess mortality and the main causes of death. The analysis of causes of death allows the identification of those illnesses contributing most to the widening of the gender gap during the famine of 1932–3. Interestingly the era of famine in the Soviet Union did not cease until after the famine of 1946–7.

Focusing on events on the Greek island of Syros in the early 1940s, the chapter by Violetta Hionidou uses that island's death and birth registration records to extend our knowledge of the demographic consequences of the famines which afflicted Greece during World War II. Census data for the period no longer exist. But Hionidou's analysis constitutes a fine illustration of the value of registration records by themselves, especially if, as in this case, they are both detailed and of high quality. Because of the singularity of circumstances on Syros, this chapter's conclusions have considerable significance for our general understanding of famine demography. Recall first that this was a situation of famine in Europe during the middle of the twentieth century, a fact which should underscore that *any* population can potentially be subject to famine, especially during times of war. For practical purposes the island's population—which was overwhelmingly *urban*—was completely cut off from the outside world. Even fishing was prohibited. So neither food, nor people, could get in or out. Mortality increased very steeply fairly soon after food supplies first became short. The main period of famine deaths was between September 1941 and November 1942. Standards of public hygiene being reasonably good on Syros, there was no real problem with infectious disease. Instead, the island's doctors certified people as dying mostly from causes which directly reflected famine—such as hunger, starvation and general exhaustion. Differentials in mortality mirrored differentials in access to what little food there was. Thus deaths in rural areas increased, but less sharply than in the towns where most people had no links at all to the countryside. Again, male mortality increased most, the excess over females being greatest between ages 15 and 40. Interestingly, this excess male mortality seems to have been particularly pronounced during the early stages of the famine. Hionidou argues convincingly that the evidence is more consistent with a physiological than a cultural explanation as to why men died more. There was also a decline in fertility corresponding to the increase in mortality. Hionidou maintains that this decline directly reflected the mounting famine stress—and that it probably operated through decreasing fecundity because of increasing malnutrition, coupled with a widespread loss of libido. Finally, the events on Syros are another example of two food crises occurring in short succession; there was a less serious famine during the first half of 1944. The second crisis saw little excess mortality, but there was a significant reduction in fertility.

Finally in this review of famines in their chronological order, we come to events in Madagascar in the mid-1980s. The chapter by Michel Garenne, Dominique Waltisperger, Pierre Cantrelle and Osée Ralijaona uses vital registration data for Antananarivo, the island's capital city, to explore the effects of a quite severe food crisis which happened during 1985 and 1986. Garenne and his colleagues tell us that after achieving political independence in 1960 Madagascar's economy deteriorated, especially from around 1971. Household incomes and food consumption fell significantly, and mortality increased slowly between about 1976 and 1984. This was a period during which the country effectively isolated itself from contact with western countries. However, the re-establishment of links in the mid-1980s led to the introduction of structural adjustment policies, and from this there followed an approximate tripling of the price of rice, the staple food, between July and December of 1985, as government food subsidies were removed. This caused a crisis for the inhabitants of Antananarivo, a large fraction of whom were already living at levels of calorie intake which were around, or below, internationally recognized minimum levels. Thus whereas in 1984 average life expectation in the city was around 51 years for males and 58 for females, by 1986 these figures had fallen to 45 and 53 years respectively. Clearly excess mortality was much greater for males than for females, the sex differential being especially sharp in young adulthood. An important aspect of the Antananarivo registration data—which are of good quality and fairly complete—relates to the detailed information on cause of death. The data show that the single category of 'malnutrition' was responsible for 55 per cent of excess deaths to people aged under 15, and 34 per cent of excess deaths to people aged 15 years and over. For both age categories deaths due to 'diarrhoea and dysentery' were the second most important cause of excess mortality. And for adults there was also a sharp increase in deaths from 'other cardiovascular diseases'. The data also indicate an increase in suicide. Garenne and his colleagues conclude with the observation that recognizing the fact and nature of a crisis are essential for remedying it. However, this 'silent' famine went almost unnoticed, in contrast to a—possibly related—outbreak of malaria which hit the city in 1988 and which *did* receive wide public attention. Interestingly too, the effects of the food crisis remained hidden in the results of the 1992 Demographic and

Health Survey mainly because, due to small numbers, the survey grouped data into time periods of five years in length, so obscuring the famine.

The final two chapters in the book are somewhat different in that rather than focusing on particular crises at specific times, instead they consider famines in comparative perspective. The chapter by Osamu Saito addresses Japanese famines in long-run historical perspective—in fact, for the period stretching from the seventh to the late nineteenth century. To do this, Saito examines carefully some novel data sources and he adopts an innovative weighting approach when gauging the changing severity of famines (and epidemics). The frequency of famines during the Tokugawa period (1603–1868) was probably less than in late medieval times. And, indeed, during the Tokugawa period there was some limited further reduction in famine frequency—even though major countrywide famines still occurred during the 1780s and the 1830s. However, famines virtually disappeared in Japan from the 1840s onwards. Saito also addresses the changing causal basis of Japanese famines. In this context the period from the fifteenth to the seventeenth century saw a gradual move away from dependency on dry-field cultivation towards the cultivation of a newly introduced 'red' rice variety which needed wet-field sites. This gradual shift in growing patterns required considerable investment in agricultural infrastructure (e.g. irrigation canals), but it meant that from being a major cause of famines, 'drought' became only a minor cause. Thus, especially from the seventeenth century onwards, it was the occurrence of cool winters (which restricted crop growth) that became the major cause of famines in Japan. Finally, Saito addresses the issue of how much famines affected population growth. Here, as he notes, particularly following the work of Watkins and Menken (1985), it has become rather fashionable to discount famines as major regulators of population growth. However, the Japanese case contradicts any such new orthodoxy. Thus focusing particularly on the Tokugawa period, Saito shows that famines *were* a major factor governing the rate of population growth. And they were much more important in this respect than were epidemics. Much of this demographic regulatory effect of famines seems to have operated through the reduction of fertility, and the effect was especially pronounced simply because the usual level of marital fertility was only moderate. Indeed, it was the elimination of famines after about 1840 that laid the basis for sustained population growth in Japan.

The final chapter in the book is by Kate Macintyre. It addresses a feature which appears in nearly all of the preceding chapters—the fact that excess male famine mortality appears to have exceeded that of females. Accordingly, Macintyre's chapter has two related objectives: first to establish, and second to account for, this phenomenon. Of course, the suggestion that the mortality of males is raised by slightly more than that of females during famines is not new. However, as she remarks, sometimes social scientists have rather shied away from the indication—indeed, occasionally they have almost denied it—perhaps partly because it seems at odds with the view that in most societies it is the women who have the worse deal in life. Accordingly, Macintyre assembles data from a lot of different famines, in very diverse populations, places, and times, to establish the point beyond reasonable doubt: famines increase male mortality by more than that of females in most cases. Moreover, this happens even

Introduction

in the most patriarchal of societies. The few studies which appear to be exceptions to the rule are usually based upon questionable data. The 'female mortality advantage' tends to be greatest between roughly ages 20 and 45 years (which, of course, are also the main years of reproduction for women). Having established that this female advantage is not the outcome of faulty data, she turns to the much more difficult issue of causation. Here there is no shortage of possible explanations—both biological and social—which she proceeds to consider.

The very frequency of greater male than female famine mortality suggests to us that, ultimately, it has a *biological* foundation. This may have arisen out of evolutionary processes, which are then conditioned, and often strengthened, by a host of other considerations in different contexts. Macintyre herself notes that studies of mammals tend to show that females have a basic mortality advantage over males during times of stress, which may well reflect their more pivotal role for purposes of reproduction and species survival. Of the several possible biological mechanisms she considers, the fact that women have higher reserves of body fat is certainly an attractive explanation. Moreover, it is interesting to note that because fat is an asset which presumably reduces with time (as the body's reserves are run down) it may help to explain Hionidou's finding for Syros that the female mortality advantage reduced as the famine itself progressed. Finally, however, Macintyre emphasizes that any biological mechanisms will be overlain by a host of possible social considerations (not all of which necessarily benefit women). In this context, she mentions women's fundamental role as child-carers and home keepers, and their sometimes more harmonious relationship with nature. She notes too that today aid agencies and famine relief operations often work on the basis of 'women and children first'. And she concludes by underlining the complexity of the phenomenon and the need for future research to employ different, yet complementary approaches.

GENERAL DISCUSSION

Having provided a foretaste of what each chapter holds, we now focus on some of the broader considerations which arose from the discussions at the meeting at the Fondation des Treilles, only some of which have been touched on in the preceding review. To avoid repetition and because they have been covered by others (e.g. see Bongaarts and Cain 1982; Hugo 1984; Watkins and Menken 1985) we will not dwell too long on the most basic demographic consequences of famines. The core facts are simple: deaths tend to increase, births tend to decrease, and people tend to migrate out of the afflicted area. However, Table 1.1 offers a more detailed listing of the demographic consequences of famines, both short- and long-term, with some comments and qualifications. Of course, the statements made in Table 1.1 are generalizations. What actually happens in a crisis will depend upon the particular circumstances which prevail.

It is often claimed that famine is an ineffective remedy against population pressure because population growth tends to fill the resultant demographic vacuum. In Finland, for example, population grew much faster after the major famine of 1868

Table 1.1. *The Demographic Effects of Famines: Some Generalizations, Comments, and Qualifications*

Generalizations	Comments/qualifications
Mortality	
1. Mortality increases during times of famine	Possible exceptions: lesser food crises; and cases where conditions associated with famine (e.g. drought) lead to a reduction in certain diseases (e.g. malaria) and/or lead to the provision of adequate famine relief measures
2. Famines usually involve an amplification of the 'normal' seasonal distribution of deaths	This amplification may be complicated and overlain by famine-induced outbreaks of particular diseases (e.g. measles, typhus). However, knowledge of the normal seasonal distribution of deaths in a population is useful for helping to limit the volume of famine mortality
3. Increased under-nutrition is the principal underlying cause of famine mortality; it reflects a lack of access to food among a part (or, rarely, all) of the population	In environments with high loads of infectious disease many famine deaths will involve such diseases; however, in low infectious disease environments many famine deaths will be attributed directly to causes such as 'malnutrition' and 'starvation'
4. Especially in poor agricultural populations, famines and epidemics often interact synergistically	Famines can cause epidemics (e.g. through migration and crowding); epidemics can cause famines (e.g. by disrupting agricultural activities). So while at the individual level there may be synergistic links between malnutrition and infectious diseases, analogous interactions can also occur at the aggregate level
5. The largest number of famine deaths happen to young children; this age group and the elderly experience the greatest absolute increases in death rates	Compared to normal times these age groups are under-represented after the famine (see effect 16 below)
6. The greatest proportional increases in death rates tend to occur at ages where death rates are relatively low during normal times	In high mortality populations this means that the greatest proportional increases may occur at around ages 10–45; but in low mortality populations infants and young children may also experience significant proportional mortality increases
7. The mortality of males increases by more than that of females	Excess male mortality is especially pronounced in the prime adult years; the near-universality of this phenomenon points to its having an underlying biological basis

Table 1.1. (Continued)

Generalizations	Comments/qualifications
	(e.g. relating to differential levels of body fat). It seems that the greater the role of starvation in mortality the stronger is this effect
8. The frequency of suicide increases during famines	There are good grounds for thinking that this happens, at least during the most severe crises. It may well be that men are more likely to commit suicide than women
9. Famine mortality varies inversely with socio-economic status	Perhaps this is obvious, but it is worth stating. The rich, at least, are usually able to access sufficient food supplies. However, famines today may be more class-specific than in the past
Fertility	
10. The build-up of famine conditions causes a lagged decline (lag duration approximately 9 months) in births	The timing of the decline in conceptions usually corresponds closely to the increase in famine stress. A fertility reduction is probably an even more common feature of famines than is a mortality increase (see effect 1 above)
11. Famines induce a decline in the frequency of marriages.	This almost always happens, as marriage plans are abandoned or postponed
12. Social and psychological factors contribute to fertility decline in all famines; biological factors tend to operate only in the most severe and lengthy crises	The first two types of factors (examples, respectively, are spousal separation through sex-selective migration and a reduction in libido) work through reduced coital frequency. Anovulation due to severe malnutrition is probably the most important of the various physiological mechanisms.
13. Soon after the end of famine there is usually a short-term increase—'rebound'—in births	Due to effect 10 above, a higher-than-usual proportion of women are at risk of becoming pregnant at the end of the famine. Moreover, the various famine-induced constraints on coital frequency and fecundity cease. Equally there is a rebound in the marriage rate as normalcy returns
Migration	
14. Migration is a feature of most famines. People move in search of food/work	Migration as a famine response has probably increased during the modern era with improvements in transport and communication. Migration tends to be selective (e.g. by sex)
15. Famine migration can have either positive or negative mortality effects, for the	Migration can weaken people and spread disease. But as economies have generally

Table 1.1. *(Continued)*

Generalizations	Comments/qualifications
migrants, those they leave behind, and therefore for the total population	become more diverse, and transport and communications have improved, so migration has probably come to have a net beneficial effect on the overall level of famine mortality
Population structure and longer term effects	
16. Because of effect 5 above, other things equal, the post-famine population age structure has proportionally more people aged 10–45 than applied pre-famine	Consequently, other things equal, the crude birth rate tends to be higher and the crude death rate lower than they would otherwise be for an extended period following the end of the famine
17. Because of effect 7 above, other things equal, the post-famine population structure is more feminine than applied pre-famine	This effect too tends to contribute to a slightly higher crude birth rate over the medium run than would otherwise prevail. It is additional to effect 13 above, which is of relatively short duration
18. Together effects 16 and 17 boost the rate of natural increase over the medium-run, speeding demographic recovery	Again, this effect is other things equal
19. Famines have long-run consequences for the health of affected survivors	Several analyses support this, most notably those relating to the Dutch 'Hunger Winter' of 1944–5 (e.g. see Lumey 1998). However, for most famines the data to demonstrate such long-lasting consequences do not exist.

than before it, filling the void left by famine deaths after a few years. And in Ireland in the half century or so following the major famine of 1740–1 population grew faster than in any subsequent period. Yet one major demographic conclusion which arose from the meeting was that it is dangerous to dismiss the role of famines in helping to control population growth in times past. Of course, during the modern era demographic growth has been the norm. And with high levels of fertility prevailing, it has been common for developing country populations to be growing at two, three, or even more per cent each year. In these circumstances the loss of quite a large fraction of the total population can be 'made up' in a short period of time. Simple arithmetic tells us that even a population growing at one per cent each year will recover a ten per cent loss in just under ten years. However, in historical conditions moderate, rather than high fertility seems often to have been the norm and populations grew slowly, if at all. And in these circumstances—particularly if there were interactions with epidemic diseases—famines could have significant effects in limiting demographic growth. Thus here Saito shows that, even without much interaction with disease (related to its geographical and social isolation) Tokugawa Japan was probably a case where famines did play a significant role in restricting demographic growth. Even a single great crisis can have very long-lasting effects. For example, the likelihood that the population of England's south, south-east, and east midlands was less on the eve of the Black Death in 1348 than in 1300 is probably due to its failure to recover from the prolonged agrarian crisis of the second decade of the fourteenth century (Hallam 1988: 1004–5). And in Ireland the mass migration that followed in the wake of the potato failures of the 1840s created its own dynamic. The sharp rise in the stock of Irish people abroad, highly concentrated in urban ghettos, produced a 'friends and neighbours' effect that accounted for part of the post-famine outflow (Ó Gráda and O'Rourke 1997). Moreover, by reducing the size of the domestic market, emigration must have also reduced the scope for specialization somewhat, and thereby reduced the population further in the long run (Whelan 1999).

The contents of this book also illustrate that food crises often come in pairs—so-called 'bang-bang' famines. Having been weakened by one food crisis a population will be more susceptible to another, unless circumstances improve. There are several mechanisms through which an initial famine may help generate a second disaster—for example, the eating of precious seed-corn, or the generation of epidemics which in turn disrupt agricultural activities.

Perhaps inevitably, much of the discussion at the Fondation des Treilles was concerned with famine *causation*. Because they involve a series of interlocking processes, it is difficult to completely isolate discussion of the causes of famines from discussion of their effects. In this context Joel Mokyr proposed the schema shown in Fig. 1.1. In this conceptual plan natural calamities (e.g. drought, flood, frost, a cold summer) and socio-political events (e.g. warfare, political isolation, policy-induced structural shifts, or economic disruption) constitute the two main proximate triggers of famines. And, of course, both these types of trigger can combine and interact. In turn, the triggers produce hunger and starvation *either* through a reduction in the total amount of food that is available to the population *or* through the creation of an imbalance between the effective demand and supply of food in the population. The latter

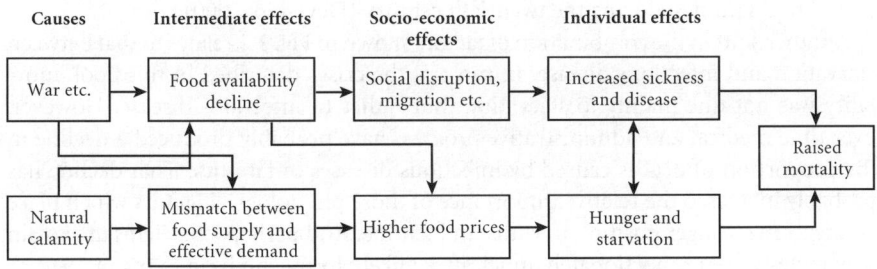

Figure 1.1. *A Simple Model of Famine Sequences*

Notes: Clearly, the above is highly simplified and incomplete. Nevertheless it is a useful way of organizing one's thoughts. Inevitably real famines involve a unique combination of sequences.

situation may arise, for example, if a large section of a poor community becomes unemployed—a case which, using Sen's (1981) terminology, would be an entitlement failure in the absence of a food availability decline (FAD).

In practice, most food crises probably involve some combination of both of the kinds of intermediate effects shown in Fig. 1.1. Food availability declines are usually implicated in famine causation (Dyson 1996: 74). In this volume FADs were involved to a greater or lesser degree in all of the famines which pre-dated the twentieth century, and in those in Burundi during the first half of the twentieth century. However, as we advance further into the twentieth century so FAD tends to play a lesser role. The famines in Russia, Greece, and Africa (as exemplified here by Burundi and Madagascar) reflect this shift.

The next component of the famine process are the economic and social effects (see Fig. 1.1). Food prices rise, people migrate, and there is social disruption. In turn, these processes generate hunger and starvation and spread disease. And again, starvation and disease will probably interact. Finally, there are the various demographic effects listed in Table 1.1, the most important of which is the rise in deaths.

Of the two proximate triggers identified in Fig. 1.1 it is certain that over time socio-political events—especially warfare—have become increasingly responsible for famines. Of course murderous famines have often been caused or exacerbated by wars in the historical past. But as the examples of much of Europe in 1740–1, Ireland in the 1840s or India in the 1870s and 1890s show, in the past peace was no insurance against the Third Horseman. Malthus, of course, envisaged famine as nature's 'ultimate response' to population outstripping food supply. However, in the twentieth century famines have owed much more to Mars than to Malthus. Socio-political considerations—like Stalinist ideology, ethnic divisions, and post-colonial strife—have mattered more than the sheer incapacity of nature to deliver food. The case for a 'Whig' interpretation of famine decline—whereby gradual economic betterment has gradually reduced the incidence and severity of famines—may fit countries such as pre-industrial England and Scotland. And in the late colonial era in Africa a combination of 'effective government, wider markets, and some increase in average wealth' has also brought a significant reduction in famines (Iliffe 1987). Yet as an account of global trends such an optimistic interpretation is much weakened by the importance of 'political famines' during the twentieth century (Devereux 2000).

Another shift in the combination of factors shown in Fig. 1.1 relates to that between starvation and infectious disease. In most of the crises described in this book mortality was not due mainly to starvation, but rather to infectious disease. However, over time medical and administrative progress have probably produced a decline in the proportion of deaths caused by infectious diseases in famines. That decline has probably increased the relative importance of those physiological factors which place women in a stronger position to withstand famine. And perhaps this helps to explain why males were proportionately much more likely to succumb on Syros in 1942 or Antananarivo in 1985–6 than in, say, Ireland or India during the nineteenth century.

A related point is that although, as Table 1.1 conveys, famines have always disproportionately targeted the poor, in the past they also killed many people who were not poor but could *not* protect themselves against infectious disease. Indeed, in the past medical practitioners, clergymen and people engaged in relief work could be particularly at risk of death. And city dwellers too were put in jeopardy by the unwelcome arrival of famished peasants seeking relief and charity. However, the studies assembled here imply that medical progress may have made famine mortality more class-specific. Developments such as penicillin, electrolytes, and antibiotics have meant that richer people at risk of succumbing to famine fevers in the past can now take preventive or curative action. Thus whereas in the past the poor could count, to some extent at least, on the enlightened self-interest of the better-off to help relieve the worst of famine, either by relieving beggars or isolating suspected carriers of disease, today the motives for such action can be weaker. Moreover, for the poor the remedies just mentioned may be available in theory, but the purchasing power to make them effective is usually lacking. Describing conditions in Ethiopia in the mid-1980s an American doctor noted the 'expensive, modern materials' destined for the army, while 'we still lack cheap vitamin pills and other medicines to cure children with illnesses from the Middle Ages' (Heiden 1992: 168).

And what of famine in the future? In considering this issue it is hard not to remark that the very meaning of the word 'famine' seems to have changed somewhat during recent years—no doubt partly reflecting changes in the 'real world'. Famine in the classical sense of widespread hunger and starvation, steeply rising mortality and, perhaps above all, social breakdown, is a relatively rare event today. Perhaps the last such episode—of famine in an almost biblical sense—occurred in Ethiopia during 1984–5. However, while still dreadful, the famines which have appeared on our television screens more recently, often from Sahelian Africa, are different, more restricted events. At least in some respects, the world has become a different place. To reiterate, the causes of most recent famines are usually much more attributable to 'man' (and unfortunately the gender of this word is all too appropriate) than to natural calamities. Warfare is usually the main contextual event, although natural events like drought may still play a role. Moreover nowadays economies are generally more diversified and there are greater chances for migration. To repeat, our knowledge of disease transmission and containment is much greater than in the past, so famine mortality tends to be restricted. International consciousness, at least potentially, is there. Supplies of food can be moved relatively swiftly, and a lot can be achieved even with small amounts of food aid. The result of these developments is that one authority has gone so far as to say that the chances of someone dying from famine in sub-Saharan Africa today have become 'vanishingly small' (Seaman 1993: 31).

But while famines in this new, more restricted sense may continue to prevail—although hopefully on a declining trend—it would be foolish to completely rule out the chances of another massive disaster—a famine of widespread starvation, a colossal number of deaths and general social disintegration. Indeed, if we adopt a sufficiently long time period into the future, then we can be fairly certain that a famine of this type *will* occur. Thus in a global economic system based on comparative advantage a calamitous famine might happen if for some reason a population became cut-off from the rest of the world. The recent events in North Korea, for example, should remind us of this. It is also possible to imagine the violent break-up of a very large country in which the circumstances and sheer scale of events means that adequate supplies of food and other assistance cannot be provided from outside. There are a few major nations in Asia to which, just conceivably, this could happen. No one really foresaw the break up of the former Soviet Union. In that instance the risk of a food crisis was reduced by the provision of food aid from the West. Environmental changes may also assume an increasing role in causing famines in the future. Thus a major sudden change in the global climate would probably produce serious FADs, with particularly grave consequences for poor countries (on the past role of climatic shifts in late nineteenth-century famines see Davis 2001).

Several other considerations might complicate responses to future famines. For example, much of the world is urbanizing, fast. Although the Soviet famines studied by Adamets give us some experience of famines in urban areas, the Soviet cities afflicted in the 1920s and 1930s were small compared to the massive and still growing urban agglomerations which are found in much of Asia and Africa today. Recall too that urban populations may have very weak links with their surrounding rural areas which, in any case, in the modern world may not supply the food that they eat. Indeed, almost everywhere nowadays urban dwellers tend to have scant knowledge of how their food is produced, where it comes from, and how it is supplied. That said, major centres also tend to command the financial and political means required to alleviate the consequences of food shortage. Yet another factor which could conceivably complicate the response to a really calamitous famine in the future is the run-down of cereal stocks by the main exporting nations, based partly on the hope—alas, not always fulfilled—that this will induce cereal importing nations to build up their own supplies.

Other crucial complicating factors are denial and complacency. The rapid recent spread of HIV/AIDS in many countries is a powerful reminder of just how much harm both these factors can do. But, of course, they also operate apropos conditions of famine. Clearly, if the build-up to a food crisis is avoided or suppressed by the government, then a famine is both more likely to occur and more likely to be large in scale. Any kind of response to famine depends upon some initial recognition that a crisis is happening. Yet the instances are legion where those in power deny that a famine is occurring. Indeed, several famines dealt with in this book suffered from this element. In this context, Drèze and Sen (1989; see also Sen 1999) have argued convincingly that famine denial is more likely to occur in the absence of an independent press. That said, even where the press has some independence, politicians and administrators are still likely to find open recognition of famine embarrassing and difficult. So in the future, as in the past, denial of famine will probably operate. And to the extent that famines increasingly have largely 'human' causes, the problem may become even more acute. Politicians find it is easier to blame a food crisis on a natural calamity than to assume some responsibility themselves. It is also an unpalatable but undeniable fact that the arrival of food aid from outside can sometimes sustain the autocrats whose actions were largely responsible for the famine in the first place (de Waal 1992).

Complacency relating to policies, is a more subtle, but related factor which may also contribute to the genesis of some future famines, both large and small. The instigation of inappropriate economic policies has been a major contributory cause to many famines in the past. And a word of caution for the contemporary world is perhaps appropriate here. For example, currently we inhabit an international system in which policies of trade liberalization and open markets hold tremendous sway. This is the way the world is moving, often with benefit. However, as the hidden famine in Antananarivo illustrates well, policies can sometimes be introduced from outside without proper consideration to their possible side-effects. Neo-liberal economic policies can ignore important institutional considerations. What the 'best' set of policies is for a particular location may not always be the same. More generally we echo the words of Nathan Keyfitz (1991: 15) that '[i]f we have one point of empirically backed knowledge it is that bad policies are widespread and persistent. Social science has to take account of them.' For sure, bad policies will contribute to famines in the future.

References

Apfelbaum, E. (ed) (1946), *Maladie de Famine: Recherches Cliniques sur la Famine Executées dans le Ghetto de Varsovie en 1942*, Warsaw: American Joint Distribution Committee.

Bongaarts, J., and Cain, M. (1982), 'Demographic Responses to Famine,' in K. Cahill (ed.), *Famine*, New York: Orbis Books.

Davis, S. (2001), *Late Victorian Holocausts: El Niño Famines and the Making of the Third World*, London: Verso.

Devereux, S. (2000), 'Famine in the Twentieth Century', IDS Working Paper 105, Sussex: Institute of Development Studies.

de Waal, A. (1991), *Evil Days: Thirty Years of War and Famine in Ethiopia*, New York: Human Rights Watch.

Drèze, J., and Sen, A. (1989), *Hunger and Public Action*, Oxford: Clarendon Press.

Dyson, T. (1996), *Population and Food*, London: Routledge.

Hallam, H. E. (1988), 'Rural England and Wales, 1042–1350', in H. E. Hallam (ed.), *The Agrarian History of England and Wales, Volume II, 1042–1350*, Cambridge: Cambridge University Press, 966–1008.

Heiden, D. (1992), *Dust to Dust: A Doctor's View of Famine in Africa*, Philadelphia: Temple University Press.

Hugo, G. (1984), 'The Demographic Impact of Famine: A Review,' in B. Currey and G. Hugo (eds.), *Famine as a Geographical Phenomenon*, Dordrecht: D. Reidel.

Iliffe, J. (1987), *The African Poor*, Cambridge: Cambridge University Press.

Johansson, S. Ryan (1999), 'Death and Doctors: Medicine and Elite Mortality in Britain from 1500 to 1800', Cambridge Group for the History of Population and Social Structure, Working Paper No. 7.

Keyfitz, N. (1991), 'Population and Development within the Ecosphere: One View of the Literature,' *Population Index*, 57(1): 5–22.

Lumey, L. H. (1998), 'Reproductive Outcomes in Women Prenatally Exposed to Undernutrition: A Review of Findings from the Dutch Famine Birth Cohort', *Proceedings of the Nutrition Society*, 57: 129–35.

McKeown, T. (1976), *The Modern Rise of Population*, London: Edward Arnold.

Ó Gráda, C. (2001), 'Markets and Famines: Evidence from Nineteenth-Century Finland', *Economic Development and Cultural Change*, 49(3): 575–90.

—— and O'Rourke, K. H. (1997), 'Mass Migration as Disaster Relief: Lessons from the Great Irish Famine', *European Review of Economic History*, 1(1): 3–25.

Ravallion, M. (1997), 'Famines and Economics', *Journal of Economic Literature*, 35(3): 1205–42.

Seaman, J. (1993), 'Famine mortality in Africa,' in J. Swift (ed.), 'New Approaches to Famine', *Institute of Development Studies Bulletin*, 24(4): 27–31.

Sen, A. (1981), *Poverty and Famines, An Essay on Entitlement and Deprivation*, Oxford: Clarendon Press.

—— (1999), *Development as Freedom*, Oxford: Oxford University Press.

Watkins, S. C. and Menken, J. (1985), 'Famines in Historical Perspective,' *Population and Development Review*, 11(4): 647–75.

Whelan, K. (1999), 'Economic Geography and the Long-run Effects of the Great Famine,' *Economic and Social Review*, 30(1): 1–20.

2

Famine Disease and Famine Mortality: Lessons from the Irish Experience, 1845–50

JOEL MOKYR AND CORMAC Ó GRÁDA

INTRODUCTION

It is commonplace to observe that one of the greatest changes of the modern age is not only that life expectancy is much longer than a century or two ago, but that there has been a radical change in the causes of death. Even in the nineteenth century, infectious disease was by far the biggest cause of death. In our own age, though these diseases have not quite disappeared and some even threaten to make a comeback, they have clearly been relegated to a secondary role in all but the poorest countries. This paper argues that this observation is central to an understanding of the nature of past famines, and of why they may differ significantly from modern famines.

There is some disagreement among scholars about what actually constitutes a 'famine'. Definitions range from 'the semi-starvation of many people' to 'extreme and general shortage of food causing distress and death from starvation among the population'. Whether famines are mostly caused by actual shortages of food or by adverse distributional shifts in what Amartya Sen has called 'entitlements' is also a controversial issue. In a series of very influential publications since the late 1970s Sen has suggested that famines are not so much crises in the *total* availability of food as in its distribution. A third dispute, prompted by the context of recent famines in sub-Saharan Africa, concerns whether violence and corruption are as much to blame for famines as the forces of nature (Aykroyd 1974; de Waal 1989; Sen 1981).

These disputes hold few resonances for the Great Irish Famine of the late 1840s. The Irish famine was not caused by war but by a series of catastrophic crop failures. Its impact was very uneven across regions and classes, but the virtual destruction of the people's main subsistence crop, the potato, for a number of successive years dominated 'entitlement' considerations. This, then, was a real famine in the old-fashioned sense of the word and not a case in which, following Alex de Waal's (1989: 25–8) distinction, a 'scarcity' was being confounded with a 'famine'. The Irish famine was a disaster with strong 'Malthusian' features: a catastrophic reduction of the food supply led to major demographic readjustment. In earlier times, famines had been commonplace in Europe, but historical demographers now agree that most of them produced only temporary population adjustments. Past famines were normally followed by a period of rapid population growth which in a fairly short time restored population levels to where they had been. Not so in Ireland.

What did people *really* die of during past famines? The short answer to this question is that they died mainly of infectious diseases. These diseases, however, came in various kinds, at different times, and with differing levels of intensity. The nosological analysis during a famine turns out to be a difficult question, raising the usual philosophical difficulties of causation. Hunger and infectious disease interact in complicated ways, some of which operated through the human body and some through the fabric of human society. In examining such issues in the context of the Irish Famine of 1846–51, we must note at the outset that this famine was in many ways *sui generis*, and that lessons learned from it may not apply to other cases in Europe or elsewhere. Furthermore, because mid-nineteenth century medical terminology and concepts differ so much from today's, contemporary evidence, both statistical and qualitative, is often difficult to interpret.

Two broad classes of causes were responsible for augmented mortality during famines. The first is directly nutrition-related, including actual starvation. More often, the Irish became victims of food poisoning due to the consumption of inferior foods that would have been discarded in normal times or nutritionally sensitive diseases brought on by impaired immunity. Either way, however, these deaths can be attributed directly to the food scarcity. The other is indirect: death was caused by the disruption of personal life and the normal operation of society resulting from famine but was not the *immediate* result of a decline in nutritional status in the strict sense. These classes overlap to some extent, but can still be kept apart.

Pure starvation was relatively uncommon during the famine years. To what extent the doctors of the time meant something similar to the modern concept of starvation remains to be seen.[1] It seems likely, however, that three or four concepts in the medical literature of the day correspond roughly to what would be regarded today as pure starvation. First, there is actually a category called 'starvation'.[2] The second category is what is known today as 'oedema' or in the language of the time, 'dropsy', a swelling due to fluid accumulation often accompanying acute starvation. A third, 'marasmus', is a general term describing the death from some form of food inadequacy of infants and small children.

Yet these premodern terms also pertain to syndromes that are not famine related. For instance, the 1841 census records only seventeen deaths from starvation for the entire year of 1840, out of a total reported deaths numbering over 140,000 for that year. In 1847 slightly over 6,000 people were reported to have died of starvation, out of nearly one quarter of a million reported deaths for that year. On the other

---

[1] An individual starves to death clinically only as a result of the attrition of protein and fatty deposits in the body causing gradual systemic atrophy, especially of the heart muscle.

[2] In his introduction to the Tables of Death (on which more below), William Wilde (BPP 1856a: 518) defined 'starvation' as 'Want, Destitution, Cold and Exposure, Neglect, Want of Necessities of Life, in Irish *Gorta*'. He also suspected that some of those reported to have died of 'infirmity, debility and old age' belonged to the same category.

hand, in 1840 dropsy and marasmus accounted for over 3,000 and over 9,000 deaths, respectively, although that year was famine-free.

Most of the other diseases that killed people during the famine were, as noted, infectious diseases. Some were opportunistic diseases that took advantage of the fall in nutritional status and the general environmental deterioration. Specialists distinguish between *individual* immunosuppression and *social* or *collective* immunosuppression (Dirks 1993: 157–63). Individual immunity declines as the body is deprived of food, especially proteins. It should be pointed out that recent research has questioned the widely held assumption that malnutrition *inevitably* leads to increased susceptibility to infection.[3] During major famines, however, there is a threshold effect whereby a switch occurs from a regime of subnutrition or even malnutrition to one of acute deprivation, in which the immune system is severely impaired. Even then, however, the effect is uneven. Some diseases are highly sensitive to food intake, others seem to operate entirely independent of nutritional status, and still others are in-between. In Ireland the potato blight reduced the *quality* of the food as well as its quantity. One consequence, unsuspected by contemporaries, was that the intake of Vitamin C, now recognized as an essential element in human resistance to disease, fell precipitously. Irish diets had always been rich in Vitamin C thanks to the potato; as diets changed after the blight, scurvy made an unexpected appearance in Ireland (Crawford 1988). Few people were reported to have died of scurvy, but the accompanying weakening of immune systems must have contributed to the onset and increased fatality of other diseases.

Community resistance to disease declined for very different reasons: as famines worsened, social structures such as formal and informal support networks and medical care broke down. Moreover, the decline in human energy output reduced the productivity of labour throughout the economy, leading to positive feedback effects that reinforced the initial shock. In addition, as Fogel and Sen have pointed out, a decline in total food supply was usually accompanied by a change in its distribution, normally to the disadvantage of the poor, people at the extremes of the age distribution, the less healthy, and possibly women (Drèze and Sen 1989; Fogel 1991; Maharatna 1996: 9–10, 174).

As resistance to disease declined, famine conditions greatly increased the 'insults' inflicted on the body. It is well understood today that such events produce an additional feedback effect: as disease reduces the body's ability to absorb certain foods, it creates anorexia, while by simultaneously increasing the demand for certain nutrients, it creates synergistic effects (Carmichael 1983; Taylor 1983). These include:

- *Digestive diseases due to decline in food quality*. As food supply declines in quantity, desperate people slid down the quality ladder, falling back on items that would normally not be eaten: seaweeds, diseased and spoiled foods, and wild plants. There is evidence that famished people in Ireland ate decomposing carrion as well as nettles, carrageen moss, and corn-weed. Such substances can mercilessly attack

---

[3] For some discussion and references, see Carmichael (1983).

the digestive system and cause a variety of diseases which could become fatal in conjunction with the weakened immune systems (Geary 2000; MacArthur 1956).

- *Digestive diseases due to changes in food composition and unfamiliar emergency foods.* This was particularly important in a potato-eating country such as Ireland in which what foods could be imported from overseas, especially the notorious 'Indian corn', were mostly unfamiliar and hard to prepare in those areas where the dependence on potatoes had been the most complete and the famine most acute. Contemporary reports described the diseases suffered by people from consuming unfamiliar and improperly prepared foods from Indian meal.
- *Infectious diseases due to population moving around.* Famine conditions frequently led panic-stricken people to quit their homes in the search for food. Mobility increases mortality for two reasons. One is that it exposes both the famine refugees and their hosts to new disease environments and microbial regimes to which they are not immune. The other is that hygienic and sanitary needs depended on certain fixed items. As people left their homes, they left behind their laundry facilities, their cooking utensils, and sanitary arrangements, however rudimentary. The result was a decline in hygienic standards. The increase of what contemporaries referred to as 'fever'—mostly typhoid, relapsing fever, and typhus—must be in large part a consequence of this phenomenon. Indeed, the many vagrants and famine refugees on the roads produced a new term for these diseases, 'road fever'.[4]
- *Infectious diseases due to hygiene deterioration as people become weak and despondent.* The impact of serious malnourishment is not immediate death and not even necessarily disease, but a decline in physical energy output. The first consequence of a decline in food intake may not have been a further decline in work effort and physical agricultural product (although that would follow eventually), but reduced energy spent on many of the standard household tasks such as laundry, the hauling of water, and cleaning. Fuel supplies, coming mostly from Irish peat bogs, declined as people could not muster the energy for the hard work involved. Personal care, childcare, and food preparation were neglected when energy levels declined. The purely physical effects of energy imbalances were reinforced here by the psychological effects of starvation such as indifference and lethargy. The impact of reduced food intake on the effort devoted to these activities contributed to the spread of so-called 'dirt diseases' (Aykroyd 1974: 13).
- *Outbreaks of seemingly unrelated epidemics such as cholera, influenza and other diseases.* Identifying to what extent these diseases are a coincidence is always a problem. The case for opportunistic disease is strong enough, but occurrences of these epidemics in the absence of food scarcity are frequent enough to allow for some coincidence.[5]

---

[4] In this regard Ireland's good roads may have been a double-edged sword: although they made it possible to rush relief food supplies to starved regions, they facilitated the creation of disease-spreading flows of famine refugees.

[5] The connection between cholera and the famine is still rather murky. Cholera outbreak took place throughout the British Isles in 1849, and so clearly were not dependent on famine conditions. There is a case for regarding cholera and famine as independent. Yet cholera rates increased sharply and accounted

THE IRISH NOSOLOGIES: A CRITIQUE

To the uninitiated, the extensive and detailed mortality tables appended to the 1851 census of Ireland (BPP 1856b) may seem like an almost inexhaustible source on the causes of death during the Great Irish Famine. Although slightly less detailed in some respects than analogous tables in the unusually rich and accurate 1841 census, the 686-page volume of tables is probably unparalleled in the range of data included. Mortality-by-cause data are cross-tabulated county by county, year by year, disease by disease, and gender by gender. A distinction is made between rural and 'civic' areas, and there are separate entries for deaths in workhouses and hospitals. The nosology is the work of William Wilde, who modelled it closely on the tables of mortality he had created for the 1841 census. It represents the best that mid-nineteenth century medical science had to offer, and while some of the diseases do not quite correspond to something a modern coroner would recognize, much of it seems to make sense.

Unfortunately, specialists have long known that the mid-nineteenth century Irish death tables leave a lot to be desired in terms of accuracy.[6] Some quick calculations and comparisons confirm the serious doubts about these tables. Indeed it is easy to become so despondent about them that the best course of action would seem to be to abandon them as misleading and useless as a source of information about the Great Famine. The main reservations historians have about these tables are as follows:

- The *total* numbers are clearly serious underenumerations because most of the numbers were collected retrospectively from surviving kin. During the famine, entire families disappeared through death, migration, or a combination of the two. Hundreds of thousands of people must therefore have expired between 1841 and 1851 with no surviving household member around to report their deaths to the census enumerators in 1851. Furthermore, given the catastrophic events after 1845, it is likely that many deaths were simply forgotten by surviving relatives. There is good reason to believe that the degree of underenumeration differed a great deal between the pre-famine years (1842–4) and the following years. To complicate matters, the totals probably included some deaths reported by families and deaths in workhouses and hospitals, so that underenumeration could have been offset to some extent by double-counting and in a few cases over reporting cannot be ruled out, although this is the exception.[7] An added complication here is that the coverage of deaths

for between 7 and 16 per cent of excess mortality during the great Indian famines of the late nineteenth century and almost 24 per cent in the Bengal Famine of 1943 (Maharatna 1996: 47–8, 154).

[6] This was stressed by William MacArthur (1956: 308–12). Not least of the surprises in Wilde's 1851 tables are the seventeen women aged 55 years and above (plus another 114 aged 50–54 years) reported to have died in childbed between 1841 and 1851, and the two youngsters of 5–9 years (plus another fourteen aged 10–14 years) who had fallen victim to 'intemperance'.

[7] The instructions given to enumerators stipulated (BPP 1856c: cxxix) that 'the enumerators will observe the period over which the inquiry extends, in order to enter with accuracy the various persons who have died since 6 June 1841, but who would, if now alive, be reckoned among the members of the existing families as relatives, lodgers, or servants, &c.' Since the form (p. cviii) stipulated that those 'who died while residing with the family' be included, institutional deaths should not have been included. It would be surprising if none were, but we don't deem this a major problem.

in workhouses, hospitals, and prisons, which accounted for about one-quarter of all recorded deaths, is likely to be quite reliable. Most such deaths were recorded in such institutions as they happened, and these records formed the basis of the summary data reported by the relevant authorities to Wilde in 1851.

To see the extent of underreporting, note that the 1841 census reported total Irish population at 8.2 million and the 1851 census at 6.6 million. Total famine mortality can be estimated by first projecting Irish population from 1841 to the eve of the famine in 1846. We then add the births that occurred in the famine years 1846–50 (adjusted for a famine-induced decline in fertility) and subtract out estimated out-migration during the famine years. This yields a total of 1.9 million people dying in Ireland in those five years.[8] The 1851 census tables report a total of 985,000 people dying. For the country as a whole, thus the reporting factor is about 52 per cent. This factor, moreover, varied substantially from county to county. The implications of underreporting are serious for a nosological analysis: if there was a correlation between the probability of having survivors and the nature of the disease to which an individual succumbed, the distribution of diseases in the 1851 mortality tables was subject to a negative bias, that is, the diseases that increased the most would be systematically underreported.

- At least some of the disease categories seem to be of a rather fuzzy nature. The 1851 census distinguishes between diarrhoea and dysentery, although it would have been difficult at the time to distinguish between the modern disease of *Shigellosis* and other acute forms of diarrhoea. Indeed, the 1841 census does not make the distinction. In the 1851 census, the ratio of reported deaths from dysentery to deaths from diarrhoea is 5.77 in Leitrim and only 2.07 in adjacent Sligo. The largest single cause of death reported in the census is 'fever', responsible for 222,000 (over 16 per cent of all reported deaths), the bulk of them occurring between 1846 and 1850. The famine years thus reveal an enormous increase in mortality rates from causes which we would consider to be *symptoms* although at the time they were considered *diseases*.
- It seems that some respondents in 1851 projected some of their famine memories back to pre-famine days, reporting famine-related diseases as if they had occurred before 1845. This can easily be inferred from a comparison of the tables for 1842 (reported in the 1851 census) and those for 1840, the last complete year reported in the 1841 census (Table 2.1). There is no reason why the figures for these two years should differ much, as underlying conditions were similar. The same phenomenon is illustrated by the report of cholera deaths; although cholera only reached Ireland in December 1848, the census reported a total of 1,376 cholera deaths in the years 1841–7 (plus a further 2,502 in 1848).[9] This projection biases the disease distribution for the years immediately preceding the famine, in that

---

[8] Given that the death rate in a typical year in Ireland before the famine was about 24 per thousand, this implies that *excess* mortality during the famine (not including averted births) came to about 1.1 million. See Mokyr (1980).

[9] This must be in part a reflection of faulty dating, but it is also possible that some survivors confounded the epidemic with some other disease. The 1841 census (BPP 1843: 'Tables of death', 182) similarly reports a steady stream of cholera deaths in the 1830s.

Table 2.1. *Comparing Pre-famine Census Data*

Disease	1840 (from 1841 census)		1842 (from 1851 census)	
	(Percentage)	(per 1000, adj.)	(Percentage)	(per 1000, adj.)
Smallpox	4.35	1.04	3.99	0.96
Dysentery and diarrhoea	1.04	0.25	2.67	0.64
Cholera	0.19	0.04	0.19	0.05
Fever	12.69	3.05	10.73	2.58
Others	12.36	2.97	12.97	3.12
Total epidemic diseases	30.63	7.35	30.55	7.34
Convulsions	5.00	1.20	4.97	1.19
Others	3.13	0.75	4.29	1.03
Total nervous system	8.13	1.95	9.26	2.22
Heart, circulatory organs	0.20	0.06	0.76	0.18
Consumption	11.39	2.73	14.40	3.46
Others	3.64	0.87	4.29	1.03
Total respiratory system	15.03	3.61	18.69	4.49
Dropsy	2.27	0.54	2.19	0.52
Marasmus	6.37	1.53	5.21	1.25
Others	2.80	0.67	3.16	0.76
Total digestive system	11.44	2.75	10.56	2.54
Urinary-reproductive, dermatological, locomotive organs	2.09	0.50	2.70	0.65
Infirmity, debility, old age	19.08	4.58	11.82	2.84
Others	2.82	0.68	3.22	0.77
Total uncertain causes	21.90	5.26	15.04	3.61
Starvation	0.01	0.00	0.27	0.06
Others	3.31	0.79	3.22	0.77
Total violent & sudden	3.32	0.80	3.49	0.84
Others and unspecified	7.21	1.73	8.96	2.15
Total		24.00	100.00	24.00

the diseases associated with famine are overreported, potentially biasing comparisons with actual famine years. How serious are these biases? A simple t-test of the hypothesis that the rates per 1,000 were the same in 1840 and 1842 does not support the rejection of the null of no significant differences. This finding suggests that the bias introduced in the 1851 census because of the disappearance of hundreds of thousands of people, while it biased the *total* counts, did not bias the distribution of pre-famine diseases intolerably. The difficulty with the famine years is more serious and will be addressed below.

- We can distinguish between categories of disease that were obviously and unambiguously associated with the famine and some opportunistic diseases (such as tuberculosis and measles) which occurred at increased frequencies as a result of the immunodepression caused by malnutrition. All the same, this still leaves unexplained some seemingly odd increases recorded in some diseases that hardly seem famine-related. For example, the number of people dying of 'rheumatism' and diseases of the bones and joints was reported as 484 in 1842 and 1,145 in 1849. Diseases that should hardly be affected by the famine such as diseases of the 'locomotive organs' and 'diseases of uncertain seat' (tumours, phlebitis, and 'debility and old age') still show a higher level of incidence for the famine years for three of the four provinces. The exception is Leinster, where the impact of the famine was weakest, suggesting that this abnormal increase in these diseases is somehow related to the famine.[10] As a proportion of the total number of deaths, these diseases declined, but their increased incidence remains rather puzzling.

- Another case in which survivors' memories seem to have let them down relates to the question 'in what season did the deceased die?' The census tables reveal that for some reason the autumn was discriminated against. Only 14.1 per cent of all deaths were reported to have occurred in the autumn, against the 25 per cent expected in the absence of seasonal variation. While many individual diseases were of course seasonal, different patterns between diseases should have reduced the susceptibility of the *total* to seasonality. Moreover, some afflictions in which seasonality should not have been much of a factor were also subject to the same bias.[11]
- The number of reported starvation deaths is surprisingly low. The total for the years 1845–50 is only 20,402. Though, as noted earlier, during famines the proportion of people dying of literal starvation is usually small, in Wilde's own words 'no pen has ever recorded the numbers of the forlorn and starving who perished by the wayside or in the ditches, . . . whole families lay down and died' (BPP 1856a: 243).

To take the Tables of Death of the 1851 census at face value would thus be a serious mistake. Yet to abandon them altogether as a source of information would leave us at the mercy of anecdotal tidbits equally if not more subject to biases of memory and selectivity. The value of the census lies first and foremost in its systematic organization, which allows us to detect certain regional and temporal patterns that at least provide a rough reflection of the nosological nature of the famine as it appeared to those who had survived it. Rather than argue that these data are in any sense accurate and reliable, we adopt the more conservative strategy of (a) drawing inferences and making comparisons where the biases just noted do not present a problem, and (b) pinpointing and adjusting for some of their worst shortcomings on the basis of what is known about Irish population statistics in this period. What emerges is not an accurate picture, but a historian's approximation, based on

---

[10] The Wilde report itself underlined the mystery of this by arguing that adverse weather conditions in 1847 were responsible for the rise in deaths from diseases such as rheumatism. While the people in question may have suffered from the diseases in question, their deaths are more plausibly attributed to famine-related symptoms, whether from reduced immunity due to malnutrition or an undiagnosed condition.

[11] Thus the proportions of people dying of 'cancer and fungus' and of 'burns and scalds' in the autumn were only 19 per cent and 17 per cent, respectively, of the annual total.

assumptions and simplifications. This reconstruction can, however, be used to shed some more light on the quantitative dimensions of the causes of mortality during the famine.

ADJUSTING THE TABLES OF DEATH

As noted, the 1851 census seriously undercounted the number of people dying both before and during the famine years. In principle there are two ways of dealing with the rate of underenumeration across counties. The simplest ploy is to assume a constant rate. An advantage of this method is that, combined with assumptions about population growth in the absence of a famine, it generates residually calculated independent estimates of famine-induced net emigration by county after 1845. For our present purposes, however, the assumption of constant underreporting will not do. As noted earlier, some underenumeration was due to the emigration of survivors, some to the deaths of entire families, some to the silence of surviving kin. Assuming constant underenumeration across counties implies, surely implausibly, that the impact of these was the same. The most serious problem with the nosologies is the possibility that certain diseases were underreported due to the disappearance of entire families. If the degree of underenumeration varied from disease to disease, the result might be an underestimate of deaths due to the most murderous of them. We thus attempt adjustments that yield estimates of underenumeration.

The underenumeration problem presents two types of biases in the data. Let $R_i = \lambda_i D_i$ where D_i are total actual dead in county i, R_i reported dead, and λ is the underreporting factor. To assume that the λs are the same across counties would overweight the distribution of diseases in counties that underreport the least and underweight those counties where underreporting was the worst. Since underreporting clearly was a function of the severity of the famine, this would bias the nation-wide distribution of disease toward underreporting famine-specific diseases. We call this *weighting* bias. Secondly, simply adjusting for underreporting will not produce a correct estimate of the disease distribution because that still assumes that the distribution of diseases among those not reported *within each county* was identical to the distribution of diseases among those actually reported. This seems implausible, since those who 'disappeared' from the census were likely to have been predominantly famine victims. We call this *truncation* bias.

To solve the two problems, we need county-specific estimates of λ. We could in principle follow for each county a procedure similar to the one outlined above for Ireland as a whole. That is, estimate total famine deaths by subtracting the actual population of each county in 1851 from a counterfactual population that would have been there given the population of 1846, normal births, and migration. The trouble with such a procedure is that while there are enough data to allow a reasonably good estimate of *total* net migration, the *county-by-county* distribution of migrants before 1850 is not known. We estimate that distribution on the basis of four alternative assumptions: the distribution of county shares in overseas migration in 1846–50 was the same as the reported one for 1851; the same as the average of 1851–5; the same

Table 2.2. *Estimates of Underreporting Coefficients (λ) by Province*

Assumption about emigration	Ulster	Leinster	Munster	Connacht	Ireland
Shares as in 1851	0.38	0.70	0.69	0.35	0.52
Shares as in 1851–5	0.42	0.64	0.68	0.35	0.52
Mean shares (weighted) 1821–41 and 1851	0.42	0.66	0.63	0.36	0.52
Shares as in 1821–41	0.57	0.68	0.50	0.37	0.52

as the weighted average between 1821–41 and 1851; and the same shares as pre-famine emigration.[12] In addition, we had to estimate the total population between the censuses on the eve of the famine. There are two alternative ways of doing this, and we worked with both.[13] We also adjust for internal migration, as reported in the 1851 census. The overall estimates of the λs are moderately sensitive to these assumptions and as there is no obvious way to choose among them, we present upper and lower bounds in Table 2.2.

The province-level data make sense in that the λs tend to be particularly low for the worst hit regions in Connacht, and high for the Leinster counties. We also ran simple regressions of the level of the λs on crude measures of the severity of the famine such as the proportion 'starvation' of all deaths reported. These regressions show a consistent negative relation between the λs and the *reported* incidence of starvation (though the latter itself is of course mismeasured). The nationwide-wide nosology resulting after adjustment for the weighting bias is provided in Table 2.3.

The adjustment, as might be expected, raises the proportion of famine-specific diseases like 'starvation' and dysentery and reduces the shares of more traditional causes of death such as consumption and 'infirmity'. Correcting for weighting problem by computing county-specific underreporting by itself is insufficient, however, because it assumes implicitly that the disease distribution for those whose deaths were not reported in the census was the same as for those who were reported in that county. This seems unlikely, as the majority of those missing from the census must have been those whose relatives had either died as well or emigrated.[14] If the likelihood

---

[12] The distribution 1821–41 was estimated by Cousens using cohort analysis: see Cousens 1965. The total outmigration in Ireland to North America in 1846–50 is reported to have been about 925,000 (Vaughan and Fitzpatrick 1978: 260). To that we added migration to England at about 40,000 people a year, based on the British census of 1851.

[13] The two alternatives are laid out in Mokyr (1985: 34–5, 68–9). Version I adjusts the prefamine underreporting of death rates by a single nation-wide adjustment factor and then computes net out-migration residually. The alternative (Version II) uses the Cousens procedure to estimate the county-by-county out-migration rates and computes the death rate distribution residually.

[14] This view is confirmed by simple regressions in which the various estimates of the degree of underreporting are regressed on measures of the sum of mortality and out-migration and in which the coefficients were consistently significant and negative. The values of λ is strongly and negatively correlated with total mortality, which suggests that death was a main determinant in the incidence of underreporting, but because of errors in measurement and the appearance of the estimated people dead in terms on both sides of the equation, these estimates are suspect.

Table 2.3. *Adjustments for Weighting Bias*

Total deaths reported	Unadjusted	Adj. with 1851 emig. shares	Adj. with 1851–5 emig. shares	Adj. with 1821–41 emig. shares
Dysentery	8.53	8.96	8.98	9.35
Diarrhoea	3.64	3.64	3.65	3.69
Fever	18.58	18.44	18.69	19.36
Starvation	2.02	2.31	2.35	2.46
Consumption	10.29	10.16	10.04	9.53
Dropsy	2.05	2.11	2.09	2
Marasmus	4.98	4.77	4.79	4.74
Cholera	3.64	3.21	3.29	3.56
Infirmity and old age	9.11	8.93	8.91	8.55
Total specified	62.83	62.52	62.79	63.24
Others	37.17	37.48	37.21	36.76
Total	100	100	100	100

Note: Table constructed by multiplying county-specific λs by reported deaths for each disease and re-aggregating.

of 'missing relatives' correlated with famine-specific diseases, as seems plausible, we would still end up underreporting these diseases. We, therefore, applied the following weighting schemes to the 'missing' dead: assume that the distribution of diseases among the missing dead was as reported in the county with highest death rate (Mayo), the counties with highest out-migration rates (Clare and Tipperary) or the counties with the highest overall population loss (Sligo and Roscommon). These shares are then multiplied by the estimated number of unreported deaths, and added to the reported ones. The results are provided in Table 2.4.

Table 2.4 gives us a notion of how serious the biases in the data are. Starvation and dysentery, clearly, are most sensitive and tend to be high when we apply the Mayo weights and the lowest when we apply the two Munster county weights. All the same, the margins are not so large as to deny us an approximate decomposition of excess famine mortality.

The central finding of this research is the decomposition of famine mortality into the contributions of the several diseases. A distribution by cause of the famine mortality can be carried out by comparing total mortality between 1845 and 1850 to normal mortality. As noted, the reported mortality from famine-diseases for the pre-famine years 1842–4 in the 1851 census is probably upward biased. We have therefore compared the disease-specific famine mortality rates with those of 1840, as reported in the 1841 census and adjusted for underreporting as before. The results, reported in Table 2.5, are thus based on the comparison of an Ireland with an 1840 nosological structure with the actual deaths reported in the 1851 census for the famine years. Table 2.5 decomposes total mortality into a 'normal' component that would have

Table 2.4. *Correcting for Underreporting*

	Mayo weights		Clare weights		Tipp weights		Rosc weights		Sligo weights	
	A	B	A	B	A	B	A	B	A	B
Dysentery	12.24	12.22	8.49	8.49	7.75	7.76	9.33	9.33	10.06	10.06
Diarrhoea	3.32	3.32	3.5	3.5	3.84	3.84	3.44	3.44	4.58	4.58
Fever	20.56	20.55	22.33	22.31	21.11	21.09	20.42	20.41	18.28	18.28
Starvation	4.82	4.8	2.11	2.11	1.75	1.75	3.16	3.16	2.66	2.66
Consumption	7.78	7.8	7.99	8	9.93	9.93	9.35	9.36	9.17	9.17
Dropsy	2.09	2.09	1.81	1.81	1.83	1.83	1.95	1.95	1.84	1.84
Marasmus	3.81	3.82	4.02	4.03	4.85	4.85	5	5	4.31	4.32
Cholera	3.1	3.1	4.26	4.26	3.34	3.34	2.26	2.26	3.4	3.4
Infirmity	7.1	7.11	7.17	7.18	8.88	8.88	8.54	8.55	8.44	8.44
Total specified	64.81	64.8	61.68	61.68	63.27	63.26	63.34	63.33	62.85	62.85
Others	35.19	35.2	38.32	38.32	36.73	36.74	36.66	36.67	37.15	37.15
Total	100	100	100	100	100	100	100	100	100	100

Note: Weights A use (1) the 1851 county emigration shares to compute the distribution of emigration rates and (2) Version I of the pre-famine death rates (see footnote 13). Weights B use the 1841 emigration share and Version II of pre-famine death rates.

Table 2.5. *Decomposition of Famine Mortality Contribution to Excess Mortality by Disease, 1846–50 (%)*

	Mayo weights	Clare weights	Tipperary weights
Hunger sensitive	40.82	28.90	29.05
Dys. and Diarrh.	28.24	21.55	20.79
Starvation	9.06	3.97	3.30
Dropsy	1.96	1.42	1.46
Marasmus	1.56	1.96	3.50
Partially sensitive	29.48	35.75	36.40
Consumption	4.64	5.03	8.67
Others	24.84	30.72	27.73
Not very sensitive	29.73	35.37	34.54
Fever	27.51	30.84	28.53
Cholera	5.7	7.88	6.15
Infirmity, old age	−3.48	−3.35	−0.14
Total	100	100	100

occurred in any event and a 'famine' component. To carry out this decomposition, we utilize the 1840 census to approximate what 'normal' mortality patterns would have looked like in the absence of the famine. We construct the number of people that would have died of each disease by multiplying the per thousand rates of 1840 by the mean population between 1846 and 1850. These are the numbers that would have died of each disease had the pre-famine *pattern* of diseases dominated the actual population of 1846–50. We subtract these numbers from the actual estimated death figures on various assumptions regarding underreporting. This table can be expanded to account for other diseases whose contribution to famine mortality is of interest such as smallpox and 'convulsions' and we plan to expand our research into that direction. The tentative results are presented in Table 2.5.

It is interesting to note that almost *every* disease listed by Wilde contributed something to excess mortality during the famine. The meaning of this finding seems clear: despite the problems of under- and mis-reporting, the famine's physiological impact on the population at large went beyond the direct and immediate effects of 'famine diseases'.

The link between malnutrition or famine and fever was controversial during the Irish Famine itself. Against Dublin surgeon Dominic Corrigan's mantra of 'no famine, no fever', the editor of the *Dublin Medical Press* in 1847 considered that 'it could easily be shown that famine and destitution are more frequently the effect than the cause of fever'. A recent survey of the role of epidemic disease is critical of both causations.[15] Further examination of Table 2.5 suggests that, roughly speaking, half of famine mortality was caused by diseases that were the result of bad nutrition (including diarrhoea, dysentery, respiratory infections, starvation, dropsy, and a few smaller diseases) and the other half from those resulting from the indirect effects of the famine on personal behaviour and social structure such as fever, cholera, and most of the diseases included in 'others.'

FURTHER ANALYSIS OF THE FAMINE NOSOLOGIES

The adjusted data can give us a better handle on many of the most interesting issues regarding the famine. Table 2.6 gives the estimated totals dying in Ireland's four provinces of five mainly famine-related illnesses between 1846 and 1851. These are what are described in the report as dysentery, diarrhoea, dropsy, starvation, and 'fever'. 'Fever' presumably includes deaths from typhoid, typhus and relapsing fever (MacArthur 1956: 265–8). The implication that the famine killed roughly twice as many people in proportion in Munster and in Connacht as it did in Ulster and Leinster is perhaps not too far off the mark.

Two plausible nosological points emerge. First, the graver the crisis, the higher the incidence of starvation and dysentery–diarrhoea, and the more likely were these to be the proximate cause of death.[16] Second, the proportion of famine-related deaths

---

[15] *Dublin Medical Press*, 29 November 1848; 17 March 1847; Geary (2000); Ó Gráda (1997: 137). It should be remembered that 'fever'encompassed a whole range of diseases, some of which, like typhoid were clearly famine-sensitive. Wilde pointed out that those who recovered from the immediate effects of starvation, contracted a peculiar and generally fatal form of typhus which no administration of food could avert (BPP 1856a: 734).

[16] An examination of the patterns at the more disaggregated level of the county reinforces that pattern.

Table 2.6. *Estimated Disease-specific Mortality Rates per Thousand (1846–50)*

Total death rates per 1,000, 1846–50	Ulster		Leinster		Munster		Connacht	
	Mayo weights	Clare weights	Mayo weights	Clare weights	Mayo weights	Clare weights	Mayo weights	Clare weights
Hunger sensitive	38.79	29.51	42.98	34.43	87.14	66.72	118.56	86.31
Dys. and Diarrh.	22.51	17.30	21.88	17.07	54.05	42.58	71.92	53.81
Starvation	5.98	2.02	5.57	1.92	16.03	7.32	26.89	13.12
Dropsy	4.05	3.63	4.13	3.75	6.15	5.22	8.12	6.67
Marasmus	6.25	6.56	11.40	11.69	10.91	11.60	11.63	12.71
Partially sensitive	81.46	86.35	94.43	98.94	130.95	141.69	147.33	164.29
Consumption	16.76	17.07	22.02	22.3	20.32	20.99	21.96	23.01
Others	64.70	69.28	72.41	76.64	110.63	120.70	125.37	141.28
Not very sensitive	48.56	52.95	63.83	67.70	98.41	108.08	120.17	135.44
Fever	31.21	33.80	35.32	37.72	69.18	74.89	87.06	96.07
Cholera	3.01	4.71	8.00	9.57	10.90	14.63	11.43	17.33
Infirmity, old age	14.34	14.44	20.31	20.41	18.33	18.56	21.68	22.04
Total	168.82	168.81	201.06	201.06	316.50	316.49	386.05	386.04

due to 'fever' tended to be fairly constant across provinces although the *incidence* of fever of course increased sharply in the worst-hit provinces.

The figures over time as well as the breakdown by province show, as one would expect, that the incidence of these diseases roughly corresponded with the severity of the famine. The proportion and numbers of those dying of fever and digestive-tract diseases rose in 1845, accelerated in the next year, then peaked in the horror year 1847. The absolute increase in the two diseases is very sharp, of course, but whereas the incidence of dysentery and diarrhoea increased by a factor of eight to twelve, as opposed to a factor of four to five for fever, they started from a much lower basis and thus the contribution of the two diseases to increased famine mortality is comparable in absolute terms. The two measures do not move tightly together, indicating the difficulty of measuring the 'impact' of a disease. To some extent famine-related diseases must have 'crowded-out' others, that is, people who succumbed to famine-related diseases would have died of other diseases in its absence. At the same time, people who were relatively well off and did not starve, still were infected by contagious diseases contracted by their less fortunate neighbours.

Table 2.7, derived from Wilde, shows the increase in reported deaths by age between 1841–5 and 1846–51 in two of the worst-affected counties, Mayo and Clare. As far as the overall ratios are concerned, again MacArthur's warning is apposite, but it is the shifts across age that are of interest here. The implication that those most affected by the catastrophe were young children and adolescents (ages 5–19 years) is interesting—though from a comparative perspective, not so surprising. The numbers also suggest that men were most at risk relative to women in their 30s and 40s.

Table 2.8 compares the age-distributions of reported deaths from the same five causes between 1841 and 1851. The implication that those who died of diarrhoea were much more likely to have been children than those dying of dropsy or fever is perhaps less surprising than the implied high share of infants and children among those dying of starvation. Again it is interesting to note that those in the prime of life (aged 15–54 years) accounted for 53 per cent of reported fever victims, but only 35 per cent of reported dysentery victims and 28 per cent of reported starvation victims. The age-distributions of reported deaths from diarrhoea, dysentery, and starvation are similar.

Table 2.7. *Reported Deaths by Age in Mayo and Clare 1846–51 as a Ratio of 1841–5*

Age	Mayo		Clare	
	Males	Females	Males	Females
<1	2.11	3.29	2.18	2.65
1–4	3.36	3.85	3.48	3.92
5–9	5.93	5.46	6.8	6.87
10–19	7.56	7.21	7.55	7.17
20–29	4.66	4.68	4.49	4.79
30–39	5.15	3.97	5.2	4.11
40–49	5.12	4.43	5.65	4.66
50–59	4.95	4.85	5.36	4.52
60–69	4.28	5.07	5.24	4.35
70–79	3.6	4.29	3.51	3.63
80+	3.43	3.70	2.98	3.01
Total	4.12	4.48	4.46	4.50

Source: 1851 Census Tables of Death.

Table 2.8. *Death from Famine-related Causes by Age in the 1840s (%)*

Age-group	Dysentery	Diarrhoea	Fever	Starvation	Dropsy
0–4	16	25	12	29	10
5–14	25	23	19	25	14
15–24	09	06	17	08	09
25–34	06	04	11	04	08
35–44	09	07	12	07	12
45–54	11	09	13	09	15
55–64	13	12	10	12	17
65+	11	14	06	06	15
Total	100 (92,657)	100 (41,212)	100 (198,078)	100 (21,664)	100 (28,332)

Source: 1851 Census Tables of Death.

KNOWLEDGE OR INCOME?

Was one of the main reasons why the Irish Famine was so much more deadly than modern events that the actual mechanisms linking famine through infectious disease to increased mortality were poorly understood? The problem can be laid out starkly by noting that famine kills through poverty and ignorance. At one extreme, when people fall below some absolute subsistence level, they will die no matter how much they know about the causes of disease. At the other, even well-fed individuals are at risk during famine if they do not understand that they are at increased risk of infection and how to avoid contagion. In between, there is a more complex area in which people are aware to some extent of the modes of infection but do not get it quite right, or are too poor or too weak to avoid them. In poor countries, even today, water quality, overcrowding, and the prohibitive cost of medical cures account for the continued incidence of infectious diseases, and their heightened role in time of famine. Extreme poverty is responsible for children catching deadly diseases even when their parents are familiar with the modes of transmission simply because they cannot afford the minimal needs for prevention.[17] Of course we are not arguing that a complete understanding of the nutritional impact of each good is feasible even today, let alone in 1846. All the same, better knowledge might have at least mitigated some of the worst effects of the famine.

It bears repeating that most victims of past famines, including the Irish Famine, were not killed directly by hunger and exposure but by micro-organisms. Neither the victims, nor the authorities, nor medical people understood this basic fact until the 1880s. Their ignorance of the exact nature of what it was that was killing most famine victims is a crucial element in determining the demographic impact of past famines. It certainly is true that even without the full knowledge of what causes disease, certain measures could have been taken that would have averted the worst. To be sure, even with such knowledge high peaks of mortality can occur. All the same, especially during a period of crisis, even a rudimentary understanding of the mechanisms of infection can be of the greatest importance in preventing or limiting massive mortality crises. Such understanding was sadly missing in the 1840s. Even as learned a physician as William Wilde did not really understand the basics of how to treat malnutrition and food poisoning, or how fever epidemics spread.[18]

---

[17] Thus in Thane, near Bombay, an Indian woman who had already lost two children through waterborne illnesses pointed out that 'to boil water consistently would cost the equivalent of US$ 4.00 in kerosene, a third of her earnings'. In Nigeria in the early 1970s (when GDP per capita was £100–£150) the cost per patient of fluids for treating diarrhoeal diseases was £4 using locally made fluids and £20 using commercial fluids. The greatest problem was getting the fluid to the patient or the patient to the fluid. See Bryceson (1977: 111); *International Herald Tribune*, 9 Jan. 1997; World Bank (1979: tables 1 and 2). On the continued importance of infectious disease, compare the excellent essays by K. David Patterson (on disease ecologies), Herbert L. DuPont (on diarrhoeal disease), and Charles W. LeBaron and David W. Taylor (on typhoid fever) in Kiple (1993: 447–53, 676–9, 1071–7).

[18] Irish doctors frankly admitted that the nature of the epidemic diseases were 'the *terra incognita* of medicine.' See Geary (2000: 319). A good example of the state of medical science is provided by Wilde's analysis of scurvy. He recognized the possible importance of the change in diet and the use of hard, dry

How much difference would better knowledge have made? The evidence provided above would suggest that more knowledge might have made a considerable difference even if it would not have prevented mass mortality. Table 2.5 suggests that at least one third of all famine mortality was caused by diseases such as fever which might have been avoided had people understood better what exactly made them ill. Both typhus and relapsing fever were transmitted by the human louse, and while avoiding lice would have become more difficult in the desperate uprooted populations gathering in poor houses, relief works, and food depots, it stands to reason that had people only known how dangerous lice were, some efforts could have been made to slow down the epidemic. This holds particularly for urban areas, as well as for deaths among the better off in the countryside. Two telling indicators of the role of 'spillover effects' from the starving rural masses to others are the excess mortality in Dublin city, and the efforts made by the authorities in Belfast to keep out famine immigrants (MacArthur 1956: 280; Ó Gráda 1999: Chapter 5). Moreover, even among those dying of dysentery and diarrhoea, death occurred through dehydration which might have been avoided in many cases had people only known basic facts such as the need to replace fluids in patients and the importance of boiling drinking water before use. Neither patients nor doctors had such knowledge.

Though the victims of the Irish Famine were predominantly poor, many who were by no means poor succumbed as well. Indeed, the Irish poor had built up some immunity to diseases such as mild typhoid fever, so that during the famine when fever struck the higher classes, it was 'universally of a much more fatal character than among the poor'.[19] At greatest risk were people such as clergymen, relief workers, and medical practitioners, whose work involved frequent contact with the diseased. In Ireland as a whole nearly two hundred doctors and medical students died in 1847, three times the pre-famine average. Catholic and Protestant clergymen also died in large numbers (Froggatt 1989: 148–50; Kerr 1996: 22–5; MacArthur 1956: 311). A better understanding of the underlying disease transmission mechanisms and the consequent need for cleaner water and greater hygiene might have saved not only non-starving middle-class victims but surely many others too.

Most of the worst afflicted regions of Ireland had very few trained doctors: in 1841 Mayo, probably the worst hit area of Ireland, counted a total of 37 physicians and 28 surgeons, or one medical practitioner for every six thousand people. This compares to, say, the town of Dublin where there was a medic for every 510 people. Yet the problem was not really one of the lack of medical personnel. More important was the low quality of medical expertise and that the people themselves did not know what made them ill nor, once they were ill, how to treat ailments that were not necessarily lethal. This was hardly specific to the remote rural areas of Connacht: years after the famine, many medical advice books still recommended a

grain instead of fresh vegetables, but then added immediately that the two peculiar causes that more than others contributed to induce scurvy were fluctuations in humidity and temperature and the 'moral depression coupled to inactivity', BPP (1856a: 513–14).

[19] *Dublin Quarterly Journal of Medical Science*, 8 (1849), 8, 16.

healthy dose of castor oil as a remedy for a child suffering from diarrhoea, without mentioning the need for rehydration. During the famine, medical people were still bleeding severely malnourished people (reportedly with 'mixed' results) and administering such medications as tartar emetic, a powerful expectorant that contributed to dehydration. The Irish misfortune was that such ignorance had to confront an unprecedented shock to the food supply system in a poor and comparatively primitive rural economy.

The belief that infectious disease 'like the ague, owes its origin to terrestrial miasms', was commonplace among medical men at the time of the Irish Famine. As noted earlier, the role played by social conditions was controversial, yet most doctors and officials realized the importance of cleanliness in the homes of the poor and of what they deemed to be pure water (Mokyr and Stein 1997). Famine, however, made hygiene and pure water more difficult to maintain and obtain. Moreover, when diseases struck, the medical profession was as powerless to cure the sick as it was to prevent the spreading of the epidemic. A contemporary account from Dublin describes treatment as follows:

> Plenty of nourishment and the free use of stimulants were found to be absolutely necessary. Wine was freely given, and with the best effects. General experience was decidedly opposed to the use of bleeding in any form. In some cases of local congestion the application of a few leeches, or the abstraction of a small quantity of blood by cupping-glasses, was found beneficial. Mercury was only given as a mild aperient or alternative, and sometimes, combined with Dover's powder, in dysentric cases it acted beneficially. Opium does not appear to have been very generally employed; 'it was only useful for allaying the vomiting of the secondary fever'. 'A combination of morphia and tartar emetic was found so valuable in cases of excitement and delirium, that it was styled a specific in the North Union sheds'.[20]

Many further examples of useless if not downright dangerous 'cures' suggested by contemporary doctors might be cited.

Medical science has advanced by leaps and bounds since the 1840s. Surely one reason why some modern famines have not resulted in mortality figures on an Irish scale is the ability of modern science to prevent or contain the worst epidemics. The decline in infectious disease consisted of two distinct stages. First, in the late nineteenth century, came the identification of pathogenic agents and their mode of transmission, and the use of this knowledge for preventive care. Then, in the 1930s and 1940s, came the emergence of antibiotics. Even the achievement of the first stage before 1846 would have saved many victims of the Irish famine.[21] For further insight into this issue we take a comparative look at the causes of death in some historical and modern famines.

---

[20] *Dublin Quarterly Journal of Medical Science* 8 (1849), 25.

[21] Bruno Latour has noted that the First World War was the 'triumph of modern hygiene. Without the bacteriologists, the generals would never have been able to hold on to millions of men in muddy, rat-infested trenches'. See Latour (1988: 112).

A COMPARATIVE LOOK

In his ghost-written introduction to one of the classics of Irish Famine historiography, historian Kevin Nowlan wrote that 'perhaps all that matters is that many, many died' (Edwards and Williams 1956: vii). Modern accounts dispute this, insisting that it does matter *how many* died, as well as *who* died and *from what cause*. Two estimates, independently derived but employing a very similar methodology, have by now firmly established the number of *excess* deaths (that is, deaths that would not have occurred in the absence of the famine) at over one million (Boyle and Ó Gráda 1986; Mokyr 1980). The actual population deficit is larger, as the famine was also responsible for emigration on a massive scale and for hundreds of thousands of averted births (children who would have been born were it not for the famine). Such numbers led Sen (1995) to declare in an unguarded aside that 'he knew of no other famine in the world in which the proportion of people killed was as large as in the Irish Famines in the 1840s'. This statement exaggerates (compare Drèze and Sen 1989: 134; Jutikkala 1955), yet it underlines the dimensions of the Irish Famine in terms of sheer demographic effect. By comparison, most of the post-colonial sub-Saharan and South-Asian famines that we see on our screens seem relatively mild. The 1.5 million or so excess deaths in Bangladesh in 1974 represented two per cent of a population of over sixty million, a loss that was made up in less than a year.[22] The widely publicized famine in the Sahel in 1973 killed perhaps 0.1 million people in an area inhabited by 25 million. The toll of the famine in Darfur, Western Sudan was slightly below 0.1 million out of a population of 27 million. Official sources indicate that the Malawi (then Nyasaland) famine of 1949–50 described by Megan Vaughan killed only a few hundred out of a population of about 2.5 million (Vaughan 1987). In the twentieth century the *truly* murderous famines tended to be man-made: the Ukrainian Famine of 1932 and Mao's 'Great Leap Forward' famine of 1959–62 killed many more people although the reference populations were also much larger. In comparative terms, a noteworthy feature of the Irish Famine is that it occurred in a country basically at peace; faction fighting and rural strife, still common in the 1820s and 1830s, had been quelled by an alliance of police and priests, and the 'rising' of 1848 lasted only a matter of hours. This tranquillity contrasts sharply with post-colonial famines in Biafra, Somalia, and Ethiopia (Drèze and Sen 1989).

If the Irish Famine dwarfed most modern famines in its relative impact, how different was its nosological profile? Comparable evidence is scarce and at first sight conflicting. Below Wilde's data, corrected and aggregated, are compared with cause-of-death data from some famines in nineteenth-century India and in Russia in the 1920s. Our reworking of Wheatcroft's data on the south Russian gubernaia of Saratov produces results uncannily similar to Wilde's (see Table 2.7). The other Russian nosologies are of poor quality, with two-fifths of the excess mortality unexplained, but they too stress the overwhelming part played by infectious diseases (Wheatcroft

---

[22] The official death toll was 26,000! Cf. Bongaarts and Cain (1982: 52); Sen (1981: 134).

Table 2.9. *Causes of Excess Deaths in Ireland, Russia, and India*

Cause of Death	Ireland, 1840s	Saratov, 1918–22	Petrograd, 1918–22	Moscow, 1918–22	Bombay, 1877	Berar, 1897	Berar, 1900	Punjab, 1900	Ut. Prad., 1908
D.D.G.[a]	24.9	19.7	10.4	16.0	9.7	30.4	37.0	3.0	−1.2
Cholera	6.8	5.1	2.0	0.7	16.5	12.1	9.6	7.6	4.6
Fever	29.2	24.1	19.3	24.6	45.9	29.0	23.9	72.2	90.9
Respiratory	4.8	9.8	19.3	20.2	n.a.	n.a.	n.a.	n.a.	n.a.
Starvation/Scurvy	10.0	5.5	12.8	n.a.	n.a.	n.a.	n.a.	n.a.	n.a.
Other, Unknown	24.3	35.8	36.2	38.5	27.9	28.5	29.5	17.2	5.7
Total	100.0	100.0	100.0	100.0	100.0	100.0	100.0	100.0	100.0

[a] Diarrhoea, Dysentery, Gastroenteritis. n.a.—not available.

Sources: Ireland: see text.
Saratov: S. Wheatcroft, 'Famine and Epidemic Crises in Russia', p. 340. The percentages are weighted averages of the annual totals for 1918–22, where the weights are Wheatcroft's estimates of annual excess mortality. Respiratory includes tuberculosis and pneumonia.
Moscow and Petrograd: Wheatcroft, 'Famines and Factors Affecting Mortality', 17–18.
India: Maharatna, *Demography of Famines*, 46–7, Table 2.6. We subtracted cause-specific death rates in baseline years from rates during famine years to get excess mortality by cause. We then calculated the percentages of the totals explained by the different causes. Maharatna's D.D.G. totals are for diarrhoea and dysentery also has data on smallpox but its contribution is small (as in Ireland).

1981a,b; 1983). The nosologies in official sources for nineteenth- and twentieth-century India are, like the Russian, far less detailed than Wilde's, though their coverage is probably better (Dyson 1991a: Table 3; 1991b: Table 7; Maharatna 1996: 18–22). In Table 2.9 the outcome is summarized and compared with our picture for Ireland in the 1840s. It indicates that most of the excess mortality during the great Indian famines of the nineteenth and twentieth centuries were also due to infection (fever, diarrhoea/dysentery, cholera, malaria), not from literal starvation. This is also true in the case of Bengal in 1943–4, where malaria was the main killer. The main difference between India in the nineteenth and twentieth centuries or between Ireland in the 1840s and Bengal almost a century later, is the smaller role of diarrhoea/dysentery in the more recent famine. Perhaps this is a sign that some of the messages of modern medicine had got through to India by the 1940s; any stronger claim is complicated by the significant role of diarrhoeal diseases in Berar in 1897–1900.[23] Unfortunately the role of literal starvation in India cannot be inferred from the tables.

In famine relief in Africa today medical supplies are deemed as important as food, and undoubtedly many lives are saved by antibiotics and rehydration. Unfortunately, cause-of-death data are very scarce. Data collected in refugee camps in Sudan in the mid-1980s make for disheartening reading; however, 17 per cent of deaths were attributed to malaria, 27 per cent to diarrhoeal disease, and another 23 per cent to respiratory disease (Mercer 1994: 34).

---

[23] Perhaps this was a product of the 'unwholesome water and food' mentioned by the local sanitary commissioner. See Maharatna (1996: 57).

A very different picture is offered by nosological evidence on a series of smaller, well-documented European famines in the 1940s. Data on the causes of death in Warsaw's Jewish ghetto before its destruction by the Nazis in July 1942 show that as the death rate there quintupled between 1940 and 1941–2, the proportion of deaths attributed to starvation rose from one per cent to one-quarter. Typhus's share remained small; however, 2.4 per cent in 1940, 4.6 per cent in 1941, and 1.7 per cent in 1942. In the towns and cities of the western Netherlands famine killed about 10,000 people during the starvation-winter of 1944–5. Here also starvation accounted for a significant share of the rise, while infectious diseases counted for relatively little. The same holds for the famine that hit parts of Greece, including the cities of Athens and Piraeus, in 1941–2. Livi-Bacci's account of famine in a part of occupied north-eastern Italy in 1918 returns a similar verdict (Burger *et al.* 1948, *passim*; Hionidou 1995; Livi-Bacci 1991: 43–6; Stein *et al.* 1975: 39–53; Winick 1994: 365–80). These famines occurred before the discoveries of Pasteur and Koch had been translated into an effective and widely available new medicine. The outcome underlines the importance of an understanding of the modes of transmission of infectious disease and of preventive measures. In these places the people at risk clearly knew the importance of keeping clean, of disinfectants, and so on. But these were relatively advanced places in economic terms, with universal literacy, a good supply of medical personnel, clean running water for drinking and washing, lots of changes of clothes, housing that was easier to keep clean (no thatch, no pigs, no mud floors), less overcrowding, and adequate cooking facilities for what little food there was.

The nosologies of the Indian and Russian famines reported above have much more in common with Wilde's than with those of famine-affected regions of Europe in the 1940s. Why? The answer must be in part that while the knowledge may have existed, behavioural patterns and consumption were subject to a great deal of inertia. It is not enough for people in some sense to 'know' what causes disease, they have to be *persuaded* to change their behaviour. In part, the answer is that the associated remedies must have been difficult to put into practice in the crisis conditions obtaining. The outcome suggests a variation of a pattern associated with the medical historian Thomas McKeown. In a series of publications dating back to the 1960s McKeown maintained, controversially, that medical science contributed little to life expectancy before the end of the nineteenth century, meaning that the decline in mortality from several infectious diseases in the developed world preceded effective medical treatment. In today's less developed world, health lags rather than leads medical science, with the result that the decline in mortality from specific causes such as gastro-enteritis, malaria, and tuberculosis has tended to lag behind technology. Economic and political progress are a precondition for modern health technologies playing their part in improving the health of the masses. In the words of leading health historian K. D. Patterson, 'more than ever, Africa's disease environment is determined by its poverty' (Patterson 1993: 452).

Ireland on the eve of the famine, with one medical practitioner for every three thousand people, was well endowed with doctors compared to much of the less developed world today, but whether this represented an advantage in terms of quality is highly dubious.[24] More important, the Irish poor knew or cared little about hygiene. Many, if not most of them, walked barefoot much of the time and were forced by poverty to rely on second-hand clothes. Most of the poor shared their accommodation with pigs, poultry, and lice, and clustered settlements made the spread of disease more likely. Their cooking and food conservation skills were rudimentary. When the famine struck, hunger made them cold and less likely to shed or change their clothes. The decline in energy meant poorer childcare, less effective care for the ill and the elderly, and possibly less fuel and clean water, which all relied on physical effort.

The gap between such conditions and those implied by the new science was enormous. Cleanliness and hygiene were luxuries that the Irish poor could hardly afford even in normal times. For the very poor, then, more knowledge and understanding would have done little. For the better-off sections of the population the benefits of the new science would have been more tangible. A better understanding of the causes of disease would have mattered more in preventing epidemics and deaths among the somewhat better off, especially in the towns.

CONCLUSION

The demographic consequences of an exogenous disaster depend on both the size of the impact and the vulnerability of the society upon which it is inflicted. The functional relation between outcome and the two determinants is, however, additive rather than multiplicative. Even seemingly invulnerable societies can be devastated if the impact is large enough. Conversely, weak and vulnerable societies may survive for long periods if they are lucky enough to avoid major challenges. Sadly, Ireland was not lucky.

Ireland's vulnerability was a result of its overall poverty, the physical impossibility of holding potatoes in buffer stocks, and the thinness of markets in basic subsistence goods due to the prevalence of the potato. But there is a second dimension to the vulnerability which compounds the first one, and that is that all populations of the time were vulnerable to an increase in the incidence of infectious diseases in case of outside shocks. The absence of a clear understanding of the nature of disease meant that the privations and disruptions of the famine quickly translated themselves into the horror-filled statistics of Wilde's 1851 'Tables of Death'.

Neither the victims, nor the authorities, nor medical experts understood that what was killing people during the famine was neither hunger nor exposure but micro-organisms. Their ignorance of the exact nature of what it was that was killing so many victims is a crucial element in determining the demographic impact of past famines. One main reason why modern famines differ from past famines is

---

[24] Myron Winick (1994: 380). In Clare in 1841 there was one physician/surgeon per 6,093 population; Mayo one for every 5,983 population; in Leitrim one per 4,853 population; in Down one per 2,245 population; in Cork, one per 1,187 population; in Belfast one per 897 population; in Dublin city one per 510 population. Compare World Bank (1979: 167–8); World Bank (1991: 142–3).

that today there are enough people who understand the role that infectious disease plays during nutritional crises (even if the victims themselves do not always). Other elements of a more effective medical understanding are the realization of the lethal effects of the dehydration caused by diarrhoea and the rehydration techniques that prevent death, and the understanding that some trace elements in the diet can play a central role in thwarting diseases such as scurvy and pellagra. The understanding of the epidemiology and etiology of infectious diseases and the physiology of their symptoms, and the knowledge of how to treat patients suffering from basic ailments such as fever and diarrhoea will remain with us even if antibiotics lose some of their effectiveness with the proliferation of drug-resistant strains. Moreover, even in the presence of severe food scarcities, the complete collapse of hygiene and personal care can be prevented. In this respect, the timing of the Irish Famine was as tragic as its dimensions; had *Phytophthora infestans* attacked only a few decades later, a better understanding of how and why excess mortality takes place following the work of Pasteur and Koch might have saved many thousands of lives.

References

Aykroyd, W. R. (1974), *The Conquest of Famine*, London: Chatto and Windus.
Bongaarts, J., and Cain, M. (1982), 'Demographic Responses to Famine', in K. Cahill (ed.), *Famine*, New York: Orbis Books.
Boyle, Phelim P., and Ó Gráda, Cormac (1986), 'Fertility Trends, Excess Mortality, and the Great Irish Famine', *Demography*, 23: 546–65.
British Parliamentary Papers (BPP) (1843), 'Reports of the Commissioners Appointed to Take the Census of Ireland for the Year 1841', [504] vol. xxiv.1.
—— (1856a), 'The census of Ireland for the Year 1851, Part V: Tables of Death: Vol. 1', [2087-I], vol. xxix. 261.
—— (1856b), 'The Census of Ireland for the Year 1851, Part V: Tables of Death: Vol. 2', [2087-II], vol. xxx.1.
—— (1856c), 'The Census of Ireland for the Year 1851, Part VI: General Report', [2134], vol. xxxi.1.
Bryceson, A. D. M. (1977), 'Rehydration in Cholera and Other Diarrhoeal Diseases', in The Royal Society, *Technologies for Rural Health*, London: Royal Society.
Burger, G. C. E., Drummond, J. C., and Stanstead, H. R., *Malnutrition and Starvation in the Western Netherlands September 1944–July 1945*, Part 1 (The Hague, 1948).
Carmichael, Ann (1983), 'Infection, Hidden Hunger, and History', in R. I. Rotberg and T. K. Rabb (eds.), *Hunger and History: The Impact of Changing Food Production and Consumption Patterns on Society*, Cambridge: CUP, 51–66.
Cousens, S. H. (1965), 'The Regional Variation in Emigration in Ireland between 1821 and 1841', *Transactions of the Institute of British Geographers*, 37 (Dec.): 15–30.
Crawford, Margaret (1988), 'Scurvy in Ireland During the Great Famine', *Journal of the Society for the Social History of Medicine*, 1(3): 281–300.
de Waal, Alex (1989), *Famine That Kills*, Oxford: the Clarendon Press.
Dirks, Robert (1993), 'Famine and Disease', in Kenneth F. Kiple (ed.), *The Cambridge World History of Human Disease*, Cambridge: Cambridge University Press, 157–63.
Drèze, Jean, and Sen, Amartya K. (1989), *Hunger and Public Action*, Oxford: OUP.

Dyson, Tim (1991a,b), 'On the Demography of South Asian Famines: Parts 1 and 2', *Population Studies*, vol. 45, 5–25, 279–97.

Edwards, R. D., and Williams, T. D. (eds.) (1956), *The Great Famine: Studies in Irish History*, Dublin: Browne and Nolan.

Fogel, Robert W. (1991), 'The Conquest of High Mortality and Hunger in Europe and America', in Patrice Higonnet, David S. Landes, and Henry Rosovsky, (eds.), *Favorites of Fortune: Technology, Growth, and Economic Development since the Industrial Revolution*, Cambridge, MA.: Harvard University Press, 33–71.

Froggatt, Peter (1989), 'The Response of the Medical Profession to the Famine', in E. M. Crawford (ed.), *Famine: the Irish Experience*, Edinburgh: John Donald.

Geary, Laurence M. (2000), ' "The living were out of their feeling": a socio-cultural analysis of the Great Famine in Ireland', in B. Ó Conaire (ed.) *The Famine Lectures: Léachtaí an Ghorta*, Boyle: Roscommon Herald, 308–28.

Hionidou, Violetta (1995), 'The Demography of a Greek Famine: Mykonos, 1941–1942', *Continuity & Change*, 10(2).

Jutikkala, E. (1955), 'The Great Finnish Famine 1696–97', *Scandinavian Economic History Review*, 3(1): 48–63.

Kerr, Donal (1996), *The Catholic Church and the Famine*, Dublin: Columba Press.

Latour, Bruno (1988), *The Pasteurization of France*, Cambridge, MA: Harvard University Press.

Livi-Bacci, Massimo (1991), *Population and Nutrition: An Essay on European Demographic History*, Cambridge: CUP.

MacArthur, W. A. (1956), 'Medical History of the Famine', in R. D. Edwards and T. D. Williams (eds.), *The Great Famine: Studies in Irish History*, Dublin: Browne and Nolan.

Maharatna, Arup (1996), *The Demography of Famines*, Delhi: Oxford University Press.

Mercer, Alex (1994), 'Mortality and Morbidity in Refugee Camps in El Fasher, Sudan 1982–89', *Disasters*, 16(1).

Mokyr, Joel (1980), 'The Deadly Fungus: An Econometric Investigation into the Short-term Demographic Impact of the Irish Famine, 1846–51', *Research in Population Economics*, 2: 429–59'.

—— (1985), *Why Ireland Starved: A Quantitative and Analytical History of the Irish Economy 1845–50*, 2nd edn., London: Allen & Unwin.

Mokyr, J., and Rebecca Stein (1997), 'Science, Health and Household Technology: the Effect of the Pasteur Revolution on Consumer Demand', in Robert J. Gordon and Timothy Bresnahan, (eds.), *The Economics of New Goods*, Chicago: University of Chicago Press and NBER, 143–205.

Ó Gráda, C. (1994), *Ireland: A New Economic History*, Oxford: Oxford University Press.

—— (1997), 'The Great Famine and Other Famines', in C. Ó Gráda (ed.), *Famine 150: Commemorative Lecture Series*, Dublin: Teagasc, 129–57.

—— (1999), *Black '47 and Beyond: the Great Irish Famine in History, Economy, and Memory*, Princeton: Princeton University Press.

Patterson, K. D. (1993), 'The Geography of Human Disease', in K. F. Kiple, *Cambridge World History of Human Disease*, Cambridge: Cambridge University Press.

Sen, Amartya K. (1981), *Poverty and Famines*, Oxford: Oxford University Press.

—— (1995), 'Starvation and Political Economy: Famines, Entitlements, and Alienation', Presented to the International Conference on Hunger, New York University, May.

Stein, Z., Susser, M., Saneger, G., and Marolla, F. (1975), *Famine and Human Development*, New York: Oxford University Press.

Taylor, Carl E. (1983), 'Synergy among Mass Infections, Famines, and Poverty', in R. I. Rotberg and T. K. Rabb (eds.), *Hunger and History: The Impact of Changing Food Production and Consumption Patterns on Society*, Cambridge: CUP, 285–303.

Vaughan, Megan (1987), *The Story of an African Famine: Gender and Famine in Twentieth Century Malawi*, Cambridge: CUP.

Vaughan, W. E., and Fitzpatrick, A. (1978), *Irish Population Statistics*, Dublin: Royal Irish Academy.

Wheatcroft, S. G. (1981a), 'Famine and Factors Affecting Mortality in the USSR: The Demographic Crises of 1914–1922 and 1930–33', Centre for Russian and East European Studies Discussion Paper Number 20.

—— (1981b), 'Famine and Factors Affecting Mortality in the USSR: The Demographic Crises of 1914–1922 and 1930–33: Appendices', CREES Discussion Paper Number 21.

—— (1983), 'Famine and Epidemic Crises in Russia, 1918–1922: The Case of Saratov', *Annales de Démographie Historique*, 329–52.

Winick, Myron (1994), 'Hunger Disease: Studies by Jewish Physicians in the Warsaw Ghetto', *Nutrition*, 10: 365–80.

World Bank (1979), *World Development Report 1979*, Washington, D.C.: World Bank.

—— (1991), *World Development Report 1991*, Washington, D.C.: World Bank.

3

The Workhouses and Irish Famine Mortality

TIMOTHY W. GUINNANE AND CORMAC Ó GRÁDA

Formal analyses of the regional variation in excess mortality during the Great Irish Famine of 1846–51 focus on county- or barony-level measures of poverty on the eve of the famine such as poor law valuation per head, average potato consumption, and literacy or urbanization rates (McGregor 1989; Mokyr 1985: Chapter 9; Ó Gráda 1999: Chapter 4). Such analyses have considerable explanatory power, even though they ignore the role of specifically local factors. In local histories of the Irish famine an indulgent landlord, an active priest, or a corrupt workhouse master might mitigate or accentuate the disadvantages captured by other measures. Indeed, local histories often claim or imply that the experience of some location or other differed from what might have been predicted on the basis of county- or province-level variables alone. In other words, agency matters. This study focuses on one issue often highlighted in such local accounts: the role of workhouse relief during the famine.

Well over two hundred thousand people, one-fifth of all famine-related deaths, perished in Irish workhouses and workhouse hospitals during the famine. According to the 1851 Irish population census, the number of workhouse deaths rose from less than six thousand in 1845 to over fourteen thousand in 1846 and nearly 67,000 in 1847. Another 156,000 died in the workhouses between 1848 and 1850. While most of the cross-tabulations describing mortality in the census refer to the decade of 1841–51 as a whole, there were relatively few workhouse deaths (20,853 out of a total of 283,765) before 1846.

Our goal here is to offer a better understanding of why workhouse mortality was as high as it was, how it varied across Ireland, and how it affected different groups in the population such as women or children. The first section of this chapter provides some background to the workhouse system and its operation during the Famine. The second section outlines several approaches to assessing workhouse management. The third section uses econometric methods and cross-sectional information on Poor Law Unions (PLUs) before and during the Famine to examine which unions were most badly hit by the crisis and to identify those that did unexpectedly badly or unexpectedly well for the reasons noted earlier. The final section concludes.

We thank Andrés Eiríksson for suggestions and for sharing data, Kevin Denny for useful comments, and Colin Pan for research assistance.

BACKGROUND

The Irish Poor Law of 1838 was modelled closely on the 'new' English Poor Law of 1834. It divided the country into 130 new administrative units known as 'unions'. These 'unions' of civil parishes were in turn subdivided into electoral divisions upon which poor rates (a local property tax) were levied. Each union was to have its own workhouse, funded by the poor rates, and managed by a board of guardians. Membership of these boards, part elected and part ex officio, was dominated by the landed and commercial elites. The guardians, who were unpaid, sought to protect the interests of the property owners who voted them in. While some guardians carried out their duties conscientiously others quickly acquired a reputation for corruption and failure to attend meetings on a regular basis. The Minutes of Drogheda Union suggests that attendances at board meetings were highest on days when patronage was being dispensed and contracts arranged, while at the height of the famine in Ballina (24 July 1847) an agricultural fair 'prevent[ed] a full attendance' of guardians.[1] Corruption on the part of rate-collectors and the workhouse staff was also sometimes a problem. On the other hand strong popular resistance to paying rates limited the scope for venality and corruption. Several unions failed to raise the rates necessary to operate the system as envisaged by the Poor Law Commissioners, and some strongly discouraged would-be inmates from becoming charges on the ratepayers.[2]

A troika of Poor Law Commissioners based in Dublin oversaw and constrained the work of the boards. By 1845 the necessary boards had been created and workhouses built, and the system was fully operational. Henceforth relief was in principle available to all those who needed it: a willingness to accept the spartan workhouse regime as laid down by the new law was deemed sufficient evidence of need. Fears that Irish poverty would make the principle of 'less eligibility' inoperable were not realized.[3] In the event few of the workhouses had ever been full to capacity before the famine struck (on the poor law in its early years see Nicholls 1856; O'Brien 1982–3, 1985). However, from 1846 on the system was subjected to challenges and strains never envisaged by its creators.

Throughout this Chapter we face a general analytical problem that is best introduced here. Death in the workhouse reflects not just conditions in the workhouses but also *the process by which some entered the institution and some did not*. Those who ended up in the workhouse are a group selected by events beyond their control (the specific impact of the famine on their household), by themselves (whether they

---

[1] *Minutes* (1995: 5); National Library of Ireland, Ms. 7,850.

[2] Thus Clifden workhouse did not open its doors to paupers until March 1847 even though 'their special attention had been called to some recent deaths in Clifden from starvation', while in Castlebar the Guardians blamed a lack of funds for their refusal to admit inmates while the workhouse contained only one-sixth of its capacity. See British Parliamentary Papers (BPP), 'Copies or Extracts of Correspondence', 8–9; *Tenth Annual Report of the Poor Law Commissioners*, 43–4, 59–64.

[3] Under the English New Poor Law, which formed the model for Ireland's system, the workhouse was to be open to any who cared to enter. The theory of the new system was that by making life in the workhouse unappealing, or 'less eligible', only the truly needy would enter. Besley, Coate, and Guinnane (1993) discuss the workhouse test in the context of incentive theory.

decided to try to enter a particular workhouse), and by the workhouse officials (who carried out legislative mandates and guardian policies, but who also had considerable discretion themselves). Thus the population in a workhouse are a 'choice-based' sample and we cannot interpret our results as an uncomplicated picture of the effects of the workhouse. Two concrete examples will illustrate. A workhouse in which everyone died shortly after admittance might seem badly managed, but this is not a sound conclusion if this workhouse only attracted those in the most extreme state of need. Similarly, a workhouse where everyone lived might seem well-run, but it could also be one in which the master refused admittance to anyone who might actually need assistance. The statistical analysis in the third section controls for these problems to some extent, but in general one should bear in mind that many individual findings can be interpreted in a number of ways.

Most of the deaths occurring from 1846 on can be attributed to the Famine. Table 3.1 compares the age profile of deaths in the workhouses as reported in the 1851 population census with those reported for the country as a whole (but excluding workhouse deaths) in 1841–51. We do not have good data on the age-distribution of workhouse inmates during the Famine, and so cannot compute proper death rates. In the absence of such rates we cannot say with certainty whether the larger number of deaths among those aged 1–4 years in the workhouse reflects poor mortality or good mortality. But the table suggests that children aged 5–14 years were particularly at risk in the workhouses. Since a much larger proportion of reported non-workhouse deaths occurred before 1846, other inferences from these data are unwarranted.

The past decade or so has seen the publication of several very useful case studies of workhouse management prior to and during the famine. These studies rely on sources such as contemporary newspapers and the Blue Books and, where possible, detailed

Table 3.1. *Reported Deaths by Age 1841–51*

Age	Workhouses		Other reported	
	Number	(%)	Number	(%)
<1	20,964	7.7	121,839	11.7
1–4	46,496	17.1	189,584	18.2
5–9	41,356	15.2	85,249	8.2
10–14	29,760	10.9	48,156	4.6
15–19	13,793	5.1	52,715	5.0
20–29	14,315	5.3	90,520	8.7
30–39	13,623	5.0	68,297	6.6
40–49	20,919	7.7	77,340	7.4
50–59	19,988	7.3	89,628	8.6
60–69	24,577	9.0	103,729	10.0
70–79	16,365	6.0	65,273	6.3
80+	9,728	3.6	47,997	4.6
Total	272,024	100	1,039,187	100

examinations of the surviving admissions registers and board minutes books of a range of unions. One of the finest is Andrés Eiríksson's assessment of Parsonstown union in King's County. The Parsonstown Guardians provided no outdoor relief after 1847 (being the only guardians in Leinster not to do so)[4] and, predictably, Parsonstown workhouse was very overcrowded as a result. In early May 1849 the workhouse, with a capacity for 1,700 inmates according to the local poor law inspector contained over 3,000 people. The inspector blamed many of the deaths in the workhouse, particularly of children, on overcrowding. Both he and the union's medical officer reasoned that the consequent shortage of clothes, staff, beds, and ventilation assisted the spread of contagious diseases. The medical officer 'even alleged that some of the temporary staff hired for a mere 6d per day to look after the increasing number of sick inmates were eating the food of the workhouse children' (Eiríksson, 1996: Chapters 7–9). The Earl of Rosse, major local landowner and the leading influence on the board of guardians, strenuously held out against outdoor relief. Eiríksson has shown that the pattern of mortality in Parsonstown differed from that in neighbouring unions, drawing attention to the late (1849) peak in deaths there. Two other striking features of mortality in Parsonstown were the high proportion of children and the high incidence of marasmus. Marasmus, a non-contagious condition largely confined to malnourished children, accounted for nearly one quarter of deaths there, as compared to 7.3 per cent in workhouses as a whole. The incidence of scarlatina in Parsonstown was also exceptional (8.6 per cent of all deaths as against 0.8 per cent nationally). Dropsy (3.9 per cent versus 3.2 per cent) and starvation (1.3 per cent versus 0.0 per cent) also featured more strongly in Parsonstown. The Parsonstown guardians blamed the mortality peaks in the workhouse on the dying state of most of those admitted. If the guardians were correct one would expect, as Eiríksson notes, the figures for admissions and deaths to fluctuate in close proximity, with rises and falls in admissions being shortly followed by similar movements in deaths. But this was not the case (see his Fig. 9.2). Eiríksson attributes the lags in deaths mainly to the transmission of contagious diseases within the workhouse.

A recent study of Lurgan workhouse (County Armagh) is also highly critical of the management. Admissions totalled 597 in December 1846 and capacity (800 inmates) had been reached by the end of 1846. Another 480 were admitted in January 1847. The workhouse was so crowded by the end of the month that admissions for the following three months were strictly limited. Nevertheless mortality in the workhouse in the early part of 1847 was very high, and soon attracted the attention of the press and the poor law commissioners in Dublin. The report by Dr Smith of the Central Board of Health concluded: 'I am of opinion that the chief causes of the evil in question are internal, and the result of effective management of the institution'. The workhouse represented 'a picture of neglect and discomfort such as I have never seen in any other charitable institution'. It later emerged that the food supplied to workhouse inmates was inadequate and barely edible (MacAtasney 1995: 85).

---

[4] Wexford almost qualifies, outdoor relief being limited to one individual for two weeks during the last nine months of 1848.

In the case of Ennistymon union the persistence of high death rates into 1851 led to a parliamentary inquiry. Ennistymon union was located in north-west Clare, where the famine was particularly severe: the union lost nearly 23 per cent of its population between 1841 and 1851. By October 1846 the original workhouse, built for 600 inmates, was full to capacity, and finding accommodation for extra inmates would prove an abiding concern thereafter. Until the end of 1850 the union's facilities were constantly overstretched, and periods of most serious overcrowding were followed, typically with a short lag, by peaks in the death rate in the house (Eiríksson 1998: 132). Ennistymon's admission books have not survived, but weekly returns in the minutes books of the Board of Guardians offer an outline profile of the inmates by age and sex. These suggest that children were less likely to survive admission into the workhouse or associated buildings than either adult males or adult females, and that adult females stood a better chance of leaving alive than males (Eiríksson 1998: 169). The median lags in days between admission and death in the workhouse in 1850–1, as estimated from data reported in the 1851 parliamentary inquiry, are reported in Table 3.2.

Such big lags suggest that a significant proportion of the deaths were due to illnesses contracted after admission, and offer strong *prima facie* evidence of mismanagement.

The admissions registers of another Clare PLU, Ennis, have not survived either, but other mostly qualitative evidence, especially the voluminous reports in a local newspaper, *The Clare Journal*, is telling enough. The board of guardians of Mullingar union (County Westmeath) have also been the subject of a critical study. Mullingar's guardians ran up substantial debts in 1846–7 and failed to provide adequate workhouse accommodation. When the letter announcing their dissolution was read to a board meeting on 5 May 1848 most of them were either at a cattle show in Dublin or at a local fair or flower show. Stringent enforcement of the workhouse test by the non-elected vice-guardians who succeeded them improved the finances of the union thereafter, but may well have increased mortality outside the workhouse. In 1848 and 1849 an increasing proportion of claimants entered the workhouse in a 'dying state' (O'Brien 1999: Ó Murchadha, 1997; 37, 45).

Table 3.2. *Deaths in Ennistymon Workhouse: Median Lag after Admission (in Days)*

Cause of death	Males	Females	All
All causes	60	59	59.5
Fever	38	47	43
Dysentery	47	55	51
Diarrhoea	87	87	87
Dropsy	43	133	55
Smallpox	56	64	61
Measles	40	43	41

Source: From data supplied by Andrés Eiríksson, derived from BPP HC 1851 [4848.] vol. XLIX.

ASSESSING MANAGEMENT

Some of those people who perished in the workhouses during the famine had entered them expressly to die, while others arrived in a dying condition. Many more died of contagious diseases such as dysentery and typhoid fever contracted in the workhouses. Indeed, given the high incidence of such diseases in many workhouses, it is conceivable that some poorly run workhouses did more harm than good during the famine. But how can we evaluate the performance of a workhouse or workhouses? The question is inherently relative. This is where case studies such as those described above, however useful and insightful, tend to fall short. For a comparative assessment, we can compare a union to its own pre-famine experience, or compare unions to each other. Neither of these comparisons is quite fair, since the strain caused by the famine varied from union to union. In the third section, we use statistical controls that attempt to compare each union's performance to what was possible given the circumstances. What measuring rods are available? Neither the number of deaths nor the death rate will do, since both were bound to rise during the famine, and both were very much functions of conditions outside the workhouses. Indeed, no measure is quite immune to outside conditions. In what follows we take several different approaches in the hope of reducing the pitfalls inherent in any single measure.

One approach is to focus on what people died of in the workhouses. Such was the pressure on the workhouse system throughout Ireland from the autumn of 1846 on, that it sometimes risked exacerbating rather than relieving the crisis. Preserving life in the workhouse entailed not only adequate food and shelter, but protecting inmates against contagious disease. Workhouse managers were expressly forbidden from admitting diseased claimants except when they had created special quarters for them at a safe distance from other inmates. Some workhouses had an adjoining fever hospital or at least separate accommodation for fever patients, but such facilities were very limited.[5] At the height of the famine it may not have been easy to identify and refuse, or segregate, all ill and diseased claimants. As Sir George Nicholls, first historian of the Irish poor law, explained (Nicholls 1856: 325–6):

It was no longer a question of whether the applicants were fit objects for relief, but which of them could be rejected and which admitted with the least risk of sacrificing life. Were persons in the last extremities of want to be denied admittance, or on the other hand were those already admitted to be made the victims of over crowding? The course which prudence dictated was the one most opposed to human sympathies ... It was the duty of the commissioners to resist all such impulsive yields, and they failed not to urge upon the guardians the necessity for such resistance on their part without which the limited means of relief at their disposal would be sacrificed ... But now unhappily, almost every person admitted was a patient—was either suffering from dysentery or fever, or extreme exhaustion, or had the seeds of disease about

---

[5] In mid-March 1847 the entire country contained workhouse accommodation intended for 93,860 inmates, 3,069 hospital places intended specifically for fever patients, and extra accommodation for 6,630. At that time there were about 120,000 inmates in the workhouses, including over eight thousand fever patients and another twelve thousand sick inmates. See BPP, H.C. 1847 vol. LV, 'Copies or Extracts of Correspondence Relating to the State of Union Workhouses in Ireland', 3rd Series, 86–7.

him. Under such circumstances separation became impossible, diseases spread, and the whole workhouse was changed into one large hospital, without the appliances necessary for rendering it efficient as such. This state of things was not a little aggravated by the illness retirement or death of many of the principal officers.

As the famine intensified in late 1846 many boards of guardians found the pressure for relief impossible to resist, even though admissions had already exceeded the accommodation provided. Thus in late December 1846 the Poor Law Commissioners in Dublin urged the Tralee guardians to heed the advice of their medical officer and to refuse further inmates, 'however distressful it may be to their feelings'. Admissions continued to mount, however, and by early March the workhouse master was suffering from fever. In Ballina two months later the medical officer of Ballina workhouse reported 40 new cases of fever in the house in the previous week, and sought to impress on the guardians the need for extra accommodation for sick inmates, then numbering nearly 500 and scattered around different parts of the house. He warned that unless the sick poor were properly cared for 'this house will become a charnel or pest house, and no man's life in it or connected with it will be for the moment secure'. But in early January 1847 at least, the accommodation problems faced by Tralee (1,068 inmates against accommodation for 1,000) and Ballina (1,029 against 1,200) seemed minor compared to those faced by Fermoy (1,408 against 900), Kanturk (1,478 against 844), or Dunmanway (839 against 400).[6] A relatively small number of unions pursued a very restrictive admissions policy in order to minimize their tax burden, but a combination of compassion and popular pressure biased many more unions towards overcrowding. The trouble was that workhouses which gained a reputation for allowing in diseased patients presumably deterred initially healthy paupers from entering them until they too were weak and sickly. The resulting selection bias in entrants to the workhouse may help explain why so many inmates died of contagious diseases. The point remains that admitting those afflicted with contagious diseases to the workhouses did them little service and risked killing others. Moreover, the symptoms of famine fever and dysentery were relatively clear. The relatively low mortality rates on emigrant ships on the Atlantic passage during the famine—with the notorious exception of ships taking the Canadian route in 1847—is surely evidence that it was not impossible to separate the diseased from the rest.

This suggests one measure of 'efficient' workhouse management: comparing the proportions of workhouse deaths attributable to contagious diseases during the famine in contiguous or similarly circumstanced workhouses. The raw material for some preliminary analysis along these lines is to be found in the Tables of Death accompanying the 1851 population census. Tables 3.3–3.5 extract some of that information, comparing causes of death in workhouses and elsewhere for several areas of Ireland. These data, the work of William Wilde for the census commissioners,

---

[6] National Library of Ireland (NLI), Ms. 7,860 (minutes of the Tralee Board of Guardians, December 1846–March 1847); NLI, Ms. 7,850 (minutes of the Ballina Board of Guardians, 1847); BPP, H.C. 1847 vol. LV [863.], 'Copies or Extracts of Correspondence Relating to the State of Union Workhouses in Ireland', 2nd Series, 7–13.

Table 3.3. *Workhouse Deaths in Selected Counties*

	Wexford	(%)	Clare	(%)	Antrim	(%)	Mayo	(%)
Epidemic, contagious, etc.	2,366	41.7	4,963	83	1,432	36.6	6,773	73.4
Sporadic diseases	2,762	48.7	728	12.2	1,490	38.1	2,100	22.8
Brain and nervous system	366	6.5	247	4.1	221	5.7	496	5.4
Circulatory organs	48	0.9	3	0.1	33	−0.8	25	0.3
Respiratory organs	1,093	19.3	264	4.4	583	14.9	528	5.7
Digestive organs	1,094	19.3	176	2.9	579	14.9	950	10.3
Urinary/generative organs	19	0.3	4	0.1	21	0.5	5	0
Locomotive organs	23	0.4	21	0.4	45	1.2	20	0.2
Tegumentary system	119	2.1	13	0.2	8	0.2	76	0.8
Other diseases	472	8.3	286	4.8	979	25.1	336	3.7
Violent/sudden (incl. starvation)	69	1.2	5	0.1	7	0.2	20	0.2
Total	5,669	100	5,982	100	3,908	100	9,229	100

are fallible. Some unions provided only very incomplete data, and there may also have been some ambiguities and inconsistencies about the identification of diseases. Still, Wilde's tabulations are worth exploiting (compare Mokyr and Ó Gráda, this volume). In the tables below 'contagious' includes fever, dysentery, diarrhoea, famine fever, and cholera—usually the main killers—as well as familiar infectious diseases such as smallpox, measles, whooping cough, and scarlatina. Famine fever included both typhus and relapsing fever, distinct diseases both transmitted by lice. The consumption of contaminated and improperly cooked food gave rise to dysentery and diarrhoeal illnesses. Most of the deaths in this category would have been due to the famine. Wilde's other categories also contain some famine-related killer diseases: these include famine dropsy and marasmus, most of the diseases of the digestive organs, and starvation in the 'violent or sudden deaths' category. Dropsy and marasmus were non-contagious conditions. Marasmus was confined mainly to young children, and arose from the reduced intake of all nutrients, particularly proteins (MacArthur 1956: 289; McConnell 1998: 387–8).

The prevalence of contagious disease and the pressure to admit sick people to the workhouse were worst in the areas most badly affected by the Famine. So it should come as no surprise that the proportions succumbing to contagious diseases in workhouses were higher in the provinces of Connacht and Munster than those of Leinster or Ulster (Table 3.3). More interesting are local anomalies or intra-provincial differences (Table 3.4). The relatively low proportion of deaths attributed to contagious diseases in both Dublin unions relative to Belfast and, to a lesser extent, Cork workhouses is interesting in this respect. Since most of the workhouse deaths were famine-related, comparing causes of death within and outside the workhouse is also instructive. The high proportion of deaths from epidemic and contagious diseases (nearly three-fifths

Table 3.4. *Workhouse Deaths in Selected Unions*

	Tralee	(%)	Listowel	(%)	Killarney	(%)	Kenmare	(%)
Epidemic, contagious, etc.	2,139	73	1,536	67	1,740	72	1,166	78
Sporadic diseases	548	19	621	27	384	16	227	15
Brain and nervous system	65	2	101	4	180	7	1	0
Circulatory organs	12	0	20	1	0	0	0	0
Respiratory organs	299	10	249	11	135	6	134	9
Digestive organs	167	6	244	11	62	3	92	6
Urinary/generative organs	2	0	3	0	0	0	0	0
Locomotive organs	2	0	4	0	5	0	0	0
Tegumentary system	1	0	0	0	2	0	0	0
Other diseases	226	8	96	4	238	10	107	7
Violent/sudden (incl. starvation)	9	0	39	2	39	2	0	0
Total	2,922		2,292		2,401		1,500	
Date open	1 Feb 1844		13 Feb 1845		5 April 1845		25 Oct 1845	
	NDU	(%)	SDU	(%)	Cork city	(%)	Belfast	(%)
Epidemic, contagious, etc.	1,972	33	1,533	30	5,745	53	2,399	48
Sporadic diseases	3,362	56	2,764	54	4,664	43	2,229	44
Brain and nervous system	530		514		143		320	
Circulatory organs	39		86		52		20	
Respiratory organs	1,917		1,425		2,221		1,030	
Digestive organs	751		580		2,222		742	
Urinary/generative organs	52		75		1		29	
Locomotive organs	56		63		18		33	
Tegumentary system	17		21		7		55	
Other diseases	689	11	777	15	392	4	382	8
Violent/sudden (incl. starvation)	11	0	2	0	4	0	11	0
Total	6,034		5,076		10,805		5,021	
Date open	4 May 1840		24 April 1840		1 Mar 1840		11 May 1841	

Source: Derived from 1851 Tables of Death (totals and percentages exclude 'causes not specified').

in Ireland as a whole when the unknowns are omitted) in the workhouses is striking. Note too the contrast between poverty-stricken Clare and Mayo, on the one hand, and Antrim and Wexford, which escaped the famine lightly, on the other. Clearly this contrast has more to do with conditions in these counties during the famine than with workhouse management *per se* (Table 3.5).

A second strategy is to focus on the time lag between admission to the workhouse and death. During the famine people who died of diseases such as dysentery and diarrhoea normally did so within days of contracting them. This implies that deaths from those diseases occurring within a workhouse several weeks and even months

Table 3.5. *Causes of Reported Deaths Inside and Outside the Workhouse 1841–51*

	Workhouses	(%)	Other	(%)
Epidemic, contagious, etc.	132,900	46.8	420,901	39.1
Sporadic diseases	67,596	23.8	388,131	36
Brain and nervous system	9,122	3.2	77,949	7.2
Circulatory organs	1,142	0.4	7,540	0.7
Respiratory organs	27,341	9.6	178,083	16.5
Digestive organs	26,638	9.4	101,294	9.4
Urinary/generative organs	626	0.2	11,425	1.1
Locomotive organs	1,476	0.5	8,679	0.8
Tegumentary system	1,251	0.4	3,161	0.3
Other diseases	23,671	8.4	142,314	13.2
Violent/sudden (incl. starvation)	602	0.2	49,155	4.6
Not specified	58,906	20.8	76,875	7.1
Total	283,765	100	1,077,286	100
Excluding 'Not specified'				
Epidemic, contagious, etc.	132,900	59.1	420,901	42
Sporadic diseases	67,596	30	388,131	38.8
Brain and nervous system	9,122	4	77,949	7.7
Circulatory organs	1,142	0.5	7,540	0.8
Respiratory organs	27,341	12.1	178,083	17.8
Digestive organs	26,638	11.8	101,294	10.1
Urinary/generative organs	626	0.2	11,425	1.1
Locomotive organs	1,476	0.7	8,679	0.9
Tegumentary system	1,251	0.6	3,161	0.3
Other diseases	23,671	10.5	142,314	14.2
Violent/sudden (incl. starvation)	602	0.2	49,155	4.9
Total	224,859	100	1,000,411	100

Source: Derived from 1851 Tables of Death (percentages in parentheses).

after admission were probably the product of contagion in the workhouse; large-scale mortality from such diseases is therefore a fair indication of mismanagement. Only where workhouse admission registers have survived is this approach relevant.[7] A third approach, again dependent on the survival of workhouse records, is to focus on the proportion of those who died who were pronounced in bad health in the admission registers. It was often claimed at the time that people on the verge of death were brought to the workhouse in order to save on burial expenses. The problem here is that most registers have been lost or destroyed and that many of those remaining lack reliable information on this score.

[7] For a guide to surviving workhouse-related material see Lindsay and Fitzpatrick (1994).

CROSS-SECTIONAL PATTERNS IN MORTALITY: POOR LAW UNIONS

Some assertions about workhouses and PLU policy can best be tested by examining cross-sectional variation in outcomes. This section uses a collection of information from the period during and directly prior to the Famine to do just that. The main sources are financial and other information taken from the reports of the Poor Law Guardians, data on population and poor law valuation abstracted from the census, and Wilde's Tables of Death. Our main goal is to examine the effect of union policy on the mortality during the Famine. To do this we experiment with several different definitions of a death rate, and use variables intended to capture matters that were under union control (such as expenditure) and matters that were beyond a union's control (such as the union's wealth and population density). The regressions themselves are instructive, as they suggest ways unions did or did not cope with the crisis in general. But equally informative are the unions whose experience is badly captured by the regressions. As noted above, Irish local historians have stressed idiosyncratic features of workhouses and unions in their discussions of why some workhouses fared better during the Famine than did others.

William Wilde's Tables of Death report the number of deaths in each of the country's 130 workhouses and associated institutions. Since these numbers were extracted for Wilde by the appropriate authorities from admission and death registers we presume that they are reasonably accurate—with one exception.[8] Our outcome variable, *DR*, is measured as total deaths in the workhouse divided by the union's total population as of 1841 times 1000 (see Fig. 3.1, Map 1). This definition answers the question 'What was the chance that a person in this union died in the workhouse during the Famine?' Clearly this death rate reflect many factors other than conditions in the workhouse. For example, a union with a too-small workhouse for its population would have a low value of *DR*.

We first model *DR* as a function of background variables beyond the poor law guardians' control. We have several controls for matters beyond the guardians' control. The variable *MAXSOUP* is the highest percentage of the union population that was fed at soup kitchens during the Famine. This variable is intended to capture the severity of the famine in the union (see Fig. 3.1, Map 2). *WEALTH* is the poor law valuation per capita in the union. This variable has two roles: wealthier unions had a better tax base, and in wealthier unions there were fewer poor people needing the union's assistance. As the Famine progressed unions were able to draw on rates-in-aid to augment local taxes (Ó Gráda 1999: 44), but for the most part each union had to contend with the crisis using its own resources. *ANYCITY* is a dummy equal to one if the union contains a city of twenty thousand or more inhabitants. *AREA* is simply the number of statute acres in the union. The first control is to adjust for the higher

---

[8] The exception is the union of Kinsale, for which the census reports over 5,000 deaths. Surviving workhouse registers suggest a figure of 1,500 at most, and that is the number we use in the regressions reported below. In other cases censal and manuscript material tally well. For more on the 1851 Tables of Death, see Mokyr and Ó Gráda, this volume.

urban mortality we would expect. The *AREA* variable controls for the difficulty of getting to the workhouse; some western areas had unions (e.g. Ballina, Tralee) that were so large that some people would not be able to travel to the workhouse. We also tried variables representing the size distribution of landholdings.

The regression result reported in Table 3.6 is a quantile or median regression. This method is strictly analogous to OLS regression except that it estimates conditional medians instead of conditional means. The reason for our choice is that there are a few influential outlying PLUs which we did not want to exclude from the analysis. The most important single determinant of death rates was just *MAXSOUP*, our proxy for the Famine's severity. Regressing *DR* on *MAXSOUP* alone produces a pseudo R-square of 0.17, and adding more controls improves the regression but does not diminish the impact of this famine-severity proxy. Of the landholding variables only *PC1*, the percentage of holdings less than 1 acre (or 0.4 hectares), entered.

We would also like some controls that capture aspects of union policy or decisions. We experimented with a range of variables representing expenditure by the union and workhouse congestion. These were measured, respectively, by the average expenditure on workhouse inmates during February of a given year (*ACFEB45*, *ACFEB46*, *ACFEB47*), and by the number of inmates divided by the workhouse's official capacity in those years. We take the costs to be a measure of union generosity. Workhouse size was fixed in the short run, but unions could through various devices—adding lofts, building temporary sheds, renting extra accommodation, converting the usage of existing accommodation—increase workhouse capacity. Overcrowded workhouses were dangerous to inmates and reflect problems in union management (Fig. 3.1, Map 4 describes congestion by this definition in 1848). There are two distinct, serious problems with these controls. One problem is timing. We have deaths during the entire famine, not by year, so we cannot match up death rates very precisely with what are annual, and in some cases rapidly changing, measures of union policy. To show how severe this problem is we computed some zero-order correlations. The correlation between *ACFEB45* and *ACFEB46* is 0.62, but between *ACFEB45* and *ACFEB47* is 0.34. The latter is still a strong correlation, but the decline suggests that areas with high average spending prior to the famine did not raise their spending during the crisis as much as those with low average spending. Changes in spending levels were systematic. In a regression not reported, we find that the percentage increase in spending between 1845 and 1847 is positively related to *MAXSOUP*, although that regressor alone only explains about 2 per cent of the variance in the dependent variable. In the event none of the average cost variables had worthwhile explanatory power, and the only congestion that mattered was that for 1846. Table 3.7 reports our results. The only policy variables to play a role turned out to be congestion in 1846 (*CONG46*) and, less explicably, expenditure per inmate in early 1845 (*ACFEB45*).

DISSOLVING BOARDS OF GUARDIANS

As already noted the board of guardians was in part elected by local ratepayers. Both the government and the Poor Law Commissioners in Dublin valued this democratic

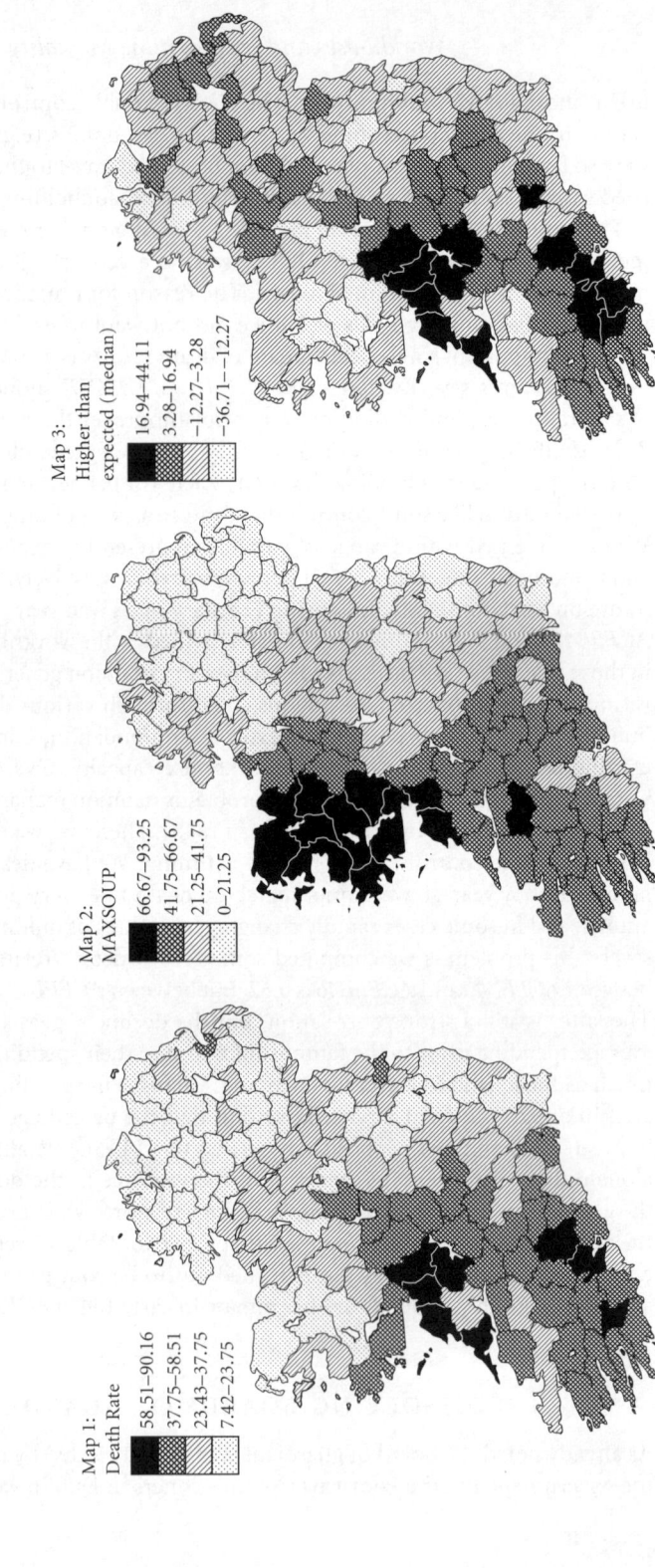

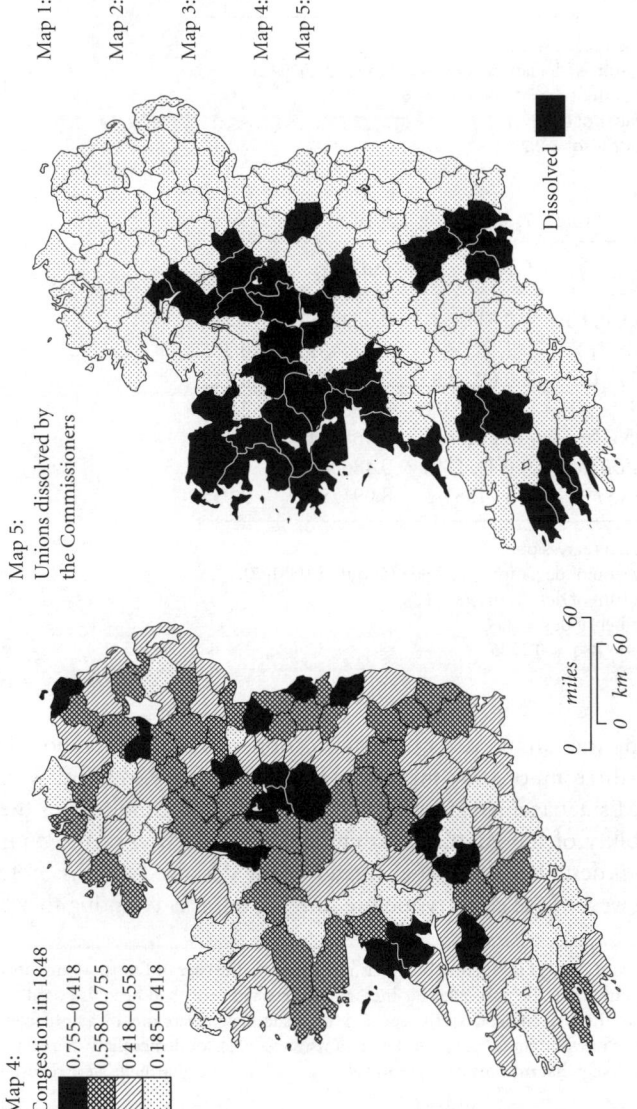

Figure 3.1. *Maps on the Irish Famine*

Table 3.6. *Accounting for the Variation in Death Rates*

DR	Coef.	Std. Err.	t
MAXSOUP	0.4548786	0.0611441	7.439
ANYCITY	7.256549	4.822481	1.505
AREA	−0.000061	0.0000216	−2.824
PC1	0.2166954	0.0959501	2.258
CONST	19.91023	3.629188	5.486

Median regression.
Raw sum of deviations 1556.445 (about 28.08942).
Min sum of deviations 1201.676.
Number of obs = 130.
Pseudo Rsq = 0.2279.

Table 3.7. *Including 'Policy' Variables*

DR	Coef.	Std. Err.	t
MAXSOUP	0.511433	0.0628932	8.132
ANYCITY	1.505591	4.524461	0.333
AREA	−0.000069	0.0000164	−4.213
PC1	0.2285325	0.0884716	2.583
CONG46	16.00754	7.468254	2.143
ACFEB45	−0.7355001	0.4864663	−1.512
CONST	24.71589	8.091285	3.055

Median regression.
Raw sum of deviations 1352.969 (about 28.033127).
Min sum of deviations 984.1634.
Number of obs = 114.
Pseudo Rsq = 0.2726.

aspect. However, during the famine years the commissioners dissolved the boards of guardians of thirty-three unions for mismanagement and replaced them with paid vice-guardians.[9] Mismanagement was loosely defined by the condition of the workhouse or the inability of the guardians to enforce the collection of the poor rates. Figure 3.1, Map 5 describes the spatial spread of the dissolved unions: note their prevalence in the west of the country. Before moving on, it is tempting to ask

---

[9] The reluctance of the commissioners to dissolve boards is illustrated by the case of Ennis, where most members attended meetings only until the particular business that interested them had been disposed of, leaving the bulk of the work to the vice-chairman. His repeated threats to resign were met by a note from the commissioners stating their unwillingness 'except under circumstances of absolute necessity' to replace the board (IUP3: 623–4). It is likely that in some cases, as in Gort and Ballina, the guardians were relieved to be dissolved.

what distinguishes unions that were taken over by the Poor Law Board and managed by vice-guardians ($VG = 1$) from those which were not. We define CONTPC as the percentage of reported deaths due to infectious diseases and marasmus. This variable tells an interesting tale. If we estimate a binary probit model (not reported) in which the dependent variable is VG, we find that the only two good predictors of takeover were a high CONTPC and a high MAXSOUP. Just these two variables, in fact, produce a pseudo R-square of 0.28 and a model that 'correctly' predicts 83 per cent of all observations. The importance of CONTPC suggests that the Commissioners looked to the cause of death as a sign that workhouses were not well-run. But taking over unions where MAXSOUP was high amounted to blaming the Guardians for events beyond their control.

Table 3.8 reports a probit regression using VG as dependent variable. Here DR is the death rate as defined earlier. This regression is very strong evidence that the poor law commissioners in Dublin were looking not at death rates or even expected death rates, but the debts run up by the PLU. And in some sense, they were blaming the PLU for the severity of the famine in that area (MAXSOUP). Note too the sign on CONG46, which would seem to indicate that the commissioners had a limited understanding that congestion in 1846 was not the unions' fault.

Probit does not have the same kind of residual as OLS or quantile regression, but one can think of worst fits than the following: the highest predicted values of Pr(VG) when $VG = 0$—or those boards of guardians with the highest probability of being replaced by vice-commissioners, but survived—and vice versa. We list below both the ten unions with the highest predicted Pr(VG) but $VG = 0$, and the ten with lowest predicted Pr(VG) but $VG = 1$.

(A) Highest Pr(VG) when $VG = 0$		(B) Lowest Pr(VG) when $VG = 1$	
Sligo	0.769	Granard	0.050
Swinford	0.767	Trim	0.067
Skibbereen	0.622	Lowtherstown	0.077
Boyle	0.503	Athlone	0.136
Kilmallock	0.491	New Ross	0.174
Tralee	0.464	Tullamore	0.202
Carrick-on-Shannon	0.436	Carrick-on-Suir	0.302
Glenties	0.404	Newcastle	0.345
Macroom	0.344	Longford	0.380

One interpretation of this outcome is that, according to the criteria used by the poor law commissioners, the guardians in unions such as Sligo, Swinford, and Tralee should have been replaced, but were not, while the boards of Trim, Athlone, and Granard were replaced, but should not have been. Detailed study of local circumstances may explain some of these 'anomalies'; some, of course, must be the product of mis-measurement or mis-specification. In the meantime, contemporary commentary in

Table 3.8. *The Probit Estimates*

VG	Robust		
	Coef.	Std. Err.	z
DR	0.0128874	0.0121959	1.057
MAXSOUP	0.0170958	0.0087871	1.946
CONTPC	1.736821	1.077332	1.612
DEBT747	0.0003099	0.0000942	3.291
CONG46	−3.062418	1.015013	−3.017
CONG48	1.874828	0.9173891	2.044
CONST	−3.362818	0.9282766	−3.623

Log likelihood = −39.077433.
Number of obs = 122.
Wald chi2(6) = 40.58.
Prob > chi2 = 0.0000.
Pseudo Rsq = 0.4054.

the Blue Books helps explain a few of them. Sligo's escape might be explained by the clean state of its workhouse and the impression that its guardians were doing what they could to reduce a debt of almost £10,000. Carrick-on-Shannon was in a bad way in late 1847 but its problems were made worse by developments clearly outside its control: the murder of a local clergyman and, almost immediately afterwards, the resignation of two rate-collectors. Tralee's problems were due to its size rather than particularly poor management; thus, it made more sense to reduce its catchment area, as was done with the creation of Dingle union in 1848, than to dissolve its board. The records suggest that Athlone and Granard were dissolved mainly for their failing to collect the rates and their consequent inability to provide extra workhouse capacity, and Lowtherstown for refusing to be guided 'by threats and menaces' from the commissioners (IUP2: 102, 120, 126–7, 728, 942–3).[10] Meanwhile Table 3.8 suggests that our simple model provides quite a good fit.

RESIDUALS

Thus far we have focused on statistical models that are designed to explore regularities in the data. But local histories tell a different tale, of a parish or region where most people survived not so much because the people were well off or the failure of the potato was limited, but because local agents saw what needed to be done and did it. Our analysis can be used to identify such cases in a fairly precise way. The difficulty with the local historian's approach is these accounts are not based on a sense of how

---

[10] Cavan, which just failed to make our list, was dissolved because of the refusal of apathetic and indifferent guardians to sanction outdoor relief despite well-attested evidence of deaths from starvation (IUP2: 233–7).

typical a particular death rate was, especially for a union with given characteristics. Our regressions estimate conditional medians, or the expected death rate given a set of characteristics such as wealth and congestion levels. We can use the regressions to ask when a union's experience was truly unusual, or implies death rates much higher than or lower than the rates implied by the union's characteristics and Irish experience as a whole.

Building on the earlier analysis, we will simply examine the residuals from the model described in Table 3.6 that are in some sense 'large'. There are many ways to define 'large' in this context, some of which rely on formal statistical criteria. Here we take a more heuristic approach and confine our attention to those observations whose residuals are *largest in absolute value*. We list below the ten biggest positive and ten biggest negative residuals from the 1st quantile regression (in descending order of absolute value); Fig. 3.1, Map 3, describes the outcome for the country as a whole. A higher death rate than predicted by the model yields a positive residual; negative residuals suggest a union that performed better than expected.[11]

'Under-performers'	Residuals	'Over-performers'	Residuals
1. Dunmanway	44.116	1. Swinford	−36.715
2. Loughrea	40.057	2. Ballinrobe	−35.468
3. Cork	39.333	3. Castlebar	−24.653
4. Gort	35.980	4. Tuam	−21.752
5. Ennistymon	33.510	5. Milford	−21.570
6. Bandon	26.353	6. Newcastle	−19.503
7. Scariff	26.000	7. Dublin South	−17.904
8. Nenagh	22.063	8. Stranorlar	−16.410
9. Fermoy	21.889	9. Carrick-on-Shannon	−14.995
10. Ballinasloe	21.109	10. Inishowen	−14.700

How does the outcome compare with contemporary and historical assessments of individual unions? Our list of poorly managed unions includes two in Clare and three in east Galway. Gort and Loughrea were the subject of contemporary criticism from Godolphin Osborne and the poor law inspectors. In February 1848 Loughrea Union's poor law inspector reported that the condition of the workhouse in early 1848 was so bad that some paupers preferred to risk death by the roadside than become inmates, while in Gort workhouse its inspector found only 'confusion, filth, and disease'. The visiting book showed no sign of any guardian having visited the interior of the workhouse since the previous March (IUP2: 563–4, 795). In Clare, the qualitative and statistical evidence concur in the cases of Ennistymon (discussed earlier) and Scariff, which until late 1847 'had enjoyed an almost perfect immunity from a poor rate' while

---

[11] We are using the residuals in a loose sense. They reflect both a particular union's difference from what was expected and shortcomings of the actual statistical model such as measurement error and specification errors.

its paupers remained dressed in rags and its staff unpaid (O'Gorman 1994: 20, 34–5, 37). The list of 'under-performers' also includes Fermoy, where according to *The Cork Examiner* mortality was proportionately higher than in Cork city workhouse, where 'we believe it was heretofore considered the greatest mortality of any union in the kingdom prevailed' (cited in Garner 1986: 75). Cork is also included in our list of poorly managed unions. Just outside the top ten 'under-performers' are Parsonstown (discussed earlier) and Kilrush, where rate-collection seems to have been lax, and the workhouse 'under Pat Kelly's mismanagement and his father's (the late master) continued interference, is in a very unsatisfactory state as regards discipline, regularity, and economy' (Eiríksson 1996; IUP3: 801–2). So far, so good. However, Carrick-on-Shannon in the north-west, deemed poorly managed by McAtasney (1997) is in our top ten 'over-performers'. And our list does not include Lurgan, Ennis, Mullingar, all three the subjects of critical case-studies mentioned earlier. As noted, McAtasney's study of Lurgan workhouse highlighted its overcrowded and filthy state and its inadequate dietary regime, and O'Brien and Ó Murchadha the careless and irresponsible behaviour of the poor law guardians in Mullingar and Ennis, respectively. Our residuals do not necessarily invalidate these local findings, but they place them in context. They suggest that the management of these workhouses was not *exceptionally* bad; the outcomes were no worse than might have been expected, given the prevailing destitution in the district in question. To an extent, therefore, local historians of the famine are writing national history in the guise of local history (McAtasney 1995; McAtasney 1997; Ó Murchadha 1997; O'Brien 1999).[12]

The list of unions that performed better than predicted also contains some surprises. Ballinrobe is second on the list though in November 1847 the vice-guardians declared the master 'wholly inefficient' and 'unable to establish any classification of the inmates'. Bookkeeping had been neglected and the house was dirty throughout (IUP2: 54). Trim, where the board was dissolved for refusing to enforce the workhouse test rigorously in December 1847 and seeking to continue outdoor relief for the able-bodied (IUP2: 455), is also an 'over-performer' by our statistical reckoning. The same holds for Galway, whose board of guardians was dissolved because the union was in debt and the guardians unwilling to provide proper clothing and bedding and acquire the accommodation necessary for more would-be inmates (IUP2: 457–8). The Commissioners dissolved Castlebar's board for their failure to collect rates due, but they clearly underestimated the difficulties facing the board, since the vice-guardians who replaced the board managed to hire a rate-collector only by allowing him a very high percentage of any money collected. In Westport for a time the vice-guardians failed to find anybody (IUP2: 57; IUP3: 572–3). Neither list above includes Tipperary, where in late February 1848 the poor law inspector proclaimed himself 'gratified' at the state of the workhouse: little was required to 'make it a model for all other Unions' (IUP3: 609).

---

[12] Manorhamilton (11.92), Lurgan (8.765), and Mohill (3.29) have small positive residuals, while Ennis (−7.714) and Carrick-on-Shannon (−15.00) emerge as 'over-performers'. Mullingar's residual was 0.30. Killarney is number 16 among the 'under-performers', though its management is commended by Foley (1987).

CONCLUSIONS

In this chapter we have offered a preliminary analysis of the role of local factors or 'agency' in determining variations in mortality across Irish regions during the Great Famine. Our focus has been on one particular aspect of agency, the workhouse regime. We have offered examples of both the case study and the comparative approach. Individual case-studies yield examples of both good and bad management. Close analysis of workhouse registers and qualitative data offers insight into crucial factors such as the quality of health care in the workhouse and the competence of the guardians. However, management quality is arguably endogenous, and this suggests the usefulness of a comparative analysis. Here we have focused on those unions which under- or over-performed, controlling for the economic and locational conditions that faced them. Our results need further refinement and qualification. But this seems to us a particularly useful direction to pursue.

References

Besley, T. J., Coate, S., and Guinnane, T. W. (1993), 'Understanding the Workhouse Test: Information and Poor Relief in Nineteenth-Century England', Yale University Economic Growth Center Discussion Paper No. 701, September 1993.

Eiríksson, A. (1996), *Parsonstown Union and Workhouse During the Great Famine: A Statistical Report*, Dublin: National Famine Research Project.

—— (1998), *Ennistymon Union and Workhouse During the Great Famine: A Statistical Report*, Dublin: National Famine Research Project.

Foley, K. (1987), 'The Killarney Poor Law Guardians and the Famine 1845–52' (unpublished M.A. dissertation, National University of Ireland).

Garner, E. (1986), *To Die by Inches: The Famine in North East Cork*, Fermoy: Éigse Books.

IUP (1968), Irish University Press Series of British Parliamentary Papers: *Famine (Ireland)*, 8 Volumes, Shannon: Irish University Press. [The pagination refers to that used by IUP.]

Lindsay, D., and Fitzpatrick D. (1994), *Records of the Irish Famine: A Guide to Local Archives, 1840–1855*, Dublin: Irish Famine Network.

MacArthur, W. A. (1956), 'Medical History of the Famine', in Edwards and Williams (eds.), *The Great Famine: Studies in Irish History*, Dublin: Browne & Nolan, 263–315.

McAtasney, G. (1995), 'The Famine in Lurgan and Portadown', *Ulster Local Studies*, 17(2): 75–87.

—— (1997), *Leitrim and the Great Hunger 1845–50*, Carrick-on-Shannon and District Historical Society: Carrick-on-Shannon.

McConnell, A. A. (1998), 'The Irish Famine: A Century and a Half on', *Proceedings of the Royal College of Physicians of Edinburgh*, 28: 383–94.

McGregor, P. (1989), 'Demographic Pressure and the Irish Famine: Malthus after Mokyr', *Land Economics*, 65: 228–38.

Minutes of the Proceedings of the Drogheda Union 1839 to March 1843 (1995), Transition Year Project, St. Oliver's Community College.

Mokyr, J. (1985), *Why Ireland Starved*, 2nd edn., London: Allen & Unwin.

Mokyr, J., and Ó Gráda C. (2002), 'Famine Disease and Famine Mortality: Lessons from the Irish Experience, 1845–1850', this volume.

Nicholls, Sir G. (1856), *A History of the Irish Poor Law, in Connexion with the Condition of the People*, London: Murray.

O'Brien, G. (1982–3), 'The Establishment of Poor Law Unions in Ireland, 1838–43', *Irish Historical Studies*, 33: 97–120.

O'Brien, G. (1985), 'The New Poor Law in Pre-famine Ireland: A Case History', *Irish Economic and Social History*, 12: 33–49.

O'Brien, S. (1999), *Famine and Community in Mullingar Poor Law Union, 1845–1849: Mud Huts and Fat Bullocks*, Dublin: Irish Academic Press.

O'Gorman, M. (1994), *A Pride of Paper Tigers: A History of the Great Hunger in Scariff Workhouse Union from 1839 to 1853*, Tuamgraney: East Clare Heritage.

Ó Gráda, C. (1999), *Black '47 and Beyond: The Great Irish Famine in History, Economy, and Memory*, Princeton: Princeton University Press.

Ó Murchadha, C. (1997), *Sable Wings Over the Land: Ennis, County Clare, and its Wider Community During the Great Famine*, Ennis: Clasp Press.

4

Famine Mortality in Nineteenth-Century Finland: Is there a Sex Bias?

KARI J. PITKÄNEN

Sex differentials in historical mortality have been examined in a large number of studies. Even though most findings indicate that mortality differentials between the sexes have been relatively small until the twentieth century, historical records have revealed some patterns and trends which have been common in historical populations. In nineteenth-century Europe male excess has been the norm in infant mortality as well as in most age groups of the adult population. In contrast, children from about 5 to 14 years of age usually show excess female mortality. In many populations the female disadvantage is evident also during women's reproductive years. Several authors acknowledge that biological factors can contribute to sex differentials in mortality, and yet, there is a wide consensus that both the historical and present mortality sex differentials are largely culturally determined (e.g. Hart 1989; Klasen 1998; Lopez 1983; Tabutin 1978; Tabutin and Willems 1998; Willner 1999).

Famines can shape considerably the patterns of mortality in the affected populations. Several studies suggest that men suffer from higher excess mortality during famines. Dyson has studied the demography of five South Asian famines, three consecutive famines in India in the late nineteenth century, the Bengal famine of 1943–4, and the Bangladesh famine of 1974–5. The available demographic data indicate that during each of these calamities proportional mortality increases were greater for men, particularly in the prime adult years (Dyson 1991a,b). A demographic survey undertaken in the Region of Darfur, Sudan, in 1986 suggests that during the famine of 1984–5 men were harder hit than women. The sex differential was most pronounced among children from 5 to 9 years of age (de Waal 1989). Boyle and Ó Gráda (1986) have provided mortality estimates which show that during the Great Irish Famine men suffered in most age categories from higher mortality than women, whereas during the pre-famine period (1821–41) women had higher mortality from childhood (beyond infancy) to age 50 and nearly uniform death rates at older ages. The analysis of the death records of Ogen-ji, a Buddhist temple in Japan, suggests that in 1837, during the peak mortality period of the Tenpo famine of the 1830s, men were harder hit than women (Jannetta 1992). Significant male disadvantages in mortality increases have also been reported during the Dutch Hunger Winter of 1944–5 and during the Greek famine of 1941–2 (Hionidou 1995; Watkins and Menken 1985: 655–6).

The authors of all the quoted studies have presented at least some reservations regarding the quality and accuracy of their data. In some cases the authors have undertaken considerable efforts to correct the likely biases in the materials (see, e.g. Boyle and Ó Gráda 1986). Nonetheless, as many students of famines have emphasized, the evidence suggesting smaller increases in female mortality is so consistent that it would be difficult to discredit these findings by simply referring to data bias. Another important pattern is that the female advantage has been reported in both historical and (relatively) modern famines, as well as in variable cultural settings. These features easily prompt the interpretation that the larger male vulnerability in famine situations is likely to be influenced by biological factors. There is some evidence to support such a conclusion. First, females may be physiologically less severely affected by food deprivation than males, at least starting in adolescence. Women are smaller and they have a lower metabolic rate and a higher body fat (Rivers 1988: 90–1; Widdowson 1976). Second, even though the evidence has been found inconclusive, it has been suggested that there may be a sex differential in the regulation of the immune system, leaving men at greater risk for infectious diseases (Hazzard 1989; Waldron 1998). Third, it has been suggested that the case-fatality rate for typhus, a common killer during famines, is greater for men than for women aged 20–50 years (Snyder 1965).

The author of this chapter has previously studied sex differences in mortality during one major subsistence crisis, the Great Finnish Famine of 1866–8 (Pitkänen and Mielke 1993). The results were compared with another period of excessive mortality, the War of Finland in 1808–9. The findings were not in good accordance with the above quoted studies. The Finnish data did not show consistent sex differences in mortality increases. Only in 1868, during the period of highest mortality increases related to the famine of the 1860s, men suffered notably more than women. The findings led to a conclusion that neither sex benefited from an inherent biological advantage over the other during the examined crisis periods. Male excess mortality in certain regions in 1868 was tentatively linked to famine-induced temporary migration which was selective by region, age, and sex.

The famine of the 1860s was a national calamity, and only a few regions escaped the disastrous effects of the catastrophe. However, there were several other crises in nineteenth-century Finland associated with harvest failures, and even though their effects were more localized, they resulted in considerable mortality increases in the affected regions. In some cases these periods of privation are clearly visible even in the national mortality figures. The historical Finnish population statistics can be used to examine the mortality impact during all these calamities in the same detailed manner as has been done in Pitkänen and Mielke (1993) for the famine of the 1860s and the 1808–9 war. In this chapter, sex differences in mortality have been studied during two other subsistence crises, the famines of 1832–3 and 1857–8. The results are compared with the famine of the 1860s (and the 1808–9 war) in order to see how common were sex biases in mortality during subsistence crises. The comparisons are also extended to the Swedish famine of 1773, the last major subsistence crisis in Sweden resulting in substantial mortality increase.

MATERIALS

The main source of information for this study is the statistical tables which the Lutheran parish ministers were required to complete beginning in 1749 as part of the Swedish population statistics. Sweden lost the Finnish provinces to Russia in 1809, but the Swedish system of population statistics was maintained in the newly established Grand Duchy of Finland during the entire Russian period (Finland became independent in 1917). The first set of the statistical tables, Population Change Tables (*väestönmuutostaulukot* in Finnish), contains information on births, deaths, and marriages. This information was given annually. The second set of the tables, Population or Census Tables (*väkilukutaulukot*) gives the population size of each parish and the age, marital status, and occupational structure of the population. Initially the ministers were required to complete the Population Tables annually. In 1752 this practice was changed and at first the Population Tables were completed only every third year, then from 1775 to 1880 every fifth year, and finally from 1880 to 1940 once every ten years. The information for these standardized statistical tables was obtained from two sets of parish registers of the Lutheran church, the so-called Communion Books (registers of the parishioners) and the Records of Births, Marriages, and Deaths. The parish records formed an excellent basis for these statistics in the sense that only a very small minority of the population did not belong to the Lutheran state church. Furthermore, the Church exercised very strict control on the population (Pitkänen and Nieminen 1984).

The age composition of the population was given in five-year intervals for all ages except those less than 5 years old. The youngest age category was divided into 3 groups: below 1, 1–2, and 3–4 years. The same breakdowns were used for the age composition of the deaths. Thus the statistical tables provide sufficient information for the calculation of age-specific death rates by sex. The basic materials (i.e., the statistical tables for individual parishes) have not been preserved in all cases. Furthermore, because of the large number of parishes (about 500 in the mid-nineteenth century) the use of the parish tables would be extremely labour-intensive. Therefore, I have used the deanery level tables, which are summary tables for a group of neighbouring parishes. There were 30 Lutheran deaneries in the beginning of the nineteenth century and this increased to 43 in the 1860s. Starting in the early nineteenth century the statistical tables were compiled separately for the cities and townships, and these administrative areas were no longer included in the deanery tables. A complete set of the deanery level statistical tables (as well as for the cities) is kept in the Archives of Statistics Finland in Helsinki.

Finnish historical population statistics are generally considered reliable. The critical piece of information for the purposes of this study is the age structure given for the population and for the deaths. As a norm, the individuals and their birth date were entered in the Communion Books soon after birth, and these entries could be used to calculate any individual's age. Therefore, apart from occasional errors, the information about ages can be expected to be reliable. The oldest continuous series of the Communion Books, however, originate in Finland from the 1720s, and in many cases the birth date of the parishioners was not entered in the records until the late 1740s. At this time, the age of the older individuals was usually estimated since in most Finnish parishes the birth records, which could be used to verify a person's age, did not extend very far in the past. As is known, in historical populations there has been a common tendency to exaggerate adult ages. A recent study (Pitkänen and Laakso 1999) indicates that this has been the case even in Finland, and therefore the age structure given in the early statistical tables is clearly biased. By the turn of the nineteenth century the effect of age mis-reporting had become negligible.

The Finnish demographic materials are well suited for the study of famine mortality because of the principle of closed registration employed in the registration during the nineteenth century (see Pitkänen 1980). Famines, by definition, are periods characterized by social disruption. As part of these developments destitute people could leave their homes in search of work and food. Many of these itinerant migrants died outside their parish of residence. Were they registered in the death records of their place of death, the comparisons between famine mortality and mortality during the 'non-famine' periods in different localities could be seriously distorted. However, according to the principles of the Finnish registration system all deaths were supposed to be reported in the death records of their parishes of legal residence. For this purpose the ministers of the home parishes had to be informed of the death of such parishioners who had been buried by the clergy of other parishes. Thus in principle the death records and the Communion Books of each parish include also those parishioners who had died while being temporarily absent from their place of residence.

In reality, however, the population registration system did not function flawlessly during the upheavals created by the crises. There is some evidence that during both the 1808–9 war and the famine of the 1860s a small portion of the deaths were omitted from the parish death records, and consequently, were not included in the mortality statistics. These were largely itinerant migrants who had died outside their parish of legal residence. Since temporary migration was highly selective by age and sex, large scale migration movements might adversely affect the results based on the mortality statistics. It is known that temporary migration reached considerable proportions in 1868, and therefore the potential effects of this phenomenon were estimated and the age- and sex-specific mortality rates were corrected accordingly. It should be stressed, though, that the inclusion of the estimated omissions rather emphasize the existing characteristics in sex-specific mortality differentials than bring forth new ones (for more details see Pitkänen and Mielke 1993).

The signs of social disruption are clear even during the famines of 1832–3 and 1857–8. Vagrancy increased in the famine stricken areas when destitute people left their homes in search for food. Nonetheless, temporary migration never grew to such chaotic proportions which characterized the famine of the 1860s, particularly the year 1868. Most itinerant migrants circled either in their home parishes or in nearby areas (Kauranen 1999: 142–7; Reports of the District Medical Officers in 1857 and 1858; the temporary migration movements are discussed in more detail below). Under such relatively more controlled circumstances omissions in the death records are not as likely. Also, the comparison of the recorded natural population increase in the population statistics with the total population increase in the censuses reveals no discrepancies, contrary to the situation during both the famine of the 1860s and the 1808–9 war (Pitkänen 1993: 34–8; Pitkänen and Mielke 1993; Official Statistics of Finland, Population Statistics vols. VI: 29 and 33). To summarize the above discussion, it can be argued that the Finnish demographic materials depict historical famine mortality with exceptional accuracy.

THREE NINETEENTH-CENTURY FAMINES

The periods of the Finnish mortality crises compared in this chapter will be briefly outlined in the following paragraphs. The famines of 1832–3 and 1857–8 have not been described previously. The War of Finland in 1808–9 and the famine of the 1860s have been earlier portrayed in greater detail in Mielke and Pitkänen (1989), Pitkänen and Mielke (1993), and Pitkänen (1993).

The Great Finnish Famine of the 1860s is relatively poorly known in international historiography, even though its late occurrence makes it particularly interesting (Ó Gráda 1992). It is even less widely known that the famine of the 1860s was not the only major subsistence crisis which occurred in nineteenth-century Finland. Even though the effects of the other famines were more localized, many of them resulted in considerable economic deprivation, nutritional distress, and mortality increases in the affected regions. In terms of their mortality impact the most severe of these local subsistence crises were the famines of 1832–3 and 1857–8.[1] In conjunction with the 1808–9 war and the famine of the 1860s these periods show the highest death rates in the nineteenth century. It should be realized, though, that the famine of 1857–8 was immediately preceded by another mortality crisis, precipitated by diseases which spread to southern Finland during the last phases of the Crimean War (Pitkänen 1993: 46–8). The mortality impact of this event was as extensive as that associated with the famine. All in all, in European perspective Finland was stricken by exceptionally frequent and violent mortality crises in the nineteenth century.

Even though the different famine periods show some variation in the regional pattern of harvest outcome and mortality, it is striking that certain areas were among the affected regions during every single famine period. These areas were the ones which most frequently suffered from harvest failure. They form a region which starts in the west from southern Ostrobothnia, extends to the Raahe and Kajaani deaneries in the north, then to central Finland, northern Savolax and northern Karelia in the east, and finally reaches the border of the province of Viipuri. This region has been

---

[1] All these famine periods have been identified in Finnish historiography; but they have not been designated as clearly defined famines by contemporaries. The historians have not used any explicit criteria in defining the existence or the absence of such occurrences. The beginning and end of the famines has been determined by using a combination of information about harvest outcome, insufficient supply of food, signs of social disruption, and above all, substantially elevated levels of mortality which contemporaries have linked to nutritional problems.

Figure 4.1. *Regions Hit Frequently by Famines in the Nineteenth Century*

Notes: Regions shaded with dark grey are areas which were frequently hit by famines (southern parts of the province of Oulu, and provinces of Vaasa and Kuopio). Regions shaded with light grey are areas which were severely affected during some famine years (central parts of the province of Oulu, north-eastern part of the province of Turku and Pori, and northern part of the province of Viipuri).

depicted in Fig. 4.1 with a dark grey shade. There are also other regions which were hit during some of the famine years. These are Satakunta in south-western Finland, the central parts of the northernmost province of Oulu, and the northern part of the province of Viipuri in the east. These areas are shown in Fig. 4.1 with light grey. The examination of the climatic conditions has revealed that the regions most severely affected by the famines are among the least suitable ones for crop production in Finland (see Solantie 1992).

All of the three famines discussed in this chapter have one common characteristic. None of these calamities resulted from a single poor harvest outcome; in every case the crisis was preceded by multiple poor years. The actual crisis was then triggered by a more severe harvest failure. Regarding the famine of 1832–3 the first year with poor harvest was in 1829. The grain harvest was rather meagre also in 1830 and 1831, and in 1832 many regions suffered from a total crop failure due to severe damage by frost (Johanson 1924: 88–90; Kauranen 1999: 30–7). As usually, the situation was worst in the regions extending from the central parts of the country to the provinces in the north (excluding the northernmost region of Lapland which was not a grain-growing area). In the affected areas the number of deaths grew to levels above the normal in September–October 1832, and the peak in mortality occurred in March 1833 when the number of deaths was about four times above the 'normal' (Fig. 4.2). The number of deaths decreased during the spring and summer until a sudden repeated upsurge in mortality took place in Ostrobothnia late in the summer.

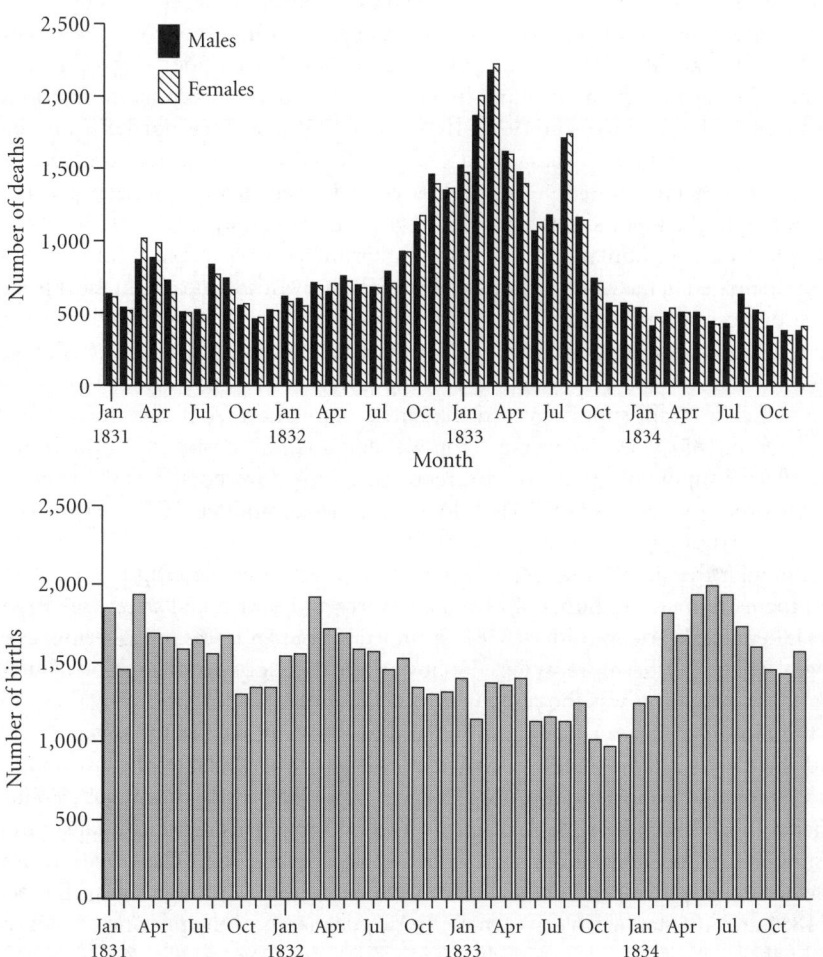

Figure 4.2. *The Monthly Number of Deaths (by Sex) and Births in 1831–4 in Regions Affected by the Famine of 1832–3*

Sources: Population Change Tables in the Archives of Statistics Finland. A listing of the affected areas has been given in the Results section of the chapter.

In this region the second mortality peak surpassed the first one. Even in these areas normal levels of mortality were again reached by November 1833 (Population Change Tables in the Archives of Statistics Finland).[2] The harvest outcome was roughly the average in both 1833 and 1834, but the misfortunes were not yet completely over. Several regions in various parts of the country suffered again from a crop failure in 1835 (Johanson 1924: 91–2). The elevated levels of mortality which can be detected in many areas in 1836 are likely to be associated with the poor harvest outcome (Population Change Tables in the Archives of Statistics Finland).

In the 1850s the harvest outcome was below the normal almost every single year in some regions, either due to cold summers, drought, autumn frost, or a combination of these factors. All administrative provinces suffered from poor crops during the decade, but again, the areas most frequently affected were regions in central and northern Finland (Johanson 1924: 103–8). In 1856 the three northern provinces of the country, Kuopio, Vaasa, and Oulu, suffered from a nearly complete crop failure. The harvest outcome was below normal even in the southern provinces. According to the reports of the provincial governors the only regions with sufficient grain to feed the populations were the southernmost areas of the country. Famine was anticipated in the worst affected regions. The harvest was meagre in most parts of the provinces of Kuopio and Oulu as well as in central Finland (the inland region east from Ostrobothnia) also in 1857, and frost had damaged the rye crop in many other regions. Due to repeated poor harvests the governors estimated that no province had sufficient grain supply to feed the entire population. A change for the better occurred in 1858 when an average crop was harvested in most parts of the country. Insufficient supply of grain was still reported by the governors, but the worst was clearly over (Johanson 1924: 103–8; Report of the Committee 1858; Reports of the District Medical Officers in 1857 and 1858).

Although the situation appeared to be very severe after the crop failure of 1856 and there are many accounts of extreme poverty and nutritional stress (see Brydolf 1944; Report of the Committee 1858), the mortality outcome was not as serious as one might expect. Furthermore, as Fig. 4.3 shows there is no such distinct period of intense mortality increase as was the case during the famine of 1832–3, or during the famine of the 1860s (see below). In eastern Finland mortality peaked in the spring of 1857, and there was another smaller increase in mortality one year later. In Ostrobothnia and Satakunta the most intense mortality peak occurred in early autumn of 1857 and a smaller mortality increase took place the next autumn. This regional dualism in the timing of the mortality increases can be detected in Fig. 4.3. The situation in the northernmost province of Oulu was somewhat different, although the spring peaks of 1857 and 1858 are visible also there. In two deaneries of the province, Raahe and Oulu, the levels of mortality were elevated throughout the years 1856–8, which may be

---

[2] Cholera visited Finland for the first time in the early 1830s. The disease reached the country in 1831, but it spread only to the southern parts of the country, mainly to the coastal regions. The epidemic had the most significant impact on mortality in the largest cities of Finland. The increases in the nation-wide mortality rates, however, were negligible. In 1832 there were only a few deaths attributed to cholera (Pesonen 1980: 148 and 158; Population Change Tables in the Archives of Statistics Finland).

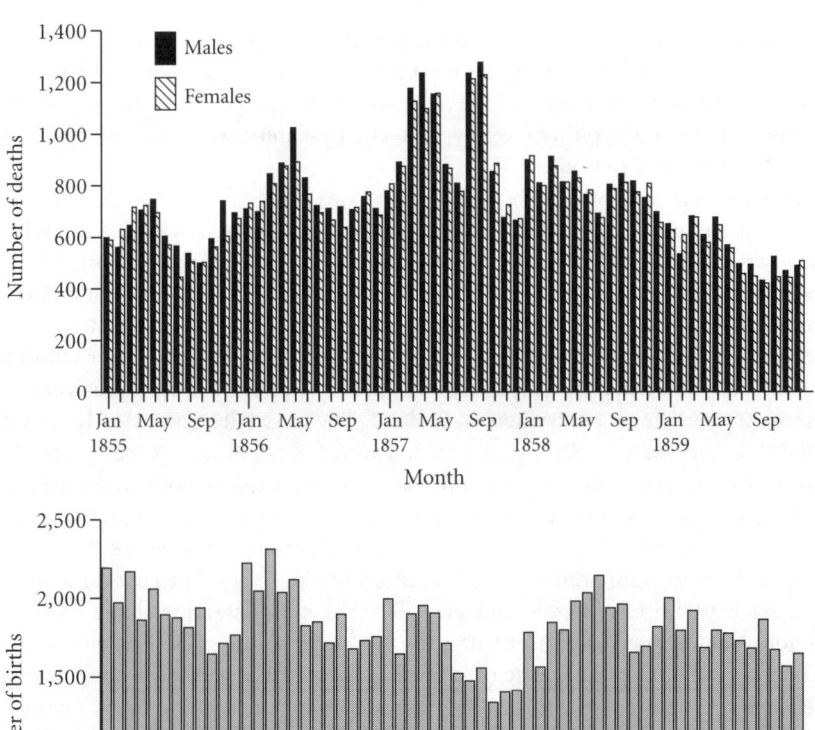

Figure 4.3. *The Monthly Number of Deaths (by Sex) and Births in 1855–9 in Regions Affected by the Famine of 1857–8*

Sources: Population Change Tables in the Archives of Statistics Finland. A listing of the affected areas has been given in the Results section of the chapter.

linked to the fact that these regions were most frequently affected by poor harvests in the 1850s. Figure 4.3 shows also other mortality peaks, particularly during the spring of 1855 and 1856. These mortality increases were limited to eastern Finland, and they affected almost exclusively children and elderly people. In 1855 the causes of death with significant increases were consumption ('lungsot' and 'tvinsot') and malaria ('frossa'). Even in 1856 the level of malaria mortality was elevated, but the increases in child mortality were caused by a measles epidemic. It is difficult to assess to what extent these mortality peaks may have been linked to problems in the nutritional status of the population. In fact, there is no unambiguous link. The harvest had not been particularly bad in 1855, and the causes of death typically associated with famine mortality in Finland, typhoid fever, typhus, and dysentery, were of small significance during both of these periods.

In the 1860s the first year with a poor harvest was 1862. As usual, the harvest failure hit mainly the population of the northern provinces: Kuopio, Vaasa, and Oulu. In many parts of the country the output was somewhat below average in both 1863 and 1864, and in 1865 there occurred the next widespread crop failure. The first year with a somewhat better harvest occurred in 1866, but even then the grain harvest was largely destroyed in southern Ostrobothnia and in Satakunta. The somewhat more abundant crop in 1866 provided only temporary relief to the peasants. The next year's crop was extremely poor almost everywhere in Finland. The crop failure was nearly complete in the three northern provinces and in Satakunta. Even in most other parts of the country the harvest deficiency was notable. Only in a few regions in the southern coastal area and in the province of Mikkeli was the grain output roughly average, although below rather than above the normal production (Pitkänen 1993: 51–3).

The 1862 crop failure did not result in mortality increases. The government organized extensive import of grain and were able to keep the situation stable.[3] Mortality did not reach elevated levels until after the 1865 crop failure. The first peak in mortality occurred during the spring of 1866 (Fig. 4.4). Although the elevated mortality levels extended from the end of 1865 through mid-year 1868, an examination of monthly variation implies that the three famine years do not form a continuum in terms of excess mortality. Even though the mortality rates were higher than normal in a majority of the rural deaneries during all three of the famine years, each year showed a distinct regional pattern. In 1866 the highest mortality rates were in the southern deaneries of the province of Oulu and in central Finland. In 1867 the highest mortality rates occurred in the western-most deaneries of Finland. In 1868 the death rates were at an extremely high level in numerous deaneries in both northern and southern Finland. An examination of the annual regional mortality patterns reveals that the areas showing the highest mortality figures were largely the same as those which had been struck most by a crop failure during the preceding year (Pitkänen 1993: 83–5).

The war of 1808–9 was a different type of crisis leading to intense mortality increases. The number of deaths grew rapidly soon after the Russian troops invaded eastern parts of the Swedish Kingdom, that is present-day Finland, in February 1808. Finnish troops retreated at a quick pace to the northern regions of the country. During the summer the Finnish army advanced towards the south and was able to recapture the central parts of the country; but after being reinforced, the Russian troops forced the Finns to retreat to what is now Sweden. The war continued until a peace treaty was signed in Hamina in September, 1809. After the peak in mortality

---

[3] There was a small peak in mortality in 1863 due to childhood diseases. However, a closer examination of the peak gives no support that it was primarily associated with the preceding year's poor harvest (Pitkänen 1993: 81).

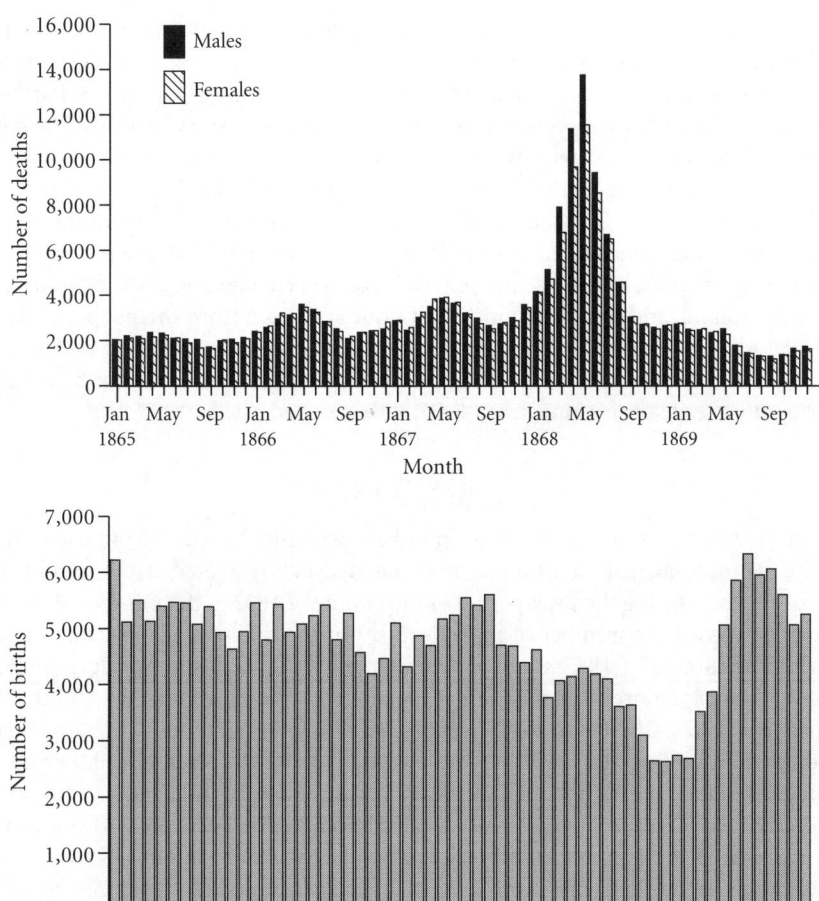

Figure 4.4. *The Monthly Number of Deaths (by Sex) and Births in 1865–9 in Finland*

Sources: Official Statistics of Finland, Population Statistics VI:2 and VI:4.

during the winter and spring months of 1809 the number of deaths started to decline reaching normal levels by the end of the year.

As is usually the case with pre-industrial warfare, the bulk of the population losses were not due to actual battles. The majority of the excess deaths occurred among the civilian population and were caused by various communicable diseases. The most significant exacerbating factor leading to high mortality rates appears to have been the contacts between both the Finnish and Russian troops and the civilian population. Soldiers were often infected with communicable diseases and were usually in proximity with the local populace of the staging areas. A war can also cause economic problems and affect adversely food production and the supply of food. Nutritional stress was reported in many regions suffering from the presence of the armies. Furthermore, poor harvests were reported in many parts of the country in 1807. The crop failure may be associated with the fact that adult mortality had started to increase already towards the end of 1807. In the northern parts of Finland the crop was damaged by frost also in 1808. Based on these accounts it is likely that the nutritional status of the population deteriorated during the war. However, in spite of the problems the situation did not develop into a famine. The Russian occupation forces bought surplus grain in Finland, and organized import of flour and grain from Russia, particularly in 1809. All this flour and grain was given as a loan or distributed as aid to destitute people. These measures were likely to have been of large significance in helping to avert a subsistence crisis (Lindström 1904; Pitkänen and Mielke 1993).

RESULTS

Figures 4.2–4.4 present the monthly numbers of death by sex during each crisis period. Under 'normal' conditions, male deaths slightly exceeded the number of female deaths. During the peak period of the famine of 1832–3 the number of female deaths surpassed the number of male deaths, but the difference is relatively small. During the famine of 1857–8 the sex differences are less consistent. During some months there are more male than female deaths, but during some other months the opposite is true. No systematic disadvantage is shown for either sex. The same holds true for the two first years of the famine of the 1860s. During the peak period of famine mortality in early 1868 a male excess is clearly visible. In fact, the death series are likely to underestimate the male disadvantage. As has been pointed out, there were omissions in the mortality statistics particularly in 1868, and it is likely that the missing deaths were disproportionately male (Pitkänen and Mielke 1993). Thus, as far as the year 1868 is concerned the female advantage often reported in famine studies is clearly detectable, but in the light of all the reported Finnish famine experiences this is an exception rather than the norm.

Examination of the total number of deaths is a very crude way to study sex differentials in famine-induced mortality, because the total numbers may conceal substantial differences between individual age categories. Therefore, excess mortality by age and sex has been analysed for all three famines, and the results have been compared with the 1808–9 war. A detailed analysis covering the famine of the 1860s and the 1808–9 war has been published in Pitkänen and Mielke (1993), and the results are not completely repeated here. As was pointed out above, the famine years of the 1860s did not form a continuum in terms of excess mortality. The years show differences also in sex-specific excess mortality, and therefore, the results are presented for each of the three famine years separately. The mortality data were analysed separately for each year of the other two famines as well, but there were no significant differences between the years 1832 and 1833 or between the years 1857 and 1858. Consequently, the results for both of these famines are presented for the two famine years combined.

The results concerning the 1808–9 war have been treated in a similar fashion for the same reason.

In order to examine excess mortality during the crises in the affected areas, age-specific mortality rates for both sexes have been compared to rates which prevailed during the absence of such calamities in the same regions. For the 1808–9 war, the 'standard' mortality is the 10-year period from 1796 to 1805. The famine of the 1860s has been compared to the 5-year period from 1861 to 1865. Both of these baseline periods contain a few mortality increases, but these are primarily attributable to various childhood diseases, such as smallpox and measles. Recurrent epidemics caused by such diseases were an essential part of the 'normal' mortality experiences of the populations. The 'standard' mortality periods for the other two famines had to be chosen with greater consideration, because in both the 1830s and the 1850s there were other mortality increases which may have been associated with poor harvests. The 'standard' for the famine of 1832–3 consists of the years 1831, 1834, and 1837–40, and for the famine of 1857–8 of the years 1851–5 and 1859–60. During the 1808–9 war the entire country has been included in the calculations, and even the ravages of the famine of the 1860s were so extensive that only the Åland Islands and the northernmost deaneries of Lappi and Kemi remained unaffected by mortality increases. In the 1830s and 1850s large regions remained unaffected during the famines. The calculations of excess mortality are limited to those deaneries which showed apparent mortality increases during the famine periods:

In 1832–3: The deaneries of Karjalan alinen, Karjalan ylinen, Pohjois-Savon ylinen, Pohjois-Savon alinen, Vaasan alinen, Vaasan ylinen, Kokkola, Pietarsaari, Raahe, Kajaani, Sortavala, Käkisalmi eteläinen, and Käkisalmi pohjoinen.

In 1857–8: The deaneries of Tyrvää, Karjalan alinen, Karjalan ylinen, Kuopion tuomiorovastikunta, Vaasan ylinen, Vaasan lääni, Pietarsaari, Raahe, Oulu, Kajaani, and Kemi.

The regions included cover roughly the three northern provinces of Kuopio, Vaasa, and Oulu (excluding the northernmost areas of the last province). During the famine of 1832–3 the affected area extended to the northern parts of the province of Viipuri, and during the famine of 1857–8 to Satakunta. The small urban populations in the affected areas have been excluded from the calculations.

Figure 4.5 shows the proportional increases in mortality by age and sex for all the crisis periods. Not only does the severity of the crises vary from one calamity to another, but also the shape of the excess mortality curves are different. The variable age patterns are largely due to differences in excess child mortality. The greater irregularity seen in the excess mortality patterns for children was caused by the variable intensity of typical childhood diseases, such as smallpox, measles, scarlet fever, whooping cough, and croup, which were responsible for a large portion of deaths among the younger segments of the population. In both 1866 and 1867 child mortality caused by these diseases did not differ much from the 'normal' levels. The peak in child excess mortality seen during the famine of the 1830s, on the other hand, resulted from an exceptionally vigorous smallpox epidemic.

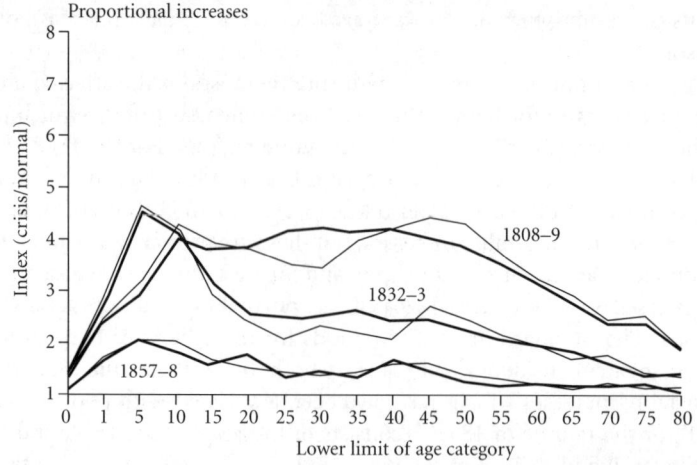

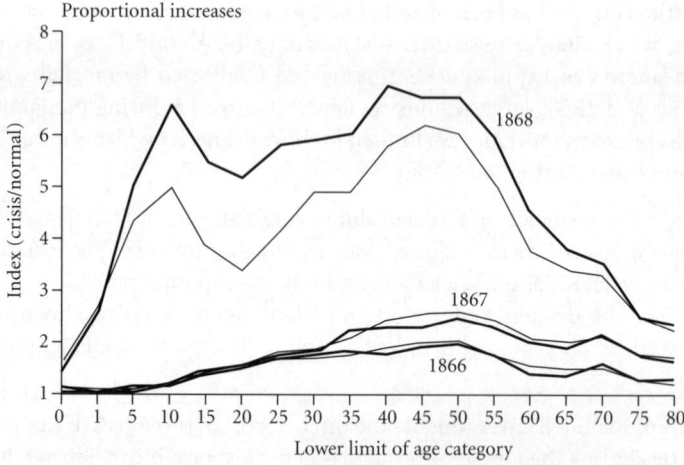

Figure 4.5. *Proportional Increases in Age-specific Mortality during the 1808–9 War and the Famines of the 1830s, 1850s, and 1860s, by Sex*

Sources: Appendix Tables 1 and 2; Pitkänen and Mielke 1993, Appendix Tables. The broad lines show mortality increases for males and the narrow lines for females. The death rates for 1868 have been adjusted to include the estimated omissions from the mortality statistics. Only regions affected by mortality increases during the crises have been included. For further details see text.

During several of the crisis periods the proportional mortality increases are roughly the same for both sexes. Nonetheless, there are certain differentials which prevail during many periods. Among younger adults men suffer from larger excess mortality, whereas the situation is the opposite for children and particularly for middle-aged adults. The year 1868 represents a peculiar pattern of sex-specific mortality increase. Apart from young children and the oldest age categories men suffered from much higher excess mortality than did women. The gap is most pronounced for adolescents and young adults.

Excess mortality has also been measured by subtracting the sex-specific standard mortality rates for each age group from the respective rates for the crisis periods. These absolute increases in the mortality rates have been depicted in Fig. 4.6. These measures tell a somewhat different story in comparison to the proportional increases. During most crisis periods there are hardly any differentials in excess mortality between the sexes. In fact, it appears that the systematic sex differentials revealed by the proportional measures reflect *differences in baseline mortality* rather than differentiated responses to crisis-induced mortality increases. In the reproductive age categories women often suffered from excess mortality during the periods of 'normal' mortality, and in such cases mortality increases of the same magnitude resulted in larger proportional increases among men. For children and the middle-aged population the situation was the opposite. Middle-aged men, in particular, show consistently significant excess mortality during the baseline periods. The age-specific death rates for the famines of 1832–3 and 1857–8 and the respective baseline periods are shown in the Appendix Tables. The data for the other two crisis periods have been published in Pitkänen and Mielke (1993).

Even though proportional increases are more commonly used to measure the extent of excess mortality, the reasons for the choice of this specific measurement are hardly ever presented. In many cases the choice does not appear to be based on any particular considerations. In fact, it can be argued that in many cases the absolute differences should be the preferred way to do such measurement.[4] The difference between the age-specific mortality rates indicates the relative frequency of the crisis-induced excess deaths in the examined population in comparison to a situation which would have prevailed without this specific risk, that is, in the absence of such a calamity. The cause-of-death statistics and the various medical reports indicate that excess mortality during the Finnish famines was largely caused by specific infectious diseases, such as typhus, typhoid fever, and dysentery (see Pitkänen 1993 and the Population Change Tables in the Archives of Statistics Finland). During 'normal' periods the incidence of such diseases was only sporadic.

However, the year 1868 shows apparent sex differentials in excess mortality also when the absolute mortality increases are examined. Male excess mortality is largest in adolescence and early adulthood even when using the absolute measure. Another period showing similar tendencies is the famine of 1832–3. Although the mortality differences between men and women are much smaller than in 1868, they are consistent for most age categories from adolescence to late middle age. However, a more detailed analysis of the data reveals considerable regional differences in the mortality response. Men were harder hit only in the western regions of the affected area,

---

[4] Another way to measure famine-induced excess mortality for various age categories is to compare a baseline with a famine period by using either ratios between male and female mortality rates or ratios between the numbers of male and female deaths. The former calculations give similar results to the proportional measure used in this chapter. The same holds true even for the latter measurement concerning those age categories in which the number of women and men are roughly the same.

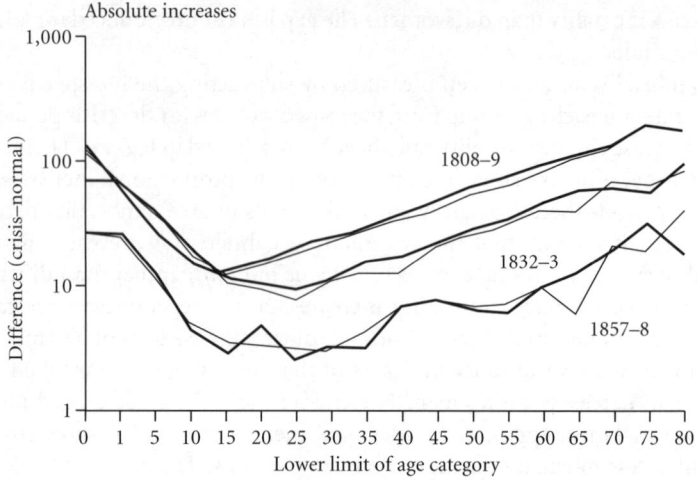

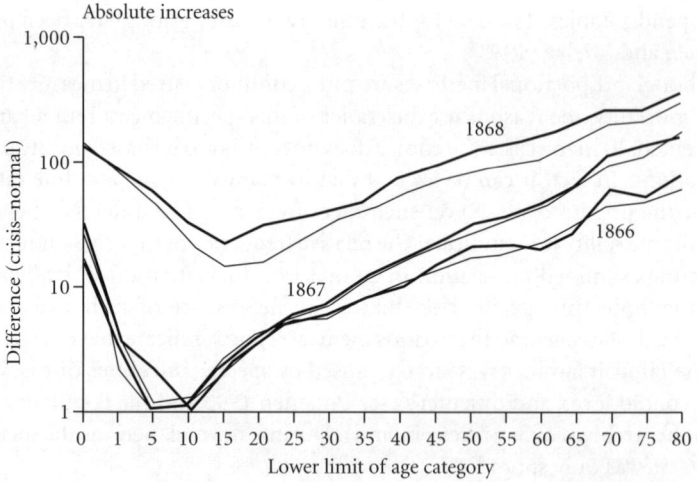

Figure 4.6. *Differences between the Actual and Standard Age-specific Mortality Rates during the 1808–9 War and the Famines of the 1830s, 1850s, and 1860s, by Sex*

Notes: Appendix Tables 1 and 2; Pitkänen and Mielke 1993, Appendix Tables. The broad lines show mortality increases for males and the narrow lines for females. The death rates for 1868 have been adjusted to include the estimated omissions from the mortality statistics. Only regions affected by mortality increases during the crises have been included. For further details see text.

particularly in southern Ostrobothnia, whereas in eastern Finland mortality increases were of the same magnitude for both sexes. The sex differentials in the west were most pronounced in the prime adult years.

A closer look at the other examined periods reveals similar regional variability during most of the crises. In the worst affected regions, that is in Ostrobothnia men suffered from slightly higher excess mortality than women during the 1808–9 war, even when measured by using absolute differences. In 1809 such sex differentials were visible throughout most of the adult ages. In 1867 a small high mortality area in Satakunta, in south-western Finland, shows higher excess mortality rates for adult men when compared to women. On the other hand, in 1868 the greater vulnerability of men is largely limited to regions which were most severely affected by mortality increases (Pitkänen and Mielke 1993).

DISCUSSION

The examination of three nineteenth-century famines in Finland and the 1808–9 war indicates that during these calamities mortality increases, particularly in absolute terms, were in many cases rather similar for men and women. Thus, the greater vulnerability of men during subsistence crises which has been reported in several studies is not a norm as far as the Finnish famine-induced mortality increases are concerned. These results are significant because they are based on good quality data, and concern populations which are well defined and fairly large.

The Finnish cases reported in this chapter are not the only ones suggesting roughly equal mortality responses between the sexes. An analysis of the 1984–5 Ethiopian famine indicated that in fact women were harder hit than men (Kidane 1989). Another example concerns Sweden. The demographic history of Sweden is quite different from that of Finland, but the countries share the same high quality historical materials. Sweden was not hit by major subsistence crises in the nineteenth century, but the country experienced a famine in 1773 resulting in significant increases in nation-wide mortality rates (Ohlander and Norman 1983).

The Swedish population statistics were used to calculate similar measures of excess mortality by sex as have been presented above for Finland. The 'standard' mortality used for the calculations is the 10-year period of 1761–70. Figure 4.7 shows that there were substantial sex differentials in the proportional mortality increases. Boys from 5 to 15 years suffered from notably larger excess mortality than girls of the same age, whereas a female disadvantage is visible for most other age categories, particularly for the middle-aged population. However, even in the Swedish case most of these features mirror differentials in baseline mortality which reveal a considerable male excess among young adults and the middle-aged population. Consequently, sex differentials in absolute mortality increases during the famine were small.

The fact that many of the crises reviewed in this chapter resulted in roughly equal mortality experiences for both women and men leads to the first conclusion of this study. The general feature of historical famines in Finland, as well as elsewhere in Europe (see Post 1990: 247–57), has been that the resulting mortality increases were largely due to communicable diseases, such as typhus, typhoid fever, dysentery, and relapsing fever. Therefore, the findings of this chapter cast doubt on the idea that men suffer from an inherently inferior regulation of the immune system. To accept such a suggestion, substantial mortality increases linked to epidemics of communicable

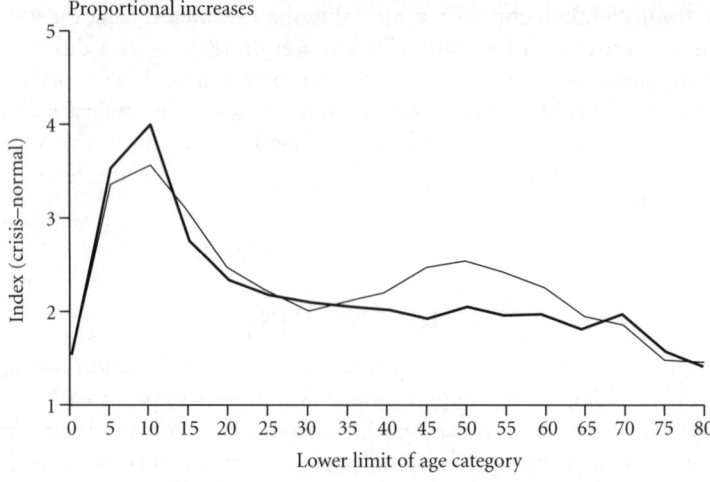

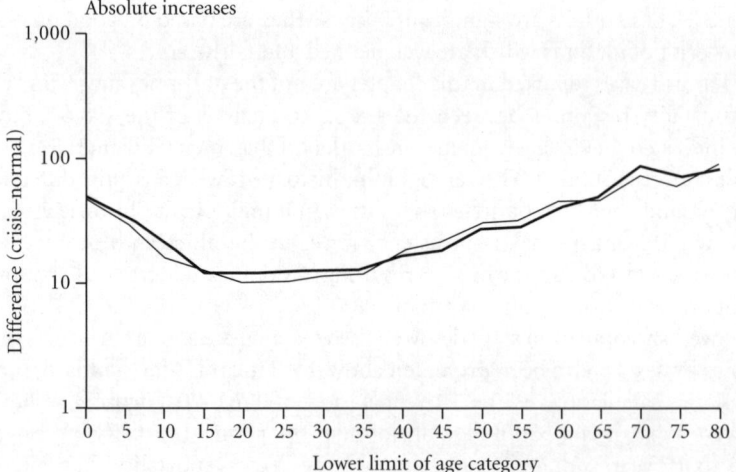

Figure 4.7. *Proportional and Absolute Increases in Age-specific Mortality during the Famine of 1773 in Sweden, by Sex*

Sources: Sundbärg 1905. The broad lines show mortality increases for males and the narrow lines for females. For further details see text.

diseases should quite consistently affect men more than women from one calamity to another and across most age categories, particularly for adults.

Although many of the Finnish calamities reviewed in this chapter failed to show consistent sex differentials in mortality response, the fact still remains that there were mortality increases which comply with the general perception of greater male vulnerability during subsistence crises. Therefore a key question is: what makes these occurrences, particularly the year 1868, different from those famine-induced mortality increases which showed no or only negligible sex differentials? Various hypotheses which have been presented in the research literature to explain greater male vulnerability will now be discussed in an attempt to answer this question. The explanations can be grouped into three wide categories. The first of them stresses largely biological differences between the sexes in responding to nutritional stress. The second category focuses on changes in fertility, and has both biological and behavioural components. The hypotheses belonging to the third category emphasize the primary role of behavioural differences between the sexes.

The significance of the biological factors could be supported by the suggestion that women are physiologically less severely affected by prolonged food deprivation than men. The implications of this sex difference appear obvious in cases when famine-induced mortality is primarily due to other causes of death than communicable diseases, but even in the case of disease-related mortality increases there are possible mechanisms which could result in a male disadvantage. First, nutritional stress could impair immune responses among men to a greater extent than among women. Second, men could suffer from higher case-fatality than women. At first glance these explanations might appear attractive considering the nineteenth-century Finnish mortality crises. The greater vulnerability of males seems to correlate with the severity of the mortality response. Male disadvantage could be detected in the high-impact regions during both the war of 1808–9 and the famine of the 1860s. Furthermore, men were harder hit than women during the famine of 1832–3, contrary to the famine of the 1850s which showed a less intense mortality response. A possible explanation is that the most pronounced mortality increases are linked to a larger male vulnerability because they also reflect the worst experiences of nutritional deprivation. A closer examination of the evidence, however, indicates that this reasoning is not convincing.

First, even though the intensity of the mortality increases was less pronounced during the famine of 1857–8, the historical accounts indicate that food shortage was severe and that masses of people were suffering from extreme lack of food (see Report of the Committee 1858; Brydolf 1944). Second, if the sex differentials result from biologically determined impairment of immune responses or if the case-fatality rates are linked to the severity of emaciation, one could expect to see consistency in these differentials across all age categories, at least at adult ages. This is largely the case in 1868, but not in 1867 or during the famine of 1832–3. Third, not all severely stricken regions showed sex differentials in excess mortality in 1868 (see Pitkänen and Mielke 1993). Fourth, during the years 1832–3 men were harder hit only in the western parts of the country, even though the nutritional circumstances must have been at least as severe in eastern Finland. In fact, the mortality increases were slightly larger in the east than in the west. Fifth, Pitkänen and Mielke (1993) have also analysed case-fatality rates among hospital patients suffering from typhus in 1868. Systematic male disadvantage could not be detected even among those patients who had come from destitute areas. All in all, the Finnish evidence indicates that the link between male-dominated excess mortality and nutritional stress is not consistent.

Figures 4.2–4.4 also show the monthly number of births for all the investigated famine periods. Fertility decline is one of the standard demographic responses during famines. The lowest number of births, however, does not usually coincide with the peak in mortality, but occurs several months later. A similar pattern characterizes all the examined nineteenth-century famines in Finland. In most cases the most intense increase in mortality occurred during the winter and spring months, whereas the nadir in births can be seen during the last months of the crisis years. A similar relation between mortality increases and fertility decline can be seen during the 1808–9 war (data not shown here, see Pitkänen and Mielke 1993). The war period differed from the famine in the respect that mortality was much above 'normal' for an extended period of time, from early 1808 until the summer of 1809. Consequently the number of births remained at low levels from late 1808 until early 1810.

The timing of the fertility decline means that during the mortality peaks a much lower percentage of women were pregnant than under normal conditions. As Dyson (1991a: 25) has pointed out, this situation could have been beneficial to women during famines and contributed to their smaller mortality increases in comparison to men. It is also noteworthy that during the famine of 1832–3 the male disadvantage in western Finland was most pronounced from about 25 to 40 years of age. The situation was rather similar even in 1867 in the affected regions, and also in 1868 the largest gap between male and female excess mortality was at the younger adult ages. On the whole, however, the Finnish data do not support the idea that women have benefited from the decreased frequency of pregnancies to a significant degree. Fertility declined in a similar fashion during all the crises periods, and yet, women were not always hit less severely. Furthermore, during the 1808–9 war, in 1832–3, and in 1868 fertility declined substantially even in those regions which showed mortality increases of the same magnitude for both sexes.

In fact, it is plausible that even though the number of pregnancies diminished during the crises, the remaining ones were more-than-usually hazardous to women's health under conditions characterized by nutritional problems and increased levels of morbidity. The District Medical Officers must have been primarily preoccupied with the catastrophic levels of epidemic mortality during the famine of the 1860s, but in spite of this a few of them mentioned in their annual reports that there had been exceptionally many miscarriages and premature births (Reports of the District Medical Officers of Uusikaupunki in 1867, and Tammela and Iisalmi in 1868). Another indication of pregnancy-related problems is that maternal mortality increased substantially during the famine of the 1860s (see Table 4.1). In 1868 the nation-wide maternal mortality rate was nearly twice the levels which prevailed before and after the famine period, and in the badly affected province of Kuopio in eastern Finland the rate was almost three times higher. Although the number of births in 1868 was about 30 per cent less than during the years immediately preceding or following the famine, more maternal deaths occurred. All in all, maternal mortality appears to be a sensitive indicator of nutritional stress and increased levels of morbidity. The maternal mortality rate prevailed at a high level even in 1869 in the provinces of Uusimaa, Viipuri, and Mikkeli. In these regions the harvest outcome was still below average in 1868.

Table 4.1. *Maternal Mortality (per 1,000 deliveries) in the Administrative Provinces of Finland, 1865–71 (95% Confidence Intervals)*

Province	Year						
	1865	1866	1867	1868	1869	1870	1871
Uusimaa	6.6 (4.6–8.6)	10.6 (7.9–13.3)	9.4 (6.9–11.9)	11.6 (8.4–14.7)	12.0 (8.8–15.1)	8.7 (6.3–11.1)	11.2 (8.5–13.8)
Turku and Pori	8.2 (6.6–9.8)	7.1 (5.5–8.6)	7.2 (5.5–8.8)	9.8 (7.6–12.0)	8.8 (7.1–10.5)	7.4 (5.8–9.1)	6.8 (5.3–8.3)
Häme	7.9 (5.7–10.1)	6.2 (4.2–8.3)	7.9 (5.6–10.2)	12.7 (9.0–16.4)	8.3 (5.9–10.7)	7.9 (5.9–10.0)	7.4 (5.5–9.4)
Viipuri	12.8 (10.3–15.3)	15.4 (12.7–18.2)	13.6 (11.1–16.0)	15.6 (12.8–18.4)	14.1 (11.2–17.0)	12.4 (10.0–14.9)	9.7 (7.6–11.7)
Mikkeli	8.8 (6.2–11.4)	14.4 (10.9–18.0)	12.0 (8.9–15.1)	16.5 (12.7–20.4)	18.9 (14.9–22.9)	10.8 (7.9–13.7)	7.9 (5.5–10.3)
Kuopio	8.5 (6.4–10.6)	8.9 (6.8–11.1)	9.4 (7.2–11.5)	23.4 (19.3–27.5)	9.4 (7.2–11.5)	7.4 (5.5–9.3)	9.6 (7.4–11.7)
Vaasa	7.7 (6.2–9.3)	8.3 (6.7–10.0)	8.0 (6.3–9.6)	11.3 (8.9–13.8)	8.4 (6.7–10.0)	5.1 (3.9–6.4)	6.8 (5.4–8.3)
Oulu	5.5 (3.7–7.3)	7.2 (5.0–9.4)	9.8 (7.3–12.3)	12.8 (9.6–16.9)	8.9 (6.5–11.4)	9.6 (7.2–11.9)	8.3 (6.1–10.5)
Finland	8.3 (7.6–9.0)	9.4 (8.7–10.2)	9.4 (8.7–10.2)	14.0 (12.9–15.1)	10.4 (9.5–11.2)	8.3 (7.6–9.0)	8.2 (7.6–8.9)
No. of maternal deaths	(528)	(566)	(569)	(629)	(603)	(523)	(547)

Sources: Official Statistics of Finland, Population Statistics VI:2 and VI:4. The number of deliveries also includes confinements resulting in stillbirths.

The remaining category of explanations focuses on patterns of social behaviour. There are two obvious behavioural mechanisms which can lead to sex differentials in famine-induced mortality increases. First, allocation of food in the household can change and result in discrimination against (or, favouring) certain groups of household members. The intra-household redistribution of food, supposing that any unequal treatment emerges in the first place, can be complex and vary from one society to another depending on household strategies and on household members' possibilities to control food resources (Drèze and Sen 1989: 55–9, 79–80). Second, due to behavioural differences certain individuals can be exposed to much harder physical stress than others.

The distribution of food in the household is difficult to examine in historical populations because direct evidence is scanty. The Finnish famine of the 1860s has been studied by using manifold source materials, including oral tradition, and yet hardly any evidence was found that indicated unequal allocation of food in the household. Discrimination appears to have been social and concerned the poorer segments of the population. Only under extreme deprivation does egocentricity seem to have become the leading force within households, but even then the family members who suffered most were those least able to defend themselves, particularly young children (see Häkkinen *et al.* 1991: 167–9, 212–15). Especially men in their prime years should have been able to safeguard their interests. Also, had specific changes in food allocation by gender been characteristic of subsistence crises in nineteenth-century Finland, it is difficult to see how they could have resulted in such variability in the mortality responses between women and men that we see in the data.

A behavioural difference between the sexes which is known to be in reasonably good agreement with the variable mortality experiences are famine-induced migration movements. As was pointed out above, vagrancy often increased during periods of deprivation. The evidence from the Finnish famine of the 1860s indicates that the stressful conditions linked to these movements could greatly boost mortality increases among itinerant migrants (Pitkänen 1992). As has been described in Pitkänen and Mielke (1993), the regional patterns of mortality are in reasonably good accordance with the known features of temporary migration in 1868. Migration from the crisis-stricken regions started to increase rapidly after the crop failure in 1867, and these movements reached massive proportions during the winter. Nothing comparable had been seen during the other nineteenth-century famines. In 1868 the itinerant migrants did not only circulate in their home parishes or in the nearby regions, but they also left their province of residence in great numbers and wandered to southern and southeastern parts of the country. Most of the migrants originated from the regions which showed large sex differentials in mortality. Migration was highly selective by age and sex, and men, particularly those in their early adulthood, were over-represented among the migrants.

Even though it is likely that temporary migration, on account of its population composition, resulted in greater mortality increases among men than women, these movements may have been just a part of a bigger picture. Temporary migration, of course, reflected the incapacity of the destitute areas to feed their poor. In part, however, the migration movements were augmented by the policies adopted by the Senate, that is, the home government of the Grand Duchy of Finland. In 1867 the government postponed their relief operations until early autumn, and even then the leading principle was not to give free aid. Finland had only a few workhouses prior to the famine, and even though there were attempts to make the residents do some work in the newly established temporary poorhouses, the results were not successful. Most of these poorhouses became no more than miserable asylums for the destitute people. The government and the province administrations, however, initiated a large number of public works to build railways, roads, and canals. These works could employ only a portion of the impoverished people, and many of these projects could not be launched until the spring. But rumours of job possibilities tempted large masses of people to migrate and seek their way to the construction sites (for a detailed description of the policies see Häkkinen *et al.* 1991).

Many of these work sites became infamous for their miserable conditions. Wages paid to the workers were low, and both morbidity and mortality reached considerable proportions. Particularly notorious were the construction sites of the Riihimäki–St Petersburg railroad, which has been said to have been built on 'the bones of its builders' (Häkkinen *et al.* 1991). The merciless policy of requiring work from undernourished people under difficult winter conditions probably contributed to the male disadvantage in mortality increases in 1868, since most of the workers who were hired to build railroads or canals were men. Even though it was also reported that women and children were hired to build roads, many historical accounts reveal that even at these sites the workers were largely men. Furthermore, it is apparent that the work assignments which were physically the most strenuous were designated to men (see, e.g., Häkkinen *et al.* 1991: 138–41).

Temporary migration, coupled with the relief policies, are conceivable factors explaining the male excess in mortality increases when attention is focused solely on the year 1868. The credibility of the explanation, however, also depends on how well similar factors could account for the observed variability in the mortality experiences across all the nineteenth-century calamities. One must acknowledge that only the famine of the 1860s has been subjected to thorough historical investigation, and a lot less is known about the other calamities. Nonetheless, what is known about the other crises is not in contradiction with the proposed explanation.

In many ways, the famine of the 1860s, and the year 1868 in particular, was exceptional among the nineteenth-century subsistence crises. First, temporary migration reached unprecedented proportions in 1868 as far as the nineteenth-century famines are concerned. Even though the destitute people left their homes during the other calamities too, the migration movements were much more local. Also, it is a plausible assumption that these migrations were less selective by sex. Nonetheless, from certain regions temporary migration had grown to sizeable proportions already in 1867. The District Medical Officer of Uusikaupunki reported in 1867 that large masses of itinerant migrants were on the move from Satakunta, that is, the region which had suffered badly from poor crops in 1866 and which showed a notable male excess mortality increase in 1867. Second, the strict governmental policies requiring work from the impoverished people in return for relief had gradually been developing during the hardships of the 1860s. It appears that in the 1850s and during the famine of 1832–3 the policies were more lenient and the primary goal was to feed starving people. During the famine of the 1830s, however, the government attempted to organize public works in the provinces of Vaasa and Oulu. These operations were much less extensive than in the 1860s, but a number of public works were undertaken (Kauranen 1999: 73–95). The possible health effects of these projects are not known, but it is noteworthy that these projects were organized in the western parts of the affected regions, which also showed a noticeable male excess in famine-induced mortality increases. The larger male vulnerability in Ostrobothnia during the 1808–9 war can also be explained by similar factors. This region was most severely affected by the military operations and showed the highest mortality increases. Most of the refugees escaping the enemy also came from this region, but such migration movements may not have been sex-selective. What may have been more significant were the tasks imposed on the civilians during the military operations. They were required to transport both goods and soldiers and carry out other tasks related to servicing the troops. The military, particularly the (Swedish-)Finnish troops, are known to have suffered severely from various infectious diseases, and civilians who were in close contact with them were exposed to these diseases. Men, especially younger adults, were most often involved in these activities (Pitkänen and Mielke 1993).

CONCLUSIONS

In this chapter the detailed and high quality Finnish demographic source materials have been used to examine sex differentials in excess mortality during three nineteenth-century subsistence crises. The results have been compared with another period of intense mortality increase, the 1808–9 war, as well as with the last major famine in Sweden which occurred in the early 1770s. The examination of the (proportional) excess mortality ratios showed for many of these calamities rather consistent differentials between the sexes. Younger adult males were usually more vulnerable than women of the same age categories, whereas the opposite was true for children and middle-aged men. These patterns of excess mortality, however, reflect differentials in baseline mortality rather than variable mortality experiences between the sexes during the calamities. When the *numbers* of additional deaths associated with the crises were used to calculate age-specific excess mortality rates the sex differentials largely disappeared. Thus, based on this measurement the sexes suffered from the calamities in rather equal terms.

A detailed analysis of the data revealed certain cases of male disadvantage even when measured in absolute terms. The most notable example is the year 1868, the most intense period of mortality increase during the famine of the 1860s. Even then the greater male vulnerability was visible mainly in those regions which had suffered most from repeated harvest failures and showed the highest excess mortality rates. A similar link is obvious also during the other examined famines, but this association is not consistent. Severe nutritional deprivation or large famine-induced mortality increases did not always result in sex differentials in excess mortality. Furthermore, a small male disadvantage could be detected even during the war of 1808–9, although the calamity was not primarily aggravated by nutritional problems.

The mortality increases associated with these nineteenth-century crises were largely due to infectious diseases. The variability in the mortality response between the different periods, affected regions, and age categories sheds doubts on the explanations attributing greater male vulnerability to inherent biological differences between the sexes, such as men's inferior regulation of the immune system or their poorer capability to resist the adverse effects of food deprivation. To credit these explanations, the male disadvantage should have occurred in a more consistent fashion. If nothing else, the operation of such biological mechanisms has been blurred by other factors. The common denominator of the occurrences of male-dominated mortality increases appears to be such behavioural patterns which have either exposed males disproportionately to infectious diseases or subjected them to harder physical stress. The male disadvantage in the mortality response is detectable under such circumstances when crisis-stricken and often starving people were required to attend public works in return for aid or military protection. These requirements were imposed to a greater extent on men than on women. The extreme example of such policies is the climax of the famine of the 1860s, when large masses of people, dominated by men, migrated over long distances trying to seek work at large railway and canal construction projects initiated by the government. Thus the evidence from the nineteenth-century Finnish subsistence crises suggests that the greater male vulnerability observed in a number of famine studies is not a biologically determined feature of such occurrences but is related to cultural factors, at least as far as historical disease-induced crises are concerned.

Appendix

Table 4.A1. *Age- and Sex-specific Death Rates in the 1830s According to a 'Standard' and During the Famine of 1832–3 in Regions Affected by the Famine (per 1,000 Population)*

Age group	Standard mortality		Years 1832–3	
	Males	Females	Males	Females
<1	249.1	200.2	322.4	305.5
1–4	35.3	33.5	100.9	97.0
5–9	11.4	10.5	51.8	49.3
10–14	6.2	5.5	26.0	23.3
15–19	5.8	5.7	18.0	16.7
20–24	7.1	7.0	18.2	16.7
25–29	6.4	7.4	16.0	15.3
30–34	7.5	8.7	19.2	20.5
35–39	9.8	10.9	25.9	24.1
40–44	12.3	12.1	30.0	25.4
45–49	15.6	12.0	38.7	33.2
50–54	22.8	17.7	52.0	44.4
55–59	32.3	25.7	67.1	56.4
60–64	47.8	39.3	94.1	79.9
65–69	67.4	56.4	124.8	97.4
70–74	101.3	88.3	161.6	157.2
75–79	153.5	140.6	210.9	204.4
80+	225.5	235.8	318.2	319.5

Source: Population and Population Change Tables in the Archives of Statistics Finland.

Note: The affected areas and the years used to calculate the 'standard' mortality rates have been specified in the Results section of the chapter.

Table 4.A2. *Age- and Sex-specific Death Rates in the 1850s According to a 'Standard' and During the Famine of 1857–8 in Regions Affected by the Famine (per 1,000 Population)*

Age group	Standard mortality		Years 1857–8	
	Males	Females	Males	Females
<1	209.6	171.9	237.4	200.1
1–4	38.8	36.0	65.4	63.7
5–9	11.6	10.2	24.2	21.6
10–14	5.4	4.8	9.9	9.7
15–19	4.9	5.2	8.0	8.9
20–24	6.4	6.3	11.3	9.7
25–29	6.9	7.1	9.6	10.3
30–34	7.4	8.1	10.7	11.2
35–39	9.0	10.0	12.3	14.5
40–44	11.0	11.5	18.5	18.4
45–49	15.2	12.1	23.0	19.6
50–54	20.7	16.7	27.3	23.7
55–59	30.6	23.6	36.8	31.0
60–64	43.0	36.0	52.9	45.9
65–69	64.4	55.7	77.3	61.7
70–74	103.1	87.1	122.8	108.1
75–79	152.0	138.8	184.4	158.2
80+	244.0	224.9	263.0	264.3

Source: Population and Population Change Tables in the Archives of Statistics Finland.

Note: The affected areas and the years used to calculate the 'standard' mortality rates have been specified in the Results section of the chapter.

References

Boyle, Phelim P., and Ó Gráda, Cormac (1986), 'Fertility Trends, Excess Mortality, and the Great Irish Famine', *Demography*, 23: 543–62.

Brydolf, Ernst (1944), 'Sverige och Finland under Nödvintern 1856–57', *Nordisk tidskrift för vetenskap, konst och industri* (new series), 20: 416–27.

Drèze, Jean, and Sen, Amartya (1989), *Hunger and Public Action*, Oxford: Clarendon Press.

Dyson, Tim (1991a), 'On the Demography of South Asian Famines, Part I', *Population Studies*, 45: 5–25.

—— (1991b), 'On the Demography of South Asian Famines, Part II', *Population Studies*, 45: 279–97.

Hart, Nicky (1989), 'Sex, Gender and Survival: Inequalities of Life Chances between European Men and Women', in John Fox (ed.), *Health Inequalities in European Countries*, Aldershot and Brookfield: Gower Publishing Company, 109–41.

Hazzard, William R. (1989), 'Why Do Women Live Longer than Men? Biological Differences That Influence Longevity', *Postgraduate Medicine*, 85: 271–83.

Hionidou, Violetta (1995), 'The Demography of a Greek Famine: Mykonos, 1941–1942', *Continuity and Change*, 10: 279–99.

Häkkinen, Antti, Vappu Ikonen, Kari Pitkänen, and Hannu Soikkanen (1991), *Kun halla lälän tuskan toi: miten suomalaiset kokivat 1860-luvun nälkävuodet*, WSOY, Porvoo–Helsinki–Juva.

Jannetta, Ann Bowman (1992), 'Famine Mortality in Nineteenth-century Japan: The Evidence from a Temple Death Register', *Population Studies*, 46: 427–43.

Johanson, V. F. (1924), *Finlands agrarpolitiska historia. En skildring av det finländska lantbrukets ekonomiska betingelser, I, från 1600-talet till år 1870*, Lantbruksvetenskapliga samfundets i Finland meddelanden, häfte 13, Helsingfors.

Kauranen, Kaisa (1999), *Rahvas, kauppahuone, esivalta. Katovuodet pohjoisessa Suomessa 1830-luvulla*, Helsinki: Finnish Historical Society.

Kidane, Asmerom (1989), 'Demographic Consequences of the 1984–1985 Ethiopian Famine', *Demography*, 26: 515–22.

Klasen, Stephan (1998), 'Marriage, Bargaining, and Intra-household Resource Allocation: Excess Female Mortality among Adults during Early German Development, 1740–1860', *The Journal of Economic History*, 58: 432–67.

Lindström, Gunnar (1904), 'Hätäavustus vuosina 1808 ja 1809', *Historiallinen Aikakauskirja*, 2: 77–83.

Lopez, Alan D (1983), 'The Sex Mortality Differentials in Developed Countries', in Alan D. Lopez and Lado T. Ruzicka (eds.), *Sex Differentials in Mortality: Trends, Determinants and Consequences*, Canberra: Department of Demography, Australian National University, 53–120.

Mielke, James H., and Pitkänen, Kari J. (1989), 'War Demography: The Impact of the 1808–09 War on the Civilian Population of Åland, Finland', *European Journal of Population*, 5: 373–98.

Official Statistics of Finland (OSF), Population Statistics, *Födde, vigde och döde åren 1865–1868 jemte en öfversigt af folkmängdens förändringar sedan år 1812 (VI:2)*, Statistiska Centralbyrån, Helsingfors.

—— *Öfversigt af folkmängdsförändringarne under åren 1869–1874 (VI:4)*, Statistiska Centralbyrån, Helsingfors.

—— *Hufvuddragen af Finlands befolkningsstatistik för åren 1750–1890, Volumes I–II (VI:29 and VI:33)*, Statistiska Centralbyrån, Helsingfors.

Ó Gráda, Cormac (1992), '"For Irishmen to Forget?" Recent research on the Great Irish Famine', in Antti Häkkinen (ed.), *Just a Sack of Potatoes? Crisis Experiences in European Societies, Past and Present*, Helsinki: Finnish Historical Society, 17–52.

Ohlander, A-Sofie, and Norman, Hans (1983), 'Kriser och katastrofer. Ett forskningsprojekt om effekterna av nöd, svält och epidemier i det förindustriella Sverige', *Historisk Tidskrift*, 103: 163–78.

Pesonen, Niilo (1980), *Terveyden puolesta—sairautta vastaan. Terveyden-ja sairaanhoito Suomessa 1800-ja 1900-luvulla*, WSOY, Porvoo–Helsinki–Juva.

Pitkänen, Kari (1980), 'Registering People in a Changing Society—the Case of Finland', *Yearbook of Population Research in Finland XVIII*, 60–79.

—— (1992), 'The Road to Survival or Death? Temporary Migration During the Great Finnish Famine in the 1860s', in Antti Häkkinen (ed.), *Just a Sack of Potatoes? Crisis Experiences in European Societies, Past and Present*, Helsinki: Finnish Historical Society, 87–118.

Pitkänen, Kari (1993), *Deprivation and Disease. Mortality during the Great Finnish Famine of the 1860s*, Helsinki: Publications of the Finnish Demographic Society 14.

Pitkänen, Kari, and Nieminen, Mauri (1984), 'The History of Population Registration and Demographic Data Collection in Finland', in *National Population Bibliography of Finland 1945–1978*, Helsinki: IUSSP–Finnish Demographic Society, 11–22.

—— and Laakso, Mikko (1999), 'The Reliability of the Finnish Mortality Statistics: A Historical Review', in Juha Alho (ed.) *Statistics, Registries, and Science—Experiences from Finland*, Helsinki: Statistics Finland, 15–37.

Pitkänen, Kari J., and Mielke, James H. (1993), 'Age and Sex Differentials in Mortality during Two Nineteenth Century Population Crises', *European Journal of Population*, 9: 1–32.

Post, John D. (1990), 'Nutritional Status and Mortality in Eighteenth Century Europe', in Lucile F. Newman (ed.) *Hunger in History. Food Shortage, Poverty, and Deprivation*, Cambridge (Mass.) and Oxford: Basil Blackwell, 241–80.

Report of the Committee for the Relief of Famine in Finland (1858), London.

Reports of the District Medical Officers in 1857 and 1858 (1858–60), *Finska Läkaresällskapets Handlingar*, 7.

Reports of the District Medical Officers in 1867 (1869), *Finska Läkaresällskapets Handlingar*, 10: 7.

Reports of the District Medical Officers in 1868 (1870), *Finska Läkaresällskapets Handlingar*, 11: 2.

Rivers, J. P. W. (1988), 'The Nutritional Biology of Famine', in G. A. Harrison (ed.), *Famine*, Oxford–New York–Tokyo: Oxford University Press, 57–106.

Snyder, J. C. (1965), 'Typhus Fever Rickettsiae', in F. L. Horsfall, Jr. and I. Tam (eds.), *Viral and Rickettsial Infections in Man*, 4th edn., Philadelphia–Toronto: J. B. Lippincott Company, 1059–94.

Solantie, Reijo (1992), 'Klimatperioder och Finlands kolonisering', *Historisk Tidskrift för Finland*, 75: 86–96.

Sundbärg, Gustav (1905), 'Döde efter kön, ålder och civilstånd i Sverige åren 1751–1900 samt Medelfolkmängden efter kön och ålder under femårsperioderna för samma tid', *Statistisk Tidskrift*, 135: 107–62.

Tabutin, Dominique (1978), 'La surmortalité féminine en Europe avant 1940', *Population*, 33: 121–48.

Tabutin, Dominique, and Willems, Michel (1998), 'Differential Mortality by Sex from Birth to Adolescence: The Historical Experience of the West (1750–1930)', in *Too Young to Die: Genes or Gender*, New York: United Nations, 17–52.

de Waal, Alex (1989), 'Famine Mortality: A Case Study of Darfur, Sudan 1984–5', *Population Studies*, 43: 5–24.

Waldron, Ingrid (1998), 'Sex Differences in Infant and Early Childhood Mortality: Major Causes of Death and Possible Biological Causes', in *Too Young to Die: Genes or Gender*, New York: United Nations, 64–83.

Watkins, Susan Cotts, and Menken, Jane (1985), 'Famines in Historical Perspective', *Population and Development Review*, 11: 647–75.

Widdowson, Elsie M. (1976), 'The Response of the Sexes to Nutritional Stress', *Proceedings of the Nutrition Society*, 35: 175–80.

Willner, Sam (1999), *Det svaga könet? Kön och vuxendödlighet i 1800-talets Sverige*, Linköping: Linköpings Studies in Arts and Science, 203.

5

Famine in Berar, 1896–7 and 1899–1900: Echoes and Chain Reactions

TIM DYSON

The condition of many of the people at the poor-houses, especially the young and old, was sad to see: shrivelled and haggard in appearance, arms thin and flabby, legs spindley and wasted in flesh, elbows and knees knobby, flattening of the buttocks, and atrophy of the mammary glands. The skin had a dirty and scurfy appearance; the hair lustreless, staring, and of the colour of dried grass, and the sufferers had often a patient and sad expression of face, like a dumb animal in pain, which was pitiable to see. (Charles C. Little, *Report on the Sanitary Administration of the Hyderabad Assigned Districts 1897*: 32)

This chapter explores the sequences and consequences associated with a pair of famines which afflicted the Berar region of central India towards the end of the nineteenth century. My choice of Berar stems from two related considerations. First, the excellent quality of the region's demographic data—particularly that deriving from its system of vital registration. Second, the fact that the general demographic history of Berar has therefore been the subject of considerable research (see Banthia and Dyson 1999; Dyson 1989a,b) which provides valuable context for the present study.

The chapter has four main sections. The first introduces Berar and its general circumstances in the second half of the nineteenth century; the demographic data sources used here are also discussed. The second section contains an annual chronology of the 1890s—the decade containing the famines—and illustrates some of the ways in which disastrous happenings compounded each other. The third section examines the demographic consequences of the famines—both in the short- and long-term. The final section concludes.

BERAR

The onetime British India province of Berar corresponds to the combined current jurisdictions of Amraoti, Akola, Buldana and Yavatmal districts in the modern Indian state of Maharashtra. In the eighteenth and early nineteenth centuries the province experienced a fairly turbulent history under the suzerainty of the Nizam of Hyderabad, before in 1853 being taken over by the British. Initially this transference of administrative responsibility was theoretically under lease from the Nizam. Therefore, during the second half of the nineteenth century Berar was often referred to in official documents as the 'Hyderabad Assigned Districts'. The province remained a distinct entity within British India until its amalgamation with Central Provinces in 1903.

With rich alluvial soils, Berar lies in the cotton zone of central India. Thus the *Berar Gazetteer* of 1870 states that: '[t]he great staple produce which the province exports, by which cultivation flourishes, traders grow rich, and the taxes are paid, is cotton' (Lyall 1870: 225). Until the middle of the nineteenth century the transport of cotton out of Berar was conducted mainly overland by pack oxen. The route taken was either directly westwards to Bombay, or 500 miles north to Mirzapur on the banks of the Ganges and then by boat a further 450 miles eastwards downriver to Calcutta. Both routes took months.

However, the onset of British administration not only brought greater social stability, it also marked the start of a period of significant infrastructural economic development—based around the increased cultivation and export of cotton. In 1867 the extension of the Great Indian Peninsular Railway meant that cotton could be transported westwards to reach the textile mills and port of Bombay in only a matter of hours. The transport of large volumes of cotton was facilitated too by the building of a network of feeder narrow gauge railways and metalled roads throughout the province, and by the rapid introduction of cotton presses. Also in 1867 a telegraph line established contact with the Liverpool market—so allowing daily communication of the world cotton price to traders in Berar. And behind much of this lay the American Civil War (1861–5) which boosted demand for Indian cotton by isolating the European textile industry from its main source of supply (see Lyall 1870: Chapter 12). That said, there is also no doubt that the commercialization of agriculture in Berar during the late nineteenth century also produced considerable social and economic dislocation. The British administration was concerned, above all, with the cotton economy and it shied away from expenditure aimed at the province's wider economic development (see Satya 1997).

Whereas in the 1830s perhaps a fifth of Berar's total cultivated area was sown with cotton, by the end of the nineteenth century this fraction had risen to about a third—an area which almost rivalled that devoted to the principal food-crop of *jowari* (great millet). The expansion of cotton after 1853 probably also benefited from the region's relatively egalitarian social structure, a favourable system of land revenue settlement, the growth of regulated markets, plus the instigation of a competitive system of credit. There can be no doubt that Berar was economically important to the British—not least because it helped to clothe the urban poor back home, while also providing employment in Manchester and other towns in Lancashire (see e.g. Bates 1984; Satya 1997).

With an expanding economy, significant numbers of migrants were attracted in—especially during the 1850s, 1860s, and 1870s. In the first decade there was still some virgin land for cultivation, but this soon disappeared. The 1881 census results revealed that 19.5 per cent of the total population were born elsewhere. And of these in-migrants there were 1.16 males for every female (Kitts 1882: 97–100). The in-migrants tended to consist either of whole families, or married men in search of a

Famine in Berar

season's work. Most of these migrants ended up working as landless field labourers—the actual picking of the cotton being done by women and children. By the 1890s about one-third of Berar's total households were categorized as landless, and a similar proportion were either cultivating tenants or smallholders—groups that were almost as poor and vulnerable as landless field labourer households (Crawford 1901a: 1). Net migration into Berar continued during the 1880s, but the indications are that it was on a reduced scale compared to the earlier decades. However, until the economic depression of the 1930s each decade saw some continued limited net movement of people—more male than female—into Berar (see Dyson 1989a: 179; 1989b: 171–2).

The collection of statistical information was a significant concern of the province's colonial regime. Clearly, agricultural and trade data were viewed as particularly important—for example, statistics on rainfall and temperature, the areas planted under different crops, and the quantities of cotton that were traded and exported. But the overall efficiency of Berar's colonial administration was also reflected in the quality of its demographic data. The province's first modern census was conducted in 1867 and it enumerated 2.2 million people. The second census was conducted in 1881; it began a regular decennial series of censuses under the Government of India which has lasted until present times.

However, it is the excellent quality of its vital registration data which really marks Berar out from most of the rest of India. General birth and death registration in the province began in 1868. From the late 1870s until the amalgamation with Central Provinces in 1903, the Sanitary Commissioner with the Government of India almost routinely highlighted Berar in his *Annual Report* as a location where the system of birth and death registration was working exceptionally well. In rural areas registration depended upon local village officers—particularly the *Patel* (headman) and *Patwari* (watchman)—to make regular notification of the vital events which occurred in their areas of jurisdiction. In urban centres responsibility for registration rested with the public at large—although, in addition, municipal functionaries were charged with keeping independent records. In both rural and urban areas an important aspect of the system were the procedures for checking the performance of these various officers. Thus it is clear from the province's annual sanitary reports that most village registers were spot-checked for accuracy (e.g. by smallpox vaccination staff) at least once each year. Moreover, internal demographic consistency checks were employed by the administration to evaluate the registration statistics. For example, birthplace data from the censuses of 1881, 1891, and 1901 were used to generate estimates of net intercensal migration; these estimates correspond closely to the volumes of migration implied by the respective census counts combined with the numbers of births and deaths registered during the corresponding intercensal periods.

The main source of the vital registration data used in this study is the *Report on the Sanitary Administration of the Hyderabad Assigned Districts* (henceforth *RSAHAD*). This volume was written and compiled annually by Berar's Sanitary Commissioner. For 1897 and earlier years this was Charles C. Little, the role then falling to one Charles L. Swaine. Both men were qualified medical doctors. A minor problem for the present research is that the published *RSAHAD* volumes for 1899–1902 lack some of the detail found in those for earlier years.[1] Perhaps the most important explanation for this deficiency was Berar's forthcoming administrative amalgamation with Central Provinces. However, the change of Sanitary Commissioner and the pressure of work associated with the two famines may also have played contributing roles. On the other hand, extra data and insight on the famines are provided by the published famine reports for Berar (Crawford 1901a,b). And, as in some other famines in South Asia (see Dyson 1991a: 10), greater checking of local vital registers seems to have occurred in the famine years.[2]

To conclude this discussion of data issues, the vital registration material for Berar in the final decades of the nineteenth century are not perfect, but the level of event coverage was certainly close to being complete. Indeed, a strong case can be made that the coverage, detail and quality of the province's registration data were broadly comparable to (and sometimes better than) those of contemporary registration schemes in South Asia—such as India's *Sample Registration System* or the *Demographic Surveillance System* which operates in Matlab Thana of Bangladesh (see Dyson 1989a,b). Consequently, in what follows the principle applied is to make only the most minimal adjustments to the raw data, adding qualifications where appropriate.

In summary, with its store of good demographic and other information, Laxman D. Satya has written (1997: 22) that during the period 1850–1900 'the state played a major role in fashioning colonial capitalism in Berar. The introduction of railways, telegraph, metalled roads and the post office provided a dynamic technological force in transforming Berar's subsistence agriculture to a major cotton producing economy.' Nevertheless Berar was devastated by famine during the final decade of the nineteenth century. So it is to this decade, and the proximate causes and demographic consequences of the two famines, to which I now turn.

BERAR, 1890–1902, A CHRONOLOGY

It is fairly common to downplay the effects of famines—and epidemics—as major determinants of the much slower rates of population growth which generally prevailed in the historical past (e.g. see Watkins and Menken 1985). However, the experience of Berar during the 1890s—and, indeed, India as a whole during parts of the nineteenth century and earlier times—certainly gives one pause for thought on this matter.

The 1891–1901 intercensal decade in Berar has aptly been described (Office of the Registrar General 1923: 4) as a period in which 'calamity begat calamity with unexampled rapidity, culminating in the famine of 1900'—a statement which neatly conjures up the idea that famines and epidemics can interact synergistically. Thus famine

---

[1] In particular, registered births by *month* of occurrence are unavailable for years 1897, 1898, 1890, 1901, and 1902.

[2] Thus Swaine reports of 1900 that '[a] comparison of the year's total work of verification (8,774) with that of the previous year shows an increase of 3,764 of inspections of registers, and that more attention was paid to this work in the year under report, and the percentage of omissions discovered was 2.6' (*RSAHAD* 1900: 2).

conditions commonly trigger epidemics, magnifying their death toll; and epidemics can make populations more susceptible to famine, for example, by disrupting agricultural operations.

Table 5.1 gives the annual registered crude birth and death rates and the implied crude rates of natural increase for years 1891–1902 inclusive. These will be used to illustrate the following discussion. The Table also gives the average annual summary rainfall statistic—because the level and pattern of precipitation was crucial to the economy and health of the people of Berar. In particular, if the main monsoon rains which usually fell from June to September were unfavourable, then prospects for field work were adversely affected and the following main *kharif* harvest around November–December was threatened too. Rainfall was also vital in determining the availability of drinking water and patterns of disease.

Whereas for the decade 1881–90 natural increase in Berar was positive—the registered crude birth and death rates (CBRs and CDRs) averaging 39.4 and 34.4 respectively—it is clear that the period 1891–1900 was very different—the registered decadal CBRs and CDRs averaged 38.3 and 43.6 per thousand. So the positive natural increase of the 1880s was wiped out in the 1890s. Indeed, in 1894, 1895, 1896, 1897—and above all in 1900—registered deaths in Berar exceeded registered births (see Table 5.1). Drawing on the annual sanitary reports (*RSAHAD*) and the 1901 Berar census report which was written by Ardaseer D. Chinoy, the Superintendent of Census Operations (Chinoy 1902: 29), it is worth examining the history of this disastrous decade, year by year.

Table 5.1. *Annual Rainfall and Vital Rates, Berar, 1891–1902*

	Year											
	1891	1892	1893	1894	1895	1896	1897	1898	1899	1900	1901	1902
Rainfall (inches)	40.3	53.2	43.6	39.6	27.3	26.6	31.3	28.1	12.9	33.1	40.3	n.a.
Crude birth rate	42.8	39.7	39.1	33.3	37.2	38.2	39.7	31.3	50.3	31.4	30.8	56.9
Crude death rate	40.7	28.9	32.7	42.0	49.8	43.7	52.6	23.4	39.8	82.4	27.7	32.5
Crude rate of increase	2.1	10.8	6.4	−8.7	−12.6	−5.5	−12.9	7.9	10.5	−51.0	3.1	24.4

n.a.—not available.

Principal sources: *Report of the Sanitary Administration of the Hyderabad Assigned Districts* (various years).

Notes: The official birth and death rates used in India at this time were calculated using a constant denominator, namely the previous census count. However, the rates shown above, and those underlying the statistics in Table 5.3, were calculated taking likely denominator changes into account. Accordingly, they differ slightly from those mentioned in the quotations which appear in the text. The rainfall figures shown for 1891–4 and 1901–2 are unweighted averages for Berar's six districts.

The year 1891 was an inauspicious year in Berar. The death rate was high and nearly equal to the birth rate. At 40.3 inches rainfall was slightly below average and unseasonable, food prices were high, and public health was bad—with heavy mortality occurring from 'fever' (some of which was certainly malaria) and relatively high mortality registered for both cholera, and dysentery and diarrhoeal diseases. Eighteen ninety two was noticeably healthier, with a sharp reduction in the death rate—partly because cholera and bowel diseases were less prevalent. However, food prices remained 'considerably high'—this time partly due to *excessive* rainfall, which damaged both the main *kharif* (autumn) crop, sown during the monsoon rains of July–September, and the secondary *rabi* (spring) crop. The next year, 1893, was not particularly bad; indeed, both the province's rainfall and death rate were about normal (Table 5.1).

However, 1894 marked the start of four consecutive bad years. The registered death rate was unusually high and the birth rate unusually low in 1894, so Berar's crude rate of natural increase was pronouncedly negative. The Sanitary Commissioner (Little) was at a loss to explain the low birth rate, except to say that it was not obviously due to high mortality and ill health during the preceding year, and that the crude birth rate decline was fairly uniform across the province's (then) six districts. But the high death rate of 1894 was easier to account for—deaths from fever were particularly numerous and there was quite a bit of influenza in the early months which reportedly killed children and old people. There was also excessive and unseasonable rainfall that damaged both crops, although food prices in 1894 were not unusually high.

The year 1895 saw further deterioration. In spite of the fairly high death rate of the preceding year the birth rate actually recovered, but the death rate rose by even more. So, again, the annual rate of natural increase was very negative (Table 5.1). Cholera, dysentery and diarrhoea together accounted for much of the rise in deaths, and fever deaths were exceptionally high too. The year's rainfall was light—although sufficient to produce a reasonable *kharif* crop. However, for two reasons the light rains of 1895 constituted bad portents for the following year. First, the prospects for the coming *rabi* crop were poor; and second, as Little presciently remarked, 'it will be in 1896, when the wells begin to dry up, that the effects of the short rainfall [in 1895] will tell on public health' (*RSAHAD* 1895: 11).

This brings us to 1896, the first year of the first famine. Note that the annual CDR was six points *below* that of 1895 and similar to that of 1894 (Table 5.1). However, not only was Little's prophecy regarding drinking water and public health in 1896 borne out, but the events of the year augured very badly indeed for those which were to follow in 1897. Whereas average annual rainfall during 1890–94 was about 41 inches, the rains of 1896 totalled only 26 inches, being even more scanty and erratic than those of 1895. This meant that there was less monsoon-related mortality (e.g. due to malaria). But it also meant that the *kharif* crop failed and food prices nearly doubled during the last four months of 1896. In short, it was obvious to everyone that there would probably be a crisis in 1897—the more so because much of northern and central India also experienced poor rainfall. Therefore, and despite its improved death rate, 1896 was regarded as an extremely bad year. In this context the following quote is instructive of (i) several significant interactions between weather and the health of the population (ii) the fact that events in Berar were heavily conditioned by the wider context within India, and (iii) the way in which famine must be seen—and usually *is* seen by its cast of characters—as a *process* which evolves through time:

[T]he short rainfall of 1895 apparently favored the development of cholera and bowel complaints in the hot weather months [of 1896], when people were in many places drinking the concentrated impurities of their wells ... while the shorter rainfall of 1896 reduced mortality during the monsoon and cold weather seasons to below the average. Another result of the short rainfall of the year was a partial failure of the *kharif* crop and almost complete failure of the *rabi*. This caused a rise in prices in the closing months of the year, not due to scarcity of grain in the province, but to the high prices prevailing in the North-West and Punjab ... the high prices at the close of the year [1896] had scarcely time to affect the mortality rate of 1896, but should scarcity rates continue, the result will be a rise in mortality [in 1897] chiefly among infants and old people. (*RSAHAD* 1896: 14)

Coming now to 1897, interestingly the registered birth rate for the *year* was about average. But Little reported that Berar's *monthly* birth rate began to decline from August—obviously related to the high food prices and likelihood of famine that had been evident at the end of 1896. In this context he remarked specifically on the rarity of finding pregnant women at relief camps and poorhouses during 1897 (*RSAHAD* 1897: 4).

Little's predictions regarding high food prices and mortality in 1897 were also borne out. The registered death rate rose to 52.6 per thousand and the rate of natural increase was very negative (Table 5.1). The main causes of heightened mortality were fever and dysentery and diarrhoea, plus some cholera. The main monsoon rains of June–September 1897 were fair, but they had *both* good and bad implications. On the good side they resulted in an excellent *kharif* harvest around the end of the year. However, on the bad side, they contributed to famine mortality:

It was the experience at all our relief camps that after the rains set in sickness greatly increased, especially fevers and bowel-complaints. Indeed, the most common termination of life in those debilitated by famine was diarrhoea or dysentery, aggravated by damp and exposure after the setting in of the south-west monsoon. Cold and damp had a most detrimental effect upon the starving poor, and those in a physically reduced condition from chronic insufficiency of food. (*RSAHAD* 1897: 7)

In conclusion, the famine of 1896–7 in Berar was, to quote Chinoy (1902: 30), one 'of high prices rather than of scarcity of food'. Many poor Beraris perished. But there seems little doubt that the bulk of the province's own inhabitants either had access to reserve pit stores of grain or obtained limited supplies through the relief works, poorhouses, and kitchens that were set up. Berar was a reputed granary at this time and it attracted grain traders from neighbouring provinces. However, it also attracted large numbers of very hungry poor (especially from Central Provinces)—who were 'too far gone from the effects of chronic starvation to be saved by food'. And, while devoid of precise statistics, the official literature leaves no doubt that in-migrants constituted a significant fraction of all deaths (see *RSAHAD* 1897: 28–32).[3] Note that the vital rates of 1897 were similar to those during the *non*-famine year of 1895 (see Table 5.1). Indeed, it is quite possible that the crude death rate in Berar in 1897 would have been lower than that of 1895 were it not for the deaths of in-migrants.

Eighteen ninety eight was a brief interlude which allowed for some degree of recovery. As Chinoy (1902: 29) stated it was '[a] year of prosperity ... [e]xcess of births over deaths, 22,608. Rainfall fair ... prices fell considerably ... Traffic [i.e. trade] increased greatly both in volume and value. Public health excellent; no epidemics.' The registered death rate fell to 23.4 per thousand. And although—following the events of 1897—the birth rate in 1898 also fell to the low figure of 31.3, the province's annual rate of natural increase was comparatively brisk (Table 5.1). The new Sanitary Commissioner, Swaine, remarked that the departure of a large number of poor in-migrants from the previous year must have served to lower the death rate. And the extremely low birth rate of 1898 must have had a similar effect. That said, it is clear too that economic and public health conditions in 1898 were genuinely favourable to a low level of mortality. For example, under the heading 'Cholera' the annual sanitary report states simply that '[t]he pleasing feature in this form is that it is blank' (*RSAHAD* 1898: 13).

This brings us to the first year of the second, much greater famine. The registered birth rate in 1899 was the highest ever recorded. Broadly speaking, it was as unusually high as that for 1898 had been unusually low (Table 5.1). We can be fairly sure that its exceptionally high level was mostly a rebound from the earlier events. The death rate in 1899 was not particularly high; indeed, it was lower than in 1891 and in each of the years 1894–7. Hence—and as in the famine of 1896–7—the death rate in the *first* year of crisis was hardly abnormal. The combination of an exceptionally high birth rate and an unexceptional death rate in 1899 produced a relatively high rate of natural increase (10.5 per thousand)—itself a partial chain reaction arising from the first famine.

However, what was exceptionally bad about 1899 was the extremely low annual rainfall of only about 13 inches. Given the occurrence of widespread drought throughout much of the rest of India, what this meant was an inevitable and much more extreme rerun of the essential events of the earlier famine. So although the initial effects of the monsoon failure included water shortages, rising food prices and the instigation of famine relief works during the last four months of 1899, it was the longer-term consequences for the following year—1900—that were really important.

The *kharif* crop in Berar at the end of 1899 was virtually non-existent because of this monsoon failure. It was measured as 251,931 *maunds* (a *maund* is approximately 82 lbs. weight) compared to the average annual out-turn for the preceding ten years (excluding 1896–97) of around 9,893,634 *maunds* (Chinoy 1902: 31). This represents a fall in agricultural production of 97.5 per cent! The scale of the

---

[3] A sizeable proportion of famine victims from Berar itself seem to have been tribal people from the hilly Melghat region in the north of the province; this region lay outside the vital registration area.

tragedy is well summarized by a single paragraph of Chinoy's 1901 census report (1902: 28):

1900.—*A calamitous year.* [emphasis in the original] Exceedingly low birth rate and highest mortality. Distress throughout the province till November, owing to the failure of the crops in the previous year. Excess of deaths over births, 146,720. Rainfall fair. *Kharif* crops good ... Prices of staple food exceptionally high till the end of October. The maximum number of persons relieved was over 601,424 or 20.8 per cent of the total population. The birth rate fell from 50.5 per mille in 1899 to 31.3, and the death rate was 82.7 as against 39.9 per mille in the previous year. The exceptionally high rate was due to famine, influx of moribund people from the Hyderabad territory, cholera, which alone carried off over 28,000 persons, and to dysentery and diarrhoea.

This quotation helps to show that, although it was very much greater, in several respects the calamity of 1899–1900 echoed aspects of the earlier famine. The failure of the monsoon rains in the first year was the trigger, although the death rate in the first year was not unusually high. The second year of famine saw the return of the rains, but it also saw the main rise in the death rate. Accordingly, the rate of natural increase was very negative—implying as much as a 5 per cent population loss in 1900 (Table 5.1).

That said, almost certainly both famines saw net in-migration to Berar because it was viewed as a place of possible relief and employment. In both crises this migration contributed to the rise in the death rate. But in 1900 the death-rate rise certainly had a very large Berari component. Finally, in neither crisis was the birth rate reduced during the first year of famine. Indeed, even in 1897 (the second year of the first famine) the birth rate was not particularly low, perhaps because the first crisis was not particularly grave. In the second famine, however, '[t]here was a marked fall in June 1900; that is, exactly nine months after distress was first felt' (Crawford 1901a: 9). So in both famines the main birth rate decline occurred in the year following the *second* year of crisis. Then, two years after the second year of famine, in both cases the birth rate in Berar recovered to reach record levels (Table 5.1). This means that the effect on fertility of both these famines stretched into the fourth year.

DEMOGRAPHIC CONSEQUENCES

Using census data, I now explore the consequences of these famines for Berar's population size, sex ratio, age-structure, marital status composition, and patterns of residence. Vital registration data are then employed to examine variation in the level and age pattern of mortality, fluctuations in causes of death, and the consequences of the famines for fertility.

Whereas the 1891 census of Berar enumerated 2,897,491 people, the 1901 census counted only 2,754,016—a decrease of 143,475, or 5 per cent. Most of this population reduction happened because of the specific events of 1900. Indeed, the vital rates in Table 5.1 indicate that at the start of January 1900 the province's population must have been very similar in size to that counted in 1891. Recall too that the excess of registered deaths over registered births in the year 1900 was 146,720.

The province's population reduction between 1891 and 1901 was over twice as great for males (−97, 526) as it was for females (−45, 949). Accordingly, the population structure became markedly more feminine—the overall sex ratio (m/f) falling from 1.061 in 1891 to only 1.025 in 1901.

Figure 5.1 compares the age and sex distributions in 1891 and 1901. Clearly in comparing them one should bear in mind that above age ten the latter distribution mostly represents survivors from the former. Also age reporting was certainly poor in Berar, and it is likely that a relatively stable pattern of mis-reporting complicates the comparison of population numbers by age at the two censuses. Nevertheless certain broad features can still be discerned. The most dramatic change between 1891 and 1901, by far, occurred at ages 0–4; this age group declined by 116,663—equal to 81 per cent of the total intercensal population decrease (of 143,475). Of course, only the 0–4 age group was cut by *both* heavier mortality and reduced fertility. The second largest population reduction (−47, 673) happened to the open-ended age group of those aged 60 years or more; and the third largest reduction (−37, 545) occurred among older children aged 5–9 years (presumably partly reflecting a somewhat reduced level of

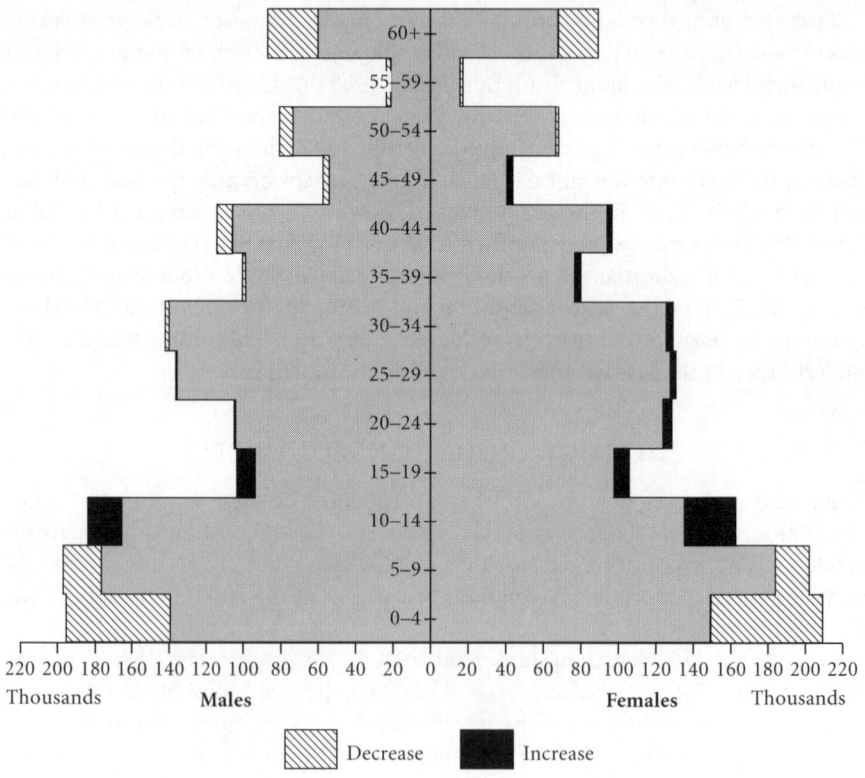

Figure 5.1. *The Age and Sex Distribution of the Population of Berar, 1891 and 1901*

fertility during the first half of the 1890s). The large reductions in population in these three age groups were partially offset by increases at some other ages—most notably at 10–14 (especially for females) and 15–19—presumably reflecting the entry into these age groups of generally larger age cohorts. In most other age groups increases in population size were small. However, it is worth remarking that for eight female, and four male age groups, the 1901 population actually exceeded that enumerated in 1891. Finally, except for the 0–4 and 15–19 age groups, the sex ratio declined (i.e. became more feminine) at *all* ages, this decline was generally greater at ages above about 35 years.

The 1890s had a profound influence on marriage patterns. Coming so soon after the major 1899–1900 famine, the 1901 census results show clear effects (see Table 5.2). At all ages a smaller proportion of women were classified as currently married in 1901 compared to what had applied in 1891. Some marriages were no doubt delayed. In this population ceremonial child marriage was the norm, and such delay must account for the rises in the percentages reported as single at young ages in 1901. But otherwise the main reason for the reductions in women currently married was the major increase in widowhood. Thus at all adult ages the declines in the proportions of women married correspond fairly closely to the rises in the proportions widowed. And, of course, the latter rises are particularly pronounced for older women (Table 5.2). The issue of child marriage complicates estimation of the fertility effects of these changes in marital status, but if ages below 25 are excluded then the value of Im* fell from 0.833 in 1891 to 0.767 in 1901 signifying a significant downward influence on fertility from increased widowhood.

The famines also produced temporary urbanization. Thus the censuses of 1867, 1881 and 1891 classified the population living in towns at 12.9, 11.6, and 12.4 per cent,

Table 5.2. *The Marital Status of the Female Population of Berar, 1891 and 1901*

Age group	Number		Single (%)		Married (%)		Widowed (%)	
	1891	1901	1891	1901	1891	1901	1891	1901
0–4	209,241	148,993	96.78	97.41	3.14	2.49	0.08	0.10
5–9	201,528	184,435	63.89	74.13	35.40	24.97	0.72	0.90
10–14	135,199	162,183	21.50	30.18	76.37	66.55	2.13	3.27
15–19	97,690	105,663	3.84	6.36	93.83	89.05	2.33	4.59
20–24	123,779	128,554	1.44	2.09	95.19	91.85	3.37	6.06
25–29	127,950	130,268	1.02	1.24	92.83	89.03	6.15	9.73
30–34	125,518	128,824	0.85	1.12	87.31	81.35	11.85	17.53
35–39	76,600	79,556	0.79	0.81	80.01	71.87	19.20	27.32
40–44	93,931	97,012	0.72	0.78	66.96	57.13	32.32	42.09
45–49	40,560	43,801	0.57	0.55	56.79	45.51	42.64	53.94

Principal sources: Census of India, 1891, *Volume VI, Berar or the Hyderabad Assigned Districts*, Calcutta, 1892; Census of India, 1901, *Berar*, Part II, Imperial Tables, Allahabad, 1902.

respectively (Dyson 1989a: 153). But in 1901 this figure rose to 15.2 per cent. There can be no doubt that this reflected famine migration, some of it emanating from outside of Berar. The sanitary report for 1900 remarks on the 'enormously high' death rates (up to 250 per thousand population) recorded for 'towns ... close to the borders of the Hyderabad State [which] were inundated with the destitute and famine-stricken from that state' (*RSAHAD* 1900: 5). Whereas during the period 1891–5 the death rates registered for towns and rural areas were very similar (differing by less than one point) in both 1897 and 1900 the death rate recorded for the towns exceeded that for rural areas by over five points, almost certainly due to registered deaths of famine urban in-migrants. However, this limited urbanization was not long-lasting—the 1911 census put the urban population back at 12.1 per cent.

Obviously census data conflate the effects of the two famines. But vital registration data permit examination of their separate effects. In this context Table 5.3 gives the registered sex-specific infant mortality rates (IMRs) for years 1891–1902 inclusive. It also gives corresponding estimates of the total fertility rate (TFR) and life expectation (again, by sex) derived by combining (i) the annual IMRs, (ii) the registered birth rates and sex-specific death rates, and (iii) census data on the province's age/sex distribution. The precise techniques and assumptions used have been detailed elsewhere and the resulting estimates shown to be robust to the (few) assumptions which are required (see Dyson 1989a). Here it will suffice to say that indirect standardization was employed to estimate annual total fertility. And the flexibility of the two parameter logit life table system (see Brass 1971) was used to produce annual sex-specific life tables which reconcile the prevailing age distributions and registered IMRs and CDRs for each year.[4] This procedure involves varying the relationship between infant and later age mortality. Therefore beta values, which essentially summarize this relationship, are presented too.

The statistics in Table 5.3 provide additional perspective on the demography of these turbulent times. Period total fertility varied from under four live births per woman in each of the years 1898, 1900, and 1901, to over six live births in 1899, and almost seven in 1902. Given the nine-month period of gestation, this range of TFR variation (from around 3.6 to 6.9 live births) was probably not greatly affected by famine migration—which was mostly relatively short term—although the TFR estimate for 1900 could be slightly inflated by such migration.

Estimated period life expectation varied from around 36–38 years in the 'good' year that was 1898, to under 20 years in 1897, and under 10 years in 1900. Here the registration of deaths of people who migrated into Berar probably does bias downwards the estimates for 1897 and 1900. However, although it is hard to be precise, the extent of this bias should not be exaggerated. In 1897 most famine migrants came from Central Provinces, and it was reported that consequently the district of Amraoti immediately adjacent to Central Provinces registered the highest death rate of 61.1 per thousand (*RSAHAD* 1897: 6). But if Amraoti is excluded then the provincial death rate would still have been 50.1 (rather than 52.6)—close to the rate for 1895 when

---

[4] The West model life table was used as standard. See Coale, Demeny, and Vaughan (1983).

Famine in Berar

Table 5.3. *Annual Demographic Estimates, Berar, 1891–1902*

	Year											
	1891	1892	1893	1894	1895	1896	1897	1898	1899	1900	1901	1902
IMR												
Male	241	202	206	249	269	224	313	179	272	416	198	297
Female	225	181	195	229	255	204	306	166	251	413	182	266
Total fertility rate (TFR)	5.51	5.10	5.01	4.22	4.66	4.74	4.88	3.81	6.13	3.77	3.63	6.93
Life expectation												
Male	24.7	32.5	29.7	23.0	19.3	22.4	17.0	36.0	24.4	8.7	31.8	27.4
Female	25.2	34.1	31.0	24.2	19.9	23.9	18.6	37.9	25.7	9.2	32.7	28.8
Beta												
Male	1.38	1.14	1.26	1.45	1.63	1.61	1.62	1.09	1.26	2.19	1.19	n.a.
Female	1.35	1.12	1.19	1.39	1.54	1.52	1.42	1.04	1.21	1.93	1.18	n.a.

n.a.—not available.

Principal sources: Report on the Sanitary Administration of the Hyderabad Assigned Districts (various years); Dyson (1989a).

Notes: The IMRs were estimated using data on the annual numbers of registered births and infant deaths and the simple assumption that 30 per cent of infant deaths in a year related to births of the previous year. The birth rate used here for 1902 differs from that used in previous research and accordingly the figures above also differ from previous estimates.

life expectation was under 20 years and there was no in-migration (see Table 5.3). Accordingly, it seems likely that life expectation in Berar in 1897 was around—and possibly below—20 years. Analogous calculations for 1900, when famine migrants came more from Hyderabad State, would only raise life expectation by a few years, because the increase in the death rate was very considerable throughout all six districts of Berar.[5] Note too that the registered IMRs in 1897 and 1900 were extremely high—at 310 and 415 infant deaths per thousand live births respectively. To the extent that registered infant deaths occurred to famine in-migrants, it is certain that many of the corresponding births to in-migrants were registered too. An estimated life expectation of somewhere about 10 years for the year 1900 may seem incredibly low, but it is important to remember both that it is a period rate, and that life expectation in Berar fell to only 6 years in 1918 (due to influenza) when migration exerted no obvious influence (see Dyson 1989a; also Mills 1989: 253).

Turning to sex differentials, Table 5.3 shows that both infant and overall mortality were usually slightly greater for males than for females. Thus the average IMRs for years 1891–5 inclusive were 217 infant deaths per thousand live births in the case of

---

[5] While probably not changing the broad picture, nevertheless it is worth cautioning that, for obvious reasons, Berar's administrators may sometimes have been a little too ready to mention the influence of famine in-migration. Certainly in the second disaster some people migrated *out* from Berar. The published registered district death rates in 1900 were as follows: 73.4 (Amraoti), 67.2 (Ellichpur), 75.3 (Wun), 110.8 (Basim), 76.7 (Akola), and 95.4 (Buldana).

females and 233 for males. The corresponding estimated average life expectancies are 26.9 years for females and 25.8 years for males—giving an average male disadvantage of −1.1 years. A male disadvantage seems to have been maintained during the main famine years, although the issue is clouded by the possible influence of differential migration. Thus in 1897 estimated female life expectation exceeded that of males by 1.6 years, although this narrowed to only 0.5 years in 1900. On the other hand, compared to 1891–5 the number of registered male and female deaths rose by 39 and 32 per cent respectively in 1897, and by 117 and 110 per cent respectively in 1900. Or to express the matter differently, during 1891–5 the average sex ratio (m/f) of registered deaths was 1.119 whereas in 1897 it was 1.176 and in 1900 1.153. In short, male mortality seems to have been affected slightly more by these famines.

Not surprisingly, the greatest proportional increases in deaths tended to occur at ages where death rates were normally relatively low—especially the age range 10–19 years. Thus compared to 1891–5, the number of male deaths registered in 1900 tripled at these ages, with only a slightly smaller proportional increase occurring for females. However, in *absolute* terms excess mortality was comparatively light at ages 10–19. Figure 5.2 shows that the largest number of excess deaths (compared to 1891–5) occurred at young and old ages (although it is noteworthy that in 1897 the mortality of children aged 1–4 only increased slightly). As can be seen, at most adult ages the number of excess male deaths greatly exceeded the number for females. Again, this could partly reflect differential migration; but there are strong reasons to believe that it was a real feature of Indian famines (Dyson 1991a: 21; 1991b: 294). In this context recall too that the 1901 population age distribution had

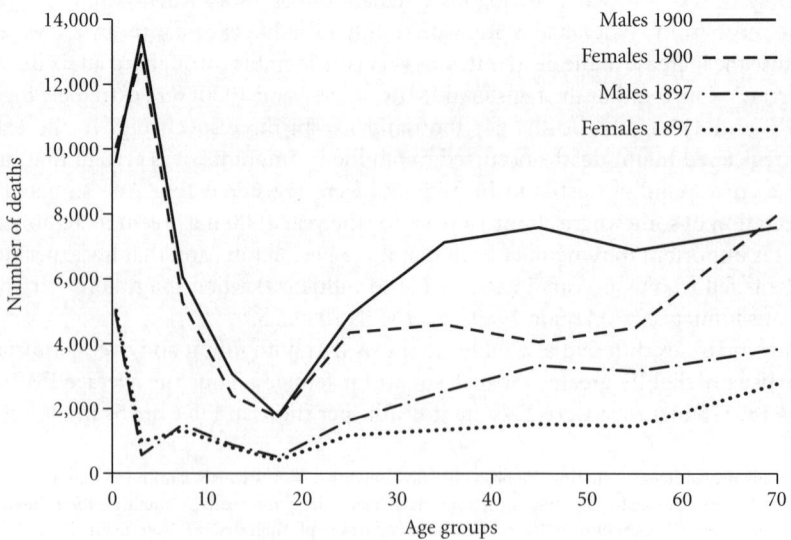

Figure 5.2. *Excess Deaths in Berar by Age and Sex (Reference = 1891–5)*

become noticeably more feminine above about 35 years, compared to that enumerated in 1891.

Returning to Table 5.3, the estimated beta values are all higher than the central value of 1.0—a figure which would denote a 'normal' relationship between early age and later age mortality (here that characteristic of the West model life table system). Indeed, the estimated values for years of heavier mortality—1895–7 inclusive and, especially, 1900—tend to be particularly high. This suggests that measured on this scale it was *adult* mortality that was most badly affected by these crises. Again, note how in both 1897 and 1900 this high beta effect was particularly pronounced for males.

Finally in the context of the age pattern of famine mortality, it is worth remarking briefly on stillbirths. The annual number of registered stillbirths per thousand live births occurring in the same year can be calculated for Berar for years 1895–1900 inclusive. The resulting rates are 50.1, 46.8, 47.3, 49.6, 46.0, and 52.3. Although the rate for 1900 (52.3) is slightly elevated, what is remarkable about this series is its relative constancy. And the figure for 1897 (47.3) is close to the average value (48.7). In this context it is worth noting that Chen and Chowdhury (1977: 415–16) found that demographic surveillance data for the Matlab area of Bangladesh indicate that neonatal mortality was little affected by the famine of 1974–5. Also, registered neonatal mortality during the Bengal famine of 1943–4 did not rise much (Dyson 1991b: 284).

Deaths in the province were classified according to six main cause of death groups. Fever was the most important single category, accounting on average for 45 per cent of all registered deaths during the 1890s (Dyson 1989b: 184); many—although by no means all—fever deaths were due to malaria. The second largest category, accounting for 29 per cent of deaths, was that of 'other causes'—a diffuse, 'catch-all' category, of rather limited analytic use. Third in importance (18 per cent) were deaths due to dysentery and diarrhoea, followed, in fourth place, by cholera (5 per cent). The two remaining cause of death groups—injuries and smallpox—were numerically tiny; neither accounted for even 1 per cent of registered deaths.

With this background, Figure 5.3 graphs total deaths and those attributed to fevers, dysentery and diarrhoea, and cholera, for each month of the period 1895–1902. The plot of total deaths conveys the theme of cumulative chain reaction very well—with a rising crescendo of death peaks, first in August of 1895, then in August of 1897 and, above all, in August of 1900.

Figure 5.3 also illustrates what has often been remarked on in the South Asian context (e.g. see Sen 1981: 213–14)—namely that famine mortality is usually an exaggeration of the 'normal' seasonal pattern of death, which in Berar peaked (and still peaks) around August/September of each year. Note too that the distribution of famine mortality is skewed towards the left. This is noticeable in 1897, and very marked in 1899–1900. During the second famine registered deaths increased in most months from June of 1898 until August of 1900, but by December of 1900 they were back to normal levels. So the build-up is long and painful, but the denouement is comparatively short.

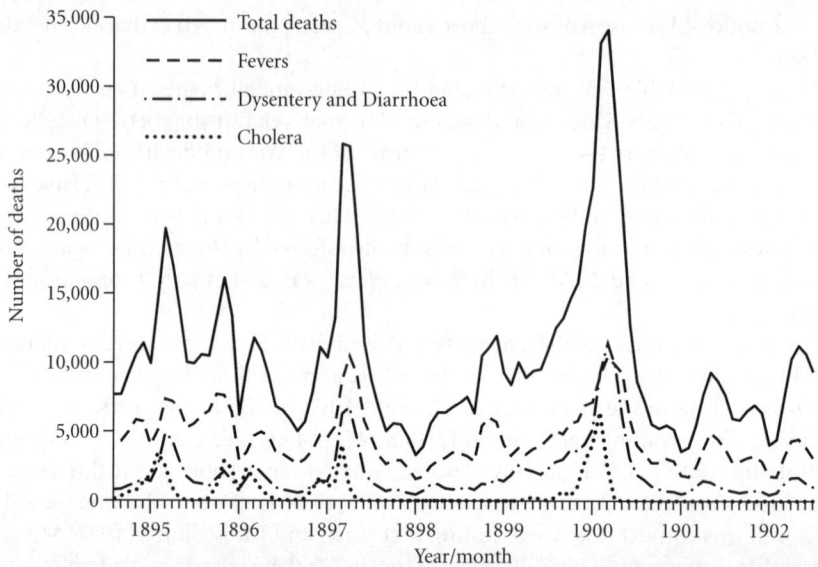

Figure 5.3. *Registered Monthly Deaths in Berar, Total and by Cause, 1895–1902*

The mortality climax was fuelled by the return of the monsoon rains and malaria, which in 1900 peaked in August.[6] Unsurprisingly, the trend of monthly fever deaths is similar to that for all deaths. And although there are periods of minor divergence— for example, during the early months of 1899—the same was true of dysentery and diarrhoea. Among other things, the reasons given for increased dysentery and diarrhoea in the famines included the consumption of bad *jowari* which had been for too long stored underground, bad water—'[t]here was a water as well as food famine in the province'—and people gorging themselves on any fresh green vegetation as soon as it appeared with the first rains (*RSAHAD* 1900: 12). Berar's administration made considerable efforts to limit cholera, mainly through surveillance and the treatment of drinking wells with permanganate of potash. Although cholera contributed to mortality during both famines, Figure 5.3 does indeed suggest that the disease was relatively confined in both scale and time.

These famines saw very few registered smallpox deaths—only 617 in 1897 and 830 in 1900. Undoubtedly this reflected widespread vaccination. By 1885 over 80 per cent of infants born in Berar were being vaccinated before reaching their first birthday, and consequently any smallpox outbreak could have only limited scope (Banthia and Dyson 1999). Swaine's remark (*RSAHAD* 1900: 10) regarding 1900 that '[t]he

---

[6] Monthly precipitation measured in inches being: 4.8 (June), 9.7 (July), 10.7 (August), and 7.5 (September). Swaine remarks of the year that '[w]hen the rains commenced the conditions became more favourable for the development of the *anopheles* mosquitoes; the prevailing type of fevers now noticed was distinctly malarial, both remittent and intermittent, and this continued to the end of the year' (*RSAHAD* 1900: 12).

district of Wun bordering on the Hyderabad State, from which a large number of unvaccinated people came, suffered the most [from smallpox]' probably contains more than a germ of truth.

From an average annual toll of 1,111 during 1891–5 the number of deaths from injuries rose to 1,335 in 1897 and 1,565 in 1900. The subcategories responsible for the increases in both years were suicides and accidents. I have remarked elsewhere on the distinct tendency for registered suicide deaths in India to peak during years of famine (Dyson 1991a: 18). The increase in the accident category may also partly reflect wrongly classified suicides plus, presumably, fatal casualties to those enfeebled by famine.

This discussion has not mentioned starvation *per se*. Yet, of course, it was usually the major *underlying* cause of death. In this context three points made by Little apropos the famine mortality of 1897 perhaps bear repetition (certainly they applied too in 1900). First, it was people's severe emaciation which meant that their hold on life was so slender that any illness could 'snap their frail support'. Second, many people who were in such a parlous nutritional state were either indifferent to food when it was available or, even if they did eat, 'were too far gone to permit of recovery'. Third, and as a consequence, that '[t]he official definition of death from starvation [which] signifies that so long as a person has food before him, or the means of procuring it, he cannot die from starvation . . . is a mistake' (*RSAHAD* 1897: 32).

The data are consistent with the view that it was generally the very weakest sections of society which experienced the greatest excess mortality. In this context, deaths were classified separately for Hindus (who constituted about 90 per cent of the population), Muslims (about 7 per cent), 'Other classes'(3 per cent), and a tiny number of native Christians. Compared to the average annual number registered during the preceding 5 years (98,845), deaths of Hindus rose by 32 per cent in 1897 and 108 per cent in 1900. The corresponding figures for Muslims (preceding average 7,402) were 28 and 86 per cent. Cattle mortality was extremely high—especially during the second famine—and Muslims could eat beef. This may help to explain the somewhat lower Muslim mortality, although it was also reported that some poorer Hindus also ate cattle flesh (Crawford 1901a: 5–16). Deaths among people of '[o]ther classes' (preceding average 5,995) rose by 65 per cent in 1897 and 179 per cent in 1900. And in the case of native Christians the usual number of registered deaths was around 30, but there were 59 deaths in 1897 and 171 in 1900. Under both '[o]ther classes' and 'Christians' fell a significant number of famine deaths to poor tribal peoples coming from hill areas from both within and outside of Berar.

Finally, a word is in order regarding the long-term effects of these famines. Of course, there was no sudden transformation of Berar's economic circumstances in the years immediately following the disastrous 1890s. On the contrary, the population remained, by most standards, extremely poor and vulnerable. Thus the average level of life expectation during 1901–10 was only 27 years—just 2.6 years higher than during the period 1891–1900. And adverse chain reactions continued to occur—for example, in both 1906 and 1907 when the province's death rate was around 50 per thousand partly because of serious outbreaks of plague.

Nevertheless, in *relative* terms, limited economic recovery was quite swift. During the famines care had been taken to harbour the most valuable economic assets—such as plough cattle. And, above all, what basic recovery really required was a reasonable monsoon leading to a better agricultural year. Thus in 1901 Berar's Commissioner felt able to write:

It may confidently be asserted that the agricultural classes of Berar, representing 75 per cent of the whole population, have recovered in a very remarkable manner from the recent famine. Except in limited tracts in the south ... where the crops sown in the year 1900 have been poor, it would be difficult to detect signs that the people lately endured a great agricultural calamity. In the province as a whole, it was found on the close of measures for famine relief that the full normal area was under crop, that the labouring classes were earning high wages, and that the public health was unusually good. (Crawford 1901a: 41)

Demographic renewal also occurred. I have remarked on the record CBR of 1902, which was mainly a short-term, 'bounce-back' effect. However, in the long-run the birth rate was unusually high during the 1901–10 decade—averaging 47 births per thousand population. By the 1911 census virtually all of the increased widowhood evident in the 1901 census results had disappeared—the value of Im^* rising to 0.821. The much more feminine population structure contributed to this unusually high birth rate. So too did the famine-induced changes in age structure. Thus whereas in 1891 women aged 20–45 constituted 39 per cent of the female population, in 1901 this had risen to 41.5 per cent. The upshot was that, in spite of continuing high mortality and new shocks, Berar's annual rate of natural increase averaged 0.81 per cent during 1901–10. And, with net in-migration, the province's population actually grew by 11 per cent between 1901 and 1911.

CONCLUSIONS AND DISCUSSION

Although in the 1890s Berar was relatively advanced in terms of certain aspects of its infrastructure, and probably the population was marginally less poor than those of neighbouring regions of India, there can be little doubt that the province's social and economic structure had experienced rapid and often disruptive alteration as a result of the swift growth and commercialization of the cotton economy. Berar's population was still extremely poor, highly dependent upon the adequacy and nature of the monsoon rains, and therefore very vulnerable to famine. Moreover, faced with these calamities the British administration was largely unprepared, and the relief measures that were provided were certainly woefully inadequate given the scale of distress.

So both the underlying causes of this pair of famines in the 1890s (about which there has been much debate) and their proximate cause (i.e. drought) were precisely the same in Berar as elsewhere in India. The relative efficiency of the province's administration may well have had some good effects—for example, in helping to limit cholera and smallpox, in providing people with perhaps a little more relief than happened elsewhere, and in the keeping of better statistical records—but these beneficial effects were limited, and they were always likely to be overwhelmed by the sheer scale of events at this time.

Two related themes of this chapter have been (i) famine as *process* and (ii) the *interconnectedness* of events. Too often food crises are analysed in rather static terms. Yet, surely, much behaviour has to be interpreted on the quite reasonable basis that people 'see ahead'. Also we have seen how patterns of rainfall, employment, migration, and disease all interact and that various interconnections sometimes take literally years to work out—for example, a drought in 1896 quite logically eventually resulting in a baby boom in 1899 (which, ironically, was also a year of drought).

Of course, such interconnections help to explain why, quite often, food crises come in *pairs*. Thus, but for the beat of a butterfly's wings, there very nearly was famine, chaos, and widespread death in Bengal in 1941. Surely one cannot analyse the famine of 1943–4 without taking account of 1941 and surrounding years. Precisely the same applies to the 1974–5 famine in Bangladesh which cannot be seen apart from the difficult events of 1971. Such pairs of food crises—bang-bang famines—should alert us to the possibility that famines and epidemics may well have combined to restrict population growth in historical times.

References

Bates, C. N. (1984), 'Regional Dependence and Rural Development in Central India, 1820–1930', PhD Dissertation, University of Cambridge.

Banthia, J., and Dyson, T. (1999), 'Smallpox in Nineteenth Century India', *Population and Development Review*, 25: 4.

Brass, W. (1971), 'On the Scale of Mortality', in W. Brass (ed.), *Biological Aspects of Demography*, London: Taylor and Francis.

Chen, L. C., and Chowdhury, A. K. M. (1977), 'The Dynamics of Contemporary Famine', in *Mexico International Population Conference, Volume 1*, Liege: International Union for the Scientific Study of Population.

Chinoy, A. D. (1902), *Berar, Report*, Census of India 1901, *Volume VIII*, Allahabad: Pioneer Press.

Coale, A. J., Demeny, P., and Vaughan, B. (1983), *Regional Model Life Tables and Stable Populations*, 2nd edn., London: Academic Press.

Crawford, J. A. (1901a), *Report on the Famine in the Hyderabad Assigned Districts in the Years 1899 and 1900, Volume 1*, Nagpur: Chambers Press.

Crawford, J. A. (1901b), *Report on the Famine in the Hyderabad Assigned Districts in the Years 1899 and 1900, Volume 2*, Nagpur: Chambers Press.

Dyson, T. (1989a), 'The Historical Demography of Berar, 1881–1980', in T. Dyson (ed.), *India's Historical Demography: Studies in Famine, Disease and Society*, London: Curzon Press.

Dyson, T. (1989b), 'The Population History of Berar Since 1881 and its Potential Wider Significance', *Indian Economic and Social History Review*, 26(2).

Dyson, T. (1991a), 'On the Demography of South Asian Famines. Part I', *Population Studies*, 45(1).

Dyson, T. (1991b), 'On the Demography of South Asian Famines. Part II', *Population Studies*, 45(2).

Kitts, E. J. (1882), *Report on the Census of Berar 1881*, Bombay: Education Society's Press.

Lyall, A. C. (1870), *Gazetteer for the Haidarabad Assigned Districts, Commonly Called Berar*, Bombay: Education Society's Press.

Mills, I. (1989), 'Influenza in India during 1918–19', in T. Dyson (ed.), *India's Historical Demography: Studies in Famine, Disease and Society*, London: Curzon Press.

Office of the Registrar General (1923), *Central Provinces and Berar, Volume XI*, Part I—Report, Nagpur: Government Press.

Report on the Sanitary Administration of the Hyderabad Assigned Districts, with Appendices (abbreviated to *RSAHAD*) (various years), Hyderabad: Residency Government Press.

Satya, L. D. (1997), *Cotton and Famine in Berar, 1850–1900*, New Delhi: Manohar Publishers.

Sen, A. (1981), *Poverty and Famines*, Oxford: Clarendon Press.

Watkins, S. C., and Menken, J. (1985), 'Famines in Historical Perspective', *Population and Development Review*, 11(4).

6

Famines and Epidemics: An Indian Historical Perspective

ARUP MAHARATNA

While episodes of catastrophic famines and epidemics abound in human history, the issue of the precise nature of the relationship between these two phenomena does not seem to be fully resolved. In fact, this age-old question has received renewed attention in the recent past—especially in the light of new discoveries and developments in scientific medical theory and historical demography. Although famines and epidemics are indeed things of the past for the Western world, the issue continues to have contemporary relevance because of recent crises in parts of the Third World (e.g. parts of sub-Saharan Africa and Asia) and because of the persistence of similar threats.

While famine is widely known to bring in its wake epidemics and excess mortality, there is evidence of independent outbreaks of epidemics—uninitiated by famine. Thus reviewing French demographic crises in the period from the sixteenth to the eighteenth century J. Meuvret wrote:

> epidemic crises unaccompanied by famine did occur; there is every reason to think however that conditions of shortage favoured the spread of an epidemic. On the other hand there were few famine years which did not lead into epidemic phases. (Meuvret 1965: 512)

However, more recently it has sometimes been argued that since famine generally represents an acute food shortage and mass starvation, a mortality crisis that may develop in its wake, out of epidemics and diseases (rather than being due to direct *starvation deaths*) should deserve separate treatment in its own right, and that this should hardly be branded as 'famine mortality' (e.g. de Waal 1989a).

In this connection the role that undernutrition plays in infectious diseases and mortality is of particular significance. Notably, the traditional view that acute undernutrition lowers human resistance against infectious disease, and thus enhances vulnerability to death, has been seriously questioned. In the modern medical literature the relationship between under/malnutrition and infectious diseases is best described as synergistic (Scrimshaw *et al.* 1968; Taylor 1985). However, since a famine

---

I gratefully acknowledge helpful comments and suggestions from Tim Dyson, Cormac Ó Gráda, and Joel Mokyr and from other participants at the Colloquium held at the Fondation des Treilles. Very special thanks are due to Joel Mokyr and Henry Sui for not only providing me with the results of Granger-causality tests, but also for helping me to interpret them. However, errors if any are my own responsibility.

usually causes a drastic decline in food consumption, the consequent undernutrition presumably initiates the synergy and hence leads to increased mortality. Furthermore, a famine often involves not only an acute nutritional crisis, but also large-scale social dislocations (e.g. population movements, overcrowding in relief camps, the breakdown of sanitary standards). And as Post has argued, during the subsistence crises of eighteenth-century Europe the breakdown of social relations—and the resulting migration, vagrancy, and overcrowding in insanitary conditions, without the benefit of adequate welfare provisions—was a major cause of mortality elevation even from diseases (such as smallpox) which are not normally identified as interacting synergistically with malnutrition (Post 1990). If higher mortality is found for the more undernourished sections of the population in a famine, this may, some scholars argue, result mainly from worse living conditions (e.g. crowding in relief camps) and a higher risk of exposure to diseases rather than from increased undernutrition *per se* (Walter and Schofield 1989). That said, recent research on some well-known major famines of the mid-nineteenth century in several of today's advanced countries—for which relatively rich and detailed historical records are available—generally assigns prime significance to famine-caused mass starvation and undernutrition as explanations for epidemics and associated mortality crises. For example, reviewing the mortality crisis during the Great Irish famine of 1845–50, Crawford has demonstrated 'inextricable links between nutrition, disease and famine', even after taking due account of the role of various social disruptions in transmitting infections (Crawford 1991). Also, a penetrative analysis of Japanese Ogen-ji temple death registers during the 1830s concludes that 'the mortality crisis of 1837 was a subsistence crisis' (Jannetta 1992: 440). Again, during the Finnish famine of the 1860s 'a synergy between malnutrition and infectious diseases' is considered to have been of prime significance in raising mortality (Pitkänen 1993: 115).

Moreover, as Mokyr and Ó Gráda (1999) have argued in their recent analysis of historical documents relating to mortality during the Irish famine of 1845–50, the vulnerability to infectious diseases and death in the face of acute starvation and famine in the mid-nineteenth century was compounded by the absence of a clear understanding of the nature of disease transmission. This can be contrasted with an overwhelming share of largely 'starvation' deaths during several major European food crises that occurred about 100 years later (e.g. the Dutch famine of 1944–5 and the Greek famine of 1941–2)—in which epidemics and infectious diseases appear to have played a relatively small role in accounting for excess mortality (e.g. Hionidou 1995, 1999). This leads to an important insight: namely that although by the mid-twentieth century these European societies were fairly advanced (e.g. in terms of their knowledge about the importance of keeping clean, of using disinfectants, and also because they had universal literacy, a reasonable supply of medical personnel, clean water for drinking and washing, and there was little overcrowding) and could avert a 'public health crisis', nevertheless a substantial rise in mortality could not be averted when a large section of their population suffered acute starvation and undernutrition.

The nutritional status of a population depends not only upon its consumption of food, but also upon other considerations including its levels of health care, education, the quality of its drinking water and the prevailing sanitary conditions (Drèze and Sen 1989: 44). Thus an increase in mortality can occur either through enhanced susceptibility to potentially fatal diseases, or through an increased exposure to such diseases, or through a combination of both. However, to reiterate, the precise nature and significance of the famine–nutrition–disease–epidemics–mortality relationship continues to be debated (e.g. see Chen *et al.* 1980; Foege 1971; Martorell and Ho 1984; Mokyr and Ó Gráda 1999; Tomkins 1986). In this context we will argue here that during a famine it is the undernutrition and associated debilitation that raises people's susceptibility to infection, while increased exposure—because of social dislocations and/or climatic considerations—also helps the spread of epidemic diseases.

INSIGHTS FROM INDIAN HISTORICAL FAMINES

Several of these issues relating to the famine–epidemic relationship have recently been examined for the Indian famines of the late nineteenth and early twentieth centuries (e.g. see Arnold 1991; Dyson 1991a,b; Dyson 1993; Lardinois 1985; Maharatna 1994, 1996; Whitcombe 1990, 1993; Zurbrigg 1992, 1998). Indeed, with its fairly long history of census taking and vital registration, India offers a good opportunity for this kind of study. Wide areas of the subcontinent experienced major famines in 1876–8, 1896–7, 1899–1900 and 1907–8. Each of these famines involved several million excess deaths.[1] And they were all precipitated by severe drought.[2]

Fairly heavy rains during the three monsoon months of July, August, and September (which result in the *kharif* crop season) and further rains in December and January (resulting in the *rabi* crop season) are generally considered to be necessary for good harvests in most of the Indian subcontinent. Given the rainfall-dependence of South Asia's agriculture, the failure of the monsoon can mean the threat of famine conditions. Dramatic price rises and massive employment losses were usually the most important proximate causes of the large and widespread reductions in food entitlements and the associated distress during these crises (Drèze 1990: 16–17; also Bhatia 1967).[3]

Using mostly registration data, Dyson has *inter alia* analysed patterns of mortality during three major nineteenth-century famines in certain Indian locations: the famine of 1876–8 in Madras Presidency, and the famines of 1896–7 and 1899–1900 in Central Provinces and Bombay Presidency (Dyson 1991a). In these famines the main mortality peak not only occurred late, but it also lasted for a short time, and 'in each case it happened in or around August [of the year following the drought]

---

[1] For a useful background discussion and information on the severity and regional spread of these famines see Bhatia 1967; Dyson 1991a; Maharatna 1996, Chapter 1.

[2] The reasons behind the emergence of such large-scale famines have understandably been the centre of long-standing debate. Factors like colonial exploitation, population pressure etc., are sometimes held to be responsible for these disasters. However, there is little dispute that the failure of the monsoon rains was the single most important proximate factor behind all of these famines.

[3] There is substantial literature on the extent to which rises in food prices reflect famine distress (e.g. Sen 1981, especially Chapters 1–5).

and was almost certainly related to the resumption of monsoon rains' (Dyson 1991a: 22). Thus, the peak of famine mortality appears to have matched the normal seasonal mortality peak—which occurred during and just after the rains.

Apropos causes of famine mortality, the importance of cholera and fever mortality was quite apparent. Dysentery and diarrhoea also seemed to be significant in some cases. Famine mortality due to cholera (and dysentery and diarrhoea) usually peaked somewhat earlier, broadly corresponding to the phase of maximum starvation and social disruption (e.g. wandering and crowding). However, as Dyson observes, 'malaria was probably the most important single component of the main death rate peaks which accompanied the return of the rains ... when field activities were resuming, employment prospects were improving, relief works were being run down and people were returning home' (Dyson 1991a: 22). He, however, adds that the occurrence of such a peak in famine mortality in a year following drought did not depend entirely upon the resumption of the rains—since mosquito breeding and disease transmission depended also on the 'particular conditions of precipitation, temperature, atmospheric humidity etc'. Another possible mechanism for outbreaks of epidemic malaria, particularly those after the resumption of the rains and normal farm activities (which, in turn, are supposed to initiate the recovery of nutritional status), that has been proposed is 'malaria refeeding'. According to this explanation, severe undernutrition may obstruct the multiplication of malaria parasites in the human body and thus brake both the development and transmission of the disease. Conversely improvements in nutritional status may induce parasite multiplication, and hence contribute to major outbreaks of malaria (see Murray and Murray 1997; Murray *et al.* 1975, 1976, 1990; Dyson 1991a: 24; see also Whitcombe 1993 and the references cited therein).

Analysing the course of mortality during the Madras famine of 1876–7 and the famines in Punjab during 1896–7 and 1899–1900, Elizabeth Whitcombe views 'famine mortality' as resulting primarily from the outbreak of malaria epidemics the scale of which was largely determined by 'cruel' whims of climate (e.g. drought followed by excessive rains as in Madras in 1877 and Punjab in 1900), the consequent abundance of surface water and humidity and the resulting exaggerated scale of mosquito-breeding (Whitcombe 1993). She argues too that excessive cattle mortality during droughts contributed greatly to the climatically enhanced mosquito-breeding because anopheles mosquitoes—being deprived of their most important host population, namely cattle—'fed almost exclusively on humans' (Whitcombe 1993: 1178). Thus Whitcombe concludes: '[a] crucial part of the explanation [for the malaria epidemics] lies not in "famine" as such, but rather in the peculiar climatic character of the famine years ...' (1993: 1177).

However, attempts to interpret excess malaria mortality in the wake of famines—almost exclusively—in terms of climatic parameters and scientific microbiological (germ) theory are fraught with difficulties. For example on the basis of her detailed study of malaria epidemics in colonial India, Sheila Zurbrigg has argued that the fact of 'selectively greater mortality from malaria among the starving' could perhaps never be disputed even by colonial administrative reports (Zurbrigg 1998: 8). Thus, even if climatic factors did play a role in accentuating mosquito-breeding and malaria infections, its role can at best be viewed as a mediating one in malaria *mortality*, which was perhaps *more proximately* related to acute undernutrition (Maharatna 1996; also Zurbrigg 1992, 1998).

Thus, these suggested mechanisms behind the relationship between famine and epidemic malaria mortality in the Indian historical context can be grouped as three hypotheses (which are not necessarily mutually exclusive):

(i) The immunity-based hypothesis: a relatively low incidence of malaria owing to the dryness of the drought year reduces the population's level of immunity; this enhances the chances of a malaria epidemic when the rains resume in the following year.
(ii) The malaria refeeding hypothesis: since a fever mortality peak appears often to have occurred after the resumption of the rains when (along with the resumption of normal farm activities) people presumably begin to experience an improvement in their nutritional level, it may be an outcome of the 'refeeding of malaria'.
(iii) The undernutrition-centred hypothesis: in view of the strong correlation found (historically) between food scarcity and fever (or malaria) mortality in parts of the Indian subcontinent, the occurrence of malaria epidemics in the wake of famines should be attributed to the occurrence of acute nutritional stress and its debilitating effects.

THREE MAJOR HISTORICAL FAMINES[4]

With this as background the present chapter now re-examines some of these issues relating to the famine–epidemic relationship. It does so in the context of several Indian historical locations which have hitherto remained largely unanalysed. In particular, we include in this analysis the famine of 1876–8 in Bombay Presidency, the famines of 1896–7 and 1899–1900 in Berar, and the famine of 1907–8 which happened in the United Provinces of Agra and Oudh (hereafter termed simply United Provinces).[5] A considerable shortfall in monsoon rains was the proximate trigger of these famines (see Maharatna 1996: Table 2.5, p. 42 for information on rainfall). Table 6.1, which presents the cause-composition of mortality both during the pre-famine and peak famine years, shows substantial excess mortality in all these locations.

In examining the development of famine distress and its relationship to the time path of mortality elevation, the sole economic measure used here is the monthly series of the average provincial price of the staple food-grain, jower (large millet). The use of rising food prices to reflect the build-up and severity of famines is a

---

[4] This section draws partly on Chapter 2 of my book, *The Demography of Famines: An Indian Historical Perspective*, 1996 (New Delhi: Oxford University Press).

[5] The selection of these locations was influenced partly by the fact that they were relatively severely afflicted by the famines, and partly because the quality of demographic data was relatively superior for these provinces. For relevant evidence see Dyson 1989a,b: Chapter 6; and 1991a; see also Maharatna 1996: Chapter 1.

Table 6.1. *Cause-specific Death Rates in the Pre-famine (baseline) and Famine Years, Historical Famine Locations*

Cause of death	Bombay		Berar			United Provinces	
	1871–5	1877*	1891–5	1897*	1900*	1901–4	1908*
Cholera	0.35	3.53	1.83	3.49	6.34	0.91	1.75
	(1.79)	(16.51)	(4.81)	(12.1)	(10.4)	(2.66)	(4.56)
Smallpox	0.80	1.69	0.13	0.21	0.29	0.15	1.26
	(4.12)	(4.62)	(0.34)	(0.58)	(0.37)	(0.44)	(6.02)
Fever	11.92	20.76	18.66	22.64	29.0	24.55	41.31
	(61.4)	(45.9)	(48.96)	(28.97)	(23.84)	(71.57)	(90.94)
Dysentery/diarrhoea	1.85	3.71	6.02	10.2	22.04	0.63	0.41
	(9.52)	(9.66)	(15.81)	(30.42)	(36.94)	(1.84)	(−1.12)
Plague						2.16	0.48
						(6.30)	(−9.12)
Injuries/accidents	0.38	0.46	0.38	0.46	0.54	0.50	0.57
	(1.97)	(0.42)	(1.00)	(0.58)	(0.36)	(1.40)	(0.37)
All other	4.12	8.53	11.07	14.84	23.25	5.40	8.41
	(21.21)	(22.9)	(29.06)	(27.44)	(28.08)	(15.74)	(52.73)
All causes	19.42	38.68	38.11	51.85	81.46	34.30	52.73
	(100)	(100)	(100)	(100)	(100)	(100)	(100)

Source: Maharatna (1996: Table 2.6, p. 46). The original sources are the Annual Reports of the Sanitary Commissioner of the respective provinces.

Notes: 1. The years marked with (*) are the prime famine years. 2. All rates are based on constant denominators being the respective enumerated populations under vital registration according to the last census prior to the famine. 3. For all baseline periods, the figures in parentheses are the respective percentage shares to total average deaths, while for all the famine years they are the respective shares to the total excess deaths. Total excess deaths for each cause of death in a famine year have been calculated over the respective average number of deaths during the baseline period. 4. In United Provinces plague began to be included as a separate cause of death only from 1902. Respiratory diseases were included as a separate cause of death only from 1905; however, the percentage share of this cause of death grouping to total excess deaths in 1908 was less than 1.

standard practice. Weekly prices of different food-grains for the districts of these provinces are available in the respective provincial Gazettes (except in the case of Berar).[6] Accordingly averages of these district-level prices for the weeks ending in the middle of each month have been calculated, and they are taken here as the monthly provincial food-grain prices.

Apropos mortality, and following other scholars, we use demographic data provided by the vital registration system. Since the inception of this system around the

---

[6] The sources of price data are as follows: Bombay Presidency: *The Bombay Presidency Gazette*, Part III, Supplement: Bombay (various years); United Provinces: *The United Provinces Gazette*, Part II: Allahabad (various years). For Berar (for which we could not find any provincial Gazettes), see *Report on the Sanitary Administration of the Hyderabad Assigned Districts*: Hyderabad (relevant years). It may be noted that prices were expressed in terms of *seers* (about two lbs. weight) per rupee.

1870s the Sanitary Commissioner of each province was responsible for producing an annual report which contained quite detailed registration material. The information on vital events was collected by village watchmen (*chaukidars*), each being responsible for a particular jurisdiction. While the quality of these data was certainly not perfect, they can still be used to examine certain specific issues even during famine periods (see Maharatna 1996: Chapter 1 and Dyson 1991a for relevant discussion). In particular, while event underregistration was a major deficiency of the registration system, this should not seriously affect our analysis of temporal (e.g. monthly) changes in mortality.

The annual distribution of registered deaths during baseline (i.e. normal) periods evinces a distinct pattern of seasonal variation (see Dyson 1991a; and Maharatna 1996: appendix A). To discount for such seasonal influences on the monthly mortality during famines, we have constructed monthly *mortality indices* (MI). These are the monthly ratios of the numbers of registered deaths to the respective pre-famine baseline average figures (the base being taken as 100), reflecting proportional, rather than absolute changes in deaths.

Registered deaths were usually classified under five major causes: cholera, dysentery/diarrhoea, smallpox, fevers, injuries, and all others. Subsequently plague and respiratory diseases were also included in the system. The distribution of registered deaths from each specified cause—both by district and by month—is available. There is no doubt that the cause of death data are not accurate, especially because village officials could hardly be assumed to have had much skill in assigning deaths to the appropriate categories. However, statistics for categories such as cholera, smallpox, and plague are generally thought to have been relatively reliable because of the very distinctive symptoms of these diseases. The category 'fevers'—under which many deaths were normally classified—seems to have been a catch-all category in the sense that several diseases which cause an increase in temperature are likely to have been included under this heading. On that count, a certain degree of mis-classification of deaths between fever and dysentery/diarrhoea seems possible (we return to this below). Also according to some intensive investigations, malaria often predisposes to respiratory diseases and dysentery/diarrhoea (see Census of India 1911: vol. XV, Pt. I, 45.). Thus as the official report on the United Provinces famine of 1896–7 noted, '[t]his heading [i.e. fever] is very general and probably includes most cases of pneumonic and lung diseases, so fatal to people of reduced stamina (especially the young and very old) employed on relief works and elsewhere' (Government of North-Western Provinces and Oudh 1897: 135). That said, malaria is generally believed to have been the most important single component of the fevers category. Thus a usual surge in fever mortality during the late-monsoon and post-monsoon months has often been attributed to the accentuation of mosquito-breeding and malaria infections following the rains.

The Bombay famine of 1876–8

The Bombay famine of 1876–8 began with the failure of both the summer and autumn monsoon rains during 1876. The summer monsoon of 1877 also failed. So drought in two consecutive years resulted in a severe and relatively prolonged famine in much of the Presidency. Figure 6.1 traces the monthly evolution of the average price of the important staple food, jower, and the mortality indices. Since food prices were expressed in terms of quantities (*seers*) per one rupee, we have reversed the direction on the Y-axis when plotting these prices. As can be seen the food price was already fairly high by the beginning of 1876 as compared to the same period of 1875. It then rose steadily to reach a peak in September of 1877 and it then stayed very high until around the end of 1879. Note that both the highest food price and maximum MI coincided in the month of September 1877. Although the closing months of 1877 and the first three months of 1878 witnessed a reduction in the MI (from its peak), the index moved in a sharply adverse direction again during June–September of 1878.

Relief operations in this famine started only around November of 1876. Given the employment losses and high prices from the beginning of the *kharif* season (i.e. June of 1876), the start of the very scant relief in November may well be considered as fairly late.

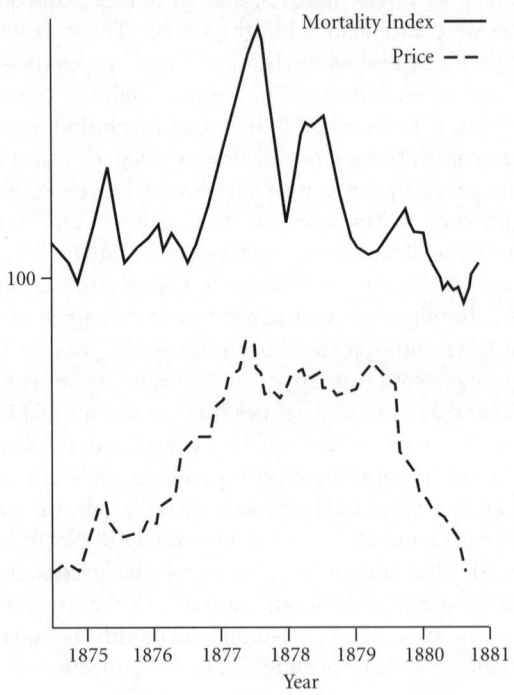

Figure 6.1. *The Price of Jower and MI by Month, Bombay, 1875–80. Ranges of Variation: MI, 94 (October 1880) to 261 (September 1877); Jower Price, 26.12 (January 1875) to 8.3 Seers per Rupee (September 1877)*

Source: See text.

Indian Famines and Epidemics

The share of cholera in the overall excess mortality of 1877 was substantially larger than in the baseline period (see Table 6.1). Notably, the proportionate share of fever deaths in excess mortality of 1877 was smaller than in the baseline period, although it was still largest both in normal and the famine years. Figure 6.2 plots the monthly numbers of deaths from cholera, fever, and bowel-complaints during 1876–8. It shows that deaths from these causes were all rising from the beginning of 1877. Cholera deaths peaked around April of 1877 and began to decline from about August; deaths from bowel-complaints peaked around September; and the fever deaths about two months later. Thus while cholera mortality mostly occurred during the pre-monsoon and early monsoon months, mortality from bowel-complaints and fever (presumably the latter in part malarial) tended to peak during and after the monsoon. This said, it is notable that all major causes of death began to rise from the beginning of 1877. Although the fever mortality peak in November of 1877 may have been partly contributed to by enhanced mosquito-breeding following the unusually heavy rains of October, its consistently rising trend over the whole year is particularly noteworthy. Mis-classification of deaths is likely, especially at this time when the registration system was still in its infancy. In particular, some deaths from cholera, dysentery/diarrhoea were possibly recorded in the fevers category. However, as the Sanitary Commissioner of Bombay Presidency in his annual report for 1877 writes, '... [i]t is impossible therefore to say how many of these [fever] deaths were due to malarial fevers, though I think there is but little doubt that the mortality recorded under this heading in the famine districts, was at all events during the latter half of the year, principally due to remittent fever' (Government of Bombay 1878: 176). By 'remittent fever' he seems to have had malaria in mind.

Furthermore, excess mortality from fever, which has often been thought to happen after the resumption of rains following a drought, can occur even in a year of drought itself (as in 1877). [Indeed, in terms of rainfall 1877 cannot be considered any better than 1876. Total annual rainfall was 36.1 and 38.6 inches respectively in 1876 and

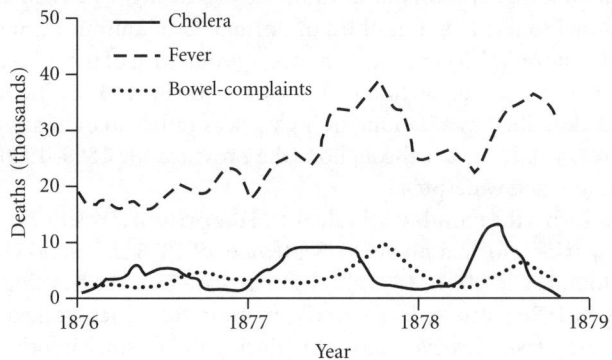

Figure 6.2. *The Monthly Distribution of Deaths by Cause, Bombay, 1876–8*
Source: See Table 6.1.

1877, while kharif rainfall (i.e. that during June–September) was in fact lower in 1877 by about 4 inches].

Assuming that fever mortality represented many of the malarial deaths, such an elevated fever mortality throughout the consecutive drought year of 1877 appears as clear testimony that the overall death toll of epidemic malaria was fundamentally contingent upon the intensity of undernutrition and debilitation following a drought and famine, rather than being due to the resumption of normal rains and/or climatically favourable circumstances for malaria transmission.

In 1878, the MI initially peaked in May—although it rose slightly higher still during the period up to September (see Fig. 6.1). In 1878, the cholera death peak in June was followed by a bowel-complaints death peak in August, which was followed in turn by a fever death peak in November (see Fig. 6.2). The delayed fever-mortality peak in 1878 was probably related to the above-normal rainfall (and consequently enhanced mosquito-breeding and malaria) especially in August and September. Figure 6.2 thus suggests that in *both* 1877 and 1878 cholera deaths tended to peak around the beginning of the monsoon; bowel-complaint deaths peaked in the mid-monsoon period; and fever deaths peaked after the end of the monsoon. All this is suggestive that although the exact timing of mortality peaks for specific diseases was perhaps shaped by climatic and other influences, the elevation of overall mortality was basically linked with trends in undernutrition and debilitation during the course of the famine.

The Berar famines of 1896–7 and 1899–1900

The Famine Commission of 1880 described Berar as 'one of the parts of India particularly free from apprehension of calamity of drought' (quoted in Census of India 1901: vol. VIII, Pt. I, 30). However, in 1896–7 the province fell under the grip of a serious famine. It experienced a considerable shortfall of rain in 1895; and the successive drought and consequent crop failure in 1896 brought famine conditions. In quick succession, Berar experienced another more severe drought in 1899 when annual rainfall amounted to less than one-third of normal. Crop output during 1899–1900 was estimated to be only 2.5 per cent of the average out-turn of the preceding 10 years (excluding 1896–7) (Census of India 1901: vol. VIII, Pt. I, 31). The Berar famine of 1896–7 was described as a 'famine of high prices rather than of scarcity of food' (Crawford 1901: vol. I, 2), but throughout the province the 1899–1900 famine was much more severe and widespread.

Figure 6.3 presents the monthly MI values and the price of jower during 1895–1901. Unfortunately, price information before September of 1896 and after December 1900 could not be found. The MIs in 1895 show some excess over the baseline level. Again, the beginning of 1896 witnessed a sharp rise in mortality which peaked around May and then fell fairly fast. However, mortality during the closing months of 1896 and the first three months of 1897 was below its pre-famine baseline level—although food prices were rising dramatically. The MI curve, however, peaked rather sharply during the monsoon months of 1897, and reached a maximum in September when food

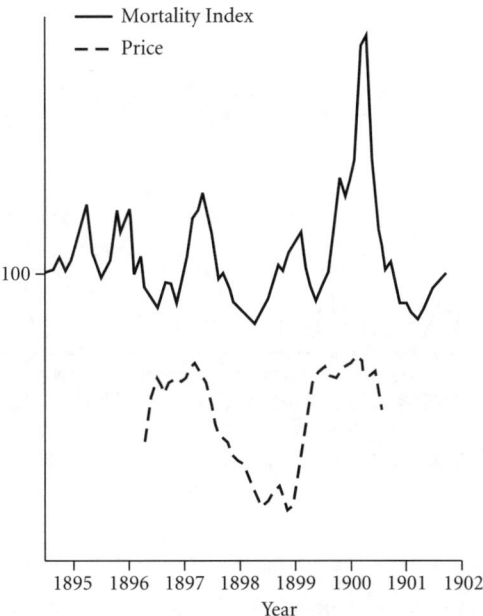

Figure 6.3. *The Price of Jower and the MI by Month, Berar, 1895–1901. Ranges of Variation: MI 43.9 (August 1898) to 423.5 (July 1900); Jower Price, 33 (April 1899) to 7 Seers per Rupee (July 1897)*

Source: See text.

prices also peaked (see Fig. 6.3). Maximum famine mortality seems to have lasted for only a short duration, that is, the latter half of 1897.

During the baseline period, cholera, dysentery/diarrhoea, and fever were the major killers among registered deaths (see Table 6.1). However, while the proportionate shares of cholera, smallpox, and dysentery/diarrhoea in *total excess deaths* in 1897 increased from their respective baseline levels, the corresponding share of fever deaths declined. Figure 6.4 suggests a quite similar time pattern of deaths from all these diseases in the main mortality year. While deaths from dysentery/diarrhoea, and from fever, peaked in September of 1897, the cholera peak occurred just one month before in August. As Berar's Sanitary Commissioner in his report for 1897 writes, '[i]t was the experience at all our relief centres that after the rains set in sickness greatly increased, especially fevers and bowel-complaints. Indeed, the most common termination of life in those debilitated by famine was diarrhoea or dysentery, aggravated by damp and exposure after the setting in of the south-west monsoon. Cold and damp had a most detrimental effect upon the starving poor, and those in a physically reduced condition from chronic insufficiency of food' (Government of Hyderabad Assigned Districts 1898: 7). The *Report* also noted that 'the number of deaths from starvation returned by village registrars numbered 377. These take no account of the deaths at poorhouses

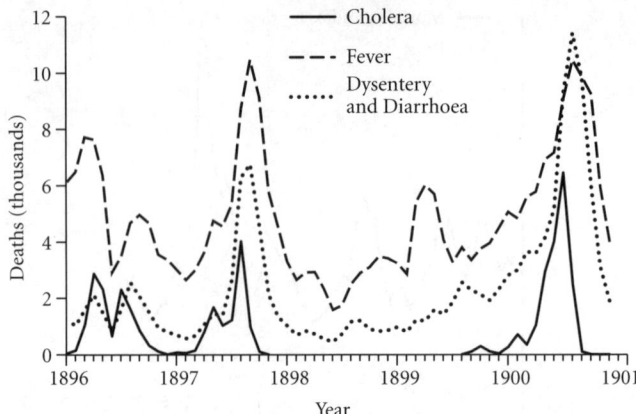

Figure 6.4. *The Monthly Distribution of Deaths by Cause, Berar, 1896–1900*
Source: See Table 6.1.

due to diarrhoea, dysentery etc., primarily the cause of chronic deprivation of food' (Government of Hyderabad Assigned Districts 1898: 32). In this connection it is worth quoting the Sanitary Commissioner's criticism of the official view on starvation deaths:

... the official definition of death from starvation signifies that so long as a person has food before him, or the means of procuring it, he cannot die from starvation. This is a mistake, for physiologically the human body may be starved of every essential to its vitality in spite of the most nutritious food if digestion has been so impaired by the effects of chronic starvation that nutrient cannot be assimilated and this form of starvation caused directly or indirectly many deaths throughout the province and explains the excess mortality under 'other causes'. (Government of Hyderabad Assigned Districts 1898: 32–33)

It is also notable that in 1897—a year of huge fever mortality—there was a marked *decline* in admissions from fever in several medical institutions of the province. This, according to the Sanitary Commissioner for Berar, largely reflected the fact that most of the excess fever mortality occurred 'amongst the famine-stricken poor, with whom the question of medical relief was secondary to that of food...' (Government of Hyderabad Assigned Districts 1898: 16). Thus the general course of the mortality rise was basically determined by the general course of famine distress and its lagged effects on human survival—albeit being partly mediated by environmental factors (e.g. post-monsoon surface water and humidity conducive to mosquito-infestation) and social disruptions (e.g. congregation at relief camps and population movements enhancing the risk of disease transmission). Mortality was below its baseline level throughout the post-famine year of 1898. While mortality was somewhat higher than normal during the early months of 1899, interestingly it was below its baseline level in late 1899—when the food price had risen dramatically (see Fig. 6.3). As in 1896, this mortality improvement during the initial phase of famine may, as suggested by the Sanitary Commissioner in his report for 1900, have been due to the dryness of the weather and the consequent lower incidence of fever (Government of Hyderabad Assigned Districts 1901: 10). Moreover there may well be a lag between the onset of famine and its excess mortality. Note that the price of food remained extremely high throughout much of 1900. From the beginning of 1900, the MI rose to reach a huge climax—peaking around July. It then declined with similar rapidity and by the end of 1900 mortality came down to its baseline level—remaining below this throughout 1901. The provision of relief reached a maximum in June of 1900, after which it fell sharply—perhaps due to the resumption of the rains and normal farm activities.

Table 6.1 shows that as in the first famine there was an increased importance of cholera, dysentery/diarrhoea, and a reduced role for fever mortality in accounting for the overall excess deaths of 1900. Indeed, as Fig. 6.4 shows, deaths from cholera, dysentery/diarrhoea, and fevers all tended to rise steadily from the closing months of 1899. According to the Sanitary Commissioner for Berar many cholera deaths (about 10,000 by his estimate) were registered under other heads (Government of Hyderabad Assigned Districts 1901: 8). While cholera deaths peaked in July of 1900—coinciding exactly with the highest MI—the other two causes reached a maximum just one month later, when deaths from dysentery/diarrhoea actually exceeded the number of fever deaths. Therefore the huge elevation of mortality which occurred in 1900 resulted not chiefly from an outbreak of malaria epidemic following the resumption of rains. In an extract from the Proceedings of the Resident at Hyderabad No. 2936 dated 12 August 1901, much of the famine mortality was attributed to the prevalence of cholera and bowel-complaints due to the 'excessive consumption of rank vegetables and foul water after the first heavy rain of the monsoon' (quoted in Crawford 1901: vol. I, 2). In fact, Mr J. A. Crawford, the Commissioner of Berar in his Foreword to the Sanitary Commissioner's report for 1900 stated that '[t]he death rate in Berar in 1900 was increased largely by the famine' (Government of Hyderabad Assigned Districts 1901, no page mark).

While scanty rainfall and related dryness of the weather may have suppressed the expected post-monsoon peak in fever mortality in both 1896 and 1899, the occurrence of peak fever mortality during the pre-monsoon months in 1900 is of interest. This, as reported by the Sanitary Commissioner of Berar, was due in large part to influenza and other simple fevers. As he wrote in his report for 1900, '[a]s the year 1900 advanced, "influenza" became prevalent, and deaths from it were registered under the head "fevers", and the number of cases of fevers also gradually commenced to increase—mostly of the type of simple continued...' He attributed this largely to 'unwholesome water and food' consumed by people who lost stamina and were exposed to heat and rain. But after the resumption of the rains, malarial fever with hepatic complications and jaundice symptoms increased till the end of the year (Government of Hyderabad Assigned Districts 1901: 10–11). Indeed, there is more evidence in the context of other historical locations that famine may have caused deaths from 'some fatal types of fever other than malarial fevers, aggravated by the debilitating effects of want of food' (see Guz 1989: 204). Thus, like the former famine, the monthly data on cause-specific deaths during that of 1899–1900 confirm a distinct correspondence between the general course of nutritional stress and the broad time path of mortality elevation (though somewhat lagged), while environmental and other factors have at best mediated in determining the exact timings of the *peaks* of mortality from specific diseases. For example, there was excess rainfall in August of both 1897 and 1900—a fact which may have contributed to peak disease (especially malaria) transmission in the following months.

The United Provinces famine of 1907–8

The famine of 1907–8 in United Provinces was brought about by the premature cessation of monsoon rainfall in August of 1907, following a generally poor start to the monsoon. In large parts of the Province, the rains lasted for only 5 to 8, instead of their usual 12 weeks. The failure of the *kharif* season in 1907 against the backdrop of some partial weather failures in the preceding two years ultimately produced famine conditions. [For details of the antecedents including partial weather failures, see Government of United Provinces of Agra and Oudh 1909a: Chapter 1.] Drought continued until January of 1908, and there was a very small *rabi* crop in early 1908 as well. According to the official report on the famine, the *kharif* harvest was only 31 per cent of normal output and only about 60 per cent in the case of *rabi* production (Government of United Provinces of Agra and Oudh 1909a: 18). The net loss in food crops in the Province in 1907–8 was estimated to be 7,000,000 tons.

The prices of food grains, which were already high during the early part of 1906 (owing to partial drought and famine during 1905–6) declined until early 1907 when they rose sharply to reach a peak later in the year (see Fig. 6.5). Due to the persistence of high prices during the pre-famine period, the majority of people who were net purchasers of food grains were already distressed and thus less able to cope with the fresh round of price rises in 1907. There was somewhat of a delay in the commencement of relief operations. This was at least partly because of the official assumption that large advances given early in the autumn (for the sowing and irrigation of the spring crops) and the 'prompt and liberal' suspensions and remissions of land revenue encouraged people to continue the sowing of spring crops until a much later period than was usual (Government of United Provinces of Agra and Oudh 1909a: 28).

As Fig. 6.5 shows, mortality was somewhat above the baseline normal level during most of 1906. There was a MI peak during the first half of 1907—largely due to the prevalence of plague. It is clear both that the MI peak of this famine was of rather short duration and that it was largely accounted for by a sharp rise in fever mortality during the last months of 1908, that is, after the resumption of the monsoon rains. As Table 6.1 also shows, although there was an increase in the relative importance of cholera in 1908, about 91 per cent of the total excess deaths were recorded under the fever category. The sharp and huge fever death peak, according to the official reports, corresponds to a malaria epidemic (Government of United Provinces of Agra and Oudh 1909a: 11; see also Government of United Provinces of Agra and Oudh 1910a). There was an enormous increase in the attendance of malaria patients at hospitals

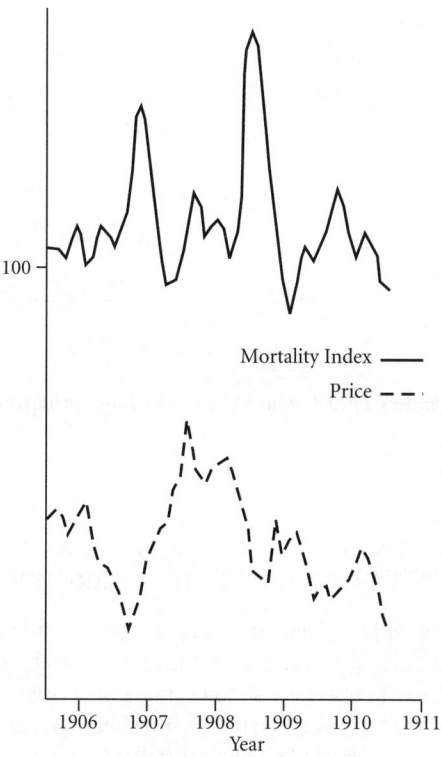

Figure 6.5. *The Price of Jower and the MI by Month, United Provinces, 1906–10. Range of Variation: MI, 84.5 (June 1909) to 244.5 (November 1908); Jower Price, 19.6 (April 1907) to 7 Seers per Rupee (December 1907)*

Source: See text.

and dispensaries: it rose from an average annual figure of 625,885 during 1904–7 to 1,369,583 in 1908 (see the Sanitary Department Resolution dated 7th July, 1910 quoted in Government of United Provinces of Agra and Oudh 1910b: 1). Note that there was no rise in the mortality from dysentery/diarrhoea, and according to the Sanitary Commissioner for United Provinces, 'this no doubt to some extent is due to the measures adopted and to the judicious feeding of the people on the relief works especially young children and suckling mothers' (Government of United Provinces of Agra and Oudh 1909b: 14). Cholera deaths peaked in September, which usually marks the end of the monsoon; fever mortality rose steeply in September and peaked around November (see Fig. 6.6). Although the cholera death peak thus preceded the huge fever mortality peak, both causes of death seem to have shared the same broad time pattern and occurred rather late.

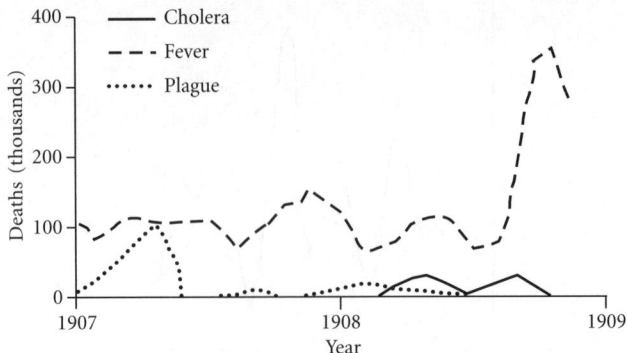

Figure 6.6. *The Monthly Distribution of Deaths by Cause, United Provinces, 1907–8*
Source: See Table 6.1.

THE CAUSALITY OF FAMINE MORTALITY: AN ECONOMETRIC EXERCISE

After the forgoing discussions sketching a broad correspondence between monthly movements of food prices and excess deaths during three major famines, we now turn to a more rigorous econometric exercise to evaluate the statistical significance of our hypothesized causality between key variables and their associated lags. In a nutshell the story that we visualize is one of deficient rainfall initially triggering food price rises and distress, which in turn, together with the mediation of climatic/environmental and other (e.g. social dislocations) factors, culminates in outbreaks of epidemics and excess deaths. Specifically, on the basis of monthly time-series data for the famine periods, we seek to test how significant was rainfall as a cause of food price rises, and how far the latter were significant in explaining the pattern of famine mortality. In doing so, here we perform what is known as Granger-Causality Test, which basically checks to see if a variable x precedes the variable y. More specifically, a variable x is said to Granger-cause variable y if, for some horizon $s > 0$, the mean squared error (MSE) of the predicted value of y_{t+s} based on past observations of y is greater than the MSE of the predicted value of y_{t+s} based on past observations of both x and y. However, if a variable is a good predictor of another, this does not imply causation as understood in common-day language. But if the Granger causing variable is determined completely outside of the economic system (i.e. is completely exogenous) then it is fairly safe to interpret Granger causality as evidence of actual causality (Chatfield 1984, Fornum and Stanton 1989).

With time-series data, the methodology for determining Granger causality involves the estimation of 'restricted' and 'unrestricted' vector autoregressions (VARs). Let us first consider the bivariate case involving variables x and y. The unrestricted VAR is a regression in which y is determined by an error term, past values of both y and x, whereas a regression in which y is determined by an error term and past values of y

Indian Famines and Epidemics

only is called a restricted VAR. To test the null hypothesis that x does not Granger-cause y one needs to estimate these two VARs, and then their respective residuals are used to form a test statistic (S), which is a distributed chi-square with p degrees of freedom, where p denotes the number of lags in the values of y (or x and y as the case may be). The exact form of S is:

$$S = T^*(SSR_0 - SSR_1)/SSR_1$$

where T is the number of observations, SSR_0 is the sum of squared residuals from the restricted VAR and SSR_1 is the analogous value from the unrestricted. If the estimated value of the statistic is greater than the chi-square critical value, the null hypothesis that x does not Granger-cause y can be rejected, and the alternative hypothesis that $x \rightarrow y$ is accepted. We have applied bivariate tests for causality of rainfall (R) on mortality index (MI) [i.e. R $\rightarrow$ MI], rainfall on number of deaths (D), rainfall on food price (P), food price on MI, and price on the number of deaths.

Because of possible equilibrium interactions between prices and mortality, it would be useful to consider Granger-causality in a more general (i.e. multivariate) setting as well. For example, one can ask if rainfall is informative to the joint stochastic process determining food prices and mortality (if so, rainfall Granger-causes prices and mortality, once one takes into account the fact that prices and mortality are determined jointly). Alternatively, one can ask if rainfall and food prices are jointly informative in predicting mortality. These are the two (actually four, given that we have used two measures of mortality, namely MI and total deaths) multivariate Granger-causality tests performed below. The methodology here is analogous to the bivariate case. Once restricted and unrestricted VARs are estimated, test-statistics can be framed by using the regression residuals. The exact form of the test-statistic (L) is:

$$L = T^*[\log(|VCV_0|) - \log(|VCV_1|)]$$

where T is the number of observations, $|VCV_0|$ is the determinant of the variance–covariance matrix estimated from the restricted VAR residuals, and $|VCV_1|$ is the analogous value from the unrestricted. The test-statistic, L, is asymptotically distributed chi-square with $n_1{}^*n_2{}^*p$ degrees of freedom, where n_1 is the number of endogenous variables in the restricted regression, n_2 is the number of restrictions (i.e. the number of variables which are potentially Granger-causing) and p is the total number of lags in the values of variables.

In interpreting the results for Granger-causality tests (as presented in Table 6.2), it is important to begin with a few practical considerations. First, results for Granger-causality tests are sensitive to the number of lags, p, included in the VAR estimation: for low values of p, the test-statistic is hardly ever rejected, while for large values of p the null hypothesis is almost always rejected. Given a rather small number of observations for all three famine periods, choosing $p = 1$ resulted in no rejections of the null hypothesis (i.e. absence of evidence of Granger-causality) for all tests considered here even at the 10 per cent level of significance, whereas choosing $p = 8$ resulted in rejections (i.e. evidence of Granger-causality) in all cases considered. Consequently, we

Table 6.2. *Estimated Values of Test-statistics and the Corresponding Numbers of Lag for Variable Values, Historical Famine Locations*

	Bombay 1876–8	Berar 1896–1900	United Provinces 1907–8
Bivariate case			
R → D	1.09 (17.32); $p = 2$	18.53## (15.8); $p = 2$	11.84## (21.13); $p = 2$
	3.23 (17.38); $p = 4$	13.12* (15.63); $p = 4$	22.74## (21.01); $p = 4$
	6.24 (17.42); $p = 6$	14.02* (15.7); $p = 6$	
P → D	1.76 (17.30); $p = 2$	13.9## (15.95); $p = 2$	1.93 (21.45); $p = 2$
	7.24 (17.29); $p = 4$	9.55# (15.7); $p = 4$	4.06 (21.52); $p = 4$
	23.26## (17.08); $p = 6$	20.75# (15.59); $p = 6$	
R → MI	6.46# (5.16); $p = 2$	3.41 (7.94); $p = 2$	4.95 (6.36); $p = 2$
	7.35 (5.33); $p = 4$	5.17 (8.03); $p = 4$	10.46# (6.3); $p = 4$
	12.08 (5.01); $p = 6$	9.48 (8.07); $p = 6$	
P → MI	0.27 (5.32); $p = 2$	4.08 (7.93); $p = 2$	0.69 (6.52); $p = 2$
	1.10 (5.49); $p = 4$	6.30 (8.00); $p = 4$	4.44 (6.49); $p = 4$
	2.41 (5.23); $p = 6$	9.97 (8.06); $p = 6$	
R → P	0.23 (−4.32); $p = 2$	2.43 (−3.84); $p = 2$	1.90 (−2.67); $p = 2$
	5.50 (−4.28); $p = 4$	19.06 (−4.11); $p = 4$	2.60 (−2.52); $p = 4$
	10.41 (−4.28); $p = 6$	23.61 (−4.23); $p = 6$	
Multivariate case			
(R and P) → D	2.62 (17.39); $p = 2$	29.14## (15.64); $p = 2$	10.09# (21.27); $p = 2$
	8.24 (17.26); $p = 4$	21.17## (15.59); $p = 4$	29.23## (20.79); $p = 4$
	28.28* (17.24); $p = 6$	27.75## (15.61); $p = 6$	
(R and P) → MI	6.38 (5.15); $p = 2$	8.34 (7.91); $p = 2$	5.42 (6.48); $p = 2$
	8.90 (5.49); $p = 4$	10.04 (8.09); $p = 4$	22.85## (6.04); $p = 4$
	17.83 (5.24); $p = 6$	18.77 (8.12); $p = 6$	
Rain → (P and D)	0.95 (12.73); $p = 2$	18.49## (11.59); $p = 2$	11.41## (18.04); $p = 2$
	6.43 (12.55); $p = 4$	25.15## (11.11); $p = 4$	54.50## (16.09); $p = 4$
	19.70 (11.87); $p = 6$	31.97## (0.71); $p = 6$	
Rain → (P and MI)	7.25 (0.34); $p = 2$	6.38 (3.83); $p = 2$	11.12## (2.88); $p = 2$
	14.16 (0.23); $p = 4$	19.75## (3.45); $p = 4$	57.41## (0.73); $p = 4$
	26.8* (-0.33); $p = 6$	32.35## (2.99); $p = 6$	

##, Null hypothesis of no Granger-causality is rejected at 0 per cent level of significance;
*, Null hypothesis of no Granger-causality is rejected at 1 per cent level of significance;
#, Null hypothesis of no Granger-causality is rejected at 5 per cent level of significance.
p = Number of lags used.
P = Food price.
R = Rainfall.
D = Number of deaths.
MI = Mortality index.
Figures in parentheses are respective values of AIC.
Source: For the mortality data the same as given in Table 6.1; see text for other sources of information.

restrict ourselves to the results for the lags of 2, 4, and 6. As well, values for the Akaike Information Criterion (AIC) are displayed for each lag specification. Essentially, the AIC is an un-nested model specification, which uses a large number of explanatory variables (here lags). Model specifications, which minimize the AIC are considered 'better'. Second, in typical time-series applications, non-stationarity of variables is of notable concern. Most macroeconomic and financial time series contain unit roots or geometric trends which must be taken out of the data, and estimating the VARs in log-levels is one way of doing this. However, because the time horizon considered here is so short (2–3 years), non-stationarity is not an issue. In fact, simple diagnostic checks show that first and second order representations of individual time series all have roots which lie well inside the unit circle. As a result, VARs have been estimated in levels (i.e. not logged). Indeed, test results on logged variables are not qualitatively different. Third, because of a small sample size for the famine episodes considered here, care should be taken in interpreting test results, particularly when null hypotheses are marginally rejected or not rejected.

As Table 6.2 shows, for the Bombay famine of 1876–8, rainfall alone does not appear to have Granger-caused any of the endogenous variables, namely MI, food price, the number of deaths; the exception is the case of R $\rightarrow$ MI where the null hypothesis of no causality can be rejected at the 5 per cent level for a lag of 2. This overall lack of causation seems consistent with the fact noted earlier that the famine mortality showed a somewhat steady rising tendency from the beginning (or even earlier) of the peak mortality year (i.e. 1877, which was again a year of deficient rainfall), thus the occurrence of substantial excess mortality preceded the usual spike of monsoon rains. Nor was there any remarkable rise in excess deaths during the wet months of 1878, which witnessed the return of the normal monsoon. While food price movements appear to have Granger-caused the number of deaths for the lag length of 6, they fail to show a significant causality on MI movements. The AIC reveals that no single lag specification dominates in any of the cases considered.

The null hypothesis of no Granger-causality is largely accepted in most multivariate tests for the Bombay famine. One notable exception is the case of rainfall being informative to joint stochastic determination of MI and price for a lag of 6 even at the 1 per cent level of significance. Note, however, that due to the large lag length, this result is based on very few observations: with 36 total observations and 6 lags, 30 usable observations are used to estimate 19 coefficients in each equation of unrestricted VAR and 13 coefficients for each restricted VAR. The other exception is (R and P) $\rightarrow$ D at the 1 per cent level for a lag of 6. But the same caveat concerning small sample size applies here as well. For the Berar famines, food prices and rainfall separately (i.e. in bivariate cases) appear to have Granger-caused the number of deaths (the test statistics across three lag specifications being significant at the 5 per cent or even at less than the 1 per cent level, especially for the lag of 2), though they both fail to appear significantly causal on the movements of the MI. Notably, however, in the multivariate case, rainfall does appear significantly causal on joint stochastic determination of MI and food prices for lag lengths of 4 and 6. This is perhaps largely due to significant causality of rainfall on food prices, especially for lag lengths of 4 and 6 (as seen in the bivariate results). This is also evident in the absence of joint causality of rain and price on MI. On the other hand, rain and prices appear jointly causal on the stochastic process for total number of deaths even at the 1 per cent level of significance.

For the United provinces famine, because of the small sample size (only 24 observations) tests results are presented only for 2 and 4 lags. In bivariate cases, rainfall appears causal on the number of deaths for lags of 2 and 4 even at less than 1 per cent level of significance, and on MI for only a lag of 4 at the 5 per cent level. This seems to reflect the fact that the total number of deaths sharply increased (like in any normal year) in September of 1907 just following the monsoon months of July and August, whereas the MI did not begin to peak until November. Furthermore, rainfall does not appear to have Granger-caused food prices. Nor do food prices appear to have had a significant causal power on total deaths and the MI. However, as multivariate test statistics suggest, rains, and prices jointly appear significantly causal both for the number of deaths (for lags of 2 and 4 respectively at the 5 and 1 per cent levels of significance) and also for the MI for a lag of 4 at even less than the 1 per cent significance level. Likewise, rainfall appears significantly informative in stochastic processes governing joint determination of prices and deaths as well as prices and the MI (for lags of 2 and 4 respectively at the 5 and 1 per cent levels of significance).

DISCUSSION AND CONCLUSION

It would now be useful to assemble and review the major points that seem to have emerged from our analysis of three major historical famines. First, an early indication of the development of famine has almost always been reflected in soaring food prices. This period of rising prices represents the onset of the so-called 'starvation phase', when people presumably pass through acute economic distress, and various social disruptions ensue. As the results of the econometric tests suggest, rainfall and food price—separately as well as jointly—seem to have somewhat greater causal power for total deaths as compared to MI. This may partly be because monthly MI values—ratios of monthly numbers of deaths, instead of death *rates*, in famine years to those for the pre-famine period—get more sensitive than monthly numbers of deaths to the defect of dealing with absolute levels rather than rates. [Note that since a large spike in deaths reduces the underlying population at risk in the following months, the monthly series of total deaths may not always truly reflect the monthly movement of *death rates*.] A relatively weak Granger-causality between food prices and the MI during famine periods, however, seems consistent with the chief features of famine mortality noted earlier, namely that the peak mortality not only occurred relatively late in the famine process (i.e. in the 'epidemic phase'), but it also occurred within a relatively short span of time, when food prices either reached a high level plateau or were only beginning to decline. In fact food prices often continued to remain quite high when mortality went back to normal levels. However, food prices and rainfall jointly (i.e. in multivariate formulations) often appear to have a significant causal power for famine mortality—perhaps indicating the importance of interactions between nutritional stress and climatic/environmental factors in shaping excess mortality during a famine.

However, a somewhat simultaneous rising trend shared by almost all recorded causes of death from the beginning of the peak mortality year, as well as an increased share of such diseases as cholera and dysentery/diarrhoea, which have an almost obvious link with undernutrition, suggests that mounting undernutrition and debilitation was fundamental to the outbreaks of various epidemics and associated excess mortality. Also, cause-composition as well as timing of famine mortality peaks, as was seen in the Bombay and Berar famines, suggest that diseases other than malaria (such as dysentery/diarrhoea, and bowel-complaints) could well be the prime killers during a famine. As the mortality experiences in the Bombay and Berar famines further show, the occurrence of a malaria epidemic following a drought-induced famine has *not* always been contingent upon the resumption of normal rains. All this calls for qualifications necessary for a malaria-centric explanation of excess mortality during past Indian famines. However, this is not to deny the mediating role that climatic variations and social dislocations might have played in hastening and spreading infectious diseases including malaria. For example, a very sharp peak in fever mortality in November of 1908 following above normal rains in September in United Provinces points to the role that monsoon rains and associated mosquito-breeding can play—particularly in determining the timing of peak malarial mortality.

As noted earlier, the absence of malaria as a separate category of death in the Sanitary Commissioners' reports (until the 1930s) always leaves us with some doubt as to whether the fever mortality-peak does indeed represent epidemic malaria. For example, Dr A. Porter, on the basis of a diagnostic investigation of famine victims admitted to hospitals during the Madras famine of 1876–8, found that a considerable number of registered fever deaths were actually due to pneumonia—which was not a recognized cause of death in the registration system. In the post-mortem room he found pneumonia ('in a more or less advanced stage') in more than 25 per cent of all cases (Porter 1889: 131). During the Punjab famine of 1899–1900 too, there is a rather strong indication that the registered fever mortality in 1900 included a large number of cholera deaths. After an enquiry into high death rates in 1900 in Hissar—a severely affected district in Punjab—the Deputy Commissioner wrote on 1 September 1900: '. . . in Rawalwas, Hissar *Tahsil* 12 deaths from cholera were reported, whereas 36 actually occurred, and that while 22 cases of fever were reported only 3 actually occurred . . . The total for the *tahsil* [Bhiwani] accordingly shows 187 actual cholera deaths to 82 reported, and 90 fever deaths against 194 reported . . . The explanation seems to be that they [i.e. *choukidars*] often dread the enquiry and trouble necessary on reported outbreak of cholera and do all in their power to minimize the matter or to avoid reporting it at all' (Government of Punjab 1901: 170–1). In another special survey of deaths in villages of United Provinces during the famine of 1877–8, sheer starvation (or 'want') was reported to be 'one dominant cause of death' (The Report of North-Western Provinces and Oudh Famine of 1877–8: 340–1).

Indeed, as was noted in the Berar famines, the largest number of deaths recorded for the month of peak MI was under the dysentery/diarrhoea category, rather than fever. Such predominance of dysentery/diarrhoea—typical 'famine diseases'—in the overall famine mortality is sometimes better corroborated by contemporary hospital records. In this context, the distribution of patients admitted to hospitals by classified causes in two districts of Ajmer–Merwara province during the famine of 1899–1900 is shown in Table 6.3. As can be seen, the percentage share of patients admitted with dysentery/diarrhoea was about 45 and 56 per cent respectively in Ajmer and Merwara, while corresponding figures under fever were only about 11 and 18 per cent. Although it is not perfectly clear if these data include the post-monsoon months of 1900 (when the outbreak of a malaria epidemic was more likely), this hospital record of admissions, considering the possibility of a better disease-categorization of famine victims in hospitals (than by village watchmen), at least calls for appropriate caution against the explanation of famine mortality *mostly* in terms of malarial deaths following monsoon rains. All this said, it is difficult to ignore that a large number of the registered fever deaths were often due to malaria, especially during the post-monsoon months. Also, some malaria deaths may have been entered under other headings as well.

The immunity-based explanation of malarial mortality in drought-caused famines (as mentioned in the previous section) can, however, be subjected to doubt in the light of our present evidence. First, as the Bombay famine of 1876–8 has shown, a malaria (as proxied by fever) mortality peak can occur even in a year of drought itself (e.g. 1877). Somewhat relatedly, especially in the Bombay and Berar famines, a broad rising trend of mortality in the course of the famine has been shared by almost all major causes of death, including fever—implying a general time pattern of famine mortality, rather than a post-monsoon epidemic of malaria *per se* being the prime explanation of famine mortality. Furthermore, Zurbrigg's regression analysis of relevant data for Punjab during 1868–1908 provides no empirical support for the immunity-centred explanation of malarial mortality following a drought and famine. In fact, no significant relationship between the previous year's autumn fever mortality and/or rainfall levels and current mortality could be found (Zurbrigg 1992: PE-13).

There are several difficulties of the refeeding malaria hypothesis too. First, since food prices almost always appear to have stayed very high during and even beyond the monsoon months in the year following drought, and since normal harvesting does not

Table 6.3. *Hospital Admissions by Major Cause during the 1899–1900 Famine, Ajmer and Merwara Districts, Ajmer–Merwara Province*

Cause of hospital admission	Ajmer district	Merwara district
Diarrhoea	4,262	5,804
Dysentery	1,429	9,821
Debility and anaemia	2,348	3,278
Fever	1,395	4,869
Ulcers	1,357	3,381
Chest diseases	845	—
Smallpox	608	—
Cholera	345	596
Total	12,589	27,749

Source: Report on the Famine in Ajmer–Merwara in 1898–1900, Ajmer, Rajputana Mission Press, 1900; pp. 70, 75.

take place until late in that year, it is doubtful whether a perceptible improvement in nutritional status of the affected population could really occur by the period of peak fever mortality. Besides, the available evidence on refeeding malaria suggests that even though the attack rate rises with 'refeeding' (i.e. recovery in nutritional level), the mortality rate depends crucially on the previous level of undernutrition. Indeed, a review of the relevant literature concludes that while a low plasma nutrient level seems to inhibit the rate of (malaria) pathogen multiplication, 'in every situation this has to be balanced against the effect of malnutrition on the immune host response' (Tomkins and Watson 1989: 24; also Zurbrigg 1998). In fact, the crux of the matter does not appear to lie so much in parasite virulence or their numbers in blood of the host as in the bodily strength of the hungry host to survive an infection, regardless of parasite levels (Zurbrigg 1992: PE-17).[7] Also, there is no evidence that malnutrition is advantageous during the recovery from infection. It is worth noting that the Indian Famine Commission Report of 1901 did attribute the enhanced fever *fatality* during these famines directly to undernutrition:

... [fevers] ... often are in origin climatic, but that their fatality is, owing to the reduced power of the people to resist them, largely due to famine (Government of India 1901: 63)

Moreover, there are fairly strong indications that poor people were more vulnerable to *malaria mortality* (e.g. Zurbrigg 1992: PE-13–14). In fact, much greater malarial death rates were reported by Christophers for the poorer classes in the late nineteenth- and early twentieth-century Punjab (Christophers 1910: 38–9). The report of an investigation of the epidemic of malarial fever in Assam during 1896 concluded that 'the poor suffer in a disproportionate degree, and have less chance of recovery, owing to their living in more crowded dwellings, and to a deficiency of nourishing diet especially of a nitrogenous nature' (Rogers 1897: 37). In a recent study of young children admitted to hospitals in an African food crisis, undernutrition, though seemingly protective against clinical malaria, appears to have been associated with a higher overall risk of death (de Waal 1989a: 103). Attention may also be drawn to the findings of an early celebrated study among 100,000 English prisoners over four years—a study which is considered to be a landmark in the history of the 'refeeding hypothesis'. In this study, while the sickness rate was found far higher for the better-fed group, those receiving least food had four times higher *mortality* than those consuming most food (Murray and Murray 1977: 472–3).

Although information on the class composition of mortality during India's past famines is particularly scant, relief records and contemporary accounts indicate that the main rural victims were often from the poor classes—small cultivators, agricultural labourers, and petty artisans (Currie 1991; also Ambirajan 1989). All this seems consistent with the undernutrition-centred hypothesis: that the death toll of epidemic malaria in the wake of a famine cannot but be fundamentally attributed

---

[7] A good illustration of this point can be drawn from a severe malaria epidemic during the Bengal famine of 1943–4—where despite low observed levels of malaria parasites and few malarial symptoms, an inordinately large number of famine victims appear to have died from malaria (Zurbrigg 1992: PE-17).

to acute undernutrition and debilitation (with enhanced susceptibility and fatality to disease).[8] Note the similar conclusion for the catastrophic malaria epidemic during the Bengal famine of 1943–4, which occurred 30–40 years later than those studied here: '[t]he overall dimensions of malaria mortality during the prime famine period cannot be dissociated from the basic fact of acute nutritional deficiency on a mass scale' (Maharatna 1996: 176; see also Zurbrigg 1998: 7–9).

This, however, is not to ignore the mediating influences of climatic variations, temperature, humidity, and other environmental, ecological, and epidemiological conditions—especially on the timing of the peak epidemic mortality. The huge post-monsoon elevation of fever mortality in several Indian locations (e.g. United Provinces)—appearing often as a magnification of the normal seasonal pattern—does suggest a mediating role played by environmental and climatic factors. The relatively low mortality that has usually been observed for the initial drought year may indeed be due to a relative absence of mosquitoes and malaria. Indeed the fact that several past famines involved small excess mortality is sometimes used to cast doubt on the inevitability of a link between nutritional stress and epidemics (including malaria). However, as has been shown elsewhere, a large part of the explanation for the occurrence of 'low-mortality' historical famines in the Indian subcontinent lies either in a relatively low severity of distress or in relatively effective and liberal relief measures or in expanded local opportunities provided by an increased diversification of the economy (Maharatna 1996: Chapter 3). Notably, in the Punjab famine of 1899–1900, a huge peak of fever mortality occurred late in 1900—certainly after the recovery of the normal monsoon (as was stressed by Whitcombe 1993), but perhaps with a crop-output even lower than that in the preceding year of severe drought.[9]

Thus resolving this question *fully*, which requires controlling for several factors such as the severity of failures both in rains and crops, climatic patterns, the nature of relief, the extent of social dislocations, and so on, is extremely difficult. Nevertheless, the foregoing discussion leads us back to the 'classical wisdom' held by contemporary scientists and administrators. Thus S. R. Christophers, the eminent malariologist of British India, while not ignoring the usual role of rainfall in creating favourable conditions for mosquito-breeding and malaria transmission, concluded his famous study of recurrent malaria epidemics in Punjab as follows: '[t]he facts certainly support the view that scarcity is a factor determining to a large degree the situation, extent, and intensity of epidemics' (Christophers 1910: 39). About seventy years later this basic point has been reaffirmed in the context of 'a most catastrophic malaria

---

[8] This is not to suggest that malaria can hardly be a killer disease among well-nourished populations. Falciparum malaria can indeed be highly fatal even for well-fed people. However, the death rates during India's many malaria epidemics following famines are so much above the contemporary mortality estimates from the disease that it is difficult to attribute the past excess malaria mortality mainly to an enhanced exposure as opposed to an increased susceptibility to the disease (Zurbrigg 1992: PE-15).

[9] While in the drought year of 1899 the cropped area in the whole of Punjab was 22.75 million acres, it declined even further to only 15 million acres in the following year of 1900, the year of peak famine mortality; see *Census of India* 1901: vol. 18, Pt I, 42.

epidemic' in Sri Lanka following a drought in 1934: 'Rainfall made the mosquitoes more abundant; famine made the people more susceptible' (Harrison 1978: 202).

To conclude: while outbreaks of epidemics and associated excess mortality in the wake of India's past major famines appear fundamentally and inextricably linked with the adverse effects (often somewhat lagged) on human health and survival of mass starvation and acute nutritional deprivation, the exact timing of peak mortality from specific diseases was partly shaped by climatic and environmental factors (e.g. the monsoon in the case of malaria, heat and lack of drinking water in the case of cholera) and partly by social dislocations (e.g. periods of maximum congregation at relief camps contributing to the spread of cholera and dysentery/diarrhoea). Consequently, a distinct dichotomy, as has recently been suggested (e.g. de Waal 1989b), into a 'starvation model' and a 'health crisis model'—as two separate explanations for famine mortality—stands as largely inappropriate. In fact, such a framing of the debate in terms of an opposition between nutrition versus public health measures creates 'a false dichotomy where in fact there is none' (Zurbrigg 1988: 9). Apropos policy implications, our analysis of India's past famine experiences suggests that there was hardly any scope for a choice between measures that restore food entitlement and those which enhance public health provisions as well as containing disease transmission. The entire excess mortality in the course of a famine—caused both directly by acute undernutrition enhancing susceptibility and fatality, and also indirectly via influences of social dislocations and climatic variations conducive to exposure and transmission—should be branded as 'famine mortality'. While this is not to downplay the role of public health measures (e.g. vaccination, maintenance of sanitation standards, control programmes for vectors), they should be a part—not quite independent—of a broader programme of restoring food entitlement to the vulnerable masses. Indeed, compared to the huge mortality tolls of these past famines, the relatively slight excess mortality during several severe droughts in many parts of Independent India has largely been attributable to the relatively effective and timely relief measures which have protected the affected populations against a drastic reduction in their food entitlements (Aykroyd 1974; Drèze 1990; Dyson and Maharatna 1992; and Maharatna 1996, Chapter 6 among others).

References

Ambirajan, S. (1989), 'Food, Famine and Hunger in Tamil Nadu: 1850–1900', in Singh, *et al.*, Volume 2.

Arnold, D. (1991), 'Social Crisis and Epidemic Disease in the Famines of Nineteenth-Century India', paper presented at the Society for the Social History of Medicine Conference on 'Famine and Disease', Cambridge: Christ's College.

Aykroyd, W. R. (1974), *The Conquest of Famine*, London: Chatto and Windus.

Bhatia, B. M. (1967), *Famines in India: A Study in Some Aspects of the Economic History of India (1860–1965)*, 2nd edn., London: Asia Publishing House.

Census of India 1901, *Report on Berar, Volume VIII*, Part I.

Census of India 1911, *Volume XV, United Provinces of Agra and Oudh, Part I, Report*, Allahabad, 1912.

Chatfield, C. (1984), *The Analysis of Time Series: An Introduction*, 3rd edn., London: Chapman and Hall.

Chen, L., Chowdhury, A. K. M. A., and Hoffman, S. L. (1980), 'Anthropometric Measurement of Protein-Energy Malnutrition and Subsequent Risk of Mortality Among Pre-School Aged Children', *American Journal of Clinical Nutrition*, 33: 1836–45.

Christophers, S. R. (1910), 'On Malaria in the Punjab', in *Proceedings of the Imperial Conference* held at Simla in October 1909, Simla: Government of India Press.

Crawford, E. M. (1991), 'Epidemic Diseases in the Great Famine of Ireland 1845–50', paper presented at the Society for the Social History of Medicine Conference on 'Famine and Disease', Cambridge: Christ's College.

Crawford, J. A. (1901), *Report on the Famine in the Hyderabad Assigned Districts in the year 1899–1900*, Hyderabad.

Currie, K. (1991), 'British Colonial Policy and Famines: Some Effects and Implications of "Free Trade" in the Bombay, Bengal and Madras Presidencies, 1860–1900', *South Asia*, 14(2): 23–56.

de Waal, A. (1989a), 'Population and Health of Eritreans in Waad Sherifei: Implications for the Causes of Excess Mortality in Famines' (mimeo), Oxford: Nuffield College.

—— (1989b), 'Famine Mortality: A Case Study of Darfur, Sudan, 1984–5', *Population Studies*, 43(1): 5–24.

Drèze, J. (1990), 'Famine Prevention in India', in J. Drèze and A. K. Sen, *Political Economy of Hunger, Volume 2*, Oxford: Clarendon Press.

—— and Sen, A. K. (1989), *Hunger and Public Action*, Oxford: Clarendon Press.

—— —— (1990), *Political Economy of Hunger*, Volumes 1 and 2, Oxford: Clarendon Press.

Dyson, T. (1989a), 'The Population History of Berar Since 1881', *The Indian Economic and Social History Review*, 26(2): 168–201.

—— (ed.) (1989b), *India's Historical Demography: Studies in Famine, Disease and Society*, London: Curzon Press.

—— (1991a), 'On the Demography of South Asian Famines, Part I', *Population Studies*, 45(1): 5–25.

—— (1991b), 'On the Demography of South Asian Famines, Part II', *Population Studies*, 45(2): 279–97.

—— (1993), 'Demographic Responses to Famines in South Asia', *IDS Bulletin*, 24(4).

—— and Maharatna, A. (1992), 'Bihar Famine of 1966–67 and Maharashtra Drought 1970–73: The Demographic Consequences', *Economic and Political Weekly* 27 June.

Foege, W. H. (1971), 'Famine, Infections and Epidemics' in G. Blix, Y. Hofvander, and B. Vahlquist (eds.), *Famine: A Symposium Dealing with Nutrition and Relief in Times of Disasters*, Stockholm.

Fornum, N. R., and Stanton, L. W. (1989), *Quantitative Forecasting Methods*, Boston: PWS-KENT Publishing Company.

Government of Bombay (1878), *Annual Report of the Sanitary Commissioner for the Government of Bombay, 1877*, Bombay: Government Press.

Government of Hyderabad Assigned Districts (1898), *Report on the Sanitary Administration of the Hyderabad Assigned Districts for the year 1897*, Hyderabad.

—— (1901), *Report on the Sanitary Administration of the Hyderabad Assigned Districts for 1900*, Hyderabad.

Government of India (1901), *Report of the Indian Famine Commission 1901*, Calcutta.

Government of North-Western Provinces and Oudh (1897), *Resolution on the Administration of Famine Relief in the North-Western Provinces and Oudh during 1896 and 1897*, Allahabad: Government Press.

Government of Punjab (1901), *The Punjab Famine of 1899–1900, Volume II*, Lahore.

Government of United Provinces of Agra and Oudh (1909a), *Resolution on the Administration of Famine Relief in United Provinces of Agra and Oudh during the years 1907 and 1908*, Allahabad: Government Press.

—— (1909b), *Annual Report of the Sanitary Commissioner of the United Provinces of Agra and Oudh for 1908*, Allahabad: Government Press.

—— (1910a), *Report on the Administration of the United Provinces of Agra and Oudh 1908-1909*, Allahabad: Government Press.

—— (1910b), *Annual Report of the Sanitary Commissioner of the United Provinces of Agra and Oudh for 1909*, Allahabad: Government Press.

Guz, D. (1989), 'Population Dynamics of Famine in Nineteenth Century Punjab, 1896–7 and 1899–1900', in T. Dyson (ed.) (1989b), *India's Historical Demography: Studies in Famine, Disease and Society*, London: Curzon Press.

Harrison, G. (1978), *Mosquitoes, Malaria and Man: A History of the Hostilities Since 1880*, London: John Murray.

Hionidou, V. (1995), 'The Demography of a Greek Famine: Mykonos, 1941–42', *Continuity and Change*, 10(2).

—— (1999), ' "Send Us either Food or Coffins": The 1941–42 famine on the Aegean Island of Syros', paper presented at Fondation des Treilles, May 1999, and published in revised form in the present book.

Jannetta, A. B. (1992), 'Famine Mortality in Nineteenth-Century Japan: The Evidence from a Temple Death Register', *Population Studies*, 46(3).

Lardinois, R. (1985), 'Famine, Epidemics and Mortality in South Asia: A Reappraisal of the Demographic Crisis of 1876–8', *Economic and Political Weekly*, 20(11): 454–65.

Maharatna, A. (1994), 'The Demography of the Bengal Famine of 1943–33: A Detailed Study', *The Indian Economic and Social History Review*, 31(2).

Maharatna, A. (1996), *The Demography of Famines: An Indian Historical Perspective*, New Delhi: Oxford University Press.

Martorell, M., and Ho, T. J. (1984), 'Malnutrition, morbidity and mortality', *Population and Development Review*, 10 (Supplement): 49–68.

Meuvret, J. (1965), 'Demographic Crisis in France from the Sixteenth to Eighteenth Century', in D. V. Glass and D. E. C. Eversley (eds.), *Population in History: Essays in Historical Demography*, London: Edward Arnold.

Mokyr, J., and Ó Gráda, C. (1999), 'Famine Disease and Famine Mortality: Lessons from the Irish Experience, 1845–50', paper presented at Fondation des Treilles, May 1999, and published in revised form in the present book.

Murray, J. and Murray, A. (1977), 'Suppression of Infection by Famine and its Activation by Refeeding — A Paradox?', *Perspectives in Biology and Medicine* 20(4, Summer).

—— Murray, A. B., Murray, N. J., and Murray, M. B. (1990), 'Susceptibility to Infection During Severe Primary Undernutrition and Subsequent Refeeding: Paradoxical Findings' (mimeo), Department of Medicine, University of Minnesota.

Murray, J., Murray, A. B., Murray, C. J., and Murray, M. B. (1975), 'Refeeding-Malaria and Hyperferramia', *Lancet*, 122 (March): 653–4.

—— —— Murray, M. B., and Murray, C. J. (1976), 'Somali Food Shelters in the Ogaden and Their Impact on Health', *Lancet*, 123 (12 June): 1283–5.

Newman, L. F. (ed.) (1990), *Hunger in History: Food Shortage, Poverty and Deprivation*, Oxford: Basil Blackwell.

Pitkänen, K. J. (1993), *Deprivation and Disease: Mortality During the Great Finnish Famine of the 1860s*, Helsinki: The Finnish Demographic Society Publications 14.

Porter, A. (1889), *The Diseases of the Madras Famine 1877–78*, Madras: Government Press.

Post, J. D. (1990), 'Nutritional Status and Mortality in Eighteenth-Century Europe', in L. F. Newman (ed.), *Hunger in History: Food Shortage, Poverty and Deprivation*, Oxford: Basil Blackwell.

Rogers, L. (1897), *Report of an Investigation of the Epidemic of Malarial Fever or Kala-azar in Assam*, Shillong: Assam Secretariat Printing Office.

Scrimshaw, N. S., Taylor, C. E., and Gordon, J. E. (1968), *Interactions of Nutrition and Infection*, World Health Organisation, Geneva.

Sen, A. K. (1981), *Poverty and Famines: An Essay on Entitlement and Deprivation*, Oxford: Clarendon Press.

Taylor, C. E. (1985), 'Synergy Among Mass Infections, Famines and Poverty', in R. I. Rotberg and T. K. Rabb (eds.), *Hunger and History: The Impact of Changing Food Production and Consumption Patterns on Society*, Cambridge: Cambridge University Press.

Tomkins, A. M. (1986), 'Protein-Energy Malnutrition and Risk of Infection', in *Proceedings of the Nutrition Society*, 45: 289–304.

Tomkins, A., and Watson, F. (1989), *Malnutrition and Infection: A Review*, London: Clinical Nutrition Unit, London School of Hygiene and Tropical Medicine.

Walter, J., and Schofield, R. (1989), *Famine, Disease and Social Order in Early Modern Society*, Cambridge: Cambridge University Press.

Whitcombe, E. (1990), 'Famine Mortality', paper presented at the British Association for South Asian Studies Annual Conference, Edinburgh, April.

—— (1993), 'Famine Mortality', *Economic and Political Weekly*, 5 June.

Wrigley, E. A., and Schofield, R. (1981), *Population History of England 1541–1871: A Reconstruction*, London: Edward Arnold.

Zurbrigg, S. H. (1988), 'Hunger and Epidemic Malaria in Punjab' (mimeo).
—— (1992), 'Hunger and Epidemic Malaria in Punjab, 1868–1940', *Economic and Political Weekly*, January 25.
—— (1998), 'Re-thinking Public Health, Food, Hunger and Mortality Decline in Indian History', *Medico Friend Circle Bulletin*, 258/259.

7

Famine Yesterday and Today in Burundi

CHRISTIAN THIBON

Burundi is a small, densely populated, hilly country in central Africa, wedged among Rwanda, the Congo, and Tanzania. Peopled in the main by two ethnic groups, the Hutu and the Tutsi, it was colonized by Germany in the 1880s and ruled by Belgium between 1916 and 1962. Its 28,000 square kilometres contained about 2 million people c.1950, making it one of the most densely populated places in Africa. The history of famine in Burundi, or at least the narrative thread most commonly retained by collective memory and in academic and official sources, at first sight suggests a classic pattern (Table 7.1). According to this version of the past, the mortality crises, food shortages, and famines associated with the colonial period were followed by a period of population growth from the mid-twentieth century on, or more precisely in the wake of the 'Manori' famine, the last famine on a national scale in 1943–4. For a time, 'Manori' seemed to mark an end to the era of famines. Since then, however, in common with many other African countries Burundi has seen the emergence of crises of an inter-tribal or socio-political character, about which there has been either a silence or, on the contrary, an overemphasis of their dimensions and their effects.

Table 7.1 reveals ambiguities and contradictions between collective and scholarly memory. The former retains evidence of the calamities of the late nineteenth century and of the great Manori famine of 1943–4, while the written record places the breaks in the pre-colonial and the inter-war periods. In both cases memories are selective, ignoring certain episodes. The difficulties encountered in the reconstitution and measurement of this history, to which may be added Burundi's paucity of hard statistical data and other evidence, and the temptation to 'africanize' the universal features of historic demography (along the lines of 'the demographic *ancien régime*'), has quickly led to the imposition of a neo-Malthusian interpretation. This interpretation associates, in analogical fashion, these past and present crises with a universal pattern, according to which past crises, resulting from an erosion of resources and a consequent reduction in the food supply, were subsistence crises due to overpopulation, while today's crises are about issues, such as access to land and diminishing returns, and are the outcome of the dislocation caused by modern inter-tribal tensions. Now, while historical reconstitution may confirm this schema, at least in its main outlines, it also revises it, revealing a diversity of crises, a complexity in their characteristics and in their effects, and in the contexts which preceded and followed them.

Table 7.1. *Crises in Collective Memory, in Oral and Written Sources*

Date	Event, popular description	Principal characteristics, oral, and written descriptions	Official/academic identification, geographical range	Principal causes given
1880/ 1919	Famines of the turn of the century, cataclysm	Depopulation in peripheral regions, famine, scarcity, high epidemic mortality, infertility, imbalance in the age distribution	National and regional	Droughts and natural calamities, illness and epidemics, war
1920s, 1930s	Famines and scarcities referred to as calamities	Excess mortality, scarcity, famine amenorrhoea, delayed marriage, migration	Regional, local food shortage, minor famines	Drought, colonial development, backward agrarian system
1943–4	The 'Manori' famine	mortality, 30,000+ victims, food shortage, internal migration	Famine, scarcity, destitution	Drought, wartime conditions
1972	Socio-political crisis of 1972, the catastrophe	150,000–300,000 victims, refugees, destitution	National, ethno-political	Genocide

The present study[1] does not seek to give an exhaustive account of the different crises. It concentrates instead on some of their forgotten or neglected features with two historiographic and interdisciplinary objectives:

(i) to correct some current impressions of Burundi and the Great Lakes region of central Africa, and
(ii) to identify the impact of crises by giving pride of place to their relations with means and strategies of survival which can be represented by the following synoptic table (Table 7.2); in this context, we aim to juxtapose demographic data and analyses on the survival strategies used in the countryside.[2]

THE FORGOTTEN FAMINES OF THE COLONIAL PERIOD

The received understanding of Burundi in the colonial period is of a country marked by a combination of demographic stagnation and recurrent crisis. These have been

---

[1] This chapter is based on research carried out at the University of Burundi in 1990–4 which is summarized in Thibon (2000). See also Thibon (1987–9, 1998).
[2] This approach is presented in the following two syntheses: Bohle *et al.* (1991); Bohle *et al.* (1993).

Table 7.2. *Agricultural Calendar, Agrarian Systems and Dietary Regimes in Central Burundi (Highland Region) in the Nineteenth and Twentieth Centuries*

Months/crops	S	O	N	D	J	F	M	A	M	J	J	A	Period
Èleusine	S-	—	—	—	—	—	—	—	R	—	—	—	Pre-colonial
Sorghum	—	—	—	S-	—	—	—	—	—	—	-R	—	Pre-colonial
Maize	S-	S-	—	—	-R	—	-R	—	—	—	—	—	Pre-colonial
Beans	—	S-	—	—	—	—	S-	—	—	-R	—	—	Pre-colonial
Livestock	R	R	R	R	R	R	R	R	R	R	r	r	Pre-colonial
Wild plants used in months of scarcity	—	—	—	R	R	R	R	—	—	—	—	—	Pre-colonial
Sweet potato	—	S-	—	—	—	—	R	R	R	R	R	R	Colonial
Maize (heath)	—	—	—	R	—	—	—	—	—	—	S	—	Colonial
Beans (heath)	—	—	—	R	—	—	—	—	—	—	S	—	Colonial
Potatoes (heath)	—	R	R	—	—	—	—	—	-S	—	—	—	Colonial
Perennial plants, banana, manioc	Rr	Rr	Rr	Rr	Rr	Rr	Rr	Rr	Rr	Rr	Rr	Rr	Colonial
Coffee plantation	—	—	—	—	—	—	—	—	—	re	re	re	Colonial
Tea	re	re	re	re	re	re	re	re	re	re	re	re	Post-colonial
Climatic and sowing season	*Agatasi*, little rainy season			*Urushana*, main sowing season			*Impeshi*, harvest			*Ici*, dry season			

Key: S, sowing/planting; R, harvest; Rr, staggered harvest; re, cash revenue; the main months of scarcity (*soudure*) are December and January.

attributed a common subsistence dimension, reflected in frequent famines, destitution, and food shortages. A common causality is also identified: in the short run, inadequate rainfall, drought, and the failure of agrarian systems and the market; and in the long run, demographic pressure. This vision was sustained by retroactive projections and it was reinforced by the memory of the last great famine of 1943–4 and by colonial discourses on the risks of overpopulation, which were taken up and given a new lease of life after independence. Nonetheless, historical research has considerably enriched our knowledge in distinguishing the crises of the turn of the century from colonial crises, and in offering more precise information about the latter.

On the subject of the wave of famines that straddled the end of the nineteenth century and strongly influenced collective memory, research exploiting the resources of oral history and the earliest written accounts has indirectly reconstituted a narrative involving scenarios of a multidimensional demographic depression over the longer run. This should not be characterized as a simple conjunction of natural calamities and foreign interventions, but stems instead from a cumulative combination of climatic accidents, microbial shocks, and internal and international political instability, all occurring in a context of undue pressure on an agro-pastoral system and of socio-political gridlock.

Agriculture, having supported exceptional demographic growth, no longer offered much margin for further growth. This improved chronological and spatial knowledge permits an appreciation of the sequence of crises—with a primacy being accorded to the destabilizing effects of epidemics and microbial short-circuits, and their indirect impacts on populations and their ecosystems. It also allows us to reconstitute the disequilibria of the structural cadres which have conditioned and stemmed from them. However, it does not yield any statistical measure beyond the purely anecdotal,[3] which therefore leaves several questions unanswered, in particular those relating to the intensity of the crises. That said, it is otherwise for the 1920s—a decade for which the sources become more varied and numerous, making possible the exploitation of the earliest statistical data and the production of the first estimates based on the parish registers of the Catholic missions.

The 1920s were marked by regional famines (1921/2, 1925/7, 1928/9) about which popular memory is more vague or even silent, unlike those which preceded or followed them. These crises tended to spread themselves across the Burundo–Rwandan surface in a concentric pattern. They were mortality crises in the classic form of a subsistence crisis intensified by epidemics, which, judging from their popular names, their cumulative scenarios, and their official descriptions, leaves little room for doubt about their catastrophic nature.

On the other hand, the hidden food shortages and the short-lived famines of the 1930s are perhaps better seen as subsistence crises of a seasonal kind, chronic food shortages against the backdrop of the last, more circumstantial, epidemic outbreaks. But in contrast with the turn of the century and the 1920s, it is the country's heartland,

---

[3] With the exception of censal and other data for certain regions and mortality records for the earliest Christians. Cf. Botte (1985).

its inhabited highlands, which were affected. There, the frequency of warnings and their geographical distribution suggest the vulnerability of an economy made unstable by colonial development, which the least climatic or other shock dramatically accentuated.

The last great 'Manori' famine constitutes a crescendo during this period. Preceded and followed by short-lived famines, it testifies to an erosion of the means of subsistence and of the capacity to survive—which culminates during the 1943–4 harvest year on the highlands where agriculture was less diversified and where mobilization for the war effort was the greatest.

This first typology therefore reveals different intensities and amplitudes. And it places in perspective the two explanatory factors—drought and overpopulation—which may or may not have affected the course of events. In the first place, vulnerability to crisis is not associated with high population densities; indeed, quite the contrary, demographic capacities constituted a resource which was mobilized during times of food shortage. Thus, the arenas of famine are to be found in peripheral spaces, depopulated or unsettled by international migrations, or in areas with a high proportion of people dependent upon wage labour. Moreover, if climatic fluctuations—such as the prolongation of the dry season—are often at the origin of crises, they are not so systematically; thus, several regions experiencing very little rain or seasonal shocks may be spared from disaster. Therefore, research has focused on two directions: first, on a more accurate qualitative and monographic reconstitution of the history of these crises, including what preceded and followed them, and the context in which they occurred; and second, on their measurement using various forms of statistical data.

FORGOTTEN ASPECTS OF THE FAMINES OF THE COLONIAL ERA

These trends concern as much the genesis and the course of events as their coming to an end. Thus, for the crises of the turn of the century, the focus of research is on certain structural dimensions. On the one hand, the epidemiological and ecological dimensions of a destabilized environment are revealed: the multiplication of epidemic and pandemic flames linking the Great Lakes to the epidemiological history of East Africa, tracing a microbial shock which affected both humans and their environment, in particular livestock, and activated a depopulation favourable to the extension of trypanosomiasis, so much so that one can really speak of an ecological crisis. On the other hand, the limits revealed by the agrarian system (limited to one or two seasons of cultivation and to the agro-pastoral binomial), and by politico-social organization, offered a breeding ground for social tensions and political conflicts which outside interventions would then underscore.

The famines of the 1920s were of an internal nature. Geopolitical conflicts were absent, at least in the case of Burundi. It was a case of 'classic' colonial famines: an accumulation of climatic and epidemiological upsets in peripheral regions and on warm land accentuating the economic disequilibria that followed colonial development and the creation of a speculative and monetary market oriented to the Congolese west. These famines reveal the impact of aggravating factors, such as the hiring away of labour and its corollary (i.e. emigration) which removed an indispensable support in times of unusual poverty or food shortage; and the negative impacts of emergency policy with mobilizations for transport and food aid. To these were added disputes between colonial authorities about the allocation of relief, and communal tensions aggravated by administrative reorganizations, social conflicts, and the coarsening of human relationships—all of which adversely affected the traditional capacities of survival and mutual help. This period also saw the first campaigns aimed at popularizing anti-famine plants.

As for the local famines and chronic food shortages of the 1930s, as with the preceding decade in each case it is the general state of vulnerability which is signalled. The slightest shock, whether natural or politico-economic in origin, gives rise to local famines, except that in this case the geographical extension seems blocked because, given the limits of the epidemic stage, their spread is contained. The last 'great' famine, occurring during World War II, brings us back to this two-sided situation: on the one hand, a climatic, economic, and political sensitivity; and on the other hand, improved nutritional and physiological capacities to resist. Thus, as in the case of the short-lived famines of the 1930s, the crisis was above all selective, affecting regional or even local populations, whose economic vulnerability was increased by the exactions of war, but sparing regions where the peasantry were quick to integrate anti-famine crops into their planting systems. These included the social strata who had access to livestock products and who were not affected by vegetal shortages, communities who lived a safe distance from commandeering zones or who had rapidly assimilated new tillage techniques and benefited from the rising prices for manioc, sweet potatoes, and bananas. On this occasion too, and in contrast with the 1930s, the government authorities operated an intelligent public relief policy. This involved: an embargo on food exports from Burundian markets, the distribution of food aid through the mission infrastructure and seed barns, the limitation of commandeering of transport associated with the war effort, the distribution of seed and agricultural implements, and anti-smallpox vaccination campaigns.

Numerical historical reconstitutions corroborate these patterns. Thus, for the famines of the 1920s, and particularly that of 1925–7, surviving colonial records show for the first six months levels of mortality for each territory which range from 4 to 12 per cent and migration rates of 2 to 4 per cent. A final estimate in 1928 suggests 40,000 famine-related deaths, or about one-seventh of the population of the territory as a whole. In the calendar year of 1929, the earliest sample demographic inquiries (see Table 7.3) conducted a little after the famine peak and the inquiries done on the Christian populations of the Catholic missions (a marginally better-off group) produce death rates of about 100 per thousand, while in other territories during the 1930s, the rates were about 30 per thousand.

Table 7.3. *Deaths in 1929 (Child and Juvenile Mortality, per 1,000)*

Place	Death rate (%)	Reference	Source
Kanyinya mission	104	Christian population ($n = 527$), 1929 cohort	Mission report, nominal list
Rugari mission	373	Christian population ($n = 318$) cohort	Mission report, nominal list
Gitega territory	101	Demographic inquiry, August 1930; sample of about 240 Agricultural year 1929/30	Territorial administration
Three sites	81 / 80		
Muyingai territory	96	Demographic inquiry, August 1930; sample of about 240, Agricultural year 1929/30	Territorial administration
Ruyigi territory	68	Demographic inquiry, August 1930; sample of about 240, Agricultural year 1929/30	Territorial administration
Rutana territory	14	Demographic inquiry, August 1930; sample of about 240, Agricultural year 1929/30	Territorial administration
Rumonge and Bujumbura territories	Unavailable		

Source: National Archives of Belgium (African section), parish registers.

So far as the famine of 1943–4 is concerned, national data are confusing. They have been subjected to various critiques and to both optimistic and pessimistic interpretations. Still, the parochial records can be exploited to reveal, apart from the aggregate movements (illustrated in Fig. 7.1) important differences between missions and seasonal movements of a kind associated with crisis mortality. They can also point to instances of excess mortality which were often preceded by warning signs from 1942 onwards, and by varying degrees of post-crisis adjustment through higher fertility levels (Table 7.4).

Case studies of individual missions identify the duration of this crisis, which is translated into excess infant mortality when it is light and by excess adult male mortality when it is severe (Table 7.5). These indices of heightened mortality and monthly death rates of over 100 per thousand are also found in the occasional enumerations carried out on certain sub-chiefdoms (*souschefferies*). While the child mortality rates for the cohorts of these years are equal to or higher than the infant mortality rates.

It is necessary, then, to place in perspective the homogeneous vision imposed on both the pre-colonial and the colonial periods. The apogee is situated in the 1890–1920 period; factors such as the epidemiological transition and the parasitical effects of policies are re-evaluated, while the potential for absorbing the crises is underlined. All the same, this simplification also applies to the post-colonial period.

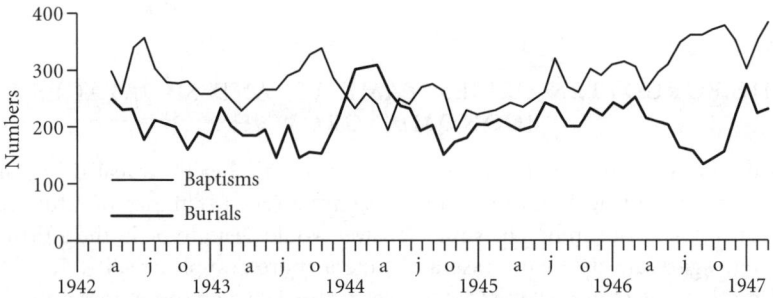

Figure 7.1. *Monthly Movements in Births/Baptisms and Deaths/Burials (Infants and Adults) in Five Rural Missions (Corrected Raw Data)*

Source: Registers of the missions of Bukeye, Kanyinya, Rusengo, Mushasha, and Kiganda. Data assembled by the Seminar on Rural History, University of Burundi (henceforth SRH).

Table 7.4. *Annual Variations in Births/Baptisms, Conceptions, and Deaths/Burials (1938–40 = 100)*

Year	Bukeye	Kiganda	Rusengo	Mushasha	Kanyinya
1938/40	100/100/100	100/100/100	100/100/100	100/100/100	100/100/100
1941	88/91/100	94/93/120	74/92/138	87/108/111	108/100/130
1942	71/73/112	75/81/154	67/84/127	93/93/164	70/100/131
1943	75/78/140	67/84/130	73/93/127	65/107/166	76/61/120
1944	37/38/265	55/78/227	74/84/120	111/107/161	88/84/88
1945	61/63/193	105/66/167	78/73/123	137/127/202	84/98/136
1946	97/98/127	116/141/149	77/91/183	153/153/248	97/89/73
1947	74/77/108	114/138/86	83/100/169	166/162/145	102/101/71

Source: Data assembled by the SRH.

Table 7.5. *Indices of Excess Mortality by Mission*

Year	Rusengo	Kanyinya	Bukeye	Kiganda
1941	3	4	2	—
1942	3	4	1	—
1943	3	4	3	—
1944	0	2	3	5
1945	1	0	3	1
1946	4	2	0	1
1947	4	0	4	0
1948	2	0	3	0
1949	4	0	0	0
1950	0	0	1	0

Source: Data assembled by the SRH. The numbers refer to degrees of severity; see Dupâquier (1979).

THE FORGOTTEN CRISES, FAMINES, AND SHORTAGES OF ECONOMIC GROWTH

Does the population growth and 'better demographic health' revealed by various national indices during the more recent past signify an end to famines, destitution, and food shortages in Burundi? The simple answer would seem to be in the affirmative. However, aggregate data can erase and hide a more complex reality. Inter-tribal conflagrations apart, at certain moments aggregate data, and sometimes non-official sources too, reveal the perturbations as the slowing of inter-censal growth, the peaking of mortality and fertility, exceptional migratory movements, situations to which collective memory or official declarations rarely refer. So, demographic growth does not signify the end of crises, but rather their gradual reduction (see Fig. 7.2).

Aggregate data drawn from mission registers and monographic studies confirm the force of these negative conjunctures, revealing short-lived local mortality crises without much impact on fertility, which affected almost all missions (the towns and one mission excepted) with more or less frequency as in 1947, 1950, 1953, 1957, 1961–3, 1966, and 1984, quite apart from the post-colonial socio-political crises of 1972–3 and 1988 (Table 7.6). Whether regarded as negative contingency or residual crisis, at the level of the individual mission these events sometimes assumed the severe characteristics typical of an *ancien régime* crisis (see Fig. 7.3). However, at other times they were barely perceptible on the scale of annual excess mortality (Table 7.7). They lasted until the mid-1980s, although becoming less frequent and less intense. They have no link—chronological, spatial, or social—with the outbreaks of inter-ethnic hostility which are the outcome of an autonomous history. For this reason, they seem residual, and their disappearance was announced in the early 1990s at a time when new local pockets of poverty were being identified.

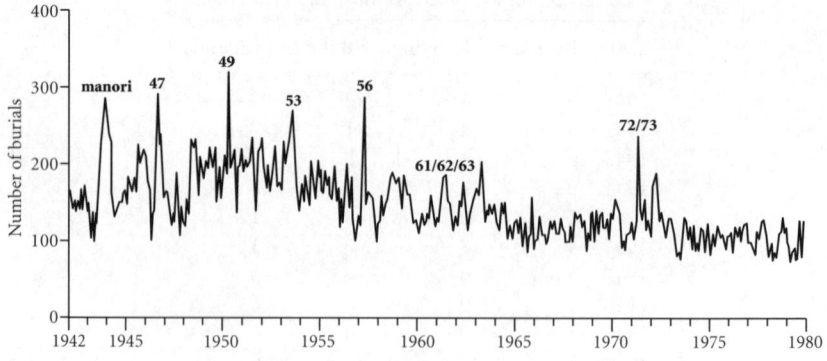

Figure 7.2. *Monthly Fluctuations in Burials in Eight Rural Missions, 1942–80*
Source: Mission registers.

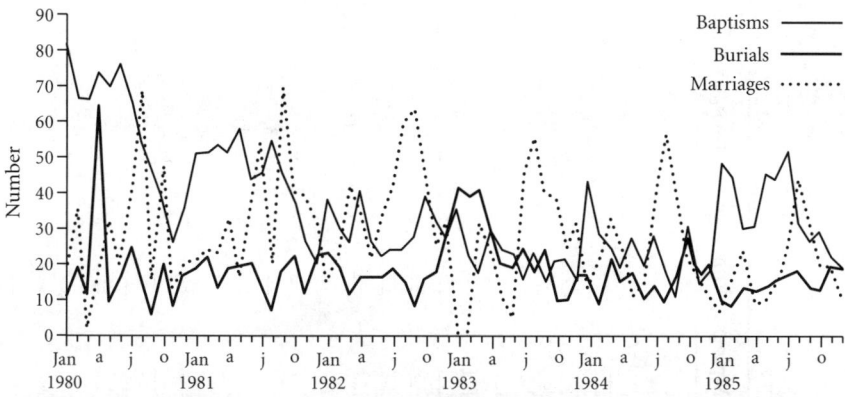

Figure 7.3. *Monthly Fluctuations in Births/Baptisms, Burials, and Marriages at Bukeye Mission, 1980–5*

Source: Mission registers.

Estimates of annual per capita calorie availability by region reflect the performance of the rural peasant economy since the 1950s (Table 7.8). They paint a rather reassuring picture—with a single cloud being Buyenzi, a populated region which has suffered reverses because of its specialization and reliance upon coffee cultivation which has meant that it has experienced declining financial revenues over time.

Apart from such general indicators, the pattern is confirmed by the evolution of the annual vital cycle, both for the population as a whole and for children aged under 7 years in nine missions which have been studied. The mission data reveal a remarkable change over four decades (1950/90) compared to the situation in the 1930s and 1940s (famine years apart). There has been a decline in end-year (September–December) mortality, which is even clearer for children. This improvement needs to be placed in the context of modifications to food and cultural regimes, the integration into the farming year of a third growing season (i.e. involving the cultivation of heath land) and the growing importance of perennial crops, including tubers, which has reduced the protein-hungry months to January–February.

Let us add that these changes were realized in the context of the structural extension of food markets and the growth of regional markets for agricultural products. Yet, these developments have not only produced positive modifications for the mode of subsistence. They have translated into two rather contradictory evolutions: On the one hand, the influence of positive changes in the immuno-parasitic equilibria favourable to children (through vaccination programmes). And on the other hand, particularly affecting the mortality of July–August, the months of harvest, an immuno-parasitic deterioration which has affected high density and high mobility populations. There are adult populations for which the sanitary statistics reveal, although in incomplete fashion, an epidemiological deterioration which chronic malnutrition can only encourage.

Table 7.6. Crises and Negative Local Shocks at the Missions

Year	Kanyinya	Kiganda	City	Rusengo	Bururi	Makamb	Bukeye	Mushasha	Mpinga	Rumonge	Gitwenge
1950	—	—	—	—	—	—	—	—	—	—	—
1951	11 (2)	—	—	—	—	—	6 (3)	—	12 (2)	—	—
1952	—	—	—	—	—	8	11 (2)	11	—	—	—
1953	—	—	—	3 (4)	—	8	—	12	3 (2)	—	—
1954	8/12 (3)	—	—	—	—	8	—	—	12 (2)	—	—
1955	10 (3)	—	—	—	—	—	—	—	12	—	—
1956	—	—	—	—	—	—	12	12	—	—	12 (3)
1957	8/12 (4)	—	—	—	—	8	3	—	8/10	—	—
1958	2	—	—	—	—	—	—	—	—	—	—
1959	—	—	—	—	—	—	—	—	—	—	—
1960	—	—	—	—	—	8 (2)	—	—	—	—	—
1961	—	—	—	12	—	—	—	12 (3)	—	—	—
1962	11 (2)	—	—	12	—	—	3/12	12	10	10 (2)	—
1963	11 (3)	—	—	—	—	—	—	—	—	—	—
1964	—	—	—	—	—	—	—	—	—	—	11 (3)
1965	—	—	—	—	—	—	*	—	—	—	12 (4)
1966	—	—	—	—	—	—	—	—	—	8	—
1967	—	—	—	—	—	—	—	—	—	—	—
1968	—	—	—	—	—	—	—	—	—	—	—
1969	1	—	—	8	—	—	—	—	—	—	—
1970	—	—	—	—	—	—	—	—	—	—	—
1971	—	—	—	—	—	—	—	—	—	—	—
1972	*	*	*	*	*	*	*	*	*	*	*
1973	*	*	*	*	*	*	*	*	*	—	*
1974	—	—	—	—	—	—	—	12	—	—	—

1975	8	—	—	—	6	—	—	—
1976	—	—	—	—	—	—	—	—
1977	—	—	—	—	—	4/11	—	—
1978	—	—	8	—	—	—	—	—
1979	—	*	—	—	—	—	—	—
1980	10	—	—	12	—	—	—	—
1981	—	—	—	—	—	11	—	—
1982	9	—	8	—	8	—	—	—
1983	—	—	—	—	—	—	8	—
1950/80	10/32	1/32	0/32	6/32	1/32	5/14	4/32	8/32	4/16	3/32	3/27

Key: * = not studied. The numbers refer to the critical month (e.g. 11 = November); those in brackets to the duration in months.

Source: Data assembled by the SRH.

Table 7.7. *Annual Indices of Excess Mortality by Mission*

	Rusengo	Kanyinya	Gitengwe	Mushasha	Bukeye	Kiganda	Bururi	Total
1950	0	0		2	1	0		2/5
1951	0	1		2	0	1		3/5
1952	0	1		2	0	0		2/5
1953	0	0		3	0	0		1/5
1954	0	0		0	0	0		0/5
1955	0	0		1	0	0		1/5
1956	0	0		0	0	1		1/5
1957	2	2		0	0	0		2/5
1958	0	0		0	0	0		0/5
1959	0	0		0	0	0		0/5
1950/59	1/10	3/10		5/10	1/10	1/10		24%
1960	2	0		0	0	0		1/5
1961	0	0		0	2	0		1/5
1962	0	0		0	0	0		0/5
1963	0	1		0	0	3		2/5
1964	0	0	2	0	0	1		2/6
1965	0	0	3	0	0	0		1/6
1966	0	0	0	0	0	0		0/6
1967	0	0	0	0	0	0	3	1/7
1968	0	0	0	0	0	0	0	0/7
1969	0	0	0	0	0	0	3	1/7
1960/69	2/10	1/10	2/6	0/10	1/10	2/10	2/3	16%
1970	0	0	0	0	0	0	2	1/7
1971	4	0	0	0	0	0	0	1/7
1972/73	*	*	*	*	*	*	*	
1974	0	0	0	0	0	0	0	0/7
1975	0	0	0	0	2	4	0	2/7
1976	0	0	0	0	0	0	0	1/7
1977	0	2	2	0	0	0	0	3/7
1978	0	0	0	0	0	0	0	1/7
1979	0	2	0	0	0	0	0	2/7
1980	0	2	0	0	0	2	0	2/7
1970/80	1/9	3/9	1/9	1/9	1/9	2/9	1/9	15%

Key: * = not studied. The numbers refer to degrees of severity; see Dupâquier (1979).
Source: SRH.

FROM ONE CRISIS TO ANOTHER, FROM FAMINE TO HUNGER

But if positive tendencies were confirmed, in particular the reduction in the periods of seasonal food shortages and a certain increased stability in the supply of food calories, and the disappearance of famines and associated mortality crises in the wake of severe shocks to the food supply happened too, this does not imply an end to hunger or (in the words of historian Fernand Braudel) '*la sortie des fatalités originaires*'.

Table 7.8. *Calorie Availability by Region*

Region	1957/58 (1)**	1967 (2)**	1970/1 (3)**	1971 (4)*	1982 (5)*	1983 (6)*	1984 (6)*	1980/5 (8)**	1983/7 (9)*	1985/90 (9)**
Bugesera				3,084	2,918	3,070			2,864	2,939
Buragane				2,123	2,206	2,140			2,114	
Bututsi				1,629	1,932	1,385	653		1,742	
Buyenzi	2,052 2,648	2,148	1,990	1,950	2,010	2,015	3,787	2,650	1,949	1,763
Buyogoma				2,307	2,188	2,360			2,107	
Bweru		2,148	2,512	2,512	2,627	2,585		2,400	2,568	3,601
Imbo				2,867	3,248	2,910	4,557		3,061	
Kirimiro		1,990		1,990	2,115	2,010	4,744	2,610	2,051	
Kumoso				2,199	2,606	2,570			2,563	
Mugamba	2,790 2,262			1,504	1,953	1,490	2,867	2,350	1,844	
Mumirwa				1,935	2,147	1979			2,024	

*Estimates; ** inquiry.
Sources: (1) Leurquin (1960); (7) Jones and Egli (1984); Thibon (2000).

These persist in two forms, one episodic, happening in the wake of socio-political crises (as in 1973, and also perhaps in 1966 following a reduction in the area under cultivation), the other being a structural consequence of modifications in dietary regimes. These developments were incubating during the entire century in line with modifications to the agrarian systems and eating regimes. Thus, they differentiated the populations according to access to staple items, both vegetable and dairy; to anti-famine plants, to sorghum and banana beers; and to plants such as beans, maize, and potatoes grown on marginal land, which account for about one-fourth of the food supply during the most difficult months of the year (the *soudure* period, typically December–February). The dividing line between the 'haves' and 'have-nots' might be regional or ethnic. Yet, more and more nowadays the distinction operates around lines of monetary cleavage, as the calculation of poverty demonstrates (see Table 7.9), and around lines of alimentary cleavage regarding access, or the lack of it, to traditional cash crops, such as leguminous plants and modern foods like cereals, rice (in particular), dairy products, and beers.

Though it may not translate itself into discernible demographic patterns (e.g. higher mortality, lower fertility, and delayed marriages) as with classic famines, this malnutrition acts like a hidden famine in reverse, an invisible famine which either escapes all measurement during part of the year or else is of a quasi-permanent fashion, because it will touch vulnerable populations at risk (i.e. strata of local or urban populations dependent upon monetary incomes; certain regional sub-groups according to criteria, such as household size; and displaced and relocated refugee populations). Its power to exclude and therefore to frustrate is all the stronger in the case of these instances, which are no longer regarded as 'natural', still less as a fatal or

Table 7.9. *Index of Poverty by Province and Calorific Supply by Region in 1990*

Province	Number of paupers (%)	Intensity of poverty (%)	Region(s)	Calorie supply >/< 2,100	Trend 1980–90
Bubanza	22	4.6	Imbo/Mumirwa	>	+/stable
Bujumbura rural	25	6.2	Imbo/Mumirwa	>	+/stable
Bururi	37	9.3	Imbo/Bututsi	>/<	+/−
Cibitoke	25	6.6	Imbo	>	+
Gitega	33	9.9	Kirimiro	2,100	stable
Karuzi	66	22	Bweru	>	+
Kayanza	44	11	Buyenzi	<	−
Kirundo	34	9.5	Bugesera	>	+
Makamba	39	11	Buragane	2,100	stable
Muramvya	24	6.6	Kirimiro/Mugamba	2,100/<	stable
Muyinga	27	6.1	Bugesera	>	+
Ngozi	42	10	Buyenzi	<	−
Burundi rural	36	10		2,100	stable

Source: Budget/consumption inquiries in rural areas 1986–90, cited in *Rapport BM*, 1996.

general failure. In the 1990s, these 'famines within' were often ignored or hidden by an obligatory optimism and by long-term catastrophic perspectives on the reversal of the Malthusian trap.

References

Bohle, Hans G., Downing, T. E., Field, J. O., and Ibrahim, F. N. (eds.) (1993), *Coping with Vulnerability and Criticality*, Sarrebrucken: Freiburg Studies in Development Geography.

Bohle, Hans G., Cannon, T., Hugo, G., and Ibrahim, F. N. (eds.) (1991), *Famine and Food Security in Africa and Asia*, Bayreuth: Bayreuther geowissenschaftliche Arbeiten.

Botte, R. (1985), 'Rwanda and Burundi 1889/1930: A Chronology of a Slow Assassination', *International Journal of African Historical Studies*, 18(1/2): 53–85 and 289–311.

Dupâquier, Jacques (1979), 'L'analyse statistique de la mortalité', in H. Charbonneau and A. Larose (eds), *Les grandes mortalités, étude méthodologique des crises démographioques du passé*, Liège: IUSSP, 83–112.

Jones, William I., and Roberto, Egli (1984), *Farming Systems in Africa: The Great Lakes Highlands of Zaire, Rwanda, and Burundi*, World Bank Technical Paper No. 22, Washington, DC: World Bank.

Leurquin, P. (1960), *Le niveau de vie des pays ruraux du Ruanda-Burundi*, Louvain: IRES.

Thibon, C. (1987), 'Un siècle de croissance démographique au Burundi', *Cahiers d'études africaines*, 27(105/6): 61–83.

—— (1988), 'Fécondité naturelle et fécondité controlée, un aperçu de l'évolution de la fécondité dans la région des grands lacs', *Annales de démographie historique*, 157–79.

—— (1989), 'L'expansion du peuplement dans la région des grands lacs au XIX siècle', *Revue canadienne d'études africaines /CJAS* 23: 23 and 54–73.

—— (1998), 'Crise démographique et crise sociopolitique au Burundi', in F. Gendreau (ed.), *Crises, pauvreté et changements démographiques dans les pays du Sud* (Aupelf/Uref, Paris), 35–51.

—— (2000), *Croissance, transition démographique et crises socio-politiques 1880/1993, une population prise au piège d'une fatalité ou de dérives socio-démographiques modernes*, Paris: Karthala.

8

Famine in Nineteenth- and Twentieth-Century Russia: Mortality by Age, Cause, and Gender

SERGUEI ADAMETS

At the beginning of the twentieth century, when Russia accounted for about one-quarter of global cereal production (Učebnik 1925), the sense that famines were becoming more serious within the country's borders was gaining wide currency among the public (Golod 1902). Peasant impoverishment and famine were at the centre of debates in the Duma from its first sessions in 1906, and they influenced the passage of important institutional and economic reforms that affected rural society. Initiated by Prime Minister Stolypin (1907) and continued until the beginning of World War I, agrarian reforms contributed greatly to the attenuation of the demographic consequences of famine during the last years of the Tsarist era. Famines reappeared in Russia during the civil war and the subsequent period of collectivization. However, the definitive victory over this scourge dates from three decades later. Did the problem of famines worsen during the course of the nineteenth century and in the Soviet era? This chapter addresses this question from the standpoint of their frequency, duration, and intensity.

FAMINE: A PREDICTABLE PHENOMENON?

During the nineteenth century, famines seemed to strike Russia in a more or less regular pattern. A volume published by the Central Statistics Committee (CSK) in 1871 referred to poor harvests in 1820–1, 1833–4, 1839–40, 1843–6, 1848–51, and 1854. The Report of the Council of Ministers drafted in 1842 implies that food shortages recurred every 6–7 years (Brokgauz and Efron 1893). During the 1860s the worst years were between 1867 and 1869. In the last quarter of the century, there were famines in 1872–3, in 1882–4, and in 1892. At the beginning of the twentieth century, local scarcities affected one or other region of Russia almost annually, and they were particularly serious in 1906 and 1911 (Buxman 1923).

In the wake of the famine of 1921–2, the statisticians of the Central Statistics Directorate (CSU) and of Gosplan tried to find rigorous explanations for the phenomenon of poor harvests and famines in pre-Revolutionary Russia. Some, like Semenov (1922), sought to link harvest fluctuations with solar activity, while others, such as Mixelsson (1920), linked them to long meteorological cycles. The majority of statisticians hoped to find a regular empirical pattern to the periodic fluctuations of good and bad harvests. This proved to be a dead-end because annual harvests fluctuated in a more or less random fashion and with considerable amplitude. However, the application of the concept of a 'cycle' opened up a new avenue for the statistical study of famines. By removing from continuous series yield differentials over identical intervals (i.e. cycles), it is possible to identify within each cycle successions of good and average harvests. This led some to suggest the existence of cycles of 4 years (Cerevanine 1919), others of 10 years (Groman 1929), and still others of 17–20 years (Mixelsson 1920). The discussion turned on whether or not the cycles were genuine, and whether they were small or large. Whatever the cyclical pattern, none of these studies suggested an intensification of famines during the pre-Revolutionary decades. Also, the models proposed may have accounted for the past, but their poor predictive power remained their Achilles heel.

World War I and the 1917 Revolution shattered an ancient empire and resulted in extremely severe food shortages in the industrial cities and in the provinces of the Volga and the Centre—regions that were most severely affected by Tsarist and Soviet requisitioning. This crisis, initially urban, was succeeded by the great rural famine of 1921–2. The effects of this famine were still felt in the periphery of the Soviet empire in 1923–4 (Čelintsev 1923–4).

In 1924, 10 territories in the Volga region were declared as disaster areas. In 1928, it was the turn of the Ukraine. In 1931, the regions of the Middle and Lower Volga and several Asiatic territories were again struck by drought, lending legitimacy to a cyclical interpretation of famine. Even so, the study of cycles was abandoned during the late 1920s, because it was deemed to be misleading and bourgeois. Conjuncturalists such as Groman, Kondratiev, and others were persecuted, arrested, and condemned. After the great famine of 1933, there was a recurrence of food shortages in 1936. The era of famine finally came to an end after that of 1946–7. Regular occurrences in the nineteenth century and the first half of the twentieth, famines suddenly ceased during the era of Khrushchev.

TRENDS IN THE GEOGRAPHY OF FAMINE

In contrast to what many observers believed, the geography of Russian famines changed considerably from about the 1870s onwards. Until the mid-nineteenth century all regions were subject to the risk of bad harvests and, consequently, famine. Pokrovski (1897) showed that the poor harvest of 1833 affected the south (below the 53rd parallel), that of 1839–40 the provinces of the Centre, while in 1845–6 the provinces of the Northwest (Pskov, Vilna, Kovno, Grodno, Moghilev, Minsk, Novgorod, and Smolensk) suffered the same fate. The southern provinces (Yekaterinoslav, Kherson, Kharkov, Poltava, and Voronezh) were hit again in 1849.

Following this chronology, let us note the bad harvest of 1853 which affected the regions of Volhynia and Podolia in the Ukraine, and those of Yaroslav and St Petersburg in Russia. In the following year, the harvest was poor in the provinces of Moscow, Volhynia, and St Petersburg. In 1855, the cumulative effect of war in the Crimea, cholera and typhus epidemics, and harvest deficits led to a rise in mortality in the West and Black Earth regions. Then, in 1868, famine affected regions bordering Finland.

However, from the 1870s onwards, the geography of famine began to change and the crisis zones became more localized than in the past. The provinces of the West and the North-west were no longer subject to mortality crises. The retreat of the famine zone reached central Russia and much of the Ukraine, and famines also became less of a problem in the Black Earth regions. The crisis zones became concentrated in the Volga region, the northern Caucasus, southern Ukraine, and Kirghizia.

In the Volga region, the first famine struck in 1872–3. It also affected other regions. In an essay of 1874 titled 'Concerning famine in Samara' the occurrence of a major food crisis was reported in Oufa, Saratov, Orenburg, the Don next to Kherson, Odessa, Bessarabia, Kaluga, Perm, and Kazan. In 1880–1, new famines affected nine provinces, mostly situated in the Volga region and in the northern Caucasus (Golod 1902). In 1883–4 another poor harvest affected six provinces in the Volga region and, most seriously, the region of Kazan (Golod 1921–2, 1923). Finally, the famine of 1892 struck thirty provinces in the Volga region, the Urals, and the northern Caucuses (Buxman 1923).

In 1897–1900, local famines affected parts of the southern Ukraine (i.e. Kherson, Tauride, and Yekaterinoslav). In 1906–7, low yields were recorded in the Volga region. The ensuing shortage affected more or less the same geographic zone as the famine of 1891–2 (Buxman 1923). In 1909, Kazakhstan was hit by a bad harvest and in 1911 once more the Volga, the Urals, and western Siberia. During World War I, although the reduction in agricultural output primarily affected the western provinces, remote areas were not immune. Thus in 1916 a severe food shortage afflicted Kirghizia, and in 1917 the Volga provinces.

The great famine of 1921–2 struck all the regions at risk, its epicentre being in the mid-Volga region. According to the final report of the Central Relief Committee for the Population in Crisis, this disaster spread over 33 provinces (Posledgol 1922). Indeed, a study of a variety of sources suggests that the disaster extended to more than half the regions of the old empire, which contained about 65 million inhabitants, of whom about 30 million were affected by famine conditions (Adamets 1995). The famine of 1932–3 struck more or less the same regions as those of 1892 and 1922, but the hierarchy of worst hit regions was reversed. Most badly affected were the territories of the Ukraine, Kazakhstan, and the northern Caucasus, while the provinces of the Volga and Black Earth regions suffered significantly less.

POPULATION TRENDS

All these famines had significant demographic effects. During the first-half of the nineteenth century, detailed annual vital statistics by diocese are available for only the Orthodox population of Russia (see Fig. 8.1). For other denominations, the total numbers of births, marriages, and deaths are available from 1826 (Sbornik 1851). In

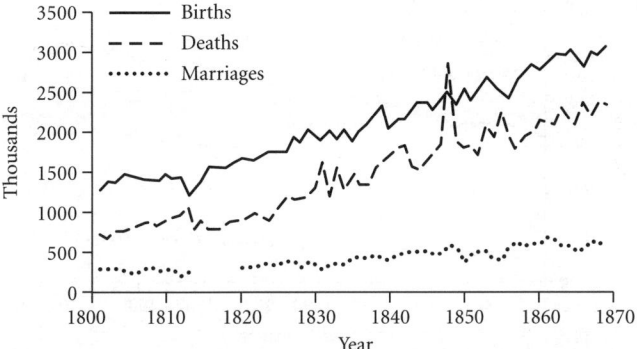

Figure 8.1. *Changes in Orthodox Population 1800–70: Annual Numbers of Births, Deaths, and Marriages*

Sources: L. Besser, L. Ballod, 'Smertnost', vozrastnoj sostav i dologoveènost' pravoslavnogo narodonaselenija oboego pola v Rossii', *Zapiski akademii nauk*, series VIII, vol. 1, no. 5, St Petersburg, 1897; V. I. Pokrovskij, 'Vlijanie kolebanija urožaev i xlebnyx tsen na estestvennoe dviženie naselenija', in: A. I. Čuprov, A. S. Posnikov, *Vlijanie urožaev i xlebnyx tsen na nekotorye storony narodnogo xozjastva*, vol. II, St Petersburg, 1897.

the early 1860s, the CSK standardized civil registration and made the recording of age compulsory. The resultant series of population trends, with breakdowns by sex and region for European Russia, were published in the annual statistical and demographic abstracts of the CSK. The final edition of the demographic abstract was published in 1917. Figure 8.2 shows data on births, marriages, and deaths from these later sources.

Demographic fluctuations gradually lessened during the second-half of the nineteenth century (Ballod-Besser 1897; Rossiïa 1991; Sifman 1977). This suggests a weakening of the impact of crises on the population, either due to the development of more effective means of resistance to disaster or to a lessening of the crises themselves. The most severe crisis, which took place in 1848, was due to cholera. In that year, counting only the Orthodox population, the annual number of deaths rose by a million and exceeded the number of births (Rašine 1956)—a feature which characterized no other crisis of the nineteenth century (Fig. 8.1).

Epidemics and famines often coincided, producing the most serious mortality crises, as in 1848, 1872, and 1892. However, apart from the years 1812–13, war never seriously disturbed Russian demographic trends during this period. The weak impact of wars on overall mortality is explained by their occurrence mostly on the periphery of the Russian empire: in the Caucasus (1830–1), the Crimea (1854–6), the Balkans (1878–9), and the Far East (1904–5).

EXPECTATION OF LIFE

The demographic statistics published by the CSK include the annual number of deaths occuring in the provinces of European Russia, broken down by age and sex.

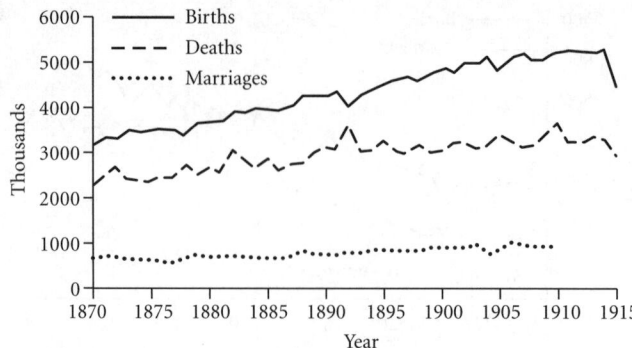

Figure 8.2. *Population Change in the 50 Provinces of European Russia: Annual Number of Births, Deaths, and Marriages*

Sources: S. A. Novoselskij, 'Vlijanie vojny na estestvenno dvizenie naselenija', in: Trudy komissii po obsledovaniju sanitarnyx posledstvij vojny 1914–1920 gg., Moscou, 1920?; S. A. Novoselskij, 'Demografija i statistika', Moscou, 1978; Institut international de statistique, Annuaire international de statistique. II. Mouvement de la population (Europe), La Haye, 1917; Statistique générale de la France. Statistique internationale du mouvement de la population d'aprés les registres de l'état civil, résumé rétrospectif depuis l'origine des statistiques de l'état civil jusqu'en 1905, Paris, Imprimerie nationale, 1907; Statistique générale de la France. Statistique internationale du mouvement de la population d'aprés les registres de l'état civil, second volume, années 1901 à 1910, Paris, Imprimerie nationale, 1913.

On the asumption that Russia's population was approximately stable, we have applied the mortality tables produced by Bortkevitch and Novoselski to the conjunctural statistics of the CSK in order to calculate annual life tables for the period 1867–1909 (Adamets 1995, 1997).

Before the end of the nineteenth century, the gap in life expectancy between Russia and other major European countries increased. In 1875, expectation of life at birth [e(0)] in Russia was about 30 years for males and 33 years for females, while in France and in England it exceeded 40 years and it approached 50 years in both Norway and Sweden (Vallin 1988). During the final decades of the nineteenth century, most western countries experienced significant reductions in mortality. However, any decline was much less impressive in Russia (see Fig. 8.3).

Although e(0) did not improve much between 1867 and 1909, it was subject to significant annual fluctuations due to endemic, but weak mortality crises. The famine of 1868 caused e(0) to drop from 28 to 26 years for males and from 31 to 28 years for females. In the absence of a disaster in 1870, e(0) recovered to reach just 31 years for males and 32 years for females. The cholera epidemic and famine in the Volga region in 1871–2 forced e(0) down again in 1872 to 25 years for males and 27 years for females (Fig. 8.3). During the following 5-year period, mortality did not fluctuate much—with e(0) varying between 29 and 30 years for males and between 30 and 33 years for females. The war between Russia and Turkey brought another crisis. And then food scarcity and smallpox resulted in yet another serious crisis in 1882. Life expectation at birth fell to 25 and 28 years for males and females respectively.

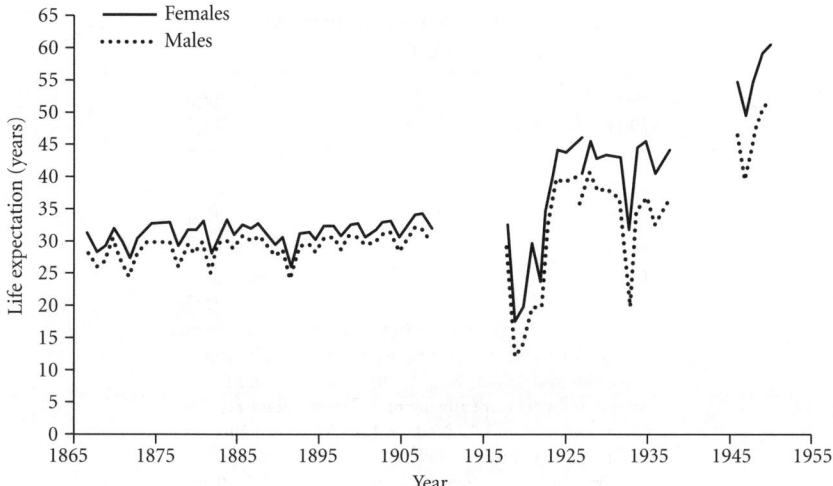

Figure 8.3. *Expectation of Life from Birth between 1865 and 1950 in the Russian Empire and in Russia*

Notes: 1867–1909 (Russian Empire); 1918–27 (USSR); 1927–50 (Russia).

However, the second-half of the 1880s was crisis-free and e(0) recovered to around its previous level.

The famine and cholera epidemic of 1892 provoked the last noteworthy mortality crisis of the *ancien régime*. From that date onwards, one sees a definite drop in mortality, albeit punctuated by major reversals (Fig. 8.3). Average life expectancy reached about 32 years for males and about 34 years for females by the years 1907–8. Then, a poor harvest in 1909, along with the cholera epidemic of 1910, slightly dampened this improvement, but mortality generally continued to decline during the following years. This is seen too in the decline in the death rate between 1907 and 1914 (Table 8.1).

The revolution of 1917 hurled Russia into a series of awful demographic catastrophes. The civil war, sanitary degradation, epidemics, as well as serious problems with transport and the provisioning of the cities, were the main factors in the first demographic catastrophe. I estimate that excess mortality reached about 10 million between 1918 and 1920, of which four million deaths were directly attributable to epidemics (Table 8.2).

Estimates of famine mortality during the years 1921–3 range from 5 to 10 million (Čelintsev 1923–4; Conquest 1986; Denisenko and Ščelestov 1994; Maksudov 1977). My model of this crisis, using epidemiological, economic, and nutritional data, puts excess mortality at more than 6 million (Table 8.2). And life expectation was probably reduced below the levels witnessed during major crises of the previous century (Fig. 8.3).

Table 8.1. *Death Rates in the 50 Provinces of European Russia (per 1,000)*

1907	28.5
1908	28.3
1909	29.5
1910	31.5
1911	27.4
1912	26.5
1913	27.2
1914	26.3

Source: 1910–12: S. A. Novoselskij, *Demografija i statistika* (Moscow, 1978), p. 122; 1913–14: estimates based on the numbers of deaths by province and their respective populations (S.A. Novoselskij, 'Vlijanie vojny na estestvennoe dviñenie naselenija', in: *Trudy komissii po obsledovaniju sanitarnyx posledstvij vojny 1914–20 gg.* (Moscow, 1920); NKZ, *Données statistiques de la santé publique et de l'organisation du secours médical dans URSS 1913–23* (Moscow, 1926) (title in both French and Russian)

Table 8.2. *USSR: Normal and Excess Mortality, 1918–23*

	Normal non-crisis	Excess				Total
		Epidemic	Military	Other	Total	
1918	3,103	136	40	847	1,023	4,126
1919	3,737	2,034	783	2,316	5,133	8,870
1920	3,343	2,069	850	1,469	4,388	7,731
1921	3,151	1,272	614	662	2,548	5,699
1922	3,292	1,389	66	1,703	3,158	6,450
1923	3,068	63	0	814	876	3,944
1918–23	19,694	6,963	2,353	7,811	17,127	36,821

Several authors have tried to estimate the scale of the demographic losses of the 1930s (Livi-Bacci 1993; Lorimer 1946; Maksudov 1977). Without knowledge of the conjunctural statistics of population change between 1931 and 1933, they have calculated the average losses for the inter-censal period (i.e. 1926–39) at between 5 and 10 million—of which perhaps 3–7 million were due to the dreadful famine of 1933.

Since the opening of the archives of the CSU, Russian researchers Andreev, Darski, and Kharkova have carried out two rigorous studies which have reconstructed the year-by-year demographic history of the USSR and Russia between 1926 and 1939

(Andreev *et al.* 1993, 1998). However, in their eagerness to highlight the demographic cost of the Stalinist era, they made some important and unwarranted corrections to the unpublished archival statistics. They assumed that in the case of Russia the under-registration of deaths fluctuated between 20 and 35 per cent before the famine of 1933, reaching 45 per cent in 1933, and falling to 10 per cent in 1938. They then added a total of 10 million deaths to the 25 million reported by the ZAGS (i.e the Civil Registers) during these years. An analogous correction for the USSR as a whole produces 18 million deaths, 6 million of whom succumbed in 1933. This last estimate of under-registration comprises two segments: 5.5 million deaths unregistered in the territories without civil registration, and 13 million in the territories covered by the ZAGS (Andreev *et al.* 1993). The first segment was taken into account by the CUNCHU (i.e. the Budget Directorate of the National Economy) in its final reports, but the second represents under-registration as estimated by Andreev *et al.* (1993).

The outcome of these calculations depends more upon the assumed correction factor than on the state of the crude statistics. Earlier calculations, unfortunately never published, produced more modest correction factors. Thus, according to Andreev *et al.* (1993), Rodina and Bekunova estimated death under-registration at 6.3 million, of which 2 million were in 1933. And Popov's commission (1944) produced an estimate of 2.4 million unregistered deaths (Andreev *et al.* 1993). Which of these various approaches is the most plausible? Should one be maximalist or prudent? The stakes are obvious: in opting for massive under-registration one maximizes the population losses, while in placing more confidence in the statistics of the CUNCHU one obtains much smaller figures of excess mortality.

There are several arguments against the maximalist estimate proposed by Andreev *et al.* (1993). First, out of a spirit of solidarity with the victims of political repression during the years 1934–7, we do not want to lend succour to their persecutors, because the poor registration of vital events was a principal point in the accusation that was made then against demographers and statisticians. On the other hand, an exaggerated under-registration would deprive available official statistics of any utility. If one-third or one-half of deaths escaped registration, would not all demographic reconstitution become mere fiction? How can one subdivide up by age, sex, or region vital events that were not registered? It bears noting that Andreev *et al.* (1993) offer no solid documentary justification for under-registration on such a huge scale.

Let us return to the key element in their case, i.e. the study of the management of the ZAGS, carried out by the CUNCHU in March 1934 in the 117 rural districts of the Ukraine and Russia. This study produced local estimates of the under-registration of births and deaths during the 1933 famine (RGAE, Kurman 1934). In the regions struck by famine the under-registration of deaths may have reached 50 per cent (RGAE, Kraval 1934). Thus, in the district of Okopski (in the northern Caucasus) according to the nominal list of those who died, there were 984 deaths in 1933, while the ZAGS registered only 557. The same level of under-registration was found in the district of Atchkarski in the province of Saratov and in Kiev. Should one regard these measures as correction factors for all the death statistics reported by the ZAGS? Or is it justifiable to apply the annual series derived by the CUNCHU?

The findings of Kurman and of Kraval, senior functionaries of the CUNCHU, were unanimous: 'the study has revealed very few cases of over-registration of deaths and a large number of cases of under-registration' (RGAE, Kurman 1934). But these cases were remarked on as extreme, chosen by the CUNCHU to counter accusations from the Central Committee of the Party which denounced 'a tendentious over-estimation of the number of deaths in the conjunctural statistics of the CUNCHU'. In the provinces which were spared serious famine, under-registration was much more modest: 7 per cent of deaths in the province of Sverdlovsk, and 10–15 per cent of deaths in Zapad (RGAE, Kraval 1935). This was also the case in most of the Ukraine. Study of 10 districts in the region of Pavlograd produced an under-registration of 6 per cent of deaths: 3,584 actual deaths as against 3,374 declared.

Taking everything into account the CUNCHU estimated that 53 per cent of the population was captured by the conjunctural statistics of the ZAGS (76 per cent in the Ukraine, 66 per cent in Russia), but it hoped to obtain definitive statistics covering 95 per cent of the population (RGAE, Kaplun 1934). In effect, the ZAGS registered 3.35 million deaths in the USSR (2 million in Russia, 1.3 million in the Ukraine, and 58,000 in Belarus). Undoubtedly, the levels of under-registration established by the inquiry of March 1934 concerned this crude statistic, deemed conjunctural by the CUNCHU. Indeed, the CUNCHU then corrected the raw statistics of death under-registration. Finally, the definitive annual toll for 1933 put the number of deaths in the Ukraine at 2.1 million (i.e. +60 per cent), in Russia at 2.9 million (+50 per cent), and in Belarus at 67,000 (+16 per cent), or a total of about 5.6 million deaths for the USSR as a whole.

The adjustments of Andreev *et al.* evidently contain an element of double counting: they have taken the data previously adjusted by the CUNCHU and factored them up again for under-registration. Finally, instead of the 2 million deaths in Russia and 3.4 million in the USSR initially registered by the ZAGS, they have obtained numbers which are the stuff of fancy: 5.2 million deaths in Russia and 11.4 million in the USSR. They offer no real documentation to support such a correction.

Hitherto our critique has focused on how the estimates of Andreev *et al.* stem from a misunderstanding. We shall now seek to find out whether the corrections of the CUNCHU were sufficient. The population of Russia was enumerated at 93 million by the census of 17 December 1926 (using the frontiers of early 1939) and it would have reached 115 million by the beginning of 1939, had it been unaffected by demographic crises.[1] In fact, the census of 1939 counted only 109 million people. The difference between the real and expected non-crisis population is a measure of the aggregate demographic losses between 1927 and 1939 (see Table 8.3). To be sure, some of this enormous deficit was generated by a drop in the number of births during the crises. Significant migrations, mainly due to the gulags and the deportation of kulaks, probably plugged the demographic hole. Andreev *et al.*

---

[1] We have assumed that the fertility levels observed between 1927 and 1931 would have persisted in the absence of a crisis. For the 1932–8 period, we have estimated non-crisis fertility as that observed in 1931. The non-crisis survival rates were obtained by linear interpolation of the ratios in the mortality tables for 1926/7 and 1938/9 (Adamets 1995).

Table 8.3. *Populations Enumerated and Expected, Demographic Losses and Under-registration of Deaths*

Population and losses	Total (in thousands)		Total
	Males	Females	
Population			
Enumerated (1)	51,594	57,804	109,397
Expected, assuming non-crisis mortality and fertility (2)	54,577	59,964	114,542
Expected, assuming non-crisis mortality and registered births (3)	53,778	59,160	112,938
Losses			
Total (2)−(1)	2,984	2,161	5,144
Due to emigration (4)	−280	−280	−560
Due to excess mortality or the under-registration of deaths (3)−(1)−(4)	2,464	1,636	4,101
Due to birth deficit (2)−(3)	799	804	1,604

(1998) estimate net Russian immigration at 560,000, an approximation, but all that is available.

In subtracting 5 million excess deaths, a figure of 1.6 million for averted births, and by adding 0.6 million for immigration, we arrive at an estimate of about 4 million deaths over and above what one would have expected in the absence of the various mortality crises. Part of this excess mortality was registered by the ZAGS. This is the 0.5 million deaths obtained by subtracting from deaths registered between 1927 and 1938, deaths expected in the absence of a crisis (columns *a–d* in Table 8.4).[2] This leaves a loss of about 3.6 million which escaped the various corrections made by the CUNCHU.

This toll represents all unregistered demographic events. But this figure of 3.6 million also measures the minimal level of under-registration of deaths, because the under-registration of births and immigration can only increase the losses attributable to mortality. How should we apportion the 3.6 million deaths between the years 1927 and 1938? Comparing reported deaths and expected non-crisis deaths offers a useful guide.

The deaths obtained by back-projection of the population from 1939 are usually less than the deaths reported by the ZAGS (columns *c* and *f* in Table 8.4).[3] On the other hand, the projection of the population, using the same death rates from 1927

---

[2] The annual ZAGS statistics were adjusted to correspond to the frontiers of Russia in 1939. Regional data are lacking for certain territories and for certain years. We estimated omissions by applying to the missing territories the death rates prevailing in contiguous regions.

[3] So that the comparison between theoretical and reported deaths is correct, one must subtract from the theoretical total, the contribution corresponding to the correction of infant and old age mortality (column *d*).

Table 8.4. *Deaths According to the Civil Register (ZAGS) and Hypothetical Non-crisis Deaths 1927–38 (in Thousands)*

Years	Deaths in ZAGS adjusted to jurisdiction of Russia in 1939 (a)	Theoretical deaths: projection from 1926 (b)	Theoretical deaths: retro-projection from 1939 théoriques (c)	Expected non-crisis deaths (d)	Correction included in the estimate of theoretical deaths (e)	Difference ((a)+(e)−(d)) (f)	Remaining under-registration rate (g)	Aggregate correction (h)	Corrected deaths (i)
1927	2,137	2,122		2,122	59	73	0.15	320	2,516
1928	1,853	2,180		2,180	57	−271	0.12	222	2,132
1929	2,111	2,204		2,204	57	−36	0.10	211	2,379
1930	2,074	2,192		2,192	57	−61	0.10	207	2,339
1931	2,080	2,156		2,156	58	−18	0.14	283	2,421
1932	2,062	2,102		2,102	57	16	0.18	365	2,483
1933	2,957	1,998	2,044	2,021	52	988	0.34	994	4,004
1934	2,004	1,918	1,966	1,966	49	87	0.15	308	2,361
1935	1,875	1,989	1,978	1,978	52	−51	0.12	220	2,146
1936	2,274	2,087	2,022	2,022	54	306	0.09	206	2,533
1937	2,194	2,199	2,108	2,108	57	142	0.07	145	2,395
1938	2,144	2,291	2,198	2,198	58	3	0.05	107	2,309
Total	25,764			25,251	666	1,178	0.14	3,588	30,018

onwards, produces the opposite result: the theorized numbers of deaths are normally higher than those reported by the ZAGS during 1927–32. This indicates that the final under-registration of deaths was not that important, and that it was more significant before the famine than during it.

Let us suppose that about 15 per cent of deaths escaped civil registration in 1927, 10–12 per cent in 1928–30, 18 per cent in 1932, and 15 per cent in the wake of the crisis, and that from 1935 onwards the level of under-registration fell steadily to reach about 5 per cent in 1938. This division corresponds quite faithfully to the hypothesis about under-registration advanced by Rodina–Bekunova according to Andreev *et al.* (1993). These correction factors produce 2.5 million more deaths than do the CUNCHU data. And for the famine itself an under-registration of about one million deaths is indicated.

In order to calculate mortality rates by age, it is necessary to first make some assumption about the appropriate allocation of the deaths that went under-registered. As far as non-crisis years are concerned, a pro rata allocation seems reasonable. However, this will not do for the famine period, since mortality patterns then probably differed from years of non-crisis mortality. I have therefore divided the one million deaths for the year 1933 in proportion to the deaths recorded by the civil registers.

Without taking under-registration into account, the civil registration statistics imply an e(0) of 28 years for males and 37 years for females in 1933, compared to 40 and 45 years, respectively, on the eve of the crisis (see Fig. 8.3). Taking into account the hypotheses about under-registration discussed above, the estimated life expectancies drop to 21 and 30 years for males and females respectively.[4] Thus, our estimates are clearly higher than those of 15 years for males and 20 years for females obtained by Andreev *et al.* (1998).

MULTIPLICATION OF DEATH PROBABILITIES BY AGE

The nineteenth century crises present two characteristic types of mortality shock. The first type (exemplified in 1868, 1882, and 1905) affected principally children and the elderly (see Fig. 8.4).[5] The second type (exemplified in 1872 and 1892) affected all age groups; this was because of the addition to famine mortality of deaths due to epidemics of cholera and typhus.

During general crises, the adult population was more affected by the rise in mortality probabilities, the peak being generally observed at about age 35 years. The multipliers were far lower for the very young and the elderly. Two hypotheses account for such a small rise in infant mortality. First, it may merely reflect the under-registration of deaths of newly born infants. Second, a compensatory mechanism may have operated whereby infant mortality was so high that famine only replaced the ordinary mortality risks by a new risk of death, without greatly affecting the overall level of infant mortality. In 1922 and 1933, the multipliers were higher than

---

[4] We distributed non-registered deaths by age pro rata to registered deaths.

[5] In order to measure the excess mortality of different age groups, we calculated the risk multipliers of death by age, linking the death rates to the rates in the immediately adjoining years.

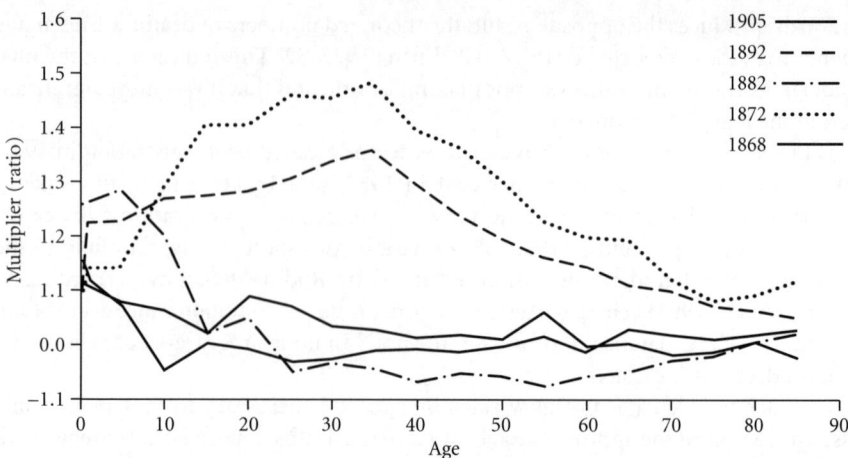

Figure 8.4. *Mortality Multipliers for Males by Age Group during the Famines of the Nineteenth Century (Ratio of the Death Rate during the Crisis to that in the Benchmark Years)*

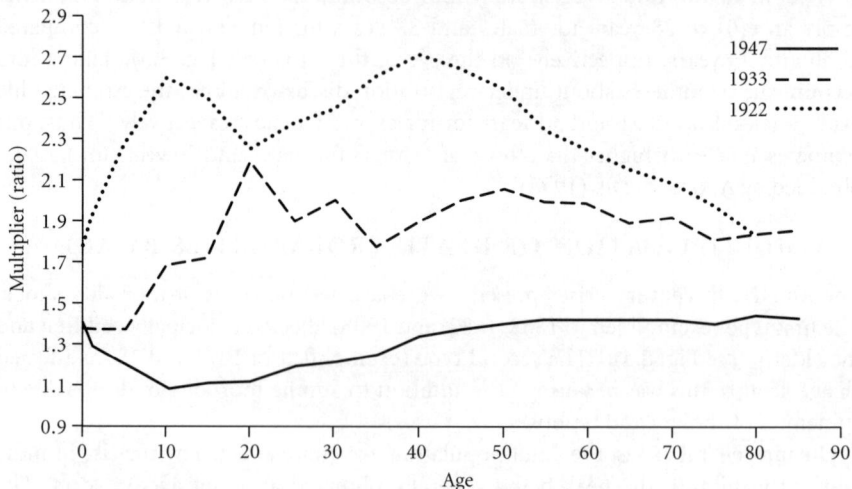

Figure 8.5. *Male Mortality Multipliers by Age Group during the Famines of the Twentieth Century (Ratio of the Death Rate during the Crisis to that in the Benchmark Years)*

during the crises of the nineteenth century (see Fig. 8.5). Children were at greater risk; and a second death peak is clearly detectable at ages 10–19 years.[6] It would seem

---

[6] We note that in 1868, Finland revealed a similar profile of mortality multipliers with a peak at juvenile ages (Pitkänen 1993). The double peak for female excess mortality is also evident during the Bengali famine of 1943–4 (Dyson 1991).

that those age groups which had benefited from a reduction in mortality in the years preceding a crisis experienced a sharp rise in deaths during the crisis itself.

Still, the multipliers in 1922 and 1933 resemble those of the general crises of the preceding century. Those which rose least were those relating to infant mortality. The peaks represent adult ages, and the multipliers were clearly lower for the elderly. The multipliers are quite different for the 1947 famine. Children under 1 year of age and the elderly population were worst hit then (see Fig. 8.5). From a minimum observed at about age 10 years, the mortality multipliers rise steadily with increasing age. The hierarchy of the multipliers therefore changed during the 1940s. The new curve is like those of the 'local' crises characteristic of the nineteenth century. The newly born, who benefited from the reduction of mortality following the war, registered the most spectacular drop in mortality in the wake of the famine of 1947.[7]

CAUSES OF DEATH

The famines of the nineteenth century were frequently accompanied by epidemic diseases. Those of 1868 and 1892 were followed by typhus epidemics and that of 1872 by cholera. The coincidence of famine and epidemic is also a feature of the crisis of 1922. Eleven epidemic diseases—typhus, relapsing fever, abdominal fever, cholera, smallpox, whooping cough, scarlet fever, measles, dysentery, diphtheria, and malaria—were the causes, by my reckoning, of 1.6 million deaths, or about half of all the excess mortality of 3.2 million (see Table 8.2).

From 1933 onwards, the registration of the principal cause of death was compulsory in urban ZAGS. This allows us to compare changes in the different cause of death structures prevailing during the famines of 1933 and 1947. In this context, I have re-grouped the deaths under 13 separate cause of death headings (see Fig. 8.6) corresponding to the main groupings of the International Classification of Diseases (ICD) and including certain causes that were particularly linked to famine situations. It can be seen that infectious and parasitic diseases were responsible for about one death in four in both 1933 and 1947. Diseases of the digestive system, and respiratory and cardiovascular diseases each accounted for between 10 and 20 per cent of deaths. The role of causes of death directly linked to insufficient food intake (designated as alimentary in Fig. 8.6) was comparatively weak: such causes accounted for less than 5 per cent of deaths in 1933 and only about 1 per cent in 1947. The proportion of deaths due to unspecified causes was more important; such deaths accounted for 10 per cent of mortality in 1933 and 6 per cent in 1947.

The distributions of deaths by cause in 1934 and in 1948 are almost the same, indicating a very simple truth: a significant part of the Russian population was spared famine and continued to experience normal risks of dying. Still, most categories of cause of death show rises for the famines of 1933 and 1947 (Fig. 8.7). The biggest proportional increase in 1933 related to the alimentary cause group—which reflected

---

[7] Infant mortality, over 200 per thousand at the end of the 1930s, fell to about 120 per thousand on the eve of the last famine.

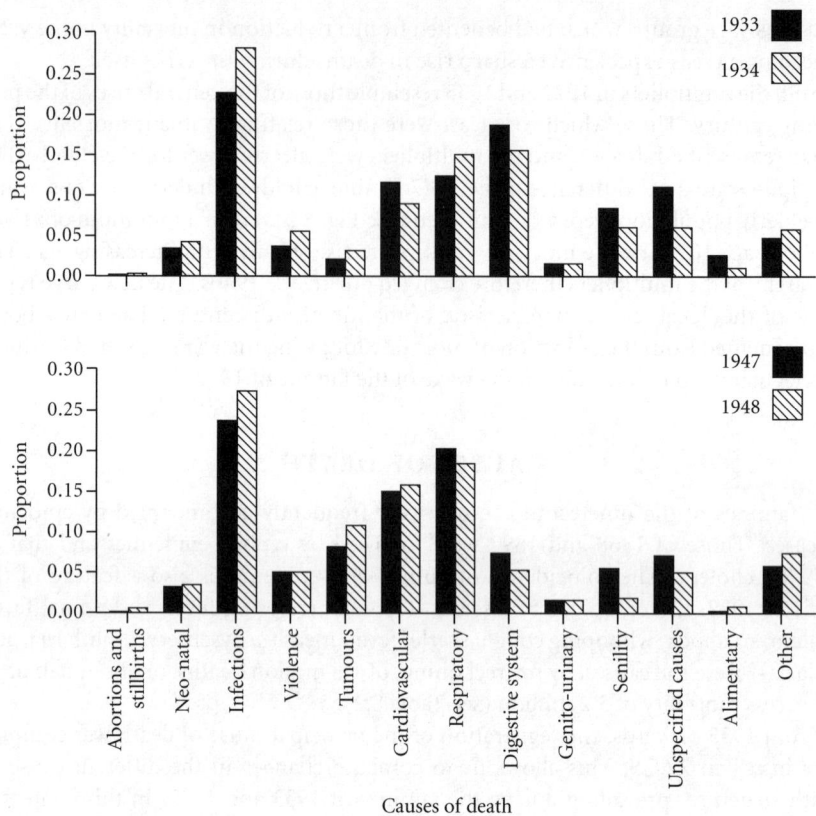

Figure 8.6. *The Main Causes of Death in 1933–4 and in 1947–8*

Sources: RGAE, f. 1562, op. 329, ed. 24, 48; 58; 2648, 3166.

insufficient and defective food intake (+300 per cent compared to 1934).[8] Deaths from unspecified causes, and senility, rose by between 100 and 250 per cent in both 1933 and 1947. Deaths due to cardiovascular and digestive disease causes also rose significantly—doubling in 1933, and rising by about a half in 1947. By contrast, deaths from cancers (i.e. tumours), maternal causes, and violence did not change much. The same holds for the infectious disease group—where the number of deaths rose by about 25 per cent during these two famines (Fig. 8.7).

MORTALITY BY SEX: AN UNCERTAIN GAP

The fact that males and females appear to face different risks of death during famines and epidemics has been the subject of many studies. Different hypotheses have been

---

[8] Insufficient food intake does not figure in the Soviet classification of cause of death after 1940.

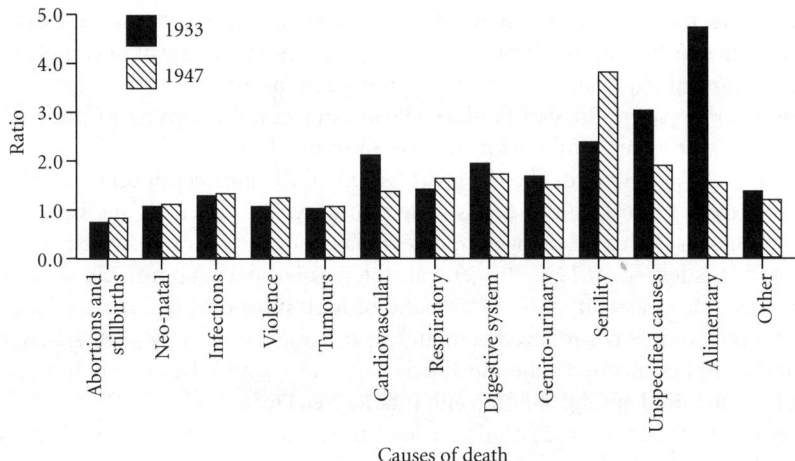

Figure 8.7. *Ratio of the Number of Deaths in 1933 and 1947 to the Respective Numbers in the Years Following the Crises (1934 and 1948)*

Sources: RGAE, f. 1562, op. 329, ed. 24, 48; 58, 2648, 3166.

proposed to explain the female advantage (see Chapter 12 of this book). Some authors have invoked a biological advantage for females, notably in terms of their greater levels of body-fat, which may give them an advantage during famines (Livi-Bacci 1991; McAlpin 1983; Rivers 1982). It has also been suggested that women's smaller body frames means that they require fewer calories in order to maintain their basic physiological functions. The reduction in fertility that typically accompanies such disasters, and which reduces their risk of dying in childbirth, and in the months following a birth may also be considered as a biological factor favouring females (Ó Gráda 1995).

It seems obvious that the biological characteristics noted above are not absolute guarantees of better survival chances for women. For example, prolonged malnutrition may quickly consume extra reserves of body-fat and reduce any initial advantage. So such a biological advantage should count more in the early stages of famine and, more generally, during mild and moderate famines. However, a careful study of famine in Finland during the nineteenth century does not support such reasoning (Pitkänen 1993).

Other scholars have proposed social, economic, and cultural factors favouring females in famines. Thus, in general, men are more likely to migrate than women during times of crisis, this being a function of how traditional societies work. Women, being possibly more attached to the home by domestic duties and childcare, tend to be less mobile. Also, men may often work outside of the home—increasing their risk of contracting an infectious diseases which may prove fatal. That said, this may constitute a disadvantage that is more theoretical than real. Thus, illnesses often affect children, who are not subject to much difference in mobility by gender. On the other hand, once contracted, airborne diseases may easily strike other members of the family in the course of daily contact. The female advantage insofar as these diseases are concerned is less certain. It may be more significant in the case of pneumonia and diseases transmitted by insects—such as typhus and malaria.

The data for some Russian famines allow us to examine several of these issues because they provide useful information on mortality by sex.

Figure 8.8 shows that for the last great famine of the nineteenth century—that of 1892—there is no real sign of excess male mortality. The mortality multipliers[9] are very similar for both sexes. However, excess male mortality is quite evident in 1933, although it is less so in 1947. In general, the Russian data support the hypothesis that excess male mortality is likely to manifest itself most during intense crises, and that this phenomenon is reduced in moderate and mild famines. Besides, excess male mortality applies mostly to the most active age groups and the elderly. It does not appear to be found among children and infants (see Fig. 8.8).

Analysis of the cause of death data allows us to identify those causes which contributed to the widening of the gender gap during these crises. Thus, comparing deaths in 1934 with those in 1933 allows us to make inferences about the role of each cause of death in overall excess male famine mortality.

In the non-famine year of 1934, the civil registration offices (i.e. the ZAGS) for European Russia registered 190,000 male deaths and 163,000 female deaths. The difference between these figures (i.e. 28,000) probably represents normal male excess mortality.[10] However, in 1933, in the same area the ZAGS counted 328,000 male and 234,000 female deaths. The male/female gap thus rose to 94,000, and the crisis added 64,000 to normal excess male mortality. The contribution of different causes of death to this increased gap varied considerably. Five cause of death groupings—infectious diseases, cardiovascular causes, respiratory diseases, diseases of the digestive system, and deaths due to unspecified causes—account for 80 per cent of the excess male mortality during the famine. On the other hand, violent deaths and cancers contributed very little to the gap. It is also apparent that the factors which accounted for the excess deaths were only weakly related to the factors which were responsible for mortality in normal times. For example, infectious diseases accounted for 28 per cent of deaths in 1934, but their contribution to excess male mortality was only 15 per cent. Also deaths due to unspecified causes accounted for 5 per cent of deaths in 1934, but a quarter of all the male excess in the famine year of 1933.

We can take this analysis a little further. Consider the case of infectious diseases. Tuberculosis accounted for about half of all the total male excess mortality from epidemic and parasitic diseases. However, childhood ailments—such as whooping cough, measles, scarlet fever, diphtheria, and smallpox—explain none of the male excess mortality, either during or after the famine. In contrast, the data indicate that

---

[9] Calculated as the ratios of the mortality rates in crisis years to those in adjoining years.

[10] In terms of life expectation, excess male mortality compared to females has been in evidence since the end of the nineteenth century and has tended to increase during the twentieth century. The gap was 2 years (in favour of females) in 1896–7, reached 6.5 years on the eve of the Second World War, 10 years in 1970–1, and 14 years in 1994 (Goskomstat 1997, 1998).

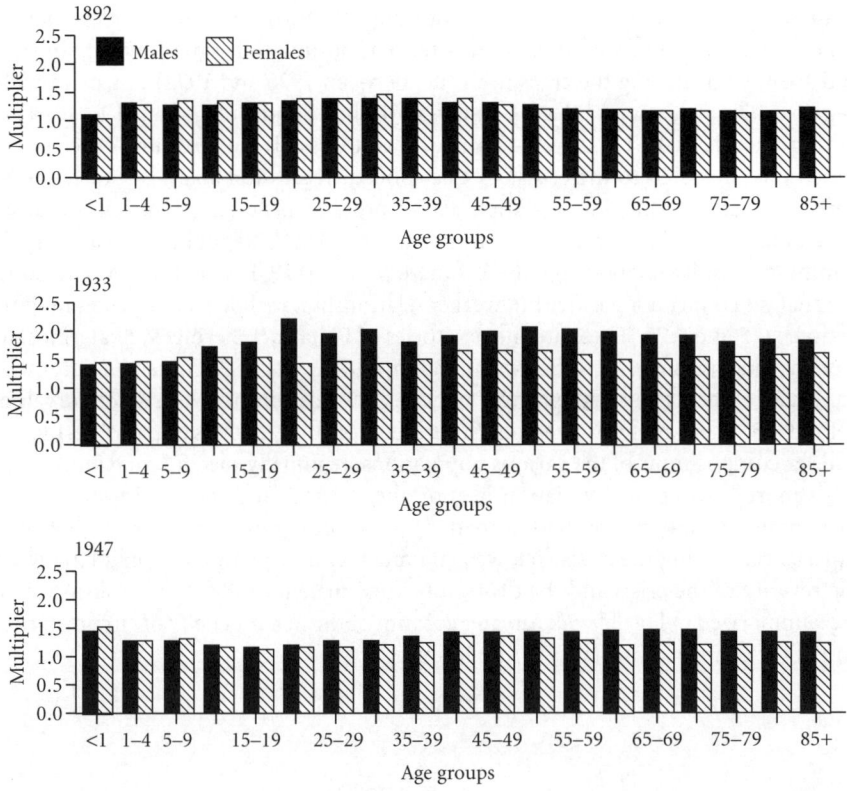

Figure 8.8. *Mortality Multipliers (Ratios) by Age Groups and by Sex during the Famines of the Nineteenth and Twentieth Centuries*

pneumonia and typhus were two to three times more virulent in the male population. And the risk of death from malaria was 50 per cent greater for males than for females.

For 1918–22, there are quite a few regional estimates of differential mortality by sex. There are series covering the whole crisis period for the cities of Moscow and Saratov. And from 1920 onwards, there are data relating to 18 territories and two cities in European Russia (CSU 1924). Similar information is available in the report of the Ukrainian sanitary inquiry which was carried out on 264,000 people during September–December 1923 (Tomiline 1925).

Examination of these data reveals that in only one case out of 143—the province of Tchernigov in 1921—is there evidence of higher female famine mortality. In all the other cases, male mortality exceeded that of females, and the scale of the male excess varied between 5 and 90 per cent. The hypothesis of higher male famine mortality is thus strongly corroborated. However, when we check whether there was a correlation between this male–female gap and the severity of the crisis, regression analysis is not always very supportive. Thus, hypothesizing a linear relationship between the overall death rate and the degree of excess male mortality, the former accounts for less than 10 per cent of the regional variation in the latter. The positive link is more evident in 1923 and 1924, while during the crisis itself (i.e. between 1920 and 1922) it is marginally negative. Does this mean that the male mortality disadvantage failed to increase during the crisis? And if there was a rise, was it possibly due to some other factor which was unrelated to the crisis? In this context, regression analysis (not reported here) suggests considerable variation across provinces. Seven provinces—Briansk, Kostroma, Kiev, Kharkov, Podolia, Toula, and the Tartar Republic—reveal a highly significant positive relationship: the R-square exceeds 0.79. For another seven regions, the analysis confirms a positive but weaker relationship, with R-square values ranging between 0.5 and 0.75. These are the territories of Poltava, Tchernigov, Ekaterinoslav, Donetz, Ekaterinburg, the Tchouvache region, and the city of Petrograd. On the other hand, half of the regions in the sample evince a weak relationship, with R-square values below 0.25. There are several reasons for the heterogeneity of the sample: differing age and sex compositions of the various populations, regionally specific contributions to crisis mortality, regional variation in mortality by age, and so on. However, if for these units we rank the correlation coefficients according to the increase in mortality experienced during the crisis (μ), we get a much clearer picture of the link between the severity of the crisis and the degree of excess male mortality. The results, which are summarized in Fig. 8.9, take greater account of the heterogeneity of circumstances and of the change in mortality through time.

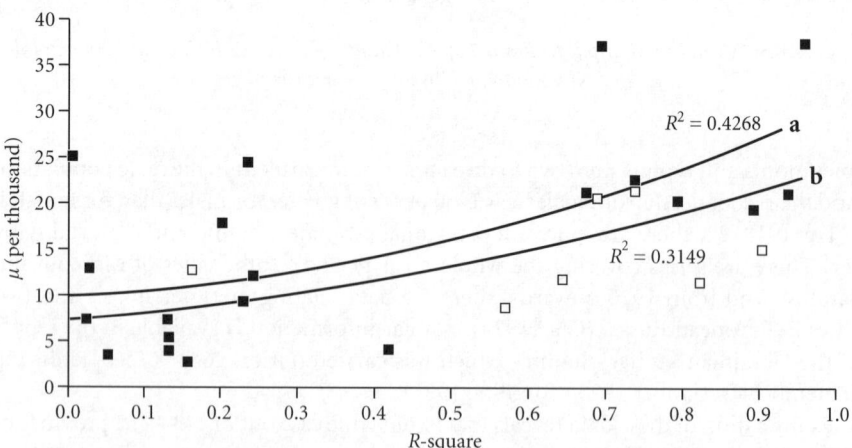

Figure 8.9. *Increase in the Death Rate during the Crisis by the Importance of the Link between Excess Male Mortality and Famine Severity (as Measured by the Value of the R-square)*

Notes: The value of μ is the difference between the maximum death rate experienced during 1920–2 and the average death rate for years 1923–4. The a line is based on regions of Russia; the b line is also based on seven provinces of Ukraine.

For all the regions, the points on the graph refer to both the severity of the mortality crisis and the degree of male excess mortality that was experienced. The first variable (plotted on the vertical axis) measures the increase in death rates during the crisis, and the second variable (on the horizontal axis) the strength of the link between the mortality rise and regional excess male mortality. It is clear that the values of the R-squares are hardly significant in those regions which experienced only mild mortality shocks. On the other hand, the link strengthens as the scale of the mortality crisis rises. So, Fig. 8.9 suggests that male excess mortality tended to increase during the famine of 1920–2, and that this tendency was strongest in the regions which were hardest-hit.

CONCLUSIONS

Famine has been a part of Russian demographic history for centuries, but it did not often escalate into really major demographic catastrophes prior to the twentieth century. The second-half of the nineteenth century was characterized by conflicting trends—although famines were no deadlier than in the past, regional inequalities in the experience of famine increased. Thus at that time most regions were no longer affected by famines, but other regions suffered calamitous food crises. And if the early years of the twentieth century were free from severe famines, this was not due to spectacular agricultural progress, but rather because of increased state interventions and progress in the struggle against epidemic diseases. Under the Soviet regime malnutrition was the norm for much of the Russian population during the 1920s and the 1930s, and there were horrific famines in 1921–3, 1932–3, and 1946–7. And in terms of the volume of excess mortality, the first two of these calamities far exceeded the famines of the nineteenth century.

References

Adamets, S. (1995), *Catastrophes demographiques en Russie sovietique entre 1918–1923: crises epidemique, alimentaire et de mortalite*, Paris: EHESS.

—— (1997),'A l'origine de la diversite des mesures de la famine soviétique: la statistique des prix, des recoltes et de la consommation', *Cahiers du monde russe*, 38(4): 559–86.

—— Blum, A., and Zakharov, S. (1995), 'Geographical patterns of soviet demographic catastrophes: some evidence of the nature of the famines compared with Russian famines', [Conference documents, 'Population of the USSR in the 1920s and 1930s in light of newly declassified documentary evidence', Toronto, 27–29 January 1995].

—— and Shkolnikov, V. M. (1995), 'A propos de tables de mortalit d'avant guerre en Russie, Ukraine et Bilorussie', [Documents of the Toronto Conference, 27–29 January 1995].

—— Blum, A., and Zakharov, S. (1994), 'Disparité et variabilités des catastrophes démographiques en URSS', *Dossiers et Recherches*, INED, 42.

Andreev, E., Darskij, L., and Khar'kova, T. (1993), *Naselenie SSSR 1922–1991* [Population of the USSR], Moscow.

Andreev, E., Darskij, L., and Khar'kova, T. (1998), *Demograficeskaja istorija Rossii: 1927–1959* [Demographic History of Russia], Moscow, 187 pp.

Besser, L., and Ballod, L. (1897), 'Smertnost, vozrastnoj sostav i dolgovečnost pravoslavnogo narodonaselenija oboego pola v Rossii', [Mortality, age structure and longevity of the two sex Orthodox population of Russia], *Zàpiski Akademii nauk*, série viii, Volume 1, 5, Saint Pétersbourg.

Brokgauz, F. A., and Efron, I. A. (1893), *'Enzyclopedičeskij slovar'* [Encyclopedic Dictionary], 'Golod' [Famine], *Volume IX*, SPb.

Buxman, K. (1923),'Golod 1921 goda i dejatelnost' inostrannyx organizatsij' [The famine of 1921 and the activity of international organisations], *Vestnik statistiki*, 5–8.

Čelintsev, A. N. (1923–4), *Selskoxozja'stvennaja geografija Rossii* [Agrarian Geography of Russia], Prague-Berlin.

Cerevanine, N. (1919), 'Evolutsija russkogo zemledelija po dannym ob urozajax [The evolution of Russian agriculture according to harvest statistics]', *Vestnik statistiki*, 8–12: 36–45.

Conquest, R. (1986), *The Harvest of Sorrow. Soviet Collectivisation and the Terror-Famine*, London: Arrow Books.

CSK (1871), *Statisti eskij sbornik* [Statistical collection], SPb.

CSU (1924), Travaux de l'administration centrale de statistique de la Russie, *Sbornik statisti eskix svedenij po Sojuzu S.S.R., 1918–1923* [*Collection of statistical data on the Soviet Union, 1918–1923*], XVIII, Moscow.

Davies, R. W., Harrison, M., and Wheatcroft, S. G. (1994), *The Economic Transformation of the Soviet Union, 1913–1945*, Cambridge: Cambridge University Press.

Denisenko, M. B., and Šelestov, D. K. (1994), 'Poteri' [Losses], in *Narodonaselenie. Entsiklopedi eskij slovar'*, Moscow.

Dyson, T. (1991), 'On the Demography of South Asian Famines', *Population Studies*, 45(1 and 2).

Great Soviet Encyclopaedia, (1930), 'Golod v Rossii' [Famine in Russia], 1st edn., Volume 17, 455–164.

Golod 1921–2 [Famine] (1923), New York.

Golod i samoderžavie [Famine et autocracy] (1902).

Golodomor 1932–1933 v Ukraini: pričiny i naslidki [Famine in Ukraine in 1932–1933: Causes and Consequences] (1995), Kiev.

Gordon, A. V. (1995), *Krestjanstvo i rynok* [The Peasantry and the Market], Moscow.

Goskomstat of Russia (1997), *The Demographic Yearbook of Russia*, Moscow.

—— (1998), *Population of Russia: 1897–1997, Statistical Handbook*, Moscow.

Groman, V. (1929),'O novom metode prognoza urožaja' [On the new method of forecasting the harvest], *Vestnik statistiki*, 2.

Ivnitskij, N. A., (1996), 'Golod 1932–1933 gg.: kto vinovat?' [The famine of 1932–1933: who was responsible?], in *Rossija XX vek: sud'by rossijskogo krestijanstva*, Moscow.

Kane, P. (1988), *Famine in China: 1951–61: Demographic and Social Implications*, New York: St Martin's Press.

Klepikov, S. A., and Ajanov, V. A. (1924), *Statističeskij spravočnik po agrarnomu voprosu. Selskoe xoziajjstvo v 1913–1920 gg.* [Statistical Abstract on the Agrarian Question. Agriculture in 1913–1920], Moscow.

Livi-Bacci, M. (1991), *Population and Nutrition. An Essay on European Demographic History*, Cambridge: Cambridge University Press.

—— (1993), 'On the Human Costs of Collectivisation in the Soviet Union', *Population and Development Review*, 19(4): 743–66.
Lorimer, F. (1946), *Population of the Soviet Union: History and Prospects*, Geneva: Völkerbund.
Maksudov, S. (1977), 'Pertes subies par la population, de l'URSS, 1918–1955', *Cahiers du monde russe et Soviétique*, Volume 18, 3: 223–65.
Manning, R. T. (1993), 'The Soviet Economic Crisis of 1936–1940 and the Great Purges', in G. A. Getty and R. T. Manning (eds.), *The Stalinist Terror: New Perspectives*, Cambridge: Cambridge University Press.
McAlpin, M. B. (1983), *Subject to Famine: Food Crises and Economic Change in Western India, 1886–1920*, Princeton: Princeton University Press.
Meslé F., and Vallin, J. (1989), 'Reconstitution des tables annuelles de mortalité pour la France du XIX^{e}me siècle', *Population*, 6: 1121–58.
Mixelsson, I. (1920), 'Vajnoe predosterejenie', [An important announcement], *Izvestija VTsIK*, 17 November 1920.
Ó Gráda, C. (1995), 'The Great Famine and Today's Famines', in C. Póirtéir (ed.), *The Great Irish Famine*, Cork: Mercier Press.
Oganovskij, N. P. (1923), *Selskoe xozjajstvo Rossii v XX veke. Sbornik statističesko-ekonomičeskix svedenij za 1901–1922 gg.* [Russian Agriculture in the Twentieth Century. Collection of statistical and economic data in 1901–1922], Moscow.
—— (1924), *Očerki po ekonomičeskoj geographii USSR* [Essay on the Economic Geography of the USSR], 2nd edn., Moscow.
Pitkänen, K. J. (1993), *Deprivation and disease. Mortality during the Great Finnish Famine of the 1860s*, Helsinki: Finnish Demographic Society.
—— and Mielke, J. H. (1993), 'Age and Sex Differentials in Mortality During Two Nineteenth Century Population Crises', *European Journal of Population*, 9.
Po povodu Samarskogo goloda [On the famine in Samara] (1874).
Pokrovski, V. I. (1897), 'Vlijanie kolebanija urožaev i xlebnyx cen na estestvennoe dviženie naselenija', [Influence of harvests and cereal price fluctuations on population movement], in Čuprov, A. I. and Posnikov, A. S. *Vlijanie urožaev i xlebnyx cen na nekotorye storony narodnogo xozjastva [Influence of harvests and cereal prices on some branches of the national economy]*, Volume II, Saint Pétersbourg.
Posledgol, C. C. (1922), *Posle goloda* [After the famine], 1.
Rašine, A. G. (1956), *Naselenie Rossii za 100 let* [Russia's Population in a Hundred Years], Moscow, 1956.
RGAE, Grossman (1935), 'O rabote CUNCHU SSSR v oblasti učeta naselenija' [On the work of the CUNCHU in the area of population enumeration], 23 June 1935, RGAE, f. 1562, op. 329, ed. 107.
RGAE, Kaplun (1934), 'Materialy k itogam estestvennogo dviženija naselenija za 1933' [Notes concerning the results of the natural movement of population in 1933], 31 March 1934; RGAE, f. 1562, op. 329, ed. 107.
RGAE, Kraval (1934), 'Pojasnenie k dokladnoj zapiske tov. Voznesenskogo 'O statistike narodonaselenija', [Clarifying points regarding the note 'On the statistics of population' by Comrade Voznesenski], 1934; RGAE, f. 1562, op. 329, ed. 107.
—— (1935), 'Narodnomu komissaru vnutrennix del, tov. Jagoda' [Note for the attention of the People's Commissar for Interior Affairs, Comrade Yagoda], 10 April 1935 ; RGAE, f. 1562, op. 329, ed. 107.

RGAE, Kurman (1934), 'Svodnyj otčet o rezultatax obsledovanija postanovki učeta estestvennogo dviženija naselenija, proizvedennogo rabotnikami CUNCHU, UNCHU USSR i Ivanovskogo oblunchu v marte 1934' [Final report on the results of an enquiry by the CUNCHU, UNCHU on the Ukraine and the oblast of Ivanovo in March 1934 concerning the statistics of population change], 4 April 1934 ; RGAE, f. 1562, op. 329, ed. 132.

—— (1937), 'O estestvennom dviženii naselenija meždu dvumja perepisjami 17. 12. 1926 i 06. 01. 1937' [Concerning the natural movement of the population between the two censuses of 17 December 1926 and 6 January 1937], 14 March 1937; RGAE, f. 1562, op. 329, ed. 107.

Rivers, J. W. (1982), *Women and Children Last: An Essay on Sex Discrimination in Disasters*, Disasters.

Rossiïa [Russie] (1991), *Dictionnaire Encyclopédique*, Leningrad, [new edition of the 54th and 55th volumes of the Encyclopedic Dictionary of F. A. Brokgauz and I. A. Efron].

Semenov, M. (1922), 'K voprosu o zakonomernosti kolebanija urozaev' [On how harvests fluctuate], *Vestnik statistiki*, 5–8.

Seminar (1998), *'Sovremennye kontseptsyi agrarnogo razvitija'* [Seminar on 'Modern concepts of agrarian development'], *Ote estvennaja istorija*, 6.

Sifman, R. I. (1977), 'Dinamika čislennosti naselenija Rossii za 1897–1914 gg.' [Population change in Russia between 1897 and 1914], in *Bračnost, roždaemost, smertnost v Rossii i v SSSR* [Nuptiality, Fertility, and Mortality in Russia and the USSR], Moscow, Statistika.

Sbornik Statističeskix svedenij o Rossii [Collection of Statistical Data on Russia] (1851), St Petersburg.

Tauger, M. (1991), 'The 1932 Harvest and the Famine 1933', *Slavic Review*, 50(1).

Tomiline, S. A. (1925), *L'hygiène Publique dans la Population Rural de l'Ukraine*, Société des Nations Organisation d'Hygiène, Geneva.

Učebnik Ekonomičeskoj geografii,(1925) 2nd edn., Moscow.

Vallin, J. (1988), 'La mortalité en Europe de 1720 à 1914. Tendances à long terme et changements de structure par sexe et par âge', INED, Paris.

Vlijanie neurožaev na narodnoe koxjajstvo Rossii [The Impact of Bad Harvests on the National Economy of Russia] (1927), Moscow, Parts 1 and 2.

Volkov, E. Z. (1930), *Dinamika narodonaselenija za 80 let* [Population Change over Eighty Years], Moscow.

Watkins, S. C., and Menken, J. (1985), 'Famines in Historical Perspective', *Population and Development Review*, 11(4): 647–76.

Wheatcroft, S.C. (1982), 'Famine and Factors Affecting it in the Soviet Union in the 1920s and 1930s', University of Birmingham, *CREES Discussion Papers*, SIPSD, 21.

Willekens, F., and Scherbov, S. (1991), 'Age-Period-Cohort Analysis of Mortality with Applications to Soviet Data', IIASA Working Paper 91/42.

Zurbrigg, S. (1992), 'Hunger and epidemic malaria in Punjab, 1868–1940', *Economic and Political Weekly*, 25 January 1992.

9

'Send Us either Food or Coffins': The 1941–2 Famine on the Aegean Island of Syros[1]

VIOLETTA HIONIDOU

The Greek famine that occurred during World War II remains largely unknown and under-researched.[2] It is mainly the politics of the famine and the involvement of Britain and, subsequently, the USA in Greek politics that have attracted most interest (see e.g. Fleischer 1986; Kazamias 1990; Kitsikis 1969, 1977; Papastratis 1984). This chapter focuses on the demographic aspects of the famine on the island of Syros. In what follows the main events that caused the famine and those that led to its conclusion will be outlined. Before proceeding with the main demographic analysis, the data and their quality will be reviewed.

CHRONICLE OF THE FAMINE

In economic terms prior to World War II, Greece was predominantly rural, with more than 60 per cent of the population engaged in agricultural occupations generating 35 per cent of the national income. Nevertheless, the country was heavily dependent upon food imports. In the period 1935–7, 45 per cent of the required wheat was imported, although by 1939, this percentage was reduced to 20.5 (Demathas 1989: 151; Diamond 1947: 5–6). These high figures resulted from a concentration on the production of cash crops such as tobacco and currants (Mazower 1991: 79–81). The primary centres of cereal production in Greece were the northern parts of the mainland, whereas the Peloponnese was the main producer of olive oil and currants. Despite wide variations, in general, the islands were usually producers of a cash crop and they also depended either on remittances and/or cash earned from seasonal/circular migration.

At the early stages of World War II and during the period of Greek neutrality, that is up to October 1940, the effects of extensive pre-war trade between Greece and Germany became apparent: imports of raw material were substantially reduced and unemployment increased (Delivanis and Cleveland 1950: 22–4). Prices rose and transportation difficulties were serious enough for urban populations to experience

---

[1] For the title, see Halares (1997: vol. 2, 132).
[2] A recently published novel has made the Greek famine more widely known (De Bernieres 1994).

difficulties in receiving agricultural supplies from rural areas (Delivanis and Cleveland 1950: 23). During the war against Italy, the situation worsened markedly. Trade with Germany ceased, economic activity declined, the cost of living increased and a black market emerged (Delivanis and Cleveland 1950: 44–7).

The invasion of Greece by the German forces was a remarkably rapid process. It began on 6 April 1941 and by the 26th day of the same month Athens was occupied. The Italians occupied the Cycladic islands in the following fortnight (Mazower 1993: 50; *The Times*, 7 May 1941, 4). On 16 April, the Greek Minister of War essentially dissolved the army (Hondros 1983: 52). At the beginning of May, large numbers of Greek soldiers were dismissed by the Germans and were provided with permits in order to return home, mainly on foot (*The Times*, 8 May 1941, 3). Soon after the occupation the country was divided into three zones, one being governed by each of the occupying powers. Thus, Bulgarians occupied the northern part of Greece on their borders, that is, eastern Macedonia and western Thrace; the Germans occupied three of the Aegean islands, Crete, the rest of Macedonia, the border area with Turkey and the Greater Athens area; while the Italians occupied the rest of the country, including the Cyclades (Doxiadis c.1945: Table 15 and comments). Within the first month of the occupation the Germans seized or bought at low prices—paying with the 'occupational marks' they circulated—all available stocks of food, tobacco, cotton, leather, and the majority of pack-animals (Mazower 1993: 24–7). The appropriation of all means of transport and fuel by the occupying authorities essentially prevented any transfer of supplies or population after the occupation.[3] Fishing was strictly prohibited, at least during the early stages of the occupation (*The Times*, 22 January 1942, 3).[4] The country was further subdivided into 13 zones between which food or population circulation was forbidden (Doxiadis c.1945: Table 16 and comments; *The Times*, 22 January 1942, 3). Thus, even the reduced harvest of 1941 could not be distributed to the most needy areas because of imposed restrictions.[5] This resulted in differences in the acuteness of the famine in various areas of the country according to the local economy of each area, with urban areas and islands being most affected by food scarcity (*The Times*, 28 October 1941, 5).

[3] The seizure of shipping by the Axis authorities was considered by *The Times* correspondent as a reason for the extreme severity of the famine on the islands (*The Times*, 28 October 1941, 5). Mazower mentions that '[t]o travel from the capital to the Peloponnese required a permit from the *carabinieri* and a booking several days in advance'. Also, that '[t]he voyage by caique (small boat) from Piraeus to Chios took 15–20 days, and could only be managed at a price beyond most people's reach' (Mazower 1993: 33). Still, by January 1942, the Bulgarians as well as the Italians refused to recognize the passes provided by the Germans, further restricting population movements (*The Times*, 10 January 1942, 3).

[4] Mazower emphasizes the especially strict prohibition imposed by the Italians on trade between the islands in the Aegean sea and the 'notoriously strict surveillance of fishing boats, which could carry information or even passengers as well as fish' (Mazower 1993: 55). At a later stage fishing was allowed, though only by fishermen, and provided that Italian soldiers accompanied them (Halares 1997: vol. 2, 129). A large part of the catch was routinely requisitioned.

[5] According to Hondros the 1941 harvest was especially poor having produced less than half the normal output (1969: 67). Diamond, citing Varvaressos, suggests that the wheat produced in 1940–1 was 80 per cent of that of 1935–7. For other cereals and pulses, it was 36 and 45, respectively (Diamond 1947: 12).

A naval blockade was imposed on Greece by the Allies as soon as the country was occupied, since it had become an enemy territory. By May the scarcity of food was visible in Athens and by June on Syros (Ntelopoulos 1987: 26; *Syriana Grammata* 1991: 241 citing the diaries of a local school).[6] In order to avoid confiscation by the occupying forces individuals and merchants concealed food either for private consumption or to be sold in the black market. When such individuals were traced retribution was extremely serious. Food scarcity resulted in increased prices while the circulation of 'occupation marks' by the Germans and 'casa mediterranea' drachma notes by the Italians led to substantial inflation.[7] Very soon, an informal bartering economy substituted the cash economy.[8] In urban centres, the black market and rationing were the only means of food supply. The latter provided bread rations varying between 0 and 256 g per day per person in Athens between October 1941 and April 1942 (Valaoras 1946: 223). Black market prices were far beyond the income of an average worker (Thomadakis 1981: 72). Moreover, unemployment was very high among the working classes since the normal channels of production virtually ceased (on Syros see Halares 1997: vol. 1, 225, citing a letter of the Catholic Bishop of Syros to the Greek Orthodox Archbishop of Athens dated 2 May 1942; vol. 2, 47 citing a letter of the Sailors' Union to the Red Cross in Athens, dated June 1944; and vol. 2, 126 oral account; on the town of Volos see Koliou 1985: 69 and 86). Moreover, unemployment benefits were not generally available (Delivanis and Cleveland 1950: 24).

The food scarcity became visible to the occupying forces from a very early point (Hoffmann 1989: 77). Among the German governing body, strong disagreements prevailed between the military and the Plenipotentiary of the Reich, G. Altenburg, and later his successor, H. Neubacher. While the Plenipotentiary, concerned by the financial and food situation of the country, proposed a reduction of imposed occupation costs, the military refused to take any action to avert or to alleviate the emerging famine (Hondros 1969: 82–3). Both Italy and Germany sent some grain to Greece in the period 15 August–30 September 1941 before the German authorities attributed to Italy the entire responsibility for providing Greece with food 'since Greece lies in Italy's sphere of influence' (Mazower 1993: 31, citing US National Archives (Washington, DC), T-821/249/829-32, 'Situazione economica e organizzazione civile nei territori occupati', 1 November 1941; Richter 1975: 155–6).

In July 1941, the US ambassador in Greece, MacVeagh, upon his arrival at New York, described the situation in Greece as 'a progression towards famine' (Iatrides 1980: 374). In August 1941, *The Times* correspondent reported people were fainting in the streets of Athens due to starvation, and the Greeks appealed to the British and

---

[6] *The Times* reported on 5 May 1941 that 'The scarcity of food, which has always existed in Greece, now threatens to reach catastrophic proportions'.

[7] Moreover, the Germans arranged with the Greek government and the Bank of Greece for the payment of large sums of drachma to the Axis powers as occupation 'expenses'. Thus, the Bank was forced to print excessive amounts of currency, which further accentuated the inflation (Thomadakis 1981: 66–7). The price of bread underwent a 23-fold increase between April 1941 and January 1942 and an 89-fold increase between April 1941 and July 1942 (Doxiadis *c*.1945: Table 63).

[8] Even the fees of doctors were paid in food (Argenti 1966: 36; *The Times*, 7 September 1942, 3).

American governments for the shipment of food for starving children (*The Times*, 16 August 1941, 3). Responding to repeated appeals from the exiled Greek government, Britain consented to allow assistance from Turkey since Turkey was within the blockade area. Some supplies arrived in Greece from Turkey in the period October 1941 to February 1942, but these did not exceed 10,000 tons of food (Kitsikis 1969: 30–1). These supplies were distributed exclusively among the Athenian population, mainly through soup kitchens for children and infants (Black 1992: 7). The food transferred from Turkey constituted the only form of relief received during that period. The estimated calorific value of the rationed food for Athens was 458 cal per person per day in July 1941; 183 during November of the same year; and 357 in March of 1942. Some 140 cal per person per day were distributed from communal soup kitchens (League of Nations 1944: 38).[9] Reports of the high death toll during the winter of 1941–2 came from Athens as well as other urban areas and the islands (*The Times*, 28 February 1942, 4). By June of 1941, the occupying forces had guaranteed the Greek government that any food sent for the Greek population would not be requisitioned. In November of the same year, the above guarantee was given to the International Red Cross (Fleischer 1986: 204–6).

The British government was very well informed of the existing situation from the beginning. A disagreement between the secretary of state for foreign affairs supporting the lifting of the blockade and the minister of economic warfare opposing it was resolved by Churchill himself who saw no need of a policy change in July 1941 since 'he was not aware of any great pressure from the United States of America' (Hoffmann 1989: 78). Pressure came initially from the Greek government in exile and the Apostolic delegate to Greece and Turkey, A. Roncalli.[10] But British policy remained unchanged, while the pleas of the anglophile Greek Prime Minister in exile were weak, and for as long as the government of the United States did not oppose the blockade. The latter, lobbied by the Greek War Relief Association that was created and run by Greek-Americans, that is Greek migrants established in the US, changed its position towards the blockade in December 1941 (Kitsikis 1977: 167–9; Fleischer 1986: 205). Eventually, under the threat of resignation by the Greek Prime Minister in exile and considerable pressure by the government of the United States, the blockade was lifted in February 1942 on the proviso that the International Red Cross would handle all food supplies to Greece (Fleischer 1986: 206–8; Hondros 1969: 97–8). On 21 March 1942, the first of a series of shipments of food approved by the British government arrived at the port of Piraeus (Kitsikis 1969: 30). Irregular shipments of wheat and flour continued to arrive until August 1942, when an agreement between all involved parties was reached and a monthly shipment of 15,000 ton of grain was secured.

---

[9] The author of this report emphasized that these averages of calorific intake were only indicative, since there was no regular system of food distribution.

[10] Hoffmann outlines Roncalli's initiatives both to the Germans and the British in his effort to allow provisions to reach the starving population (Hoffmann 1989). Nevertheless Hoffmann's account rather glorifies the effectiveness of these initiatives (Hoffmann 1989: 80). On the steps taken by the Greek Prime Minister in exile, E. Tsouderos, see Tsouderos (1946).

Regular shipments of foodstuffs—managed and distributed by the International Red Cross mission—started arriving in November 1942 (Hondros 1969: 85). According to estimates of the Joint Relief Committee, the average daily distribution of food in 1943 did not exceed 825 cal per person and the total calorie intake for the urban population was 925 (Diamond 1947: 22–3). The Cyclades received relief in late 1942, but this was essentially suspended between December 1942 and January 1944 due to the ban imposed by the Allies on the use of small vessels for the transport of foodstuffs (Note concernant l'interdiction d'effectuer des envois en Epire, aux Cyclades, aux iles Ioniennes et aux Sporades, Commission de Gestion pour les Secours en Grece, Folder 3, Deas Archive, Benaki Museum, Athens). Athens and Piraeus enjoyed uninterrupted relief with only a short-term suspension during December 1944, which rapidly led to increases in mortality (Laiou-Thomadakis 1980: 38; Valaoras 1946: 217).[11] The relief operation targeted those areas that suffered most during the peak of the famine, that is large towns and some of the islands. Thus, while the countryside fared quite well during the peak of the famine—compared to the towns and the islands—in the following winter of 1942–3 these areas were 'literally weeping for bread' (Sosnowski 1962: 227, citing the Report of the Swedish delegate who visited Greece during the War (Proceedings of the Trial of the Major War Criminals before the International Military Tribunal, Nuremberg 1947, VII, 527)).[12]

In summary, a chain of events that started with the occupation of the country led to extreme scarcity of food among the Greek population during 1941–2. No single cause for this can be pinpointed. Rather, the combined effect of a multitude of events led to the famine. These included the occupation; the requisitioning of food; the continuance of the blockade throughout the peak of the famine; the apathy of the governing bodies and the Greek government; the extent of the black market; unemployment and the concomitant lack of cash for the working classes; and, finally, extreme inflation.

SYROS

Syros is one of the Cycladic islands and it had a population of 25,952 in 1940. Hermoupolis, the capital town of the island and of the Cyclades was essentially created in the early 1820s when successive waves of Greeks sought refuge from the Ottoman forces (Kardases 1987: 29). The old town of Ano Syros is situated on a steep hill close to Hermoupolis, which is a port town (on Ano Syros see Loukos 1994). The dominance of Hermoupolis over Ano Syros has not only been numerical—a population of 18,925 compared to 2,763 in Ano Syros in 1940—but also financial, with all the existing industries as well as the commercial activities being concentrated

---

[11] The provision of food and aid in the post-liberation era was closely linked to the politics of the time and the civil war (Laiou-Thomadakis 1980: 37–8).

[12] So, for example, in grain-producing Macedonia the 1942–3 winter excess of deaths is considerably larger than that of the previous winter, in contrast to the situation on the islands and in the Athens/Piraeus area (Helger 1949: 614–15; Mazower 1993: 39).

there. Nevertheless, in both cases, the occupational profile of the population was 'urban'—with farmers residing almost exclusively in the countryside. Moreover, the urban population of both towns rarely possessed any land in the countryside (*Syriana Grammata* 1991: 230).

The major point of differentiation between the two towns was, and is, religion. Hermoupolis is inhabited overwhelmingly by people of Greek Orthodox faith and Ano Syros by Catholics. The rest of the island's population is almost exclusively Catholic.

Hermoupolis was by far the most important port of Greece in the mid-nineteenth century, although its significance had begun to decline in the 1870s. The importance and wealth of Hermoupolis during the nineteenth century was also reflected in the level of social infrastructure. The town boasted a hospital as early as 1823, a post office and the first insurance company in 1829, the largest quarantine area in Greece by 1842, numerous schools, a theatre, and orphanages (Traulos and Kokkou 1980: 28–32). In the 1930s, some industries still operated in Hermoupolis attracting a number of workers. 'Popular kitchens' offering food to the 'poor' began operating at the end of 1937. Run by the municipal authorities, the kitchens were financed by a special tax imposed by the municipal authority on the most affluent members of the society (Archives of Cyclades, Municipal Archive, D/A/Filanthropia-Koinoniki Pronoia 3, letter dated 24 November 1937, from the Prefect to the Mayor).

The island of Syros was chosen for this study for a multitude of reasons: it combined rural and urban populations, it was 'closed' to migration during the occupation, it is known to have experienced high mortality during the famine, and, most importantly, it possesses good data to which I now turn.

DATA

In examining the demographic aspects of the famine the civil registration records (i.e. relating to births and deaths) are used here. During World War II, and the Civil war which followed, the collection by the Central Statistical Office of the reports of vital statistics from the local registrars was suspended until 1955. (On the vital registration system of Greece, see Hionidou 1993: 21–5; Valaoras 1980.) Because of this there is no accurate figure of famine deaths for the whole of Greece other than some, sometimes arbitrary, estimates such as 100,000, 200,000, 250,000, and 450,000 (the first two referring to the 1941–2 'winter', the third referring to famine victims between 1941 and 1943, and the last referring to the period May 1941–April 1943) (Black 1992: 8; Fleischer 1986: 196; Helger 1949: 625; Mazower 1993: 41; Valaoras 1946: 225). It was in mainland Greece, where the combined effects of resistance, Civil War and migration were the greatest, that civil registration was most disrupted. But, in some areas, such as the islands of Mykonos, Syros, and Chios, registration itself was not interrupted (for Chios see Argenti 1966: 45).

For Hermoupolis, as for Mykonos, such data are continuously available from 1859. The information provided in the death certificates includes the full name of the deceased, the parish of death, place of birth, place of residence, date of death, age of the deceased, cause of death, and the name of the doctor who certified the death. The registered deaths concern only those who died on the island and thus soldiers who perished elsewhere are not included. Any visiting person, on the other hand, would be included in the registered deaths. Persons visiting for short periods of time—such as when seeking medical help in the hospital—were recorded as being in Hermoupolis only temporarily.

The constraints imposed by the occupying forces on the mobility of citizens ensured that the island's population was a 'closed' one from the beginning of the occupation period—that is, in May 1941—and at least until the end of the famine. This did not preclude movement within the island. Whoever possessed a house in the countryside probably did move there, either before or soon after the arrival of the occupying forces (Halares 1997: vol. 2, 126 and 260; *Syriana Grammata* 1991: 224). Still, this concerned only a small fraction of the population, namely the well-off. In any case, such people were the least at risk of death from starvation. Less affluent families and individuals also moved to the surrounding countryside, usually residing in rented accommodation, in order to avoid the bombardment of Hermoupolis. Nevertheless, their links with the town were closely maintained.

Civil registration, and specifically death registration, was not seriously disturbed during World War II on Syros. At the time registration would take place in the municipal buildings of the two towns and in the community offices of six villages/communities. In all cases but Hermoupolis, a problem of death under-registration would be very unlikely, if only because of the small sizes of the populations involved. Such a problem could have been present in Hermoupolis, and indeed has been suggested by at least one author. In arguing that 8,000–9,000 deaths occurred in Hermoupolis, which is the number recorded in the municipal memorial to the famine victims, Halares, a local historian, utilizes the records from both parish and civil registration. Making unfounded statements concerning the number of burials for those parishes for which no data survive, he concludes that extensive under-registration of famine deaths occurred and suggests that the Italians had every reason to conceal the real extent of the famine (Halares 1997: vol. 1, 166–7).[13] In the same book, however, there is an abundance of references from oral testimonies to the postponement of burial so that the family could utilize the deceased's ration card (Halares 1997: vol. 2, 82–3, 138 and 278). There are no references either to abandoned corpses or to secret burials, although there are some references to corpses of people with no relatives to tend to them.[14] A different explanation for the delay of burials is given by a verger: the

---

[13] For example, based on oral accounts there were 30–40 deaths daily. Assuming that this was taking place every day for seven months, he estimates that 7,350 deaths occurred during the famine (Halares 1997: vol. 1, 166). While oral accounts can offer a wealth of information, numerical estimates are usually not trustworthy. Moreover, even if such a high daily number of deaths occurred at some point, most certainly it did not last for seven months. This is part of a dispute between Catholic and Greek Orthodox local historians as to who suffered most during the famine. See Loukos (1998).

[14] Secret burials would have been rather difficult because of the curfew imposed at night. Halares refers to four corpses which were eventually collected by a municipal carriage and which were subsequently buried in a communal grave (1997: vol. 2, 82–3). In another oral account, a reference is made to

daily number of deaths was so high that the priests could not perform burials fast enough, and therefore the dead remained unburied in houses for a number of days (Roussos 1946: 24). Then neighbours would carry the dead to the cemetery where they remained until the workers could bury them (Roussos 1946: 24). Thus, the delay of burial in some cases is certain, though this delay probably did not extend beyond about 10 days.

The municipal office, where civil registration took place, seems to have been concerned about the scale of the famine, and also—possibly—about the reporting of deaths during the famine. Thus, figures were drawn up on a bimonthly basis both of the daily number of deaths as reported in the civil registers and of the daily number of burials that took place in the Greek Orthodox Cemetery of *Agios Georgios* (Archives of Cyclades, Municipal Archive, D/E/Thanatoi/10). With only two exceptions the number reported in the civil registration was always higher (Loukos 1998: 196).[15] The explanation for this is probably straightforward: any Catholics who resided and died in Hermoupolis would have been buried in the Catholic cemetery and thus not be included in the Greek Orthodox cemetery books.

In 1945 an article in a local newspaper by a lawyer who lived through the famine in Hermoupolis gave an account of the famine figures referring to the 1940–4 period. The author provided a rough estimate of approximately 500 non-registered deaths having taken place during that period (Drakakes 1945). More recently a local journalist managed to trace the death certificates of persons known to him as having perished during the famine (*Syriana Grammata* 1991: 251).

Soon after the early stages of the famine, the local graveyard was filled and had to be expanded. For reasons of lack of space and because burials of the 'poor' were funded by the municipality, common graves were used, although always within the local cemetery. Nevertheless, it seems that with only a few exceptions, persons received the last rites and their deaths were registered both in the church books and in the municipal books.

The situation in Athens and Piraeus—with a joint population of 956,813 in 1940 (Valaoras 1946: 215)—was under much less control. For example, the bodies of deceased persons were secretly abandoned either in public cemeteries or in the streets by relatives in order to keep the ration cards (Mazower 1993: 38; Milliex 1982: 84). Thus, burials were taking place without the appropriate permit and such deaths often remained unregistered (Junod 1942: 17; Skouras *et al.* 1991: 288–9). In other cases, bodies would be found in houses days after the death had taken place and in the absence of any relatives who could indicate the identity of the deceased (Junod

---

approximately 10 persons—all immigrants from Santorini—being buried unofficially because 'we did not have the strength to take them to Hermoupolis' (*Syriana Grammata* 1991: 227).

[15] These comparisons were taking place from February 1942 to May 1943. The difference between the two figures ranged from 1 to 19, except for May 1942 when it was as high as 42. In the two cases where burials exceeded registered deaths, the excess was not more than two deaths. The existing correspondence between the cemetery supervisor and the Mayor during the famine does not suggest any irregularities. The former submitted biweekly lists of the buried 'poor', that is persons whose families could not afford their burial (Archives of Cyclades, Municipal Archive, I/Nekrotafeio/9).

1942: 17). Burials were expensive and difficult to arrange in Athens and Piraeus due to the lack of transport and fuel (Mazower 1993: 41). Occasionally the dead would be buried unofficially (Ntelopoulos 1987: 125 referring to the burial of a baby). Even more important, death was much easier to conceal from people and the local priest in such a large urban area. Consequently, and in contrast, the uninterrupted death registration data available for Hermoupolis allow us to study the demographic characteristics of an acute, urban famine.[16]

DEMOGRAPHIC ASPECTS OF THE FAMINE

With a crude death rate (CDR) of 17.3 per thousand population, the famine arrived at a time when Hermoupolis had been experiencing low mortality for at least a decade, although higher than the national average rate of approximately 14 per thousand in 1935–9 (Table 9.1) (Valaoras 1960: 132). The crude birth rate (CBR) had experienced a decline from 25.9 to 22.4 per thousand between the late 1920s and the late 1930s, and was markedly below the national average of 27.6 during 1935–9 (Valaoras 1960: 132). A fairly high infant mortality rate of 159 infant deaths per thousand live births still prevailed in the early 1930s. The countryside was radically different to Hermoupolis in respect of mortality, having half the CDR of Hermoupolis but an almost identical CBR (22.4 and 23.6, respectively, during 1938–9).[17] The town of Ano Syros was very similar to Hermoupolis—with somewhat lower mortality (15.7 as opposed to 17.3), but also somewhat lower fertility (19.2 as opposed to 22.4).

In defining the length of the famine, the monthly number of deaths was drawn up for the period 1939–45 (Fig. 9.1). The peak of the famine happened in the middle of a bitterly cold winter. In January 1942, 484 deaths occurred in contrast to 35 during the same month of 1939. A baseline number of 50 monthly deaths has been assumed as representing normality. This was exceeded for the first time in September 1941, and the number remained above 50 until November of 1942. Interestingly, this baseline number was exceeded once again in the period January–July 1944. This should be noted as a secondary, considerably less serious famine. Its causes should be sought in the interruption of the relief provided by the International Red Cross. This interruption was due to the objection of the Allies to the transport of foodstuffs to the Cycladic islands by means of caiques (small boats) (Helger 1949: 388). The interruption began in November 1942 and lasted throughout 1943, although supplies provided earlier covered the needs of the population until February 1943. Provisioning re-started in January 1944, but significant amounts of food only arrived during

---

[16] The only drawback in such a study is the non-availability of an age structure of the population at, or around the time of the famine. This applies to the whole of Greece because the 1940 census returns were destroyed before their analysis was completed. Only the population figures by sex have been published for every community, town, and prefecture. The nearest dates to the famine when an age structure of the population is available are those of 1928 and 1951.

[17] The rather clear-cut rural–urban split in mortality levels prior to the famine was most probably real, with crowded living conditions and a less than perfect water supply system in Hermoupolis being responsible for the higher levels of mortality compared to the countryside.

Violetta Hionidou

Table 9.1. *Crude Death and Birth Rate Measures for Syros*

	1865–70	1926–30	1938–9	Famine	1949–53	Ratio
a. *The CDR on Syros and the ratio of the famine to the pre-famine rate*						
Syros island			15.7	112.2		7
Hermoupolis	33.4	18.6	17.3	138.3	8.4	8
Ano Syros			15.7	100.4		6
Countryside			8.6	26.6		3
Males			16.8	143.2		9
Females			14.6	85.0		6
b. *The CBR on Syros and the ratio of the famine to the pre-famine rate*						
Syros island			22.3	14.9		0.7
Hermoupolis	39.3	25.9	22.4	15.0	21.0	0.7
Ano Syros			19.2	12.4		0.6
Countryside			23.6	16.1		0.7

Sources: The rates for 1865–70 and 1926–30 were derived from Kolodny (1969: 275). The figures of births and deaths used in the calculations of all the other rates were obtained from the civil registration records of Syros.

Notes: The population on 1 January 1939 was estimated from the 16 October 1940 national census figures and the births and deaths that occurred between the two dates. Similarly, the population on 15 February 1942 (the middle point of the famine period) was calculated from the population figures of 1 January 1942 and the deaths and births that occurred between the two dates. The population figures for 1 January 1942 were obtained from the census organized by the occupying forces of the Cycladic islands (Archives of Cyclades, Italian Archive, 203). The population figure used to compute the 1949–53 rates was that of the 1951 national census.

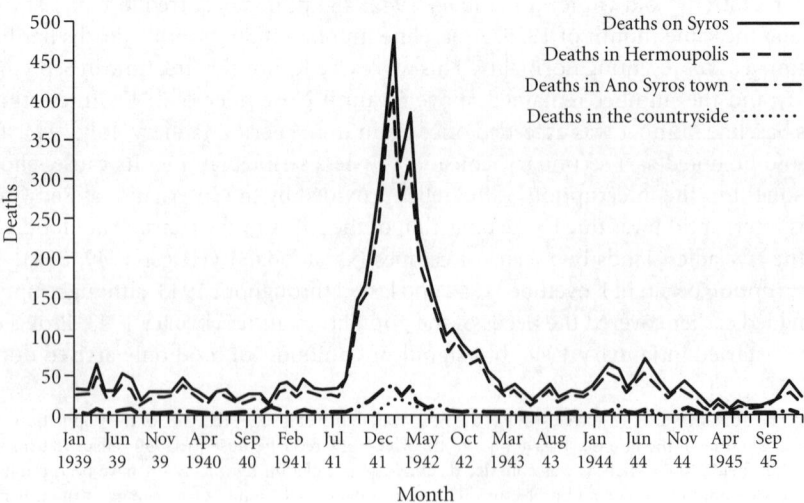

Figure 9.1. *The Monthly Number of Deaths on Syros, 1939–45*

Source: Civil registration records.

the second trimester of 1944 (Helger 1949: 144–5). Although some foodstuffs were brought into the Cyclades by the Italians in 1943, these were obviously not sufficient to avoid increases in mortality (Helger 1949: 388). The timing of the mortality increase coincided with the period when food availability in terms of production was at its lowest level, that is during the winter and spring. Similarly, a secondary famine was also observed in Athens, although this occurred in the autumn of 1944 and its cause was clearly political (Laiou-Thomadakis 1980: 27). The neighbouring Cycladic island of Mykonos did not experience such a secondary mortality peak and excess mortality in the major famine there had receded by June 1942 (Hionidou 1995). The variability of the observed experience points to the importance of local circumstances. Significantly, access to the countryside—and its produce—must have played an important role. So for Mykonos the links between the urban centre and the countryside were very strong—in many cases through the ownership of small land parcels by town dwellers. This not only had a positive effect in alleviating the famine during the summer months of 1942, but it also ensured that no further increases in mortality occurred. The same early return to 'normality' is suggested by the data for Ano Syros town, and the countryside of the island of Syros. While both clearly experienced the famine, their populations recovered much earlier than did that of Hermoupolis.

Figure 9.1 also outlines the geographical variation of the famine within Syros. While it is clear that all suffered from its consequences, it is also obvious that the inhabitants of Hermoupolis suffered the most. This is to be expected considering the occupational profile of the inhabitants of each region, as revealed from the pre-war death certificates and other secondary sources. Those people residing in the countryside were engaged in agriculture and despite some requisitioning most of them would still manage to conceal some produce either for their own consumption or to exchange for other goods. The relative force of the famine is shown clearly in the ratio of the famine to the pre-famine CDR (see Table 9.1). While this ratio is 3 for the countryside (i.e. the famine CDR was three times that of the 1938–9 CDR) for Ano Syros the ratio was 6 and for Hermoupolis it was 8.[18] The intermediate position of Ano Syros may be attributed in part to the inclusion of two farming villages, *Episkopeio* and *Kini*, within its administrative boundaries, and also to the much closer relationship of the town of Ano Syros to the countryside—a relationship present at both the personal level, with family ties connecting the two, but also in relation to religion.[19] Where the ties were especially strong, some movement from Ano Syros to the countryside must have also occurred. Hermoupolis, on the other hand, was rather cut-off from the countryside,

---

[18] In Table 9.1 the population on 15 February 1942 (the mid-point of the famine period) was calculated from the population figures of 1 January 1942 and the deaths and births that occurred between the two dates. When the 16 October 1940 census population figures are used to calculate the population on 15 February 1942 the results naturally differ (e.g. the CDR for the whole island becomes 102). Most importantly, however, the ratios of the CDRs of the geographical areas retain their relative values, thus not affecting the conclusions drawn here. The ratios of the CBRs are all 0.6. Most interestingly, for males the CDR ratio is reduced to 7 while for females it remains the same.

[19] The population of Episkopeio and Kini accounted for 13 per cent of the Ano Syros population in 1928.

its only link being the ownership of rural villas by the wealthiest Hermoupolites. The lack of links between the inhabitants of the countryside and those of Hermoupolis is reflected in the numerous oral accounts which refer to the rather harsh punishment meted out by farmers to any Hermoupolites who were found attempting to steal agricultural products (Halares 1997: vol. 2, 31).

Despite the strong geographical variation in mortality, the effect of the famine on fertility was surprisingly uniform. The ratio of the pre-famine to famine CBR ranges only between 0.6 and 0.7 for all three areas (Table 9.1). Thus, in examining fertility during the famine it makes sense to concentrate on the whole island population.

The monthly numbers of births and deaths show some interesting features (Fig. 9.2). First, there is a strong concentration of births during the first three months of the year. This seasonal pattern, though sustained through the famine, was certainly disrupted in 1943, although it was back in force in 1944.

Second, the absence of a sizeable decline in births during the famine but a downturn immediately after it suggests the absence of an 'early response' to the famine. That is, despite the early signs of food scarcity—reported as early as April 1941—the sexual activities of the population were not suspended. Examination of the precise timing of conceptions provides some clarification (Fig. 9.3). The peak of conceptions in 1941 occurred in April–May, coinciding with the return of soldiers from the front. Moreover, this was the time of the 'usual' peak in conceptions. What followed was a decline in conceptions where the trough was reached at the same time as the mortality peak. A gradual recovery in conceptions followed until December 1942 when almost

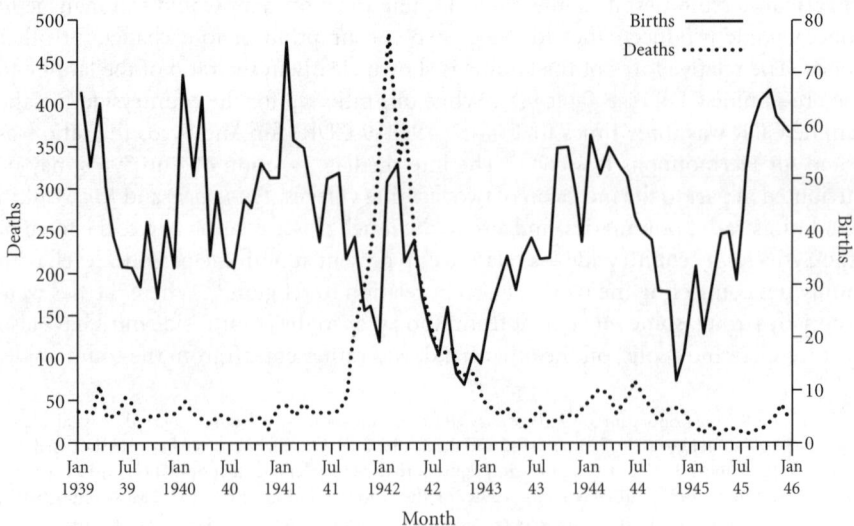

Figure 9.2. *The Monthly Number of Deaths and Births on Syros, 1939–45*

Source: Civil registration records.

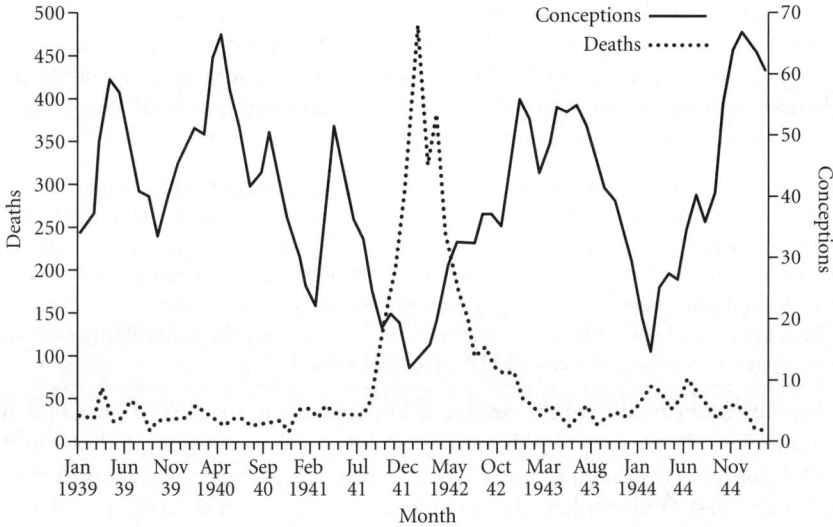

Figure 9.3. *The Monthly Number of Deaths and a Two-month Moving Average of Conceptions on Syros, 1939–44*

Source: Civil registration records.

pre-war levels were attained. These were then more or less sustained until June 1943. It may be no coincidence that these high levels of conceptions broadly coincided with a general optimism about the course of the war and a concomitant temporary improvement in the Greek monetary situation which came to an end by May 1943 (Delivanis and Cleveland 1950: 12).

What followed—starting in late 1943—was a serious food scarcity that led to moderate increases in mortality. The reaction was rapid and effective: the trough in conceptions reached in February 1944 was very similar to that which occurred during the previous famine. The fact that this second 'famine' was extremely modest in relation to the first—in terms of mortality—does not seem to have been important. The 'monetary chaos' that started in May 1944 must also have contributed to the decline in conceptions. That said, this chaos lasted until November 1944, by which time conceptions had reached a major peak (on the Greek war economy see Delivanis and Cleveland 1950). Thus, the main cause of the decline in conceptions must have been the second 'famine', although its moderate effect on mortality may preclude a physiological explanation. Rather, the 'knowledge' and 'fear' of famines that the population had accumulated from the earlier famine made this 'early' reaction possible. The above, I would suggest, indicates that the reduction in conceptions during situations of moderate—in mortality terms—famines is largely due to psychological causes and their effect on the libido of individuals. While the physiological effect is important in acute famines and especially during their mortality peak, during the rest of the time it is this psychological effect that overwhelmingly determines coital frequency and thus the conception rates of the population.[20] Even during the same famine the observed decline in conceptions may have different causes for individuals or groups within the population. Thus, during the 1941–2 acute famine in Athens for a middle-class Athenian who was among those 'hungry, though they certainly [ate]' the causes of libido loss were psychological rather than physiological (Theotokas 1982: 300):

Since the fall of 1940, the intensity of the events, the agitation of the place and afterwards the horror of the famine, the general thoughts, expectations and agonies and most of all 'the disease of the century' occupy my psyche and do not allow me to re-enter into the sphere of my private emotional life. I do not command myself on that. So, my sexual life is reduced, for a year and a half now, in a purely physiological occupation without any traces of emotion, without the curiosity of getting to know human beings, curiosity that I strongly possessed in other times. (Theotokas 1982, entry 335 of 2 February 1942)

The different causality of the decline in conceptions in the two famines of Syros is also tentatively suggested by the recovery rate of conceptions: a rapid one in the second 'famine' whenever the psychological causes ceased to exist, and a more gradual one in the first famine when the physiological effects of malnutrition had to be reverted.

Mention should be made here about the possible effect of birth control and/or its differential utilization by various groups. Our understanding of contraceptive knowledge and use in Greek pre-war populations is very limited. However, if the findings concerning the neighbouring Cycladic island of Mykonos are to be taken as a guide to the situation on Syros, then the probable methods used included condoms, *coitus interruptus*, abortion, and breast feeding (Hionidou 1998). During the war, it would have been impossible to purchase condoms and rather difficult to obtain abortions. Breast feeding was extensive on Syros, and the more so during the war for infant feeding purposes (Halares 1997: vol. 1, 125; vol. 2, 323 and 184). This, in a situation of low nutritional intake for mothers, would have further reduced their ability to conceive, thus leaving *coitus interruptus* as the main candidate for birth control. Still, a significant finding of the Mykonos study was that, when practising contraception, couples were usually aware of only one such method (Hionidou 1998: 79). If that were the case on Syros too, then even if those utilizing *coitus interruptus* and breast feeding continued to do so, a portion of the population practising birth control prior to the war were probably unable to during the war and the famine. Nonetheless, large declines occurred in conceptions—suggesting that contraception was not a significant factor in the observed outcomes.[21] A lack of knowledge of contraceptive methods and/or a lack of contraceptive devices during the war period is also reflected in the extremely high rates of illegitimacy recorded on Syros. Starting from 6 per thousand live births in 1939, the illegitimacy rate increased to 58 in 1942,

---

[20] The rest of the time refers to the early stages of an acute famine, low mortality famines, but also situations of 'repetitive famine', that is cases where individuals experience more than one famine in their lifetime. Such an example would be the Indian populations of the nineteenth and early twentieth centuries (Maharatna 1996).

[21] This will be examined in subsequent parts of this project with the use of interviews.

112 in 1943, and 115 in 1944. These rates are outstandingly high when compared to those of pre-war Greek populations (D'Agata 1942: 115).

MORTALITY BY AGE AND SEX

Significant variations in mortality by sex and age are particularly important aspects of the famine. Considerably higher mortality among men was observed both for Athens/Piraeus and Mykonos (Valaoras 1946; Hionidou 1995). The same was true of Syros, although to a somewhat smaller extent than that of Mykonos: the ratio of the famine/pre-famine CDR was 9 for males as opposed to 6 for females (Table 9.1). The respective ratios for Mykonos were 13 and 8. Male deaths during the famine constituted 59, 63, and 67 per cent of all deaths on Syros, Athens/Piraeus, and Mykonos, respectively. Nevertheless, this variation seems to have been a result of the differential length of the famine. So if we truncate the famine period to the first six months—which is the duration of the famine on Mykonos—then the percentage of male deaths increases to 65 for both Syros and Athens/Piraeus (for Athens/Piraeus the data provided by Valaoras (1946: 218) have been used). This suggests that males succumbed more than females particularly during the early stages of the famine. This is clearly indicated by the gradual decline in the percentage of male deaths over time during the famine period on Syros (Fig. 9.4). While in September 1941 almost 70 per cent of deaths involved males, by November 1942 only 50 per cent did. Similarly for Athens/Piraeus the percentages were 68 in the period October–December 1941, and

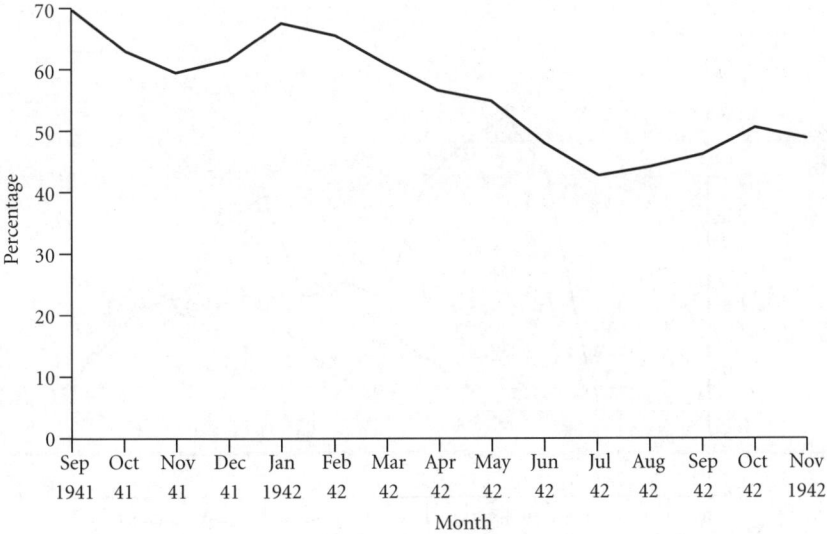

Figure 9.4. *The Monthly Percentage of Male Deaths, Syros, September 1941–November 1942*
Source: Civil registration records.

64, 56, and 53 in the first, second, and third quarters of 1942. The excess mortality of males, but also their earlier weakening—in comparison to females—were apparent to contemporaries: 'Men did not have the strength to lift [anything]. It was the women ... who carried the dead' (oral account from *Syriana Grammata* 1991: 233); 'It is men who die mainly, the workers' (from a letter dated January 3, 1942 sent by the Catholic Archbishop to the Commander of the Occupation Army, *Syriana Grammata* 1991: 280); 'Men were either in bed [ill] or walking with sticks due to total exhaustion' (Stefanou 1973: vol. 2, 81). It should be mentioned that there were no additional demands on the energy of males either in comparison to females or with the pre-war situation.

This male vulnerability does not seem to have been consistent across all ages. During the famine young adult males—those aged 15–35—experienced considerable excess mortality compared to young adult females and in comparison with the pre-famine situation (Fig. 9.5). Middle-aged men—aged 35–54—also experienced excess mortality in relation to women, but to a lesser extent. For the rest of the age groups, pre-famine sex differences were sustained. The male to female ratios of deaths by age on Syros during the famine are very similar to those of Athens/Piraeus, but less so to those of Mykonos (Table 9.2). Again, if the length of the Syros famine is artificially truncated to six months, then the ratios become similar to those of Mykonos. The similarity of the sex differentials between different places and the distinctiveness of the mortality of young men suggests that these differentials were not culturally driven. If a cultural explanation were in force this would be expected to favour males of all

Figure 9.5. *The Ratio of Male to Female Deaths by Age Group, Syros*

Table 9.2. *Ratios of Male to Female Deaths During the Greek Famine of 1941–2*

Age group	Athens/Piraeus, Oct. 1941–June 1942	Mykonos, Dec. 1941–May 1942	Syros	
			Sep. 1941–Nov 1942	Sep. 1941–Feb. 1942
0–4	1.1	1.0	1.3	1.6
5–19	1.3	2.4	1.7	2.4
20–39	2.4	3.1	2.4	2.6
40–59	2.6	3.6	2.0	3.1
60+	1.4	2.0	1.1	1.4

Sources: The ratios for Athens–Piraeus and Mykonos are from Hionidou (1995: 292). For Syros, the civil registration records were used.

ages and especially young boys. This is not obvious in childhood, that is at ages 0–14, where the ratio of male to female deaths is almost identical to that of the pre-famine period. If some preference for males did exist, then this concealed a further physiological/biological disadvantage for them. Moreover, one explanation that is usually provided for the relatively low mortality of females does not hold for Syros. It has been argued that due to an early reduction in conceptions, the number of pregnant and breast feeding women during famine is low and these women are less vulnerable than would otherwise have been the case (see e.g. Dyson 1991: 294). On Syros, fertility did not decline significantly during the famine and thus young adult women were as vulnerable as in 'normal' times. Also, during the famine women on Syros and Mykonos were breast feeding, and for longer durations than in non-famine conditions (Halares 1997: vol. 2, 323; and vol. 1, 125).

MORTALITY BY CAUSE

The question of what causes death during a famine is probably one of the most significant, yet for many famines it remains unanswered. However, in the case of Syros, a cause of death—occasionally, a secondary cause as well—was recorded in virtually all death certificates throughout the period covered by this study. The overwhelming majority of causes during the famine were assigned by seven—most of them municipal—doctors, although no less than 21 doctors certified some deaths at the time.[22]

An overall absence of epidemics during the famine was indicated in the *WHO* account of health in Greece during World War II (Anon 1942–4: 664). Similar to the famines of Mykonos and Athens/Piraeus, the overwhelming majority of deaths on

---

[22] They do not seem to have followed a specific cause of death classification that I am aware of. It is interesting to note that each doctor seems to have had some 'preferences' regarding the terms used. For example, the Greek for 'general exhaustion' was the preferred term used by Alivizatos, whereas Douratsos used extensively the term meaning 'lack of food'.

Table 9.3. *The Main Causes of Death during the Famine and their Percentage Contribution to Overall Mortality, Syros, 1941–2*

Cause	Percentage
Starvation, hunger oedema, general exhaustion, cachexia	70.3
Diarrhoea, enteritis, gastro-enteritis, dysentery	5.0
Old age related causes	4.4
Tuberculosis	4.1
Typhus	0.1
Typhoid fever	0.1
No cause stated	0.0

Source: Civil registration records of Syros.

Syros—70.3 per cent—were attributed either to literal starvation, hunger oedema, general exhaustion, cachexia, or other associated causes (Table 9.3). (For Mykonos and Athens/Piraeus, see Hionidou 1995: 293–4; Skouras *et al.* 1991: 291; Valaoras 1946: 221.) There is an abundance of references from oral and literary accounts of the time about the widespread oedema and swollen bellies (*Syriana Grammata* 1991: 249, oral account of a doctor; Halares 1997: vol. 2, 127). Along similar lines, the director of the Cycladic public health centre on Hermoupolis stressed the large numbers of civilians suffering from 'cachexia and general weakening and whose health has been damaged to an almost irreversible point' (Archives of Cyclades, Municipal Archive, I/Demosia Ygeia/Eksanthematikos tufos, no 369, letter dated 15 April 1942). He also mentioned that during the previous month many cases of vitamin deficiency, scorbuto, and pellagra had appeared. Moreover, the municipal authority of Hermoupolis had created a special unit for 'those suffering from oedema' for whom medical care was provided by the municipal doctors as well as some additional food.

The second most important registered cause of death (either primary or secondary) was 'diarrhoea'. There were only three deaths from typhus during the famine period. Although there is an abundance of references to the poor state of hygiene, clothing and housing of the poor, the cleanliness of the town streets, and the dominance of lice, no references to any major epidemics have been traced in the archival material, in the local newspaper, or in existing oral accounts (Similar references can be found for Athens/Piraeus: Junod 1942: 15, Ntelopoulos 1987: 34; Reader Zervos 1991: 64). For both Syros and Athens/Piraeus, there are many references from secondary sources about the occurrence of typhus, in the spring of 1942 in Athens and in the summer of 1943 on Syros (Valaoras 1946: 221; *Syriana Grammata* 1991: 226, an oral account of a person who went through typhus). But neither of the two outbreaks seems to have been particularly deadly. The quick reaction of the public health services of both the government and on Syros must have been partly responsible for this. As early as November 1941, the major hospital in Hermoupolis offered free vaccination against typhus (Archives of Cyclades, Municipal Archive, I/Demosia Ygeia/Eksanthematikos tufos, no 2277 letter to the Mayor). Not surprisingly, 'those who happily proceeded to have it were the middle and upper classes, but not the working classes among whom are most of those suffering' from typhus (Archives of Cyclades, Municipal Archive, I/Demosia Ygeia/Eksanthematikos tufos, no 2277 letter to the Mayor dated 21 December 1943). Thus, the director of the public health centre on Syros requested the Mayor to inform the public that vaccination would be freely available from all municipal doctors rather than at the hospital.

To summarize, it is clear from the above that the apparent absence of major epidemics in Greece during the 1941–2 famine—suggested by oral accounts, diaries, and the published material of the time—seems to be valid. As a contemporary observer in Athens remarked 'the hygiene situation ... was so satisfactory during the winter [of 1941–2] and ... no epidemics of the ones the people were afraid of occurred until the end of May, when typhus made a short appearance' (Milliex 1982: 86).

Interestingly, for Syros and Greece in general, there are ample references in secondary sources to extremely high rates of TB prevalence immediately after the war. (For Athens/Piraeus see Skouras *et al.* 1991: 293–5.[23]) For Syros, 20–25 per cent of the population was quoted as suffering from TB in 1946 (*Tharros*, 10 December 1946). This issue remains to be examined using not only the death certificates, but also the hospital records for Hermoupolis.

DISCUSSION

The findings of this chapter enhance those for Mykonos and Athens/Piraeus.

The effect of the famine on the fertility of Syros was very similar to that observed on Mykonos, that is, a lack of any significant decline in conceptions immediately prior to the famine when food scarcity was already evident. This suggests that the cause of an early response—when such a response occurs—is entirely due to behavioural rather than physiological reasons. What the Syros data allow us to observe is the reaction of the population in a subsequent instance when famine was imminent: there was an immediate response through a substantial decline in conceptions as soon as food started becoming scarce. On this second occasion, the population, having already acquired a 'knowledge' of famine from the previous instance, responded immediately, even though the second 'famine' was of a much smaller scale.

The excess mortality of males on Syros has been established, thus confirming not only oral accounts, but also the Mykonos and Athens/Piraeus findings. Males seem to have succumbed more, but they also succumbed earlier in the famine than did females. Interestingly, males comprised 65–67 per cent of all deaths during the first six months of the famine in each location. Young adult males seem to have experienced higher relative mortality increases during the famine. A possible contributory reason for this may have been the general weakening of the Greek soldiers because of the lack

---

[23] According to a survey conducted by the Greek Red Cross in Athens, 19 per cent were found infected among those examined in the period 1 September 1942 to 31 December 1943. In a second survey that took place between 1 July 1945 and 30 April 1946, 51 per cent were found to be infected.

of sufficient food provisions during the period of combat, and also because many of them had to return home on foot from the country's northern borders (Hoffmann 1989: 77). Moreover, once they were back they joined the ranks of the unemployed and became members of one of the most vulnerable social groups (Halares 1997: vol. 2, 126, oral evidence). The absence of migration and the continuation of childbearing during the famine remove some of the reasons suggested by other studies for the sex differentials in mortality. The findings of this paper certainly point to a biological advantage of women during the early stages of acute famines.

The almost complete absence of epidemics and the attribution of almost three quarters of all deaths to literal starvation or associated causes is a rather unusual finding among famine studies, but not so where the Greek famine is concerned. The absence of any major epidemics during the Greek famine is well established. A question that may be raised concerns the sincerity of Greek doctors when reporting on the cause of death, given that the country was under foreign occupation. For Syros, there is no evidence in the examined archival material that there was any pressure from the Italian Occupation authorities or from the Italian-friendly Mayor in 'manipulating' circumstances. Instead, it seems to have been a rather 'laissez faire' situation. Even in the official newspaper of the Occupation authorities no such effort was seriously made. When the Mayor was asked by the Italian administrator to submit daily accounts of deaths, because of the immense increase in mortality, he presented the total number of deaths as well as the cause of death for all causes except those clearly associated with starvation (Archives of Cyclades, Italian Archive, 209, various letters dated January 1942). The picture that emerges is one of detachment between the Greek municipal officials, such as those who were concerned with the collection of vital statistics and the running of the hospitals, and those of the Occupation authorities. Even the Italian doctor, presumably of the occupying forces, who assigned the cause to a total of 14 deaths during the famine, reported two deaths as being due to 'cachexia' and 'marasmous'. Thus, I would be much more inclined to question the reported causes of death in famine situations where the government, for one reason or another, has a clear motive to suppress the reporting of starvation as a cause of death, such as in the cases of historical Indian famines or the Ukrainian famines of the 1930s.

Finally, in this chapter the vulnerability of urban populations to such crisis situations has also been revealed. The case of Hermoupolis is somewhat exceptional within Greece, in that for historical reasons its population did not have any access to land in the countryside. The result was a much longer duration of the famine than would otherwise have applied.

References

Anon (1942–44), 'Health in Europe: Greece', *Bulletin of the Health Organisation. League of Nations*, X: 662–4.

Argenti, P. (1966), *The Occupation of Chios by the Germans and their Administration of the Island, 1941–44*, Cambridge: Cambridge University Press.

Black, M. (1992), *A Cause for Our Times: Oxfam, the First 50 Years*, Oxford: Oxfam and Oxford University Press.
D'Agata, C. (1942), 'Nuzialità e natalità in Grecia nel periodo precedente la seconda guerra mondiale', *Genus*, 5(3–4): 103–18.
De Bernieres, L. (1994), *Captain Corelli's Mandolin*, London: Secker & Warburg.
Delivanis, D., and Cleveland, W. C. (1950), *Greek Monetary Developments 1939–1948*, Bloomington: Indiana University.
Demathas, Z. (1989), 'H ekselikse vasikon megethon tes ellenikes oikonomias, 1935–1939 (The evolution of basic indicators of Greek economy, 1935–1939)', in H. Fleischer and N. Svoronos (eds.), *H Ellada 1936–44. Diktatoria, Katoche, Antistase. Praktika A Diethnous Sunedriou Sunchrones Istorias. (Greece 1936–44. Dictatorship, Occupation, Resistance. Proceedings of the First International Conference on Modern History)*, Athens: Morfotiko institouto ATE, 145–59.
Diamond, W. (1947), *Agriculture and Food in Greece*, UNRRA, Operational Analysis Paper 19.
Doxiadis, K. (*c.*1945), *The Sacrifices of Greece in the Second World War*, Athens.
Drakakes, A. T. (1945), 'Gegonota kai sumperasmata (Events and conclusions)', *Eleutheria* 35: 1.
Dyson, T. (1991), 'On the demography of South Asian famines, Part II', *Population Studies*, 45(2): 279–97.
Fleischer, H. (1986), *Stemma kai svastika: H Ellada tes katoches kai tes antistases 1941–1944 (Crown and Swastika: Greece of Occupation and Resistance, 1941–1944)*, Athens: Papazeses.
—— and Svoronos, N. (eds.) (1989), *H Ellada 1936–44. Diktatoria, Katoche, Antistase. Praktika A Diethnous Sunedriou Sunchrones Istorias. (Greece 1936–44. Dictatorship, Occupation, Resistance. Proceedings of the First International Conference on Modern History)*, Athens: Morfotiko institouto ATE.
Halares, D. N. (1997), *Ta katochika (On the Occupation)*, 2 Volumes, Athens: Vogiatzis.
Helger, B. (ed.) (1949), *Ravitaillement de la Grèce pendant l'occupation 1941–1944 et pendant les cinq mois après la libération*, Athens: Societé Hellénique d'éditions.
Hionidou, V. (1993), 'The Demography of a Greek Island, Mykonos 1859–1959: A Family Reconstitution Study', Ph.D., University of Liverpool.
—— (1995), 'The Demography of a Greek Famine: Mykonos, 1941–1942', *Continuity and Change*, 10(2): 279–99.
—— (1998), 'The Adoption of Fertility Control on Mykonos, 1879–1959: Stopping, Spacing or Both?', *Population Studies*, 52: 67–83.
Hoffmann, P. (1989), 'Roncalli in the Second World War: Peace Initiatives, the Greek Famine and the Persecution of the Jews', *Journal of Ecclesiastical History*, 40(1): 74–99.
Hondros, J. (1969), 'German Occupation of Greece 1941–44', Ph.D., Vanderbilt University.
—— (1983), *Occupation and Resistance, The Greek Agony 1941–44*, New York: Pella Pub Co.
Iatrides, J. O. (ed.) (1980), *Ambassador MacVeagh Reports: Greece, 1933–1947*, Princeton: Princeton University Press.
Junod, A. (1942), 'Rapport sur la situation en Grèce', 31 January 1942, Public Records Office, FO371/32460.
Kardases, V. (1987), *Syros. Staurodromi tes Anatolikes Mesogeiou, 1832–1857 (Syros. Crossroads of Eastern Mediterranean Sea, 1832–1857)*, Athens: Morfotiko idruma Ethnikes Trapezes.
Kazamias, G. A. (1990), 'Allied Policy Towards Occupied Greece: The 1941–42 Famine', DPhil, University of Bradford.

Kitsikis, D. (1969), 'La famine en Grèce (1941–42). Les conséquences politiques', *Revue d' Histoire de la Deuxième Guerre Mondiale*, 74: 17–41.

—— (1977), *Ellas kai ksenoi, 1919–1967 (Greece and Foreigners, 1919–1967)*, Athens: Estia.

Koliou, N. (1985), *Agnostes ptuches katoches kai antistases 1941–44 (Unknown Aspects of Occupation and Resistance)*, Volos: Nitsa Koliou.

Kolodny, E. (1969), 'Ermoupolis-Syros. Gennesis kai exelixis mias ellenikes nesiotikes poleos (Hermoupolis-Syros. The birth and evolution of a Greek island town)', *Epeteris Etaireias Kukladikon Meleton*, H: 249–86.

Laiou-Thomadakis, A. (1980), 'The Politics of Hunger: Economic Aid to Greece, 1943–45', *Journal of Hellenic Diaspora*, VII: 27–42.

League of Nations (1944), *Food Rationing and Supply 1943/44*, Geneva: League of Nations.

Loukos, C. (1994), 'La petite ville face a la grande: Le cas d'Ano Syra aux XIXe siecle', *Ariadne*, 7: 151–64.

—— (1998), 'Thanatoi apo peina ste Syro, 1941–44. Muthoi kai pragmatikotetes (Deaths from Hunger on Syros, 1941–44. Myths and Reality)', *Deltio Kentrou Ereunes tes Istorias tou Neoterou Ellenismou*, 1: 191–202.

Maharatna, A. (1996), *The Demography of Famines. An Indian Historical Perspective*, Delhi: Oxford University Press.

Mazower, M. (1991), *Greece and the Inter-war Economic Crisis*, Oxford: Clarendon Press.

—— (1993), *Inside Hitler's Greece, The Experience of Occupation 1941–44*, New Haven and London: Yale University Press.

Milliex, R. (1982), *Emerologio kai marturies tou polemou kai tes katoches (Diary of the War and the Occupation)*, Athens: Themelio.

Ntelopoulos, K. (ed.) (1987), *To emerologio katoches tou Minou Dounia (The Diary of Occupation of Minos Dounias)*, Athens: Estia.

Papastratis, P. (1984), *British Policy Towards Greece during the Second World War, 1941–1944*, Cambridge: Cambridge University Press.

Reader Zervos, S. (1991), *One Woman's War. A Diary of an English Woman Living in Occupied Greece 1939–1945*, Athens: Athens Centre Academic Press.

Richter, H. (1975), *1936–1946: Duo epanastaseis kai antepanastaseis sten Ellada (Two Revolutions and Counter-revolutions in Greece)*, Athens: Exantas.

Roussos, N. (1946), *Ta apomnemoneumata enos kandilaptou (The Memoirs of a Verger)*, Syros.

Skouras, F., Chatzedemos, A., Kaloutses, A., and Papademetriou, G. (1991), *H psuchopathologia tes peinas, tou fovou kai tou agxous (The Psychopathology of Hunger, Fear and Stress)*, Athens: Odusseas (Originally published in 1947).

Sosnowski, K. (1962), *The Tragedy of Children Under Nazi Rule*, Poland: Zachodnia Agencja Prasowa.

Stefanou, M. P. (1973), *Syrianes selides (Pages of Syros)*, 2 Volumes, Athens.

Theotokas, G. (1982), *Tetradia emerologiou (1939–1953) (Diary pages 1939–1953)*, Athens: Estia.

Thomadakis, S. (1981), 'Black Markets, Inflation, and Force in The Economy of Occupied Greece', in J. O. Iatrides (ed.), *Greece in the 1940s: A Nation in Crisis*, Hanover: University Press of New England, 61–80.

Traulos, I., and Kokkou, A. (1980), *Ermoupolis. H demiourgia mias neas polis ste Syro stis arxes tou 19ou aiona (Hermoupolis. The Creation of a New City on Syros at the Beginning of the 19th Century)*, Athens: Emporike Trapeza tes Elladas.

Tsouderos, E. I. (1946), *O episitismos 1941–1944 (The Provision of Supplies 1941–1944)*, Athens: Papazeses.

Valaoras, V. G. (1946), 'Some Effects of the Famine on the Population of Greece', *Milbank Memorial Fund Quarterly*, 24(4): 215–34.

—— (1960), 'A Reconstruction of the Demographic History of Modern Greece', *Milbank Memorial Fund Quarterly*, 38: 115–39.

—— (1980), 'National Primary Socio-economic Data Structures. V: Greece', *International Social Science Journal*, 32(2): 343–58.

Varvaressos, K. (1943), *Greece's Ability to Pay*, First UNRRA council session.

10

The Demographic Impact of a Mild Famine in an African City: The Case of Antananarivo, 1985–7

MICHEL GARENNE, DOMINIQUE WALTISPERGER,
PIERRE CANTRELLE, AND OSÉE RALIJAONA

Famines have been recurrent throughout human history. Their occurrence has diminished only recently because of increases in food production, improved management of food stocks, the diminishing isolation of most parts of the world, greater international trade, better and faster transport, as well as increased international awareness, higher sensitivity towards human rights, and greater international solidarity. However, even in the second half of the twentieth century severe famines occurred in South Asia, China, and sub-Saharan Africa. If earlier famines were primarily due to climatic factors, plant diseases and poor crisis management, recent famines seem mostly to have been due to serious mismanagement by the state (i.e. bad governance) and to the voluntary or forced isolation of a country—often the consequence of international or civil war. The latter scenario applies particularly apropos famines in sub-Saharan Africa during the past quarter of a century.

The demographic impact of major famines has been well documented. In relation to nineteenth-century Europe, key studies have dealt with the 1846–50 famine in Ireland (Boyle and Ó Gráda 1986), the 1866–8 famine in Sweden (Pitkänen and Mielke 1993), and the local famines during World War II in Holland and the Warsaw Ghetto (Livi-Bacci 1993). The largest famines in the twentieth century occurred as a consequence of severe mismanagement in the so-called 'communist' countries—in Russia during the early days of Stalinism (Blum *et al.* 1997; Livi-Bacci 1993) and in China during the Great Leap Forward of 1959–61 (Kane 1988; Peng 1987). A large number of studies have dealt with recurrent famines in the Indian Subcontinent (Alamgir 1980; Chowdhury and Chen 1977; Das 1949; Dyson 1991; Sen 1981). Work has also been conducted on more recent crises in sub-Saharan Africa, such as the 1973–4 famine in the Sahel (Caldwell *et al.* 1988) and events in southern Sudan (de Waal 1989), Malawi (Vaughan 1987), and Somalia (Seaman 1987).

Beyond the total number of deaths attributable to famines, several demographic issues have been debated—in particular, as regards the age and sex patterns of famine mortality, and to a lesser extent the causes of famine deaths. In absolute numbers famines seem to affect primarily the young and the elderly, changing the level, but not the overall age pattern of mortality. However, it is often found that relative increases in mortality are higher among young adults than among other age groups. In her comprehensive study of famine mortality by gender that is found elsewhere in this book, Macintyre finds fairly consistent evidence for excess male mortality—that is, a relative advantage for females during famines—even when the opposite applies before and after the crisis. Changes in cause of death patterns during famines have been poorly studied. However, beyond severe malnutrition and exhaustion, attention has been drawn to increases in deaths from certain infectious and parasitic diseases which are closely linked to nutritional status—in particular diarrhoeal diseases, and two other ailments that are typical of famines: osteomalacia (i.e. bone demineralization) and hypothermia. In addition, it has been a recurrent observation that malaria makes a come-back after famines in tropical countries. This has been seen in India and in the Sahel after the droughts of 1973–4 and 1983–4. Such a resurgence of malaria may be due to epidemiological factors (e.g. populations of mosquitoes are reconstituted when the rains return after a drought), but it may also be linked to decreased resistance of the people after a prolonged period of low food intake.

If major famines have fascinated researchers, very little work has been conducted on the demographic impact of mild famines. Yet such food shortages have commonly existed in rural areas prior to industrialization. And nowadays they seem to occur even in urban areas of developing countries, and especially amongst the most deprived groups of people, as a result of poverty, changing economic policies, fluctuating prices, and other causes of economic change. Consequently, the aim of the present study is to document a mild famine and its demographic impact in Antananarivo, the capital city of Madagascar.

HISTORICAL CONTEXT

Madagascar is a fairly large island, about the size of France, located in the Indian Ocean off the coast of Mozambique. It has been populated over the past 10 centuries or so by people coming from both Indonesia and Africa, and it was colonized by France for a short period of time (1896–1960).

Since Independence in 1960 Madagascar has experienced a series of political crises, including several coups, student riots, and farmer rebellions. Its political regime has not been stable since Independence, and there have been major changes in both the country's political orientation and its economic policies. The first 12 years following Independence (i.e. 1960–71) were relatively stable politically, but with poor economic management this period ended with student and farmer riots. In the second period (i.e. 1972–83), power was assumed by a series of Marxist-like radicals, often arising out of the military. During this time, the country's official economic policy was modelled on that of China and Russia. This period also ended in a severe economic crisis with a serious rebellion by farmers in rural areas and radical protests among students in the cities. A third period started in 1984. This involved re-establishing links with Western countries (especially France), opening the economy to international trade, and the introduction of a series of economic reforms (i.e. structural adjustment policies) which were still proceeding during the late 1990s (Pottier 1993).

Since 1960 Madagascar's economic performance has been very poor (Pottier 1993). Macro-economic data suggest that the gross national product (GNP) per capita, corrected for parity purchasing power (PPP), declined by half between 1960 and 1995. Thus, the World Penn Table gives a figure of US$1,191 per capita in 1960 and only US$608 in 1992 (measured in constant 1985 prices). However, the fall has not been steady. During the first phase (i.e. 1960–71) GNP per capita stayed at about the same level; during the second phase (1971–83), it fell by about a third; and in the third phase (1983–92), it declined by about a further quarter. These macro-economic estimates have been confirmed by an analysis of household expenditure in the capital city. Using various consumption surveys, Ravelosoa and Roubaud (1996) have estimated that household consumption declined by about 45 per cent in constant prices over the period 1960–95. They also found little change during the first period (i.e. between 1961 and 1969), but a major decline in the 1970s and 1980s which seems to have continued until 1995.

Falling incomes translated into declining levels of food consumption in Antananarivo. Although the share of household income devoted to food increased significantly, from 32 per cent in 1961 to 48 per cent in 1993–4, total food consumption fell. Thus, over the period 1961–95 consumption of rice—the main staple food—declined by 21 per cent, that of bread by 42 per cent, that of fruit by 32 per cent, that of vegetables by 40 per cent, and that of meat by 51 per cent (Ravelosoa and Roubaud 1996). Not only did total food intake go down, but the quality and balance of the diet deteriorated too. As a result, total calorific intake was estimated at only 1,661 kcal in 1995, that is, 21 per cent below the minimum international recommendation. A large part of the population of Antananarivo was therefore living far below international food intake norms, indeed quite close to those required for bare survival.

In addition to these long-term declines in income and food intake, there were major fluctuations in food prices which probably further worsened the nutritional status of the population for short periods. Unfortunately, these short-term changes in nutritional status have not been studied. However, a time series of market prices for rice is available for Antananarivo. Of particular significance is a major price rise lasting for about 2 years—from July 1985 to June 1987. Outside this period, the price of rice averaged about 217 units of the local currency unit. The price started to increase steeply in July 1985 and reached 640 units in December, that is, about three times above the usual price. Given that in these years about 47 per cent of the average household budget was used to buy food, and that about 35–45 per cent of the food budget was devoted to rice, it is clear that many households were not able to cope with the price increase. We do not have a breakdown of income by social group; however, it can be anticipated that among the poorest strata of the population the price increase far exceeded their economic capacity to pay.

In addition to the food crisis, Madagascar experienced a major surge in malaria at about the same time. The disease was highly prevalent on the island before 1945, but it came near to eradication after the major anti-malarial campaigns of the late 1940s and the early 1950s. As a result, malaria mortality remained very low until about

1983. However, the incidence of malaria started to increase markedly in 1984 and peaked in 1988. Subsequently, the incidence of and mortality from the disease have decreased somewhat and stabilized, but at much higher levels than was the case prior to 1984.

As will be seen below, these broad economic, nutritional, and epidemiological changes are reflected quite clearly in the mortality statistics of Antananarivo.

DEMOGRAPHIC DATA

Mortality data for Antananarivo—a city of about three quarters of a million people in 1995—come from the vital registration system (VRS). Vital registration in Madagascar was started in the nineteenth century at the initiative of Queen Ranavalona II following a severe epidemic of plague. The system was improved during the period of French colonization and today registration of births and deaths is known to be virtually complete in the large cities, although less so in rural areas. Unfortunately, the vital registration data are poorly documented and little analysed.

For Antananarivo city, the research team of Cantrelle, Ralijaona, and Waltisperger organized the data entry of all death certificates for the whole period from 1976 to 1995 with financial assistance from UNICEF and Le Centre Français sur la Population et le Développement. Data from the later part of the period (1984–95) have been documented and analysed in a recent publication (Waltisperger et al. 1998). However, the data used for the present analysis cover the whole period 1976–95.

Death rates were computed by dividing registered deaths (by age and sex) by the population at risk. For the numerators, only deaths registered in Antananarivo of people resident in the city were kept for the final analysis (i.e. about 82 per cent of the total deaths registered). Denominators were estimated from the two available censuses—that is, those of 1975 and 1993. Populations by age and sex were interpolated between these two enumerations by assuming a constant rate of growth for each 5-year age group and separately for each sex. The data used here differ only slightly from the earlier estimates of Waltisperger et al. (1998). The hypothesis of a constant rate of population growth is consistent with what is known about the population dynamics of the city. Annual age specific death rates were computed for each of the 20 years between 1976 and 1995. Yearly life tables were then computed by applying standard formulae to the age specific death rates.

Causes of death were coded using the ninth revision of the International Classification of Diseases. A total of 1,970 individual causes of death were identified in the registration records and these were then grouped in 60 smaller categories for purposes of analysis. However, most of the tables presented here are based upon an even smaller number of grouped categories.

Standard errors were computed for certain life table values—in particular, the estimated life expectancies. The statistical testing of differences was systematic. Standard formulae were used to test for differences between means (for life expectancy), probabilities (for quotients), and risk ratios (for sex ratios and ratios of death rates).

DATA QUALITY

As previously noted by Waltisperger *et al.* (1998) vital registration in Antananarivo appears to be virtually complete, both for births and for deaths. However, as an independent check child mortality estimates relating to the age group 0–4 years from the VRS were compared with estimates obtained from the two demographic and health surveys (DHS) which were conducted in Madagascar in 1992 and 1997. The DHS estimates were recomputed by us for quinquennia ending in the years 0 and 5 during the 15 years prior to each DHS. The results are presented in Table 10.1. The estimates from vital registration are always slightly higher than those of the DHS, although most differences are not significant due to the small number of deaths that were captured by the DHS (with the exception of the earliest period of the second DHS (i.e. 1981–5)). In fact, it seems that the vital registration data permit an estimate of the level of underestimation in each DHS survey. Thus both surveys appear to have been virtually complete apropos the 5-year period immediately preceding the survey. The 1992 DHS seems to have missed only a few deaths in earlier periods: about 7 per cent during the period 6–10 years before the survey, and 12 per cent in the period 11–15 years prior to the survey. However, the 1997 DHS seems to have missed somewhat more deaths: about 10 per cent in the period 6–10 years before the survey, and 25 per cent in the period 11–15 years before. In any case, there is no evidence of under registration of child deaths in the vital registration data for Antananarivo.

The quality of the data on cause of death is harder to gauge—since there is no single 'gold standard' for purposes of comparison and also because each population has its own cause of death profile and associated trends. However, in general, it can be said that the cause of death profile indicated by the registration data for Antananarivo appears to be consistent with what is known about the city. And the major recorded

Table 10.1. *Comparison of Death Rates Computed from Vital Registration Data with Estimates Obtained from the DHS of 1992 and 1997, Antananarivo*

Period	DHS		VRS		Comparison (DHS/VRS)	
	q(5)	Deaths	q(5)	Deaths	Ratio	t-Test
DHS, 1992						
76–80	0.121	52	0.137	10,767	0.88	−0.912
81–5	0.162	79	0.174	15,115	0.93	−0.624
86–90	0.132	64	0.136	12,924	0.97	−0.248
DHS, 1997						
81–5	0.130	65	0.174	15,115	0.75	−2.338*
86–90	0.122	67	0.136	12,924	0.90	−0.900
91–5	0.111	72	0.100	10,309	1.11	0.861

Note: The comparisons relate to the 15-year time periods prior to each of the surveys.
*$P < 0.05$.

epidemics (e.g. of measles, whooping cough, and malaria) show up clearly in the cause of death trends. The proportion of deaths of undetermined cause was moderate (8.4 per cent for children, 8.9 per cent for adults aged 15–59 years, and 18.5 per cent for the elderly (i.e. those aged 60+)). Only one registered cause of death was a source of concern: 'Alveolitis of the jaws' (ICD-9 code = 526.5). In developed countries, this is a rare cause of death, usually resulting from complications arising after the extraction of teeth (often the third molar). However, this was clearly not the situation in Antananarivo. Instead, this cause of death appeared in large numbers in the death records, mostly for children, but it was also common for young adults. And this cause was epidemic—being concentrated during the 1985–7 crisis. At the moment we do not have an explanation for the prominence of 'alveolitis of the jaws' in the cause of death data for Antananarivo. But a preliminary investigation suggests that it may have been a consequence of the severe malnutrition that was experienced during the period. A similar disease occurs to animals when they eat inappropriate foods, such as tough plants. What people may have eaten during the 1985–7 food crisis is unclear and needs further investigation. However, this cause has been added to that of malnutrition in the following analysis.

RESULTS

Antananarivo experienced major changes in mortality over the 20 years from 1976 to 1995 (see Table 10.2). Between 1976 and 1984, mortality increased slowly but steadily, more for children than for adults, and among adults more for men than for women. Over this period life expectancy for both sexes combined dropped by about 6 years, from an estimated value of 59.7 years in 1976 to 53.6 years in 1984. The short period of 1985–7 was a time of deep crisis, both for children and for adults, and there was a further rapid drop in life expectancy of about 5 years during the peak crisis year (average life expectancy was only 49.0 years in 1986). The following years (1988–91) were a time of rapid recovery, with estimated life expectancy reaching 60.0 years in 1991. The four years of 1992–5 saw stagnation, with the last estimated value for both sexes combined being about 60 years in 1995. In summary, during the final three years of the period (i.e. 1993–5) life expectancy in Antananarivo was about the same as it had been during the first 3 years (i.e. 1976–8).

The impact of the 1985–7 famine

During the main famine years of 1985–7 life expectancy was far below the prior declining trend ($P < 0.05$), indicating a very serious mortality crisis. Compared to the baseline period (here taken as an average of both of the periods 1976–8 and 1989–95) mortality in 1986 was 57 per cent higher for males and 41 per cent higher for females. The highest mortality increase for both sexes occurred at ages 30–34 (+161 per cent for males, and +49 per cent for females) and at ages 5–9 (+161 per cent for males, and +146 per cent for females).

Table 10.2. *Trends in Demographic Estimates Obtained from Vital Registration Data, Antananarivo, 1976–95*

Year	Life expectancy at birth e(0) (years)		Mortality of children 0–14 years, $_{15}q_0$		Mortality of adults 15–59 years, $_{45}q_{15}$	
	Males	Females	Males	Females	Males	Females
1976	58.2	61.3	0.137	0.123	0.274	0.230
1977	57.2	60.6	0.149	0.135	0.277	0.237
1978	57.8	61.1	0.135	0.120	0.301	0.224
1979	52.5	56.5	0.187	0.165	0.344	0.281
1980	54.3	58.0	0.176	0.154	0.303	0.242
1981	52.8	56.9	0.197	0.178	0.330	0.250
1982	52.6	57.5	0.184	0.171	0.353	0.239
1983	51.9	58.2	0.208	0.178	0.326	0.224
1984	50.8	56.5	0.192	0.176	0.380	0.261
1985	47.3	54.8	0.216	0.198	0.437	0.259
1986	44.9	53.2	0.216	0.196	0.511	0.316
1987	51.3	56.8	0.160	0.147	0.430	0.308
1988	53.2	56.3	0.175	0.168	0.344	0.288
1989	56.7	60.3	0.135	0.132	0.314	0.252
1990	55.6	61.5	0.140	0.125	0.362	0.231
1991	57.5	62.6	0.121	0.109	0.332	0.240
1992	57.5	62.9	0.114	0.098	0.346	0.237
1993	55.9	61.1	0.130	0.120	0.348	0.241
1994	58.8	63.3	0.113	0.105	0.301	0.217
1995	56.9	62.1	0.110	0.104	0.371	0.237

Comparing the observed number of deaths in 1985–7 with the expected number—that is, those that would have happened on the assumption of the mortality profile of the baseline period—allows us to estimate the net effect of the crisis, that is, the mortality attributable to the famine (see Table 10.3). The difference between the observed and the expected number of deaths indicates an excess of 7,636. A majority of these deaths occurred among children aged under 15 years (3,873) and among adults aged 15–59 years (2,625).

Sex differences

For broad age groups Table 10.4 summarizes the relative increases in deaths and changes in the sex ratio of deaths during 1985–7 compared to the baseline period. In a little more detail, during the year 1986 the difference between male and female mortality increased compared to the baseline period, and was the greatest among those aged 30–34 years. The sex ratio of death rates (i.e. male death rate/female death rate) increased from 1.32 to 1.81 among those aged 15–44 years ($P < 0.05$), indicating

Table 10.3. *Estimates of the Excess Number of Deaths Caused by the 1985–7 Crisis, Antananarivo*

Age group	Males			Females			Both sexes, excess
	Observed	Expected	Excess	Observed	Expected	Excess	
Children 0–14 years	5,526	3,470	2,056	4,889	3,072	1,817	3,873
Adults 15–59 years	4,749	2,815	1,934	2,798	2,107	691	2,625
Adults 60+ years	2,948	2,234	714	2,702	2,278	424	1,138
Total	13,223	8,519	4,704	10,389	7,457	2,932	7,636

Note: Observed = number of deaths registered; expected = number of deaths in the population if mortality had been that of the baseline period (i.e. 1976–8 + 1989–95).

Table 10.4. *Relative Increase in Mortality and Sex Ratios of Deaths during the 1985–7 Crisis, Antananarivo*

Age group	Relative increase in deaths (crisis/baseline)			Sex ratio of deaths (male/female)		
	Males	Females	Both sexes	Crisis mortality	Baseline mortality	Excess mortality
Children 0–14 years	1.59	1.59	1.59	1.13	1.13	1.13
Adults 15–59 years	1.69	1.33	1.53	1.70	1.34	2.80
Adults 60+ years	1.32	1.19	1.25	1.09	0.98	1.68
Total	1.55	1.39	1.48	1.27	1.14	1.60

that excess mortality was higher for men than for women during the crisis. The sex ratio of death rates also increased among adults aged 45 and over, although to a lesser extent (from 1.45 during the baseline period to 1.67 during the crisis years, $P < 0.05$). There was virtually no change in the sex ratio of death rates among children (which was 1.13 in the baseline period and 1.14 in the crisis years).

Similarly, the excess number of deaths was much higher among adult males than among adult females. Thus as Table 10.3 shows computation of deaths attributable to the famine in 1985–7 compared to the baseline experience indicates that three times more young adult men died (1,934 deaths) than did young adult women (691 deaths), whereas the numbers were of similar magnitude among children (2,056 boys and 1,817 girls). Of course, such excess male mortality among young adults is typical of famines.

Causes of death

The trend in mortality attributed to malnutrition on the death certificates reveals the nutritional crisis very clearly indeed (Fig. 10.1). Among adults, in particular,

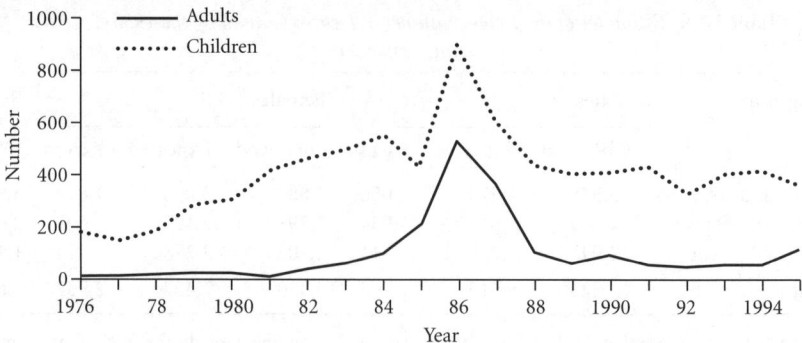

Figure 10.1. *Trends in Registered Deaths Attributed to Malnutrition, Antananarivo, 1976–95*
Source: Vital registration records.

deaths due to malnutrition were rarely recorded prior to 1984. But they increased dramatically thereafter and peaked in 1986 before then virtually disappearing after 1988. Among children deaths from malnutrition existed even in 1976–8, as is the case in most developing countries at such a level of mortality. However, they increased steadily from 1979 to 1984 and also peaked in 1986. Child deaths from malnutrition then declined quickly after the crisis year, and in 1991–5 regained the level experienced during the early 1980s. Many other causes of death also peaked in 1986—in particular, diarrhoeal diseases and acute respiratory infections, two conditions which are often closely associated with malnutrition.

The excess mortality during the 1985–7 food crisis, compared to the baseline period, can be decomposed by cause of death (Table 10.5). For children aged less than 15 years most of the increase can be attributed to malnutrition (41.9 per cent) and to related diarrhoeal diseases (25.8 per cent), acute respiratory infections (11.1 per cent) and other infectious and parasitic diseases (18.0 per cent). However, other causes contributed as well, although they were of lesser importance; in this group are violent deaths other than motor vehicle accidents (MVAs) (2.0 per cent), malaria (0.6 per cent), and tuberculosis (0.7 per cent). For adults (i.e. those aged 15 years and over) the picture was somewhat similar, with the largest share also being attributable to malnutrition (35.0 per cent) and its correlates like diarrhoeal diseases (23.4 per cent) and acute respiratory infections (10.6 per cent). Other diseases also played an important role among adults, in particular cardiovascular diseases (14.0 per cent), tuberculosis (7.6 per cent), malaria (3.4 per cent), and maternal mortality (1.8 per cent). As among children, violent deaths other than MVAs also contributed to excess mortality (3.5 per cent).

In summary, the 1985–7 crisis appears to have been primarily due to the direct effects of food shortage and its consequences for malnutrition, diarrhoeal diseases, acute respiratory infections, and other infectious and parasitic diseases. In addition, indirect effects relating to cardiovascular diseases, deaths from violence and maternal mortality also added to the overall picture for adults.

Table 10.5. *Causes of Death Responsible for the Mortality Increase in the 1985–7 Crisis, Antananarivo*

Causes of death	Number of deaths in 1985–7			(%)
	Observed	Expected	Excess	
Children aged 0–14 years				
Malnutrition	2,254	931	1,323	41.9
Diarrhoea, dysentery	2,389	1,575	814	25.8
Acute respiratory infections	1,417	1,067	350	11.1
Tuberculosis	70	47	23	0.7
Malaria	138	119	19	0.6
Other infectious and parasitic	908	341	568	18.0
Violent deaths (other than MVA)	272	209	63	2.0
Other and unknown	2,967	2,254	712	—
Total	10,415	6,542	3,873	100.0
Adults aged 15+ years				
Malnutrition	1,190	120	1,069	35.0
Diarrhoea, dysentery	1,137	421	716	23.4
Acute respiratory infections	872	547	324	10.6
Tuberculosis	509	278	231	7.6
Malaria	413	308	105	3.4
Other infectious and parasitic	146	127	19	0.6
Maternal causes	231	176	56	1.8
Cardiovascular diseases	3,505	3,078	426	14.0
Violent deaths (other than MVA)	612	504	108	3.5
Other and unknown	4,583	3,874	708	—
Total	13,197	9,434	3,763	100.0

The malaria epidemic

Malaria mortality in Antananarivo was very low until 1984. This was true both for children and for adults (Fig. 10.2). It then started to increase rapidly and peaked in 1988. Registered deaths from malaria then fell quickly, stabilizing at an intermediate level after about 1991. Malaria seems to have played only a minor role during the 1985–7 crisis. However, it seems to have played a big role in the mortality experienced during 1988 (see Table 10.6). Compared to the baseline period, in 1988 malaria accounted for 24.6 per cent of the excess mortality among children, and 69.3 per cent of the excess mortality among adults (i.e. those aged 15 years and over). Indeed, referring to the absolute numbers one can argue forcefully that virtually all of the excess adult mortality which occurred during 1988 (411 deaths) was attributable to malaria (Table 10.6).

In the three main epidemic years (i.e. 1987–9) malaria caused the deaths of 708 people (526 adults and 182 children). And the epidemic did not stop then; rather the disease remained an important cause of death during the period 1990–5.

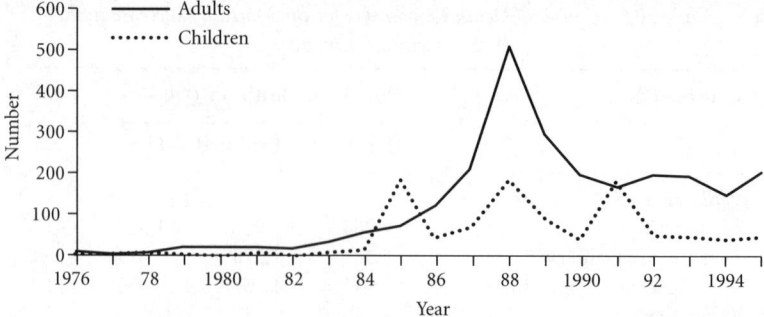

Figure 10.2. *Trends in Deaths from Malaria, Antananarivo, 1976–95*
Source: Vital registration records.

Table 10.6. *Causes of Death Responsible for the Mortality Increase in 1988, Antananarivo*

Causes of death	Number of deaths in 1988			(%)
	Observed	Expected	Excess	
Children 0–14 years				
Malaria	190	41	149	24.6
Malnutrition	474	322	152	25.2
Diarrhoea, dysentery	638	545	92	15.3
Acute respiratory infections	454	369	85	14.0
Tuberculosis	10	16	−6	−1.0
Other infectious and parasitic	248	118	130	21.4
Violent deaths (other than MVA)	75	72	3	0.5
Other and unknown	1,154	781	373	—
Total	3,242	2,264	978	100.0
Adults 15+ years				
Malaria	514	104	409	69.3
Malnutrition	117	40	77	13.0
Diarrhoea, dysentery	202	143	59	10.0
Maternal	105	60	46	7.7
Acute respiratory infections	168	186	−19	—
Tuberculosis	68	94	−26	—
Other infectious and parasitic	41	43	−2	—
Cardiovascular diseases	885	1,045	−160	—
Violent deaths (other than MVA)	160	171	−11	—
Other and unknown	1,458	1,420	38	—
Total	3,717	3,306	411	100.0

Excess mortality in the country as a whole

Similar trends in excess mortality in 1985–7 and in 1988 can also be seen in the DHS data for children aged less than 5 years of age—not only for Antananarivo, but also for the country as a whole. This indicates that both these crises were apparent nationwide. Unfortunately, however, detailed data by age, sex, and cause of death are not available for the rest of the country.

DISCUSSION

Madagascar presents a typical case of mismanagement and bad governance lasting for many years. Such was typical of the situation found in many African countries during the post-colonial era. However, decreases in GNP per capita and food intake were probably more severe in this country than was the case in many others. One result of this mismanagement was the 1985–7 famine, which severely hit the capital city. The famine seems to have occurred mostly as a consequence of a sharp increase in the price of rice—which was too rapid and pronounced for most households to be able to cope with. This happened at the time of price liberalization—that is, when government subsidies were stopped and the rice market was being left to the private sector after more than a decade of state control. The crisis lasted 2 years and it had major demographic consequences. It appears that no mechanism existed to help people cope with the price changes until a new equilibrium was reached.

Instances of economic changes leading to famine and excess deaths in a large city have rarely been documented. However, it is probable that similar developments have occurred in other locations, at least among the urban poor.

The 1985–7 food crisis in Antananarivo bears all the characteristics of famine mortality as observed elsewhere: in absolute numbers, more deaths occurred among young children; in relative terms, the greatest increase in mortality happened among young adults; there was a stronger mortality impact on males than on females, and in particular a much stronger impact on young men than on young women. Higher famine mortality among young men may be attributable to biological effects, in particular relating to male body composition which contains much less fat than that of females and may thereby provide males with less resistance to nutritional stress. That said, there may also be a behavioural component—for example, if in desperate situations men tend to move about more, or are more prone to adopt risky forms of behaviour.

Sex differences in mortality during famines merit greater attention. Of particular importance in the present case was the excess mortality of young men in 1985–7, followed by a period of their experiencing lower than expected mortality *vis-à-vis* females during 1988–9. This could be due to a 'harvesting effect', that is a selection of vulnerable males during the famine crisis. Other examples of sex selective harvesting effects have been documented for respiratory infections (such as the 1918 influenza), but they do not seem to have been described for circumstances of severe malnutrition.

During the 1985–7 crisis, other than deaths linked to malnutrition, the causes of death did not change with only a few exceptions. Maternal mortality increased, probably as a direct consequence of the food shortage. More surprisingly, violent deaths (other than MVAs) increased. This was primarily due to suicide and various types of poisoning. This may well be a consequence of situations of extreme poverty, where desperate people commit suicide, or where people in severe distress eat toxic foods. Excess mortality during 1985–7 was estimated at about 7,600 deaths. In relative terms the impact of this famine was comparable to that of the 1974–5 famine in Bangladesh which has been widely discussed. However, the Antananarivo famine has been largely ignored.

It is striking that malaria came back at about the same time in Madagascar's recent history. Although this may have been independent of the famine, there may have been some links. For instance, reorganization of the state and the public health system may have had consequences for various measures to control malaria. More importantly, organisms weakened by 2 years of food shortage may have been more receptive to malaria and this may have been conducive to an epidemic explosion.

Perhaps more striking still, the 1987–9 malaria epidemic, which killed about 700 people in the city in three years, has been well documented and studied. Indeed, several scientific publications and many articles in local and international newspapers have appeared on the subject. However, the more silent food shortage which killed perhaps 11 times more people has been ignored. News coverage and scientific publications do not always follow a demographic logic, although demographic numbers are widely used in the press. Diseases or causes of death which for some reasons are considered to be shameful tend to be ignored, another classic example being cholera in Africa.

Unfortunately, the overall economic situation in Madagascar does not inspire optimism, even though economic growth has been positive in later years (1996–8). A situation similar to the 1985–7 crisis could occur again, since the political circumstances of the country are far from stable and the economic situation remains fragile. That said, the market is freer now, the country is less isolated, and it is probably more able to cope with a crisis than was the case a decade or two ago. In order to mitigate the demographic impact of a possible future food shortage Madagascar will need to establish mechanisms to monitor economic and nutritional changes, and to organize assistance for the most deprived sections of the society. This will require recognition of the rights of the poor to a decent food intake, what Sen (1981) calls an 'entitlement'. Actions to mitigate the effect of famines have been described for more than two centuries, and used with some success in places like India. In this respect, recognition of the magnitude of the problem is critical to the organization of action. And denial is arguably the most serious difficulty which needs to be solved before a society can cope efficiently with such an important challenge to public health.

References

Alamgir, M. (1980), *Famine in South Asia: The Political Economy of Mass Starvation*, Cambridge, Mass.: Oelgeschlager, Gunn and Hain.

Blum, A., Ely, M., and Zakharov, S. (1992), 'Démographie Soviétique: 1920–1950, une redécouverte', *Annales de Démographie Historique*, 7: 7–22.

Boyle, P. B., and Ó Gráda, C. (1986), 'Fertility Trends, Excess Mortality and the Great Irish Famine', *Demography*, 23(4): 543–62.

Caldwell, J. C., Reddy, P. H., and Caldwell, P. (1988), *The Causes of Demographic Change*, Madison, Wisc.: University of Wisconsin Press.

Chowdhury, A. K. M., and Chen, L. C. (1977), 'The Dynamics of Contemporary Famine', in *Mexico International Population Conference, Volume 1*, Liège: International Union for the Scientific Study of Population.

Das, T. K. (1949), *The Bengal Famine of 1943 as Revealed in a Survey of the Destitutes in Calcutta*, Calcutta: Calcutta University Press.

de Waal, A. (1989), *Famine That Kills: Darfur, Sudan 1984–85*, Oxford: Clarendon Press.

Drèze, J., and Sen, A. (1989), *Hunger and Public Action*, Oxford: Clarendon Press.

Dyson, T. (1991), 'On the Demography of South Asian Famines', Parts 1 and 2, *Population Studies*, 45(5–26): 279–98.

Kane, P. (1988), *Famine in China: 1951–61, Demographic and Social Implications*, New York: St Martins Press.

Livi-Bacci, M. (1991), *Population and Nutrition. An Essay on European Demographic History*, Cambridge: Cambridge University Press.

—— (1993), 'On the Human Costs of Collectivization in the Soviet Union', *Population and Development Review*, 19(4): 743–66.

Ó Gráda, C. (1995), 'The Great Famine and Today's Famines', in *The Great Irish Famine*, Cathal Poiteir (ed.), Cork: Mercier Press.

Peng, X. (1987), 'Demographic Consequences of the Great Leap Forward in China's provinces', *Population and Development Review*, 13(4): 639–70.

Pitkänen, K. J., and Mielke, J. H. (1993), 'Age and Sex Differentials in Mortality During Two Nineteenth Century Population Crises', *European Journal of Population*, 9: 1–32.

Pottier, P. (1993), Madagascar: les traits marquants de son évolution macro-économique de 1960 à nos jours. Document de Travail No. 1993-02/T, DIAL, Paris.

Ravelosoa, R., and Roubaud, F., (1996), La dynamique de la consommation dans l'agglomération d'Antananarivo sur longue période (1960–1995), et les stratégies d'adaptation des ménages face à la crise. *Economie de Madagascar*, No. 1, Octobre 1996, 9–39.

Sen, A. (1981), *Poverty and Famines, An Essay on Entitlement and Deprivation*, Oxford: Oxford University Press.

Seaman, J. (1987), 'Famine Mortality in Ethiopia and Sudan', in *Proceedings of the IUSSP Seminar on Comparative Mortality Changes*, Youndé, Cameroon 19–23 October, London: Oxford University Press.

Vaughan, M. (1987), *The Story of an African Famine: Gender and Famine in Twentieth Century Malawi*, Cambridge: Cambridge University Press.

Waltisperger, D., Cantrelle, P., and Ralijaona, O. (1998), La mortalité à Antananarivo de 1984 à 1995, *Documents et Manuels du CEPED*, No. 7. Paris.

11

The Frequency of Famines as Demographic Correctives in the Japanese Past

OSAMU SAITO

In the first edition of his book *An Essay on the Principle of Population*, Thomas Robert Malthus regarded famines as 'the last, the most dreadful' of all positive checks on population growth (Malthus 1798: 51–2). In its later editions, however, he became concerned more with factual aspects of the matter, especially with the issue of how frequently famines occurred in relation to plagues and other epidemics. Using data assembled by Dr Thomas Short, he noted in the sixth edition of his book that the periodic returns of epidemics were 'at the interval of about 4 1/2 years', while the mean interval between the visits of great famines and dearths was 'about 7 1/2 years'. Malthus suggested that 'plagues, violent diseases, and famines have been certainly mitigated, and have become less frequent' than in past times (Malthus 1826: II, 308 and 315). It is not quite certain if the later Malthus jettisoned his earlier view that famines were a mighty corrective to overpopulation, but few will question the later Malthus' stance that the frequency of famines was one of the factors accounting for changing rates of natural increase of populations in the past.

Against this background, the present chapter has three aims. The first is to ascertain how famine frequency changed over the long run in Japanese history. The chronology of famines on the Japanese archipelago begins with ancient events. It is therefore possible for us to place early modern famines, of which we have more records, in a very long, historical perspective. The early modern period in Japan usually refers to the era under the rule of the Tokugawa shogunate which occurred during 1603–1868, but my focus here is chiefly on the period after about 1700, during which time the country's population exhibited little growth.

Second, an effort is made to give an account of the changing causes of Japanese famines over the long run, and especially between the periods before and after 1600.

This is a revised version of a paper prepared for the IUSSP workshop at the Fondation des Treilles, which was a development from a paper presented at the IUSSP Conference on Asian Population History, held at the Academia Sinica in Taipei during January 1996. I am grateful to the discussants and the participants at both occasions for comments and suggestions. Thanks are due also to Prof Minoru Yoshimura of Yamanashi University for allowing me to share a paleoclimatological database which he and his colleagues are compiling, Dr Yukinobu Kitamura of Hitotsubashi University for his advice on statistical methods, and Mrs Mihoko Tanaka for her research assistance.

Frequency of Famines in the Japanese Past 219

The data used show that until the seventeenth century both droughts and cold summers were major causes of famine. In the Tokugawa period, however, it became rare that a famine was caused by short rainfall. Instead, most of the recorded famines during that period were occasioned by cold summers. Climate data indicate that adverse weather conditions did not always lead to a famine, and that this became increasingly apparent during the early modern period.

Third, the chapter assesses the relationship between population change and famine during the eighteenth and nineteenth centuries. As suggested above, the movement of population totals was stagnant between the early eighteenth and the mid-nineteenth century. It was not until the 1840s that the population started to increase again. Typically then, Malthusian assessments are made. The question, however, is whether or not famines actually prevented the population from increasing for a 150-year period in Japan's early modern history.

Recent general historiography, however, shows that against this long-held Malthusian tradition, there is a revisionist view which plays down the importance of famines as demographic correctives. Empirical studies have found that deaths from starvation were never numerous. Instead, it was usually infectious disease outbreaks and decreases in conceptions which accounted for much of the demographic crisis triggered by harvest failure. Moreover, Susan Watkins and Jane Menken have demonstrated that even taking these effects into consideration, the impact of a famine on the rate of change of population was never great. Thus, assuming that a famine was of 2-year duration, that the mortality level increased by 110 per cent, and that the population was characterized by a moderate level of fertility and a rather low life expectancy and an initial annual rate of population growth of 0.5 per cent, then their simulations indicate that the size of the population would decrease by just 9 per cent, and that the time required to regain the initial population size would be only 11 years. With these unspectacular results, they suggest that in order to explain the long-run, stagnant growth of populations in the past, we should turn our attention from crisis mortality to 'the low rate of natural increase set by normal levels of mortality and fertility', and that 'the control of normal mortality, the day-to-day causes of death, rather than the elimination of the one-time or extremely rare large-scale killer, is far more responsible for the onset of modern population growth' (Watkins and Menken 1985: 666–7).

In the Japanese context too, Akira Hayami, the doyen of Japanese historical demography, has questioned the Malthusian views held by earlier generations. He has argued that the sporadic falls in population totals and the overall population stagnation of the eighteenth and early nineteenth centuries should not be attributed to a series of 'short-term famines'. Even at the time of the Tenpo famine of the 1830s, one of the Four Great Famines in the Tokugawa period, Hayami, suggested that disease rather than crop failure accounted for the accompanying population decrease (Hayami 1986). Recently, however, a criticism has been made of Hayami's interpretation. Having examined temple records in a remote, hill area at the time of the Tenpo famine, Ann Jannetta has concluded that while epidemic patterns were not very different from those of non-famine years, two new disease terms appeared at the height of the famine period. And both these terms seem to have been related to symptoms associated with the 'final stages of starvation', suggesting that starvation did indeed take place during the 1830s (Jannetta 1987, 1992). Also Masao Takagi has examined death records from areas of the north-east at the time of the Tenmei and Tenpo famines and showed that in most of the villages examined the death rate increased to the range of between 40 and 80 per thousand, and that in some villages it reached as high as 200 per thousand or more during the peak year of the Tenpo famine (Takagi 1996). More recently, a study by Futoshi Kinoshita of another village in the north-east notes that the community experienced mortality crises more frequently than was previously thought, but on the other hand supports Hayami's view that the crises were more often associated with epidemics than with harvest failures (Kinoshita 1998).

It is interesting that, however different their conclusions, all these Japan specialists have been less concerned with the overall effect of famines on population growth than with the effect on mortality. That said, it is important to realize that any judgement about the role played by famines as demographic correctives should be based on what impact such occurrences had on the size of the population. Indeed, for the period after 1721, the results of the Tokugawa shogunate's efforts of taking population surveys enable us to examine the relationship between the frequency of famines and the actual changes in population size. The present chapter will make this examination, controlling for the effects of epidemics on the overall rate of population change. The results show that while the genuine effect of famines was never great in comparison even with the simulated effect suggested by Watkins and Menken, the frequency of famines may in fact explain much of the population change between 1721 and 1846 and also part of the subsequent population upturn. The chapter will suggest that the key to understanding this seemingly paradoxical result is the fact that the general level of Tokugawa marital fertility was low. Japan's experience at this time points to an important causal link, largely unnoticed by the Watkins–Menken paper,[1] namely that the lower the background level of fertility, the greater the weight of famines' fertility effect, and hence the greater the impact of the elimination of periodic famines on population change.

THE CHRONOLOGY OF FAMINES

Since the Meiji Restoration of 1868, several source books have been compiled to record the history of natural disasters in Japan during the period stretching back to the seventh century. The compilers of these source books examined gazetteers, pamphlets, memoirs, diaries, and other literary materials in search of information about famines and crop failures, and evidence about the occurrence of epidemics and natural hazards like floods, cold summers, and droughts. The first source book of this kind was published in the late nineteenth century (Ogashima 1894), and a more

---

[1] In one simulation exercise, Watkins and Menken did show that other things held constant, the lower the initial growth rate the greater the decline in population size caused by a famine. They did not comment on this suggestive result, however (Watkins and Menken 1985: 663).

comprehensive volume dealing with crop failures and famines was compiled in the 1930s (Nishimura and Yoshikawa 1936). There are also some modern publications which are based, either entirely or partly, on these two earlier volumes.

It is unsurprising that there are far more entries in the 1936 volume than in that published in 1894. However, the former does not cover the Meiji period, while the latter extends its coverage until the late 1880s. Both include not only 'famines' but 'poor harvests' as well; however, a majority of the additional entries in the 1936 volume are actually crop failures. This raises, first, the practical problem of defining a 'famine'. In dictionary terms, it is a scarcity of food accompanied by hunger and starvation. However, it is not always easy to determine if a particular historical occurrence was in fact a famine in this sense. Individual events were described with various words and ideographs. Given the difficulties associated with such diverse wordings and terms, I decided to select cases where either 'hunger' or 'starvation' or a substantial 'death toll' are mentioned, although inevitably there still remain some ambiguous cases.

Secondly, there is a question of magnitude. A common method to measure the magnitude of a famine is to use death statistics. Thus, an increase of 110 per cent in the death rate (chosen by Watkins and Menken in their simulations) should surely be considered indicative of a harsh famine, although in the most severe cases the mortality rise might be even greater still. In the case of pre-1868 Japan, however, it is impossible to adopt this approach. Even for the Tokugawa period, no aggregate vital statistics are available unless attention is turned to village-level records. Therefore, no weights are applied to individual famines according to their magnitude.

Thirdly, it is important to know whether a famine was a countrywide phenomenon or just a local disaster. Here, there can be three categories of crisis: local, regional, and countrywide. Local famines may be defined as those which were restricted to a single province. Since it is likely that most local famines, especially those during earlier periods, were omitted from recordings, they are not counted as famines here. Regional famines were those which affected four or five provinces together; and countrywide famines were those which hit a wider area still. Note that although the term 'countrywide' is used, this does not necessarily imply that the whole country was actually affected. In this context, the most common expression we encounter in the source books is 'famine in various provinces', but it is unlikely that all the 60 or more provinces of Japan were actually affected.[2] A 'countrywide' famine in my terminology is simply a famine which hit (or is supposed to have hit) various provinces across the country. In almost all cases, this meant a famine affecting provinces in both eastern and western Japan. The only known exception is the famine of 1755; this was one

---

[2] It is interesting to note in this respect that according to Poing-ti Ho's account of the 268-year history of famines in Hubei province of China, there was only one occasion where 36 out of the 71 districts were hit by famine simultaneously. On another occasion, 10 districts were affected. But all the other major famines were recorded in districts of less than 10 (Ho 1959: 292–300). In the Japanese records, unfortunately, no such precise lists of areas affected are available. The names of provinces hit by famine are often given, usually with 'and so on'. In my construction of Table 11.1, therefore, I set the dividing line at five; that is a famine is classified as 'countrywide' if the number of provinces affected by the famine was 5 or more, and as 'regional' if the number was less than 5.

of the most disastrous of the Tokugawa period, but it took place exclusively in the eastern half of the country. Thus, I have classified all those 'famines' identified into two categories—'countrywide' and 'regional'—and given a weight of 1.0 to the former and 0.5 to the latter.

Finally, there is one more factor which must be taken into account, that is, the duration of the famine. In Japan, most famines were limited to one harvest year. The typical sequence of events started with a crop failure in the autumn, this was followed by cases of hunger and starvation lasting from winter through until early spring as the grain stocks ran out, and then finally there were deaths from infectious diseases as the temperature and humidity began to rise (Kikuchi 1994; Tamura 1996). However, famines which were regarded as 'great famines' tended to last over two or more years. During such a famine period, not all years were actually marked by harvest failure. However, that said, according to contemporary accounts of such famines, signs of hunger and other famine symptoms continued to hover throughout the period. Therefore, I have counted all such years as 'famine years' in the context of great famines. For example, the Tenmei famine produced disastrous effects across the country throughout the entire period from 1782 to 1787; consequently because of its total duration, I have accorded this famine a weight of 6 points. The Tenpo famine, another 'great famine' of the Tokugawa period, began with a serious crop failure in the autumn of 1833. In the western half of the country it ended in 1836, but people in the east continued to starve in both 1836 and 1837. So in this case, 1 point has been accorded to each of the first four years of famine, and a weighting of 0.5 points has been given to 1836 and 1837. In other words, the Tenpo famine was weighted as a crisis of 5 points. However, comparing the Tenmei and Tenpo famines the small difference between 6 and 5 points should not be regarded as really reflecting a known difference in magnitude.

With this as background, Table 11.1 summarizes the results of this exercise by century. The first point to be noticed is unexpectedly wide fluctuations in all three columns. For example, it is odd to see the number of countrywide famines decrease abruptly from 25 in the ninth century to just 3 in the tenth century. Similarly, a sudden rise in the regional famine series from 2 in the fourteenth century to 12 in the fifteenth century and then 22 in the sixteenth century, appears dubious. It seems to be more a reflection of the changing ability of the central administration to govern. Indeed, during the tenth century, the centralized, Chinese-style *ritsuryo* state system gave way to a loosely structured, de-centralized land appropriation system of *shoen*. A lack of effective central control was one salient feature of the successive stages, during which time systematic recordings of information could probably not be expected. Such a period lasted for centuries, between the heyday of the *ritsuryo* system in the eighth and ninth centuries and the Tokugawa period. However, it may be that even before the year 1600 the availability of information started to improve. Judging from the rise in the number of countrywide famines from the twelfth to the fifteenth century, such an improvement may have started in the middle of the medieval period. In the case of regional famines, the sudden increase in the fifteenth and sixteenth centuries

Frequency of Famines in the Japanese Past

Table 11.1. *Summary of Famine Records for Japan for the Period from the Seventh to the Nineteenth Century*

Century	Incidence of famine		Weighted total (3)
	Countrywide (1)	Regional (2)	
7th	6	2	7
8th	28	16	36
9th	25	24	37
10th	3	3	4.5
11th	3	1	3.5
12th	8	3	9.5
13th	7	3	8.5
14th	10	2	11
15th	14	12	20
16th	8	22	19
17th	11	3	12.5
18th	9	3	10.5
19th	4	4	6
Total	136	98	185

Sources: Nishimura and Yoshikawa (1936), cross-checked with Ogashima (1894: Pt. 1). The former volume lists far more famines and crop failures than the latter, and most of the cases listed in the latter also appear in the former. However, there are some famines included in the latter, but not found in the former source (in fact, 11 such cases in column (1) and 9 in column (2)).

Notes: (1) The table does not cover Ryukyu and Hokkaido. The former was annexed in the late Tokugawa period, while part of the latter was included in the Tokugawa territory from the beginning, but its full-scale colonization did not start until the Meiji era. (2) The 'nineteenth century' here means the period 1801–85. (3) Given the difficulty of determining whether or not all the regions were actually struck in a particular 'countrywide' famine year, and exactly how many counties were affected on each occasion, a weight of 1.0 has been given to a countrywide famine and 0.5 to a regional famine.

may well be an indication that more books and diaries were written at local levels as literacy gradually rose.

However, what seems certain from Table 11.1 is that the frequency of famines during the Tokugawa period was low compared with the situation in ancient times. In the seventeenth, eighteenth, and nineteenth centuries there were 24 countrywide and 10 regional famines—giving a total weighing of 29 points. This means an average of 9.7 per century compared to 36.5 points in the eighth and ninth centuries. To express the point differently, during the ancient period there was a countrywide famine once in 3 years, whereas the overall frequency was once in every 10 years during 1600–1900 (the data series ends in 1885, but it is unlikely that any famine occurred between 1885 and 1900). This contrast is consistent with estimates which have been made for life expectancies in both ancient and Tokugawa times. Tokugawa life expectancies seem in most cases to have been in the thirties, perhaps in the high thirties (Saito 1997). For ancient Japan, W. W. Farris has applied model life table parameters to fragments from household registers taken by the *ritsuryo* government during the eighth century, and suggested that life expectation ranged from about 28 to 33 years. However, a close look at the methods and results raises the possibility that the actual level may have been lower. The author had to reject some of the cases in which the estimated life expectancy was considerably below 20 years, because this was the lowest limit in the model life tables which were used. Since the expectation of life could actually drop below 20 in various historical populations, Farris's estimates can in fact be taken to suggest that the average level of life expectancy in ancient times was well below 28 years. Such a level was certainly 'pitifully low' compared with that experienced by Tokugawa peasants (Farris 1985: 42–3).

A second point from Table 11.1 is that famines during the Tokugawa period may well have become less frequent even if compared to late medieval times. Thus, the average of weighted famine points for the fifteenth and sixteenth centuries is 19.5 per century; this figure drops to 12.5 in the seventeenth century. All these famine points are undoubtedly understated. Given the fact that the amount of information available exhibits a sudden increase with the establishment of the Tokugawa administration, however, the late-medieval points are likely to have been much more seriously understated. This implies that the decline in famine frequency was even more substantial than Table 11.1 suggests. Again, this conclusion is not inconsistent with a piece of evidence which is available for the late-medieval period. A seasonality analysis of temple death records in an area east of present-day Tokyo for the period 1394–1592 shows that there were more deaths in spring and summer than in autumn and winter (Tamura 1996). As noted above, this spring–summer pattern of death seasonality appeared in typical famine years. Since the spring–summer pattern of deaths is known to have appeared only in specific famine years during the late Tokugawa period, this implies that famine was far more frequent in the fifteenth and sixteenth centuries than in the early nineteenth century.

A third point is that even within the Tokugawa period there seems to have been a diminishing frequency of famine. Thus, the weighted total in Table 11.1 decreases from 12.5 in the seventeenth century, to 10.5 in the eighteenth, and finally to just 6 points in the nineteenth century. It is a little difficult to discuss the modest change between the seventeenth and eighteenth centuries, for it is likely that famine events were still under-recorded before 1700. However, as far as the latter half of the period is concerned the trend is unmistakable. Thus, towards the end of the Tokugawa regime, there were fewer famines. According to Table 11.1, the century total of famine points was almost halved from the eighteenth to the nineteenth century. Moreover, a little more than half of the eighteenth-century weighed famine years were accounted for by the Tenmei famine and five out of the six famine years in the nineteenth century by the Tenpo famine. In fact, after the 1840s there were no famines except for two rather regional events. Famine, as scarcity of food accompanied by widespread hunger and starvation, disappeared from Japanese history.

SHIFTING CAUSES OF FAMINE

Table 11.2 breaks down the famine frequency data by the causes of famine. Excerpts included in the source books enable us to identify in most, if not all, cases what triggered the recorded famine. There are more uncertain cases in the period before 1600 than in the period after that year. However, if it can be assumed that those cases where the cause of famine was unknown were not very different from cases where the cause was known, then Table 11.2 points to one very important fact. This is that the role of drought as a cause of famine declined over the entire 1,300-year period. In ancient times, both droughts and cold summers ravaged the country periodically, but it was drought which proved the more disastrous for the population; and this probably remained so during medieval times. The turning point was the seventeenth century when the frequency of famines started to decrease. In the eighteenth and nineteenth centuries no famines were occasioned by drought while the number of famines continued to decline. All this suggests that the fall in the importance of drought as a major cause of famine led to an impressive decline in famine frequency. On the other hand, the phrase 'long and continuous rain' became increasingly prominent in the famine records. This description has always been associated with cool summers, which could result in a poor harvest even when rainfall was not excessive. Cool summers were hazardous to farming throughout ancient and medieval times, but because of the diminishing importance of drought it became virtually the only cause of famine in Japan during the eighteenth and nineteenth centuries.

The period from the fifteenth to the seventeenth century saw a gradual but unmistakable shift in the centre of population gravity. During medieval times, there were comparatively more dry-fields than wet paddies in Japan. Most such dry-fields were found on hillsides and in mountainous uplands. In lowland areas too there were farm

Table 11.2. *The Proportions of Famines Triggered by Droughts and Cold Summers for the Period from the Seventh to the Nineteenth Century*

Period	Famine year total	Number of cases triggered		
		Drought	Cold summer or long and continuous rain	Other/unspecified
7–9th	80	32 (40)	21.5 (27)	26.5 (33)
10–14th	37	14 (38)	7.5 (20)	15.5 (42)
15–16th	39	11.5 (29)	6 (15)	21.5 (55)
17th	12.5	3 (24)	5 (40)	4.5 (36)
18th	10.5	0 (0)	9.5 (90)	1 (10)
19th	6	0 (0)	5.5 (92)	0.5 (8)

Sources: See Table 11.1.

Notes: (1) Famine years have been taken from the weighted totals in column (3) of Table 11.1. The proportions of drought or cold summer years have been calculated on the basis of this weighted series. (2) The figures in parentheses are the percentages of the famine year totals.

fields, but most of them were concentrated on slightly elevated ground in marshes, old river-beds, and natural levees. The crops planted there were dry rice, barley, millet, buckwheat, beans, and other plants. The cultivation of wet rice, on the other hand, was a rather unstable activity. This was particularly so in the flood plains. It is documented that in early medieval times water control was so difficult that crops could only be grown once in, say, every three years. This meant that in fertile lowland fields harvests were vulnerable to any slight change in climatic conditions. So, during times when the rains were overlong it was quite probable that the harvest would fail. But if, on the other hand, conditions were extremely dry, the result was likely to be the same, that is harvest failure.

The situation started to change gradually during the period between the fifteenth and the seventeenth centuries. A crucial consideration behind this change was the introduction of a new rice variety from abroad. It was called *akamai* (literally 'red rice'). This new rice originated from Champa, an area in present-day Vietnam, and it was—unlike other indigenous *japonica* rice varieties—a long-grain, *indica* type. Most of the *indica* 'red' varieties were early ripening and were characterized by their ability to withstand poor water conditions and low levels of fertilizer application. Despite its taste, the planting of this new red variety was advantageous because it was drought-resistant, it could be harvested before the typhoon season, and it could also be grown in marshy fields. It is now documented that this variety was widely grown mostly in lowland swamps, and especially in western parts of the country (Arashi 1974).

Another aspect of progress around this time consisted of converting swamps into 'drainable' fields. This process took much longer, because the conversion was made possible only by the construction of dikes, creeks, conduits, culverts, and sluice-gates. These works were needed to provide supplemental water if there was insufficient supply, and also to drain excess water at times. Given these infrastructural investments it was possible to introduce new, high-yielding rice varieties of the short-grain, *japonica* type, which in most cases were late-planting and relatively quick-maturing, and which responded well to higher levels of fertilizer application. The consequence of all this was an increase in the double-cropped area, which in turn stabilized harvests and increased farm incomes. These changes increased the security of peasants from the effects of weather fluctuations. Since the process started from the western provinces of the country, it was the north-east that remained vulnerable to weather changes during the Tokugawa period, areas where cool summers were much more of a problem than in the warmer west.

CLIMATE AND FAMINES

Was this overall agrarian shift associated with changing climatic conditions? Did it happen because the temperature became more favourable? To help address these questions, Fig. 11.1 plots a measure of long-term climatic change from the mid-fifteenth century onwards.

The index of warmness shown in Fig. 11.1 is derived from records of the 'divine crossing' (*omiwatari*) occurring on Lake Suwa, which is located in Shinano province.

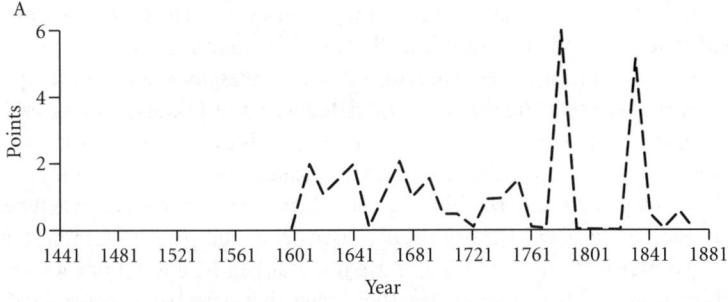

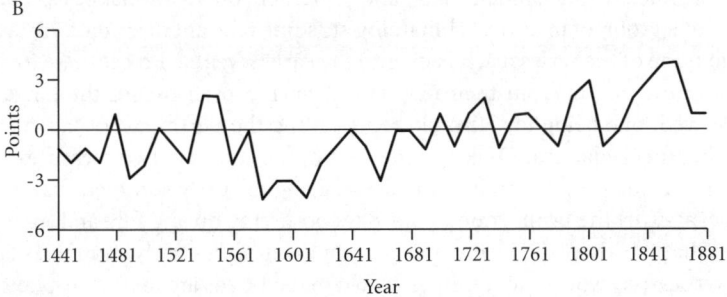

Figure 11.1. *Climatic Change and Famines, 1441–1881: (A) Famine Points and (B) Warmness Index*

This crossing is a crack on the ice surface created by the pressure of freezing, and records of it enable paleoclimatologists to determine whether the year in question had a cold or a warm winter. The index shown is that prepared by Koichiro Takahashi and Junkichi Nemoto, and is defined as the difference between the numbers of warm and cold winters per decade (Takahashi and Nemoto 1978: 184–5). Much of the period covered by Fig. 11.1 falls in the so-called 'Little Ice Age', but it is apparent that there was a particularly cold period between the 1580s and the 1610s. The seventeenth century was a period of recovery, and there then occurred a secular warming trend. Indeed, recent work reveals that the average July temperature in the nineteenth century was about 1°C higher than in the eighteenth century (Mikami 1996). This pattern of change in the index of warm winters, according to Takahashi and Nemoto, is in broad agreement with that indicated by sun spot data.

Figure 11.1 also shows my weighted famine points by decade. Given the degree of reliability of the late-medieval figures, these are not shown for the period before 1600. From this graph, it seems that in the seventeenth century famines occurred more or less regularly, and they gradually became less frequent during the eighteenth century. Although the late eighteenth and nineteenth centuries were characterized by two extremely severe famines that devastated the country for several years, the overall tendency was still a decreasing one. On the face of it, this long-run trend is not inconsistent with the warming tendency. However, a close examination of the peaks and troughs of the two graphs indicates that there is no correlation between the warmness and famine series. This suggests that it was not the winter temperature, but the summer temperature that was associated with the Tokugawa famines. Indeed, Takahashi and Nemoto prepared another index for this to be checked, that is an index of lean years; this second index is in fact associated more closely with the famine series. However, given the possibility that their lean-year index was constructed from historical sources similar to those used to construct the present famine table (i.e. Table 11.1) it may be that the two series are not really independent of each other.

Clearly, it is desirable to employ weather series that have been constructed on the basis of completely independent data, and preferably on an annual basis. Thanks to the work of a group of historical climatologists some relevant diary data are available, although none of the series reach back into the early seventeenth century (for details, see Yoshimura 1993). From their database, I have chosen two of the longest time series derived, one being for Hirosaki representing the north-east of Japan, and the other being for Ikeda, near Osaka, in the west of the country. Two measures are now examined: (a) the proportion of rainy days during the early summer, that is in May and June; and (b) the proportion of fair days occurring during July and August. It is assumed that the lower the former proportion the drier the early summer, that is the *tsuyu* (wet season) when rice seedlings grown in seed-beds are to be transplanted into flooded fields; while the lower the latter proportion the cooler the high summer, a time when for the plants to mature properly some summer heat is essential. For both measures the top panel of Table 11.3 sets out the means, medians, and first quartiles for the two places. Judging from the mean and median values it was generally wetter and sunnier in Ikeda than in Hirosaki, while the coefficients of variation indicate that weather conditions fluctuated a little more widely in Ikeda than in Hirosaki. Since preliminary checks revealed that there were no time trends in the series, it is possible to identify those years with a dry May–June period and those with a cool July–August period by adopting the first quartile as the cut-off point. Accordingly the middle panel of Table 11.3 examines how many famine years happened to be years of either dry *tsuyu* or cool summer, and the bottom panel examines how many years of dry *tsuyu* season and how many years of cool summer coincided with famine years.

Several interesting points arise from Table 11.3. First, the middle panel confirms that in both eastern and western Japan famines were occasioned more by the occurrence of a cool summer than by a drought. A majority of famines in both Hirosaki and Ikeda happened in years when the July–August period was short of sunshine. Only four or five out of the 14 or 16 famine years identified coincided with a dry *tsuyu*, and a close look at the available records suggests that in most cases such dry seasons had no causal bearing on the occurrence of famine. Secondly, the bottom panel of Table 11.3 indicates that not all unfavourable weather situations led to a famine. While it is unsurprising that only a fraction of the dry seasons happened to be famine years, as many as 30 out of the 40 cool summers in Hirosaki and 28 out of the 38 cool summers in Ikeda did not result in any region-wide famine. In 1806, for example, Hirosaki's proportion of sunny days dropped to 0.29, which was followed

Table 11.3. *Short Rainfall, Cool Summers, and Famines: Hirosaki and Ikeda Weather Records, 1714–1864*

	Hirosaki (representing the north-east)	Ikeda (representing the west)
Proportion of rainy days in May–June		
Mean	0.274	0.351
Median	0.270	0.352
C.V.	0.237	0.305
1st quartile	0.230	0.279
(N)	(150)	(145)
Proportion of fair days in July–August		
Mean	0.541	0.589
Median	0.549	0.597
C.V.	0.194	0.216
1st quartile	0.468	0.500
(N)	(149)	(146)
Famine years		
N	16	14
Of which		
Years with dry May–June	5	4
Years with cool July–August	10	10
Years with dry May–June		
N	39	43
Of which: with famine	5	4
Years with cool July–August		
N	40	38
Of which: with famine	10	10

Sources: The Hirosaki and Ikeda files were supplied by Professor Minoru Yoshimura, Institute of Geography, Faculty of Education, Yamanashi University. For famine years, see Table 11.1.

Notes: (1) C.V. denotes the coefficient of variation (i.e. the standard deviation divided by the mean). (2) The proportion of rainy days is defined here as the weighted total of days with 'little rain', 'rain', and 'heavy rain' divided by the number of days in the month. For details of the weights adopted, see Yoshimura (1993). A year of 'dry May–June' is a year in which the proportion of rainy days corresponds to the first quartile or under. (3) The proportion of fair days is defined as the unweighted total of 'fine' and 'partly cloudy' days divided by the number of days in the month. A year of 'cool July–August' is a year in which the proportion of fair days corresponds to the first quartile or under. (4) Missing years are 1720 (May–June only), 1755, 1788, and 1858–60 for Hirosaki; and 1799 and 1800 (July–August only) for Ikeda.

by another cool summer when the proportion remained below average, that is 0.37. In Ikeda, 1846 and 1847 were similar years, in which the proportion of sunny days dropped below average, being 0.34 and 0.41, respectively. These measures indicate disastrous summers which could well have triggered a region-wide famine of at least 2-years duration. However, no widespread famine reports are known to exist for those years. This should not be taken to imply that bad weather had little to do with the occurrence of a poor harvest. In such cool years people did experience poor harvests;

however, the point is that such lean years did not invariably result in hunger and other phenomena closely associated with famine.

Much has been written about historical famines. However, very little is known about what we might term 'averted famines', that is very unfavourable weather patterns and harvests which could have resulted in famine, starvation, and deaths, but in fact did not. What prevented famines from occurring in such unfavourable circumstances? What measures, whether intentional or unintentional, were taken in responding to such situations at the level of the government, community, and the family? Such issues need to be addressed by future research. However, what is certain at this stage is that unfavourable weather conditions were rather poor indicators of famines in the eighteenth and nineteenth centuries in Japan, and that this became even more so towards the end of the latter century.

POPULATION, FAMINES, AND EPIDEMICS

Once a famine broke out, it must have had an impact on population numbers. The third task of this paper is to gauge how great this impact was as compared to that of epidemics. Before undertaking this task, however, we must look at the data on both population and epidemics.

The country's population totals are available from the early eighteenth century onwards. The Tokugawa government took the first population survey in 1721, the second in 1726, then there was one six-yearly until 1846 (with the exceptions of 1738, 1810, and 1816). The survey excluded samurai and outcast populations. The population groups covered were peasants, craftsmen, and merchants, which together represented about 85 per cent of the nation's population. In some daimyo territories a younger age group was not included in the enumeration. All this means that the Tokugawa population totals cannot be compared with Meiji figures, since the latter covered the entire population. But it is widely held that if one's focus is not on absolute levels, but rather on changes during the 1721–1846 period, then the survey data are usable (Minami 1978; Sekiyama 1958: Chapter 2).

The first reliable chronological table of epidemics before the Meiji Restoration was compiled by Fujikawa (1912). This table can be extended to the early Meiji years by referring to other source books (such as Ogashima 1894). It appears that the Fujikawa table includes less prevalent epidemics, but it is not a straightforward matter to assign appropriate weights (analogous to those used above for famines) to individual disease outbreaks—since neither case fatality nor mortality figures are available. However, it is documented that the country had previously been closed to the outside world and was thus insulated from rampant pandemics. And it is also known that cholera, influenza, and other infectious diseases which arrived after the first overseas contact led to some unprecedentedly serious disease impacts. Particularly devastating were three cholera outbreaks in 1858, 1862, and 1879; so I assign 2 points to each of these events (Fujikawa 1912: 215–34 and 262–8; Jannetta 1992: 155–72; Kosei-sho Imukyo-ku 1976: 25–31).

Table 11.4 sets out the data used for the analysis. For population change, two measures are considered. One is the difference between two population size figures in adjacent surveys, expressed in per-year terms; the other is the annual rate of change over the same interval. Since Meiji population statistics enable us to compute rates

Table 11.4. *Population Change, Famines, and Epidemics, 1721–1885*

Period	Population change		Famine frequencey (points p.a.)	Epidemics frequency (points p.a.)
	Rate (% p.a.)	Increment (000 p.a.)		
1721–6	0.37	96.8	0	0.20
1726–32	0.23	62.2	0	0.33
1732–44	−0.24	−64.1	0.08	0.33
1744–50	−0.15	−39.2	0.17	0.67
1750–6	0.09	25.5	0.17	0.17
1756–62	−0.09	−25.0	0.08	0
1762–8	0.21	55.2	0	0.17
1768–74	−0.17	−43.7	0	0.67
1774–80	0.01	3.5	0	0.33
1780–6	−0.59	−154.2	0.67	0.50
1786–92	−0.13	−32.5	0.33	0.17
1792–8	0.39	96.7	0	0.17
1798–1804	0.10	25.2	0	0.67
1804–22	0.21	54.4	0	0.33
1822–8	0.38	99.8	0	0.5
1828–34	−0.08	−22.8	0.17	0.67
1834–40	−0.72	−191.0	0.67	0.67
1840–6	0.63	165.0	0	0.17
1846–73	—	—	0.04	0.52
1873–9	0.69	—	0	0
1879–85	0.83	—	0	0.5
1721–1864				
Mean	0.025	6.21	0.130	0.372
S.D.	0.332	89.6	0.216	0.224
1721–1885				
Mean	0.099		0.117	0.360
S.D.	0.395		0.208	0.230

Sources: Population: For 1721–1846, Sekiyama (1958: 123) with Minami (1978: 178); and for 1873–85, Somu-cho Tokei-kyoku (1987: 48–50). Famines: the same as for Table 11.1. Epidemics: Fujikawa (1912: 56–65), cross-checked with Ogashima (1894: Pt. 7).

Notes: (1) Population change has been calculated as a compound rate from the two end-year population totals. (2) The famine column is a weighted series as explained in note 3 of Table 11.1. (3) In the case of cholera epidemics a different weight has been adopted. There are at least seven cholera outbreaks during the period in question, of which those of 1858, 1862, and 1879 were particularly devastating. In view of the extremely high case fatality, a weight of 2.0 has been given to these 3 years. (4) The means and S.D.s (i.e. standard deviations) for famine and epidemics points have been calculated omitting the period 1846–73.

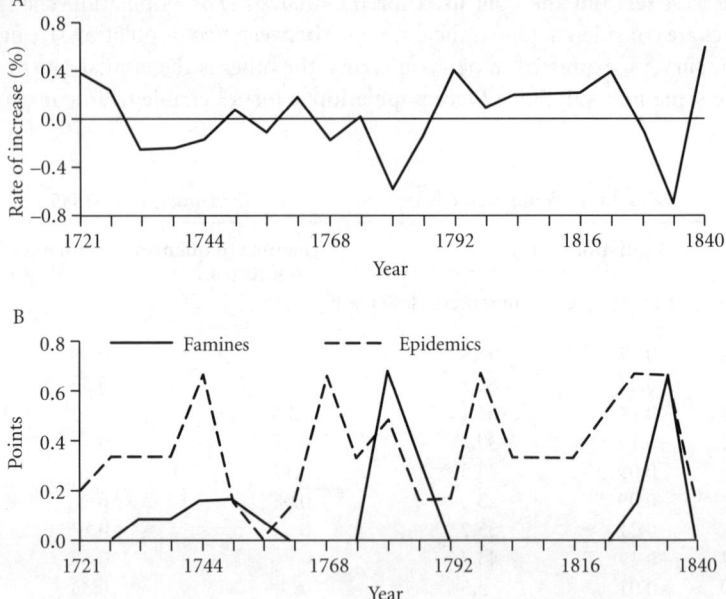

Figure 11.2. *Population Change (A), Famines and Epidemics (B), 1721–1846*

of change from 1873 onwards, the second column includes two additional 6-year observational periods (i.e. 1873–9 and 1879–85) with a missing quarter-century in between. Also, the famine and epidemic columns, expressed in per-year terms, extend to 1885. Three of the four series—that is the rate of population change, and the points totals for famines and epidemics—are shown in Fig. 11.2 for the period 1721–1846.

In Fig. 11.2A, the two deep troughs in the population series around 1780–6 and 1834–40 correspond to the great Tenmei and Tenpo famines. During the Tenmei 6-year period, the country's population declined by 925,000 (i.e. an annual average of 154,000) while over the Tenpo period the reduction was 1,146,000 (i.e. 191,000 annually). It is apparent that there was not much growth in Japan's population until 1846. Table 11.4 indicates that over the entire period until 1846 the mean annual increment in population was positive but meagre (i.e. 6,000); the corresponding mean rate of population increase was 0.025 per cent per year. If the growth rate is calculated over the period until 1885, it rises to 0.099 per cent, reflecting the fact that the modern population take-off happened in the second half of the nineteenth century. Indeed, independent estimates suggest that the population grew at 0.4 per cent annually during the missing quarter-century (Saito 1988), and this was followed by higher rates of increase in the 1870s and 1880s (see Table 11.4).[3]

---

[3] Since the population covered by the Tokugawa government's surveys cannot be compared with that in Meiji population statistics, it is not easy to know the rate of increase in population during this quarter-century. However, by excluding provinces where it is known that young children were customarily excluded

The famine and epidemic columns in Table 11.4 indicate that in the period before 1846 famines occurred on average every 7.7 years, while the corresponding frequency of epidemics was every 2.7 years. Compared with the figures Malthus quoted in the sixth edition of his *Essay* (i.e. 7.5 and 4.5 years) the famine frequency was not much different from the historical experience in historical Europe, but it is clear that epidemics were more frequent in Tokugawa, Japan. Although such a comparison may not be rigorous, it is probably safe to conclude that famines were not particularly frequent in eighteenth- and nineteenth-century Japan. There were more epidemics during the same period, although a majority of them were benign. It was only from the 1850s onwards that outbreaks of infectious diseases caused a substantial death toll. That said, comparison of Fig. 11.2A and B reveals that the frequency of epidemics cannot explain much of the fluctuation in the rate of population change. It is apparent that the famine graph is more closely associated with that of population change for the period 1721–1846. Moreover, Fig. 11.2B shows that the famine and epidemic point plots are not related to each other. This suggests that in Tokugawa Japan, the interaction between famines and epidemics was not important. It was only in times of the great Tenmei and Tenpo famines that the epidemic frequency was also high; and, interestingly, Fujikawa did note that there was evidence that this interaction emerged in those particular famines (Fujikawa 1912: 56, 59, and 63). However, judging from the weak correlation between the two series in Fig. 11.2B there were no serious epidemics in a majority of the Tokugawa famines.[4]

In order to gauge the demographic impact of famines and epidemics, a multiple regression analysis has been employed. The explanatory variables are the famine frequency and the epidemic frequency, both of which are expected to have negative effects. In this formulation, all positive effects are expressed in a non-negative constant term, which may be interpreted as reflecting the degree of *potential* population growth attained when neither famine nor epidemic struck the country. In another equation, a 'time trend' has been taken into consideration, since the data in Table 11.4 suggest that there may have been a slight upward trend in the rate of population change over the period in question. In this latter formulation, the degree of potential population growth gradually increases with time. As there are also two measures of the dependent variable, four equations are estimated. Table 11.5 summarizes the results of the four regression exercises.[5]

---

from enumeration, I linked the population figures for all the other provinces in 1846 to those for the commoner population in the 1881 statistics, the latter being one of the few that provide us with cross-tabulations by status and province. By allowing for the number of samurai who changed their status after the Restoration, I arrived at the estimated average rate of population change of 0.4 per cent per year for the period 1846–81 (Saito 1988).

[4] The correlation coefficient between the famine and epidemic series is 0.295 for 1721–1846, and 0.298 if the post-1846 periods are included. Neither of the coefficients is statistically significant at the 5 per cent level.

[5] There are two implicit assumptions in this analysis. One is that there should be no 'multi-collinearity' problem. Since the correlation coefficient between the two independent variables was not statistically significant (see note 4) this condition is met. Second, there may have been an effect of population size at time $t-1$ on population change from $t-1$ to t. I have checked this possibility by adding one more

Table 11.5. *Accounting for Varying Rates of Population Change in Japan, 1721–1885: Regression Results*

	(1)	(2)
A. 1721–1846 (Y: Increment per year)		
Constant	83.46 (3.57)*	56.24 (2.32)**
X_1: Famine frequency	−307.8(−5.24)*	−325.4(−6.14)*
X_2: Epidemics frequency	−100.4(−1.77)**	−129.1(−2.47)**
X_3: Time trend	—	0.678 (2.20)**
R^2 (adjusted)	0.689	0.752
N	18	18

	(3)	(4)
B. 1721–1885 (Y: Rate of change)		
Constant	0.389 (3.60)*	0.158 (1.67)
X_1: Famine frequency	−1.328(−4.52)*	−1.339(−6.39)*
X_2: Epidemics frequency	−0.376(−1.41)	−0.458(−2.40)**
X_3: Time trend	—	0.0038 (4.17)*
R^2 (adjusted)	0.585	0.789
N	20	20

Source: See Table 11.3 above.

Notes: (1) The 1846–73 period is not included in equations (3) and (4). (2) The figures in parentheses are the corresponding *t* ratios. (3) Those marked *are statistically significant at the 1 per cent level and those marked ** at the 5 per cent level, both on the basis of one-tailed tests.

Several points arise. The results of the equations without time trend, (eqns 1 and 3) reveal that the constant is estimated as positive and famine frequency as negative, and that both coefficients are statistically significant. But the results for epidemic frequency are mixed: the *t* value does not attain significance (eqn 3). With the time trend included, on the other hand, the overall performance is improved (eqns 2 and 4). In equation 4, judging from the size of the *t* statistic, the acceleration in the potential rate of population growth is proved to have been operating over the entire period until 1885, although the significance level for the constant is reduced. It is interesting to note that the frequency of epidemics is now estimated significantly and with the expected negative sign, reflecting the possibility that the impact of epidemics became more severe after the 1850s (Table 11.5).

An important conclusion from these results is that the potential rate of population growth in eighteenth- and nineteenth-century Japan was rather low. Even if no

---

variable on the right-hand side of the equation, population size at $t - 1$, with the observation periods 1721–6, 1732–44, and 1804–22 excluded (all have differing intervals). However, no specification has been estimated with a statistically significant coefficient of the added variable.

famine or epidemic had occurred equation 2 implies that the country's commoner population—which stood at 26 million in 1721—would have grown only by 56,000, or at 0.2 per cent per year. Including the effect of the time trend this potential rate increased over time, reaching 0.5 per cent during the mid-nineteenth century; recall that this was the level that Watkins and Menken chose for their simulation exercises to represent a long-run stagnant population regime characteristic of a pre-modern society. Looking at the statistics from equation 4 the result becomes a little different—the potential rate of growth beginning at less than 0.2 per cent and then rising to 0.6 per cent. However, even with these levels we can safely conclude that Tokugawa Japan's population growth potential cannot be said to have been substantial.

Another point to note is that in all four regression exercises, the size of the famine coefficient is much larger than that indicated for epidemics (see Table 11.5). Undoubtedly, a famine had a greater effect than an epidemic on the actual rate of population change, presumably this was partly because of the less lethal nature of infectious diseases in Tokugawa Japan under the self-imposed seclusion regime.

What is more noteworthy, however, is that the frequency of famines was more influential in explaining the changing tempo of population change than that of epidemics *despite* the comparatively weak demographic impact that the Tokugawa famines exerted. Imagine that a 2-year famine was compounded by the spreading of infectious diseases. Even if the time trend is ignored, equation 4 in Table 11.5 indicates that the population size at the end of the famine would be smaller by only 4 per cent. Compared to the 9 per cent decline predicted by Watkins and Menken in their simulation with a similar set of assumptions, this impact should be regarded as mild. Nonetheless, the regression analysis suggests strongly that Japan's stagnant population, and the fluctuations in its size during the eighteenth and early nineteenth centuries, were conditioned by the chronology of famines.

CONCLUSION

An important conclusion from this paper is that the demographic effect of Tokugawa famines cannot be underestimated. This statement should be set against the historical background that, because of the attenuation or near elimination of drought-induced famines, hunger, and starvation had become much less frequent by the early Tokugawa period. Nevertheless, the famines during the eighteenth and early nineteenth centuries did in fact accentuate the population process despite the mild demographic impact that a single famine could exert.

Moreover, the start of population growth during the late nineteenth century can also be predicted from the regression results reported in Table 11.5. Equations 2 and 4 indicate that the rate of population growth after 1846 must have been in the range of 0.3–0.4 per cent per year if there was no region-wide famine, and if the frequency of epidemics increased from that of one in every 2.7 years to one in every 2 years. The two conditional clauses are closer to what actually took place during the quarter-century after 1846. And, as noted earlier, the estimated rate of population growth during the same quarter-century is 0.4 per cent per year. Therefore, all this suggests that, contrary to what Watkins and Menken claimed, the elimination of famines was indeed 'responsible for the onset of modern population growth' in the Japanese context.

There are two reasons why such seemingly contradictory results are possible. First, the coefficient of the famine variable in the regression equation captures not just its mortality effect, but its fertility effect as well. There is evidence that much of the calculated effect of famines in Table 11.5 reflects fertility effects. Thus, recent work by Masao Takagi reveals that at the time of one of the worst famines nutritional intake could be as low as one-seventh of the normal level. According to his analysis of a village official's account book of relief distribution for six months of the year 1836 in a famine-hit north-eastern farming village, the estimated caloric intake per capita per day must have been a little more than 320 kcal. With such a meagre intake, it is hardly surprising to see that no births were recorded in the year after this relief operation was undertaken (Takagi 1999). Contemporary observers too pointed out that famines reduced the number of births. When a famine hit the northern-most province of Japan in 1615, it was noted in one samurai diary that there were many miscarriages in that year and very few births for the next two years. At the time of the Tenmei famine, one writer suggested that women in the North-east suffered serious menstrual disorders as a result (both cases are quoted in Nishimura and Yoshikawa 1936: 225 and 710). Such happenings may well have been related to malnutrition caused by harvest failure, which was summed up by a contemporary vulgar rhyme: 'starving skin and bone, giving no birth' (quoted in Sekiyama 1958: 167, no 24). However, there was another dimension to this fertility link. In his autobiography, Matsudaira Sadanobu, a chief councillor in the Shogunate government, looked back to the Tenmei famine years when he had been *daimyo* of an area in the North-east. He noted that because of the famine, the country's population decreased 'by 1.4 million' compared to the previous survey year. 'This decrease was not due to deaths at all. They were all out from the registered place, some became (unlicensed) monks and itinerant priests, some homeless, some unregistered workers in Edo—all floating populations' (Matsudaira 1942: 114). The decrease by 1.4 million from 1780 to 1786 is grossly exaggerated—as noted earlier, the actual difference was 92,000. And his claim that there were very few deaths from starvation and related diseases is incorrect, for in the same biography he writes that in neighbouring domains hundreds of thousands of people died of famine. However, his remark points to one important mechanism why births were reduced by famines. Men and women were separated—with men on the move in search of food and jobs. Since these 'floating' people were not counted in any population registers it is very difficult to get information about them, although there is various literary evidence that a famine swelled the number of such people (see Kikuchi 1994).

Second, it should be remembered that the growth potential of the Tokugawa population was weak. There is evidence that the background level of mortality was on the low side by pre-modern standards. Although the ranges of the available estimates of infant mortality and life expectancy are rather wide, an infant mortality rate of about

180 per thousand live births and a life expectancy at birth of around 39 years are probably not far off the mark for the Tokugawa village population (both sexes combined; see Saito 1997). On the other hand, marital fertility was low. Ken'ichi Tomobe has estimated that the total marital fertility rate for a country sample of villages was 5.8 live births, and that it was even lower (i.e. around 4.3) for villages in eastern Japan (Tomobe 1991). The low rate of potential growth in population, therefore, was conditioned by low marital fertility. Since it is well documented in the historical demography literature that short-term fluctuations in grain prices and birth rates were closely correlated, and since there is evidence that this was so in Tokugawa Japan (Uemura 1978; Feeney and Hamano 1990; Tsuya and Kurosu, 2000), this implies that not only severe famines, but also the numerous minor and 'averted' famines (i.e. crop failures that did not result in widespread hunger and starvation) did indeed reduce fertility rates and hence the rate of natural increase.

If my argument that much of the observed correlation between the chronology of famines and rates of population change during the eighteenth and nineteenth centuries is explicable by the fertility effects of famines combined with the low level of marital fertility is correct, then this implies that the onset of population growth in Japan after the 1840s was fertility-led and that this was particularly so in the North-east and other eastern provinces that were hard hit by a series of lean years lasting until the 1840s. This latter proposition can be tested, at least partially. And indeed analysis shows that provincial rates of population change estimated for the quarter-century period following 1846 are best accounted for by a fertility measure (such as the woman–child ratio) in 1881, and that the north-eastern and northern Kanto provinces were among the fastest-growing and highest-fertility population groups (Saito 1988).

To conclude, the Japanese historical experience examined in this chapter suggests a somewhat different causal relationship between famines and low population growth rates than that which is commonly entertained. In the case of Japan, it was *because* of a low rate of natural increase set by the normal level of Tokugawa fertility, and *through* the fertility effect of famines, that a series of famines and their elimination were a major determinant of both the stagnant and upturn phases of population change in the country's past.

References

Arashi, Kaichi (1974), *Nihon akamai ko*, Tokyo: Yuzankaku.

Farris, W. W. (1985), *Population, Disease, and Land in Early Japan, 645–900*, Cambridge, Mass.: Harvard University Press.

Feeney, G., and Hamano, K. (1990), 'Rice Price Fluctuations and Fertility in Late Tokugawa Japan', *Journal of Japanese Studies*, 16: 1–30.

Fujikawa, Yu (1912), *Nihon shippeishi* (reprint edition), Tokyo: Heibonsha, 1969.

Hayami, A. (1986), 'Population Change', in M. B. Jansen and G. Rozman (eds.), *Japan in Transition: from Tokugawa to Meiji*, Princeton: Princeton University Press.

Ho, Ping-ti (1959), *Studies on the Population of China, 1368–1953*, Cambridge, Mass.: Harvard University Press.
Jannetta, A. B. (1987), *Epidemics and Mortality in Early Modern Japan*, Princeton: Princeton University Press.
—— (1992), 'Famine Mortality in Nineteenth-century Japan: The Evidence from a Temple Death Register', *Population Studies*, 46: 427–43.
Kikuchi, Isao (1994), *Kikin no shakaishi*, Tokyo: Hasekura Shobo.
Kinoshita, F. (1998), 'Mortality Crises in the Tokugawa Period: A View from Shumon Aratame-cho in Northeastern Japan', *Japan Review*, 10: 53–71.
Kosei-sho, Imu-kyoku (1976), *Eisei tokei kara mita isei hyakunen no ayumi*, Tokyo: Gyosei.
Malthus, T. R. (1798), *An Essay on the Principle of Population*, 1st edn., London: in E. A. Wrigley and D. Souden (eds.), *The Works of Thomas Robert Malthus*, Volume 1, London: William Pickering, 1986.
—— (1826), *An Essay on the Principle of Population*, 6th edn, London, in E. A. Wrigley and D. Souden (eds.), *The Works of Thomas Robert Malthus*, Volume 2 (I) and Volume 3 (II), London: William Pickering, 1986.
Matsudaira, Sadamitsu (ed.) (1942), *Matsudaira Sadanobu's Uge no hito koto, shugyo-roku*, Tokyo: Iwanami Shoten.
Mikami, T. (1996), 'Long Term Variations of Summer Temperatures in Tokyo since 1721', *Geographical Reports of Tokyo Metropolitan University*, 31: 157–65.
Minami, Kazuo (1978), 'Tenpo 11-nen zenkoku jinko chosa ni tsuite', in his *Bakumatsu Edo shakai no kenkyu*, Tokyo: Yoshikawa Kobunkan.
Nishimura, Makoto, and Yoshikawa, Ichiro (eds.) (1936), *Nihon kyoko-shi ko*, Tokyo: Maruzen.
Ogashima, Minoru (ed.) (1894), *Nihon saii-shi*, Tokyo: Nihon Kogyokai.
Saito, Osamu (1988), 'Jinko hendo ni okeru nishi to higashi: Bakumatsu kara Meiji e', in Odaka Konosuke and Yamamoto Yuzo (eds.), *Bakumatsu-Meiji no Nihon keizai*, Tokyo: Nihon Keizai Shinbunsha.
Saito, O. (1997), 'Infant Mortality in Pre-transition Japan: Levels and Trends', in A. Bideau, B. Desjardins, and H. Perez Brignoli (eds.), *Infant and Child Mortality in the Past*, Oxford: Oxford University Press.
Sekiyama, Naotaro (1958), *Kinsei Nihon no jinko kozo*, Tokyo: Yoshikawa Kobunkan.
Somu-cho, Tokei-kyoku (1987), *Nihon choki tokei soran*, Volume 1, Tokyo: Nihon Tokei Kyokai.
Takagi, Masao (1996), '19-seiki Tohoku Nihon no "shibo kiki" to shusshoryoku', *Shakai keizaishigaku*, 61, 567–98.
—— (1999), 'Kiga to eiyo kyokyu: 19-seiki chuki Tohoku chiho no ichi noson', *Nihon kenkyu*, 19: 159–201.
Takahashi, K., and Nemoto, J. (1978), 'Relationships between Climatic Change, Rice Production and Population', in K. Takahashi, and M. M. Yoshino (eds.), *Climatic Change and Food Production*, Tokyo: University of Tokyo Press.
Tamura, Noriyoshi (1996), 'Shibo no kisetsusei kara mita chusei shakai', in his *Nihon chusei sonraku keiseishi no kenkyu*, Tokyo: Hasekura Shobo.
Tomobe, Ken'ichi (1991), 'Kinsei Nihon noson ni okeru shizen shusshoryoku suikei no kokoromi', *Jinkogaku kenkyu*, 14: 35–47.
Tsuya, N. O., and Kurosu, S. (2000), 'Mortality Responses to Short-term Economic Stress and Household Context in Early Modern Society', in T. Bengtsson and O. Saito (eds.), *Population and Economy: From Hunger to Modern Economic Growth*, Oxford: Oxford University Press.
Uemura, Masaharu (1978), 'Kinsei ni okeru hokyo jotai to shussho-su, shussho seihi', *Osaka Daigaku keizaigaku*, 27(4): 66–85.

Watkins, S. C., and Menken, J. (1985), 'Famines in Historical Perspective', *Population and Development Review*, 11: 647–75.

Yoshimura, Minoru (1993), 'Ko-kiko no fukugen to rekishi-tenko detabesu', *Chigaku zasshi*, 102: 131–43.

12

Famine and the Female Mortality Advantage

KATE MACINTYRE

The possibility of a 'female advantage' in mortality during famines[1] has been proposed in the past, though often dismissed simply as a feature of data bias. Unfortunately, the authorities who observe the phenomenon and who most argue its validity also rarely take the time to analyse *why* there might be a female advantage, nor do they address what specific factors might explain it. On the contrary, the explanations given are often brief and tentative, and they are followed by warnings about the quality of the data and the lack of information about the social and political context of the famine. This chapter has two objectives. First, I present a critical review of historical famine literature and identify evidence for a female advantage. Using secondary sources, this section establishes that the weight of evidence does indeed indicate an advantage for women in mortality as a consequence of famine. The evidence comes from a wide range of famine studies, both cross-national and over time. My second objective is to examine how authors have explained this female advantage and develop a conceptual framework that may help us to understand this phenomenon. I explicitly distinguish socio-political and cultural factors from biological factors, so that demographers may begin to explain the phenomenon of differential mortality not only by sex, but also by gender—an approach influenced by the literature on 'gender roles and responsibilities' in society.

The use of gender as a key variable has influenced research in many disciplines and topic areas, though it has rarely been applied to demographic analyses of famines. The importance of gender research for famine studies, though, can be set in the context of other related studies in sociology, economics, and social history. Researchers have emphasized, for example, the economic contribution of women to society, high rates of poverty among female headed households, the exclusion of women from farming extension activities despite their significant roles in agriculture, and the differential impacts of environmental degradation on women (e.g. see Agarwal 1992; Deere 1982; Moser 1989). Differential knowledge and roles of men and women in relation to the environment, and women's particular contribution to rural resource conservation

---

[1] The 'female advantage' is defined as a high (m/f) sex ratio of mortality, where the age-specific death rates for women are lower than those of men. It is a relative term, since famines involve excess mortality for both sexes and, usually, at all ages. This chapter uses the term 'female advantage', though it may be as appropriate to use 'male disadvantage'. However, I employ the term for the same reasons that analysts refer to 'son preference' rather than 'daughter discrimination'.

efforts have also been observed (Agarwal 1990). Some scholars suggest that women possess special knowledge and affinity with the natural environment, which may in turn affect their chances of survival during times of crisis.

The growing body of gender-informed research, and the literature on son preference and women's status lead one to conclude that women, especially poor rural women, enter famine at a major disadvantage compared to men. If women in normal times have less access to land, food, and health care, are more likely to be excluded from the cash economy, are more likely to suffer from malnutrition and severe anaemia, and are highly vulnerable to abandonment by husbands, then a logical deduction is that during a crisis women will suffer even more. But the opposite appears to be the case in relation to the severest of crises—famine. The paradox is that while women probably enter famines in a more physical and socially vulnerable condition than men, they seem to survive famines somewhat better. Is the explanation purely biological, or do survival strategies and institutional or socio-cultural factors tend to protect women?

This chapter tries to unravel this paradox. It combines literature from both the biological and sociological fields to better explain gender differentials in mortality during famines. The final picture is still unclear, and the colours run, but the central intention is to discuss an area of singular importance to famine scholarship, and one that for many reasons has been left, until recently, relatively untouched.

THE LITERATURE ON FAMINE MORTALITY

Harrison's phrase 'the variability of vulnerability' (1988: 14) captures the problem at the centre of this analysis. Researchers have often noted and analysed the variability of the risk of death in terms of age: the very young and the very old are highly vulnerable during famines (Dyson 1991; Harrison 1988; Razzaque 1989; Watkins and Menken 1985). They have also noted the age-specific mortality variability both between families under similar conditions and within families (de Waal 1989). Even close siblings can experience differing outcomes in sickness and death during times of famine (de Waal 1989; Rivers 1988).

Other variables, such as income and ethnicity, have also been the focus of study. Sen (1981) built his thesis of entitlements on the theory that poverty not only caused famine, but that the poorest suffered the most too. Razzaque (1989) in his study of famine mortality in Bangladesh during 1974–5 showed that the mortality of the poor increased 117 per cent while that of the 'rich' only increased by 28 per cent. An analysis of the Chinese famine years around 1960 shows that minorities suffered much higher infant mortality rates than did other non-minority populations in several heavily affected provinces (Kane 1988). In sum, part of the demographic story behind famine indicates that people at the extremes of age are at high risk, and that poverty and ethnicity can also contribute significantly to vulnerability. But what of the sex-selectivity of mortality rates during famine? Here demographers appear to be somewhat unsure.

Many historians and demographers have mentioned sex-specific mortality ratios for famines (e.g. see Boyle and Ó Gráda 1986; Chowdhury and Chen 1977; de Waal 1989; Dyson 1991; Drèze and Sen 1989; Livi-Bacci 1991; Rivers 1988; Sen 1981; Watkins and Menken 1985). But most do little more than mention the subject. This may be partly due to the weaknesses of the data, but it may also reflect the weakness of our theories for explaining sex-specific causes of differential mortality during famines. It is also surely a feature of the highly contextual and isolated factors that operate in each famine; many are not studied as cross-national phenomena, but as context-specific entities that require individual explanations about their causes and consequences. Thus, unless evidence is particularly strong regarding the selectivity of survival, there may be a natural hesitancy about emphasizing the findings. Accordingly, the first step in this chapter is to compile evidence regarding the existence of a famine mortality advantage for females.

Table 12.1 summarizes the literature on famine mortality. The famines are listed in temporal order, beginning with the Finnish and Irish famines of the nineteenth century and ending with the recent famines in the Horn of Africa. The table includes a column as to whether or not a female advantage was noted by an author. Although this is not a comprehensive list of all historical famines, it does include most of those for which we have sufficient data to draw demographic conclusions. A brief summary of the explanations offered for the sex differential by the authors listed is given in the last column. Only a few authorities are listed for each famine, although some crises have attracted numerous studies. The authors represented include those who reported sex-specific mortality data and who presented arguments to explain the differential levels of mortality. Note the almost uniform response 'Yes' in the third column. The female advantage has been identified on nearly all continents and across time. A second feature of the table is the range of explanations given. This is the subject of the second part of this chapter.

Prior to the mid-nineteenth century data on sex-specific mortality are available for only a few famines. However, some biblical references to famine do include comments specifically relating to men. For example, '[i]f a country sins against me by being unfaithful and I stretch out my hand against it to cut-off its food supply and send famine upon it and kill its men and their animals' (Ezekial 14: 13). But most such references tend to be sex-neutral; for example, 'This is what the Lord Almighty says: "I will punish them. Their young men will die by the sword, their sons and daughters by famine" ' (Jeremiah 11: 22). Wrigley and Schofield (1981) in their study of England's population history based on parish records—which includes multiple mortality crises—spend no significant time examining data differentiated by sex. The relatively rich data from Japanese parishes prior to the nineteenth century also reveal little concrete evidence of a sex differential in mortality, although there is some evidence that in the major famine of 1837 there were more male than female deaths (Jannetta 1992).

The first famines for which we can have some confidence regarding the data on sex-specific mortality are the Finnish and Irish crises of the mid-nineteenth century. These famines provide us with some of the richest demographic evidence of a female

Table 12.1. *Famines and the Female Mortality Advantage: A Summary of the Literature*

Famine country/year	Authors—selective	Female advantage identified (yes/no)	Explanation
Ireland 1846–50	Boyle and Ó Gráda (1986); Fitzpatrick (1997)	Yes	Biological: body fat and fertility, entitlement/socio-cultural
Finland 1860s	Pitkänen and Mielke (1993)	Yes	Migration
India 1890s	Dyson (1991); McAlpin (1983)	Yes	Migration, famine foods, prostitution, and biological: body fat, fertility decline
Greece 1941–2	Valaoras (1946); Hionidou (1999)	Yes / Yes	None given, Biological: body fat; differential access to food
Warsaw 1940s	Livi-Bacci (1991, 1993)	Yes	Biological: body fat/immune responses
Dutch Famine 1944	Henry (1990)	Yes	Biological: body fat/immune responses
India–Bengal 1943–4	Sen (1981)	No	Artefact of poor data
Russia 1930s	Livi-Bacci (1993)	Yes	Poor conditions affect men more—for example, labour camps and deportation
Malawi 1949	Vaughan (1987)	Insufficient data to measure mortality	Evidence of sex-specific survival strategies suggest female advantage
China 1959–61	Kane (1988); Sands and Buelow (1999)	No / Yes	Female infanticide gave male children advantage (one province only) / Biological: body fat
Bangladesh 1974–5	Chowdhury and Chen (1977); Razzaque et al. (1990)	No / Yes	/ Migration of males, fertility decline
Ethiopia 1984–5	Lindtjorn et al. (1993); Lindtjorn and Alemu (1997); Kidane (1989)	Yes / No	Women migrated to relief camps / No explanation
Sudan 1984–5	de Waal (1993)	Yes	Boys coming in contact with diseases, other migration factors
Madagascar 1985–7	Garenne et al. (1999)	Yes	Biological: 'a harvesting effect'—differential vulnerability to infectious diseases
Somalia 1992	Collins (1995)	Yes	Biological: body fat, and position of women in society (gender)

mortality advantage. In Finland these periods include the war years of 1808–9 and the famine years of 1832–3 and 1857–8, as well as the Great Finnish Famines of the 1860s. Pitkänen and his colleagues have examined these crises in a series of publications, and they conclude that generally the female mortality advantage in Finland was small but consistent, at least for certain age groups and regions (Pitkänen and Mielke 1993; Pitkänen 1999). Their explanation is that the high levels of migration of young adult males led to higher excess mortality through exposure to disease in the towns and cities.

While the Great Irish famine of 1845–51 has attracted considerable attention from demographers and historians, only recently have the gender differentials in mortality been investigated in any depth (Fitzpatrick 1997). This is due to what Ó Gráda (1999: 101) calls the 'very tricky business . . . [of] estimating the relative impact of the crisis on men and women'. He admits, however, that the quantitative evidence, though limited, does point to a female advantage for most of the years of the crisis, and across most of the regions of Ireland (Ó Gráda 1999). He is certain too that while men do appear to have been at a disadvantage, in relative terms this disadvantage was small. Ó Gráda calls this a 'slight male edge' (1999: 102), although the gender ratios of mortality in rural areas over the 5 years of the famine range from 1.13 to 1.25.

Data from two Indian famines of the 1870s show that women had lower excess mortality than men in both Bombay and Madras. The death rates, for example in the Madras relief camp, were 595.3 per thousand for women and 796.4 per thousand for men. McAlpin accounts for these differential mortality statistics as supporting evidence for 'the hypothesis that females have greater biological capacity to resist the rigours of famine—a capacity that is not offset by social factors' (McAlpin 1983: 63). This same account of excess male mortality is also taken as evidence that men succumbed more to infectious, epidemic diseases (largely cholera in India during the 1870s) than did women (McAlpin 1983: 64). Dyson (1991) in his study of South Asian famines in the late nineteenth and early twentieth centuries also argues for a slight but consistent female mortality advantage in most areas. Thus in Berar between 1890 and 1900 the population sex ratio declined for all ages except the 0–4 and 15–19 age groups. This decline in the sex ratio is even more evident in older age groups. Dyson states that 'at most adult ages, the number of excess male deaths greatly exceeded the number for females' (Dyson 1999: 12).

In contrast, Sen's conclusions concerning gender differentials in mortality during times of famine are rather ambiguous. Thus, in his book *Poverty and Famines* (1981), when addressing the Bengal famine of the 1940s, he dismisses the idea of a female advantage, although he has since drawn a more tentative conclusion (see below). In relation to the Bengal disaster Sen concludes that the famine mortality was a 'magnification of normal mortality'—in terms of both the age and sex differentials. One table, however, clearly shows that for the most severe year of the famine (1943) women's death rates dropped compared to their pre-famine (i.e. 1941–2) level while those of males rose. Sen's dismissal of this as reflecting the biases of data collection evident in colonial India is built on the grounds that there are some 'rather contrived explanations . . . proposed to explain the supposed contrast of sex ratios' (Sen 1981: 212).

These explanations are described in a footnote (p. 213). They include women's better capacity to find employment, their having possession of goods which can be exchanged for money or food, and even their being in charge of the cooking pot. It seems strange to dismiss evidence on the grounds that the explanations seem personally unappealing (Sen uses the phrase 'my favourites' (1981: 211)). But perhaps these explanations will appear a little less 'contrived' if they are examined carefully. Indeed, in later work Drèze and Sen discuss famine mortality and acknowledge that 'there is considerable dispute as to whether the intensity of female deprivation increases in famine situations' (1989: 55).

Demographers studying famines have sometimes detected a distinct female mortality advantage for some age groups and not for others. Thus Pitkänen and Mielke (1993) report considerable differentials in the sex ratios for excess mortality in 1868 in Sweden for what they call 'high impact regions', and especially for young adult men (i.e. those aged under 30). However, the authors' investigation of hospital data reveals very little difference between the sexes in case-fatalities due to famine-related diseases (especially typhus) in any other age group. Likewise, a study of the demographic impact of the Bangladesh famine of 1974–5 by Chowdhury and Chen suggests that the normal 'disadvantage for females (under the age of 10) appears to have been exaggerated during the 1974–5 famine, but disaster diminished or even reversed the disadvantage to older women in most age groups by raising male death rates more than females death rates' (1977: 415). Also, while examining the demographic impact of famine on population size, Watkins and Menken conclude that 'in most situations, where reasonable data are available, the sex and age differentials in excess mortality appear to favour women and young adults, so that the capacity for reproduction is preserved' (1985: 656).

Results from the Russian famine of the 1930s, which had an enormous demographic impact, have only recently begun to be compiled (see Livi-Bacci 1993; Wheatcroft 1999). Livi-Bacci reports that 'about 60 per cent of excess deaths were male (but the share is higher for the population over age 10 in 1937)' (1993: 752). Thus Livi-Bacci too suggests that males suffered higher excess mortality at all ages and particularly past childhood. He briefly accounts for this by saying that 'this is consistent with the fact that males were hit harder by the repression and suffered more from the hardships of deportation and labour camps'. The estimated numbers of excess deaths for people aged over 10 indicate a range of between 0.6 and 1.8 million deaths in the case of women compared to between 2.0 and 3.2 million in the case of men. Despite these large mortality differentials, Livi-Bacci (1993: 753) still suggests that future research is needed to 'establish whether ... males were more seriously affected than females'. My reading of his data is that probably we do not need to 'establish' the fact, but we do need to explain it.

In another 'great' twentieth-century famine, that in China during 1959–61, there are conflicting reports on the matter, depending upon the region of focus. Ashton *et al.* (1984) report that there is some evidence of a female mortality advantage, especially in the older age groups. Sands and Buelow (1998) portray a considerable advantage. They suggest that females had on average a 20 per cent higher survival rate than males, but that there was sizeable variation both between and within provinces. In contrast, Kane reports that little female advantage can be found for the province of Anhui (Kane 1988). She argues that girls born between 1955–6 and 1959–60 'seem to be missing in particularly large numbers'. She accounts for this by using contemporary reports of increased female infanticide and discriminatory feeding practices for girls. The example of the Chinese famine points to the need for more context-specific, local investigations that can reflect the variety of experiences and outcomes.

Interesting results have emerged from data gathered during World War II, mainly from small, discrete regions, which suffered extreme hardship. These studies also support the notion of a female advantage. The Dutch Hunger Winter (1944–5) drove mortality for females up by 73 per cent, and that for males up by 169 per cent (Henry 1990). Wartime conditions in Greece also appear to have affected men more than women (Hionidou 1999; Valaoras 1946), although few explanations for the differentials were noted. A recent analysis of famine on the islands of Mykonos and Syros finds a uniform male disadvantage (Hionidou 1999) for the peak famine periods. Male deaths constituted 59 per cent of famine deaths on Mykonos and 67 per cent on Syros. Hionidou also reports that men appear to have succumbed earlier in the famine than women, although she does not say why. Because mobility and migration were restricted and epidemic disease appears to have been minimal, these island populations constitute the closest we have to quasi-laboratories for controlled experiments in mortality during famine. Meanwhile, in another horrendous wartime event, that of the Warsaw ghetto (1941–2), women again appear to have survived marginally longer than did men (Livi-Bacci 1991).

Finally, we turn to the more recent famines of sub-Saharan Africa, particularly those in the Horn of Africa. Ethiopia, Somalia, and Sudan have all suffered from famine conditions during the past 30 years; indeed, some populations in this area of the world are still suffering. Unfortunately, the data from these famines are inadequate, particularly when one is trying to disaggregate by sex. In Darfur and Sudan, de Waal (1989) observes significant differences between male and female death rates, which are extreme in the 5–14 age group and at older adult ages (i.e. those over 30). In contrast, the case of Ethiopia appears to offer a rare example of a female mortality *disadvantage*. Thus Kidane (1989) examines the demographic consequences of the 1984–5 famine. He uses survey data from before the famine (1981) and compares them to data collected from famine victims in 1984–5. Comparing famine with pre-famine mortality, he concludes that mortality was greater for females than for males, and that the sex ratio of mortality was biased towards males in all age groups except the very youngest, meaning that they survived in greater numbers than did females. However, the author's analysis is marred by the fact that his data (total sample just 774) come from survivors of refugee camps who were interviewed during a period of rehabilitation in resettlement areas in 1985. And the author admits that this study population were not representative of those most affected by the famine. Data from Somalia in 1992–3 have recently been published which point to a slight female mortality advantage, although again the data are restricted to small and unrepresentative populations (Centers for Disease Control 1992; Collins 1995).

ARGUMENTS FOR A FEMALE ADVANTAGE

In the previous section I have presented evidence of a consistent sex differential favouring women during famines in countries all around the world. I now examine three basic arguments for this observed sex differential in mortality which emerge from the famine literature. The first argument is that this phenomenon is the result of biased evidence, that is the data collected during famines may be so poor that they consistently miss particularly female deaths. Alternatively, biological and sociocultural determinants may underlie a real female advantage. These explanations are briefly described in this section and illustrated in the next.

Data collection

One explanation is that this 'observed' female advantage is actually a result of consistently poor data collection, resulting in a selection bias. This bias is present during normal times, but it may be exaggerated by famine conditions, for example by the chaos that data collectors may operate under during famine times. Women are commonly under-reported in many censuses in predominantly non-industrial, agrarian societies. And either due to discrimination or ignorance, women may be counted even less dependably during times of famine; their deaths being forgotten, not noticed or underreported in greater numbers (e.g. UN 1998). These biases could operate at any age, but they may be especially important at the relative extremes: for example, before marrying and after becoming a widow. This thesis says, therefore, that due to under-reporting of famine (female) deaths there may be an inflated number of women and girls who *appeared* to survive famine. Conversely, a seeming female mortality advantage could conceivably result from male deaths being over-reported. For example, in situations where there is high internal population mobility, especially of men in search of food or work for their families, it is conceivable that their deaths are reported both at their home locations and their places of death (e.g. the city where they have gone to search for work). This phenomenon would mean that male deaths would appear to have been higher in number than they actually were.

Biological mechanisms

Several important biological explanations may account for the greater survival of females of many different species during times of stress. The underlying thesis, as Watkins and Menken (1985) argue, is that females are needed in greater numbers in post-famine/stress periods in order to retain the ability of the species to reproduce. Essentially, the survival of a mammal population depends upon there being more wombs than sperm producers, since in a short period of time, one sperm producer can fertilize many wombs. Thus it is more important to have a larger proportion of females alive than males. Although simple to accept theoretically, it is not so easy to explain how this argument operates in practice, that is, what the actual mechanisms are that make differential survival possible, and how they come about. In human populations, at least, these ideas are extremely difficult to test. Current theses in this area highlight women's higher levels of body-fat (a metabolic efficiency argument), an explanation related to immune responses that may be differentially genetically programmed and which may generate greater male vulnerability to some infectious diseases, and fertility decline.

According to the body fat hypothesis, described by Henry (1990), Livi-Bacci (1991), and Rivers (1982), the female advantage is directly related to the higher proportion of body fat carried by women, compared to men, which improves their survival rates. This is often described as a series of biological factors that insulate women from the effects of nutritional deprivation (Fitzpatrick 1997). Rivers suggests that females 'ought to be less vulnerable to deprivation, having smaller needs for energy and most nutrients, because they are smaller than men' (Rivers 1982: 91). Women may also have an advantage through a lower metabolic rate, plus a higher body fat content. At the same body weight, women have more fat, which theoretically means that they may live longer on their energy reserves, and thus protect their vital organs from collapse. Compared to men, women should survive acute deprivation better, mainly because they need less energy to support their weight. Conversely, men with a higher lean body mass, which elevates their nutritional needs just to maintain their basal metabolism, may use their body fat stores up quicker, and they may need more energy and nutrients daily just in order to maintain their basic functions (i.e. to keep body organs going) (see Hoyenga and Hoyenga 1982).

Several authors cite experiments done on rats, lions, reindeer, and other mammals that 'often show male mammals more vulnerable to starvation and death than females' (see Hill *et al.* 1986; also Rivers 1988: 91). Other reports from mammalian studies describe the greater proportion of muscle in male bodies compared to female (36 per cent in women compared to 44.8 per cent in men) (Ó Gráda 1999). Given that muscle simply adds to the body mass of an individual, it is not a physiological advantage to have more of it during times of malnutrition and food deprivation. Finally, men and women may process micro-nutrients differently, with women processing them quicker and needing fewer in a crisis (L. Adair, personal communication, 1999). This explanation, however, may well interact with socio-cultural explanations which argue that women and men have differential access to micro-nutrients during crises, as discussed below.

Since in famines many individuals die not of actual starvation, but of infectious or communicable diseases, it is logical to wonder whether the gender gap in male and female response to the physical onslaught of these diseases may partially explain the differential death rates. Research shows girls are more likely to survive some diseases than are boys (Garenne and Lafon 1998). In particular, excess male mortality due to typhoid, malaria, anthrax, schistosomiasis, and polio has been noted. Of these diseases, the first two are frequently cited in connection with famine. However, other diseases, such as measles, smallpox, whooping cough, and cholera, show considerable female *disadvantage*—especially in the age range 15–30. Data used in the study by Garenne and Lafon were taken from over 100 countries for the period between 1959 and 1989; but the relevance of the conclusions for famine conditions may be doubtful.

Nevertheless, a sex differential in cause-specific mortality, which the authors hypothesize may be due to differential immune responses, may, in the case of malaria and typhoid at least, be especially important during some famines.

The final biological explanation discussed here is that declining fertility, which frequently accompanies famine, may release women from the stress and dangers of pregnancy and child birth, and hence lower their mortality. A famine-induced reduction in the risk of pregnancy due to amenorrhoea, malnutrition, physical separation of spouses, or a drop in sexual drive due to reduced energy may lead to a consequent drop in maternal mortality. A reduction in fertility, however, is unlikely to account for all of the female mortality advantage observed in famines. Although maternal mortality is high in many countries that have experienced famine, it is not high enough to account for the saving of lives that this differential suggests. It could, no doubt, contribute to the gender mortality gap, since the drop in pregnancy rates means a reduction in the stress and discomfort of pregnancy, and a reduction in the numbers of very young children who need to be fed and protected (Ó Gráda 1999).

Socio-economic and cultural mechanisms

The final set of arguments that may account for the female advantage arise from a broad group of non-biological factors. These may operate at the individual or household levels, within larger institutions, or be due to national and even international contexts.

At the individual level, numerous survival strategies have been identified by social scientists trying to understand how communities cope during stressful periods. The arguments relevant to famine demography are those relating to gender-differential survival strategies. For survival strategies to work in favour of one gender, the strategy must either be protective of women, and/or increase the vulnerability of men. The general strategies described below include: migration, differential coping strategies for access to food (either through knowledge of wild or 'famine' foods, or through access to the cooking pot by women), the willingness and ability to turn to prostitution, or the action of seeking care or assistance, and in particular the willingness to seek shelter in institutions such as relief camps, workhouses, or standard health care settings.

Migration is a common coping mechanism practised by numerous societies during crises. It appears that this strategy is more frequently used by men to seek work and/or food to send back to their families. For several reasons migration may put them at greater risk of illness or death than women. The migration flow is, of course, always 'emigration'—that is, out of the crisis area. Migrants are at greater risk because they may come into contact with deadly infectious diseases—for example, measles, typhoid, cholera, and malaria—earlier than women, especially if men are seeking work in overcrowded towns with little infrastructure to handle large numbers of immigrants. Migrant males may also be at a higher risk due to increased energy use in travelling or increased risk of accident during travel or at work. Even suicide may be more prevalent among dislocated men. Conversely, women who stay behind use fewer energy resources, they remain within the security network of other familiar families in similar situations, and—if the out-migration of their men is successful—they receive financial remittances or other material support.

Another mechanism reported with a gender-specific component in different societies is differential access to food. The search for wild foods, often known explicitly as 'famine foods', is sometimes seen as one of the main strategies that allow women a greater advantage during famine in terms of the variety and quantity of nutrition available to them. It is also possible to hypothesize that women's common role as cook and food preparer may provide some material advantage for them and their girl children, since they are in charge of the cooking pot itself. (See El Bushra and Piza-Lopez (1994) for a more complete description of survival strategies in emergencies.)

The strategy of women turning to prostitution to feed themselves and their children is also commonly observed in economic crises. Despite evidence that prostitution is practised by both genders, women and girls may more easily consider prostituting their bodies because it is more readily accepted in terms of the social and behavioural norms found in most societies. Once again, this explanation is unlikely to account for more than a small proportion of enhanced female survival, since the act of prostitution may also put women at very considerable additional risk.

Finally, women, in their roles as reproducers and protectors within the family, and being the usual first guardians of children, are more likely to take sick children, and themselves, to a health post or hospital. This may benefit women in some circumstances. Women are also more likely to seek care and help in crises, because cultural norms generally make them responsible for the well-being of children. They may have less pride than men, which may make them more likely to seek help at relief camps or, as in nineteenth-century Ireland, in workhouses.

Finally, at the national and international levels practices and policies may exist to protect women and children more, mainly because societies perceive them to be more vulnerable than men. In many relief or refugee situations policies operate that favour accepting women and children before the acceptance of men (El Bushra and Piza Lopez 1994). These practices reflect cultural norms, for example the accepted wisdom that women are guardians of the next generation, or that they are more physically vulnerable (the 'weaker' sex) and thus must be afforded greater protection.

DISCUSSION

To illustrate these arguments and assess which may be more appropriate in our search for explanations for the female advantage, I turn again to the famine literature. The main explanations—data biases, biological considerations, and socio-cultural factors—are examined. And I apply the framework shown in Fig. 12.1 to illustrate the various factors and highlight key research questions.

Systematic bias in vital event reporting is a constant threat to the quality of data on famines, and most authorities spend considerable time discussing the quality of their data. If women's deaths are indeed consistently under-reported, relative to men's, and if we can assume that female births have *not* also been systematically under-reported, then we can assume that an artefact of data collection may in fact explain

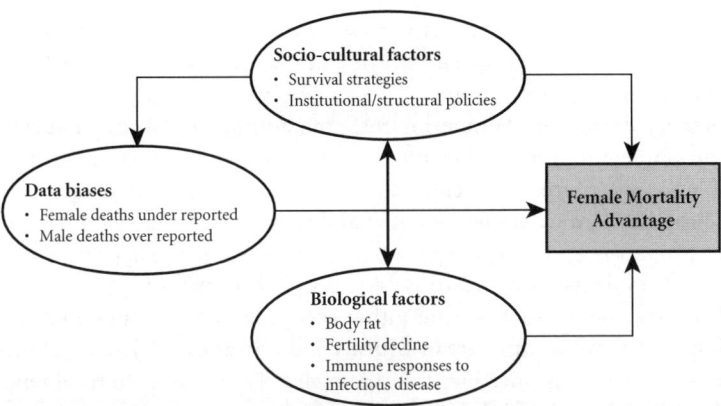

Figure 12.1. *A Conceptual Framework of the Female Mortality Advantage in Famine*

the observed female advantage. Sen in his Bengal famine analysis (1981) argues that data bias is the explanation most likely to explain gender differentials in survival. Few other authors, however, report a serious data bias in this respect against women. One example of under-reporting is Ethiopia in the 1980s (the exact date was unclear in the article). The authors show that during the famine and dislocation prompted by the policy of villagization in the 1980s between 17 and 46 per cent of total deaths went unregistered (Lindtjørn *et al.* 1993). The under-registration of deaths in this case was strongly associated with neo-natal deaths, but unfortunately the authors do not present a breakdown of the sex of the infants that died.

Data bias, however, is unlikely to be a significant explanation for the female advantage for two reasons. First, the pattern of female advantage is consistent across numerous countries (ranging from China to Holland, from Sudan to Russia) and across time (from the early nineteenth century to the 1980s). For data bias to be a serious explanation, sources of error would have to be cross-cultural and cross-temporal. Second, the female advantage recorded in many famines is reasonably substantial, and none of the reports of data bias can explain more than a slight female advantage in mortality at the macro level. Thus, while some societies do discriminate against women and to such an extent that some under-recording of their deaths as adults is likely, I do not think it is reasonable to assume that a systematic and large increase during crisis periods can explain the phenomenon in every society observed in famine conditions.

The biological arguments are compelling and they surely explain some of the systematic, consistent, and cross-cultural phenomenon that is seen in Table 12.1. The body fat thesis is tempting in its simplicity, but still largely empirically unfounded in *homo sapiens*. Several authorities doubt the value of the hypothesis, and argue that its effects need to be disaggregated between a short-term protective mechanism and a long-term effect. Evidently, the former seems to work, but the latter may not. As Fitzpatrick says, 'Though a significant advantage in normal times and in the early months of scarcity, this capacity [to store body fat] must have become rapidly irrelevant to both sexes as under-nourishment persisted and intensified among the Irish poor' (Fitzpatrick 1997: 59).

In Somalia, during the famine in 1992, the author of a study of survival rates and anthropometry of men and women *in extremis* found that women appeared less vulnerable to severe famine oedema. But once oedema was controlled for, the body mass indices (BMI) were similar for men and women (Collins 1995). Men also had a poorer prognosis and died at greater rates than women. This rare study, based on data from patients admitted to Baidoa hospital in 1992–3, appears to confirm the body fat argument. However, the author concludes that a greater number of male admissions—many of whom were in critical condition and could not walk unaided—could have reflected a gender bias towards males. There was a cultural tendency to carry men to the hospital for help, whereas the women were probably left to die. As Collins points out, more research is needed, with reliable data, before the proportion of body fat can be established with confidence as a primary determinant of survival.

Regarding the fertility decline thesis, evidence shows that fertility often drops in the early stages of famine. Chowdhury and Chen (1977) found, for example, a significant decline in fertility during the two Bangladesh famines occurring between 1966 and 1975 (though they do not pursue the idea of sex differentials in mortality as a result of the decline in fertility). Dyson, in his historical reconstruction of the Bengali and Indian famines of the nineteenth century, calculated that the drop in fertility was a good predictor of the severity and duration of the famines. He also points to the possibly lowered risk from maternal mortality for women consequent on this drop in fertility (Dyson 1991: 12). Boyle and Ó Gráda (1986) also estimated that the fertility decline that accompanied the Irish famine can be translated to over 300,000 averted births from 1846–51. However, if these averted births are used to estimate the 'averted' maternal deaths, using a high estimate of the Irish maternal mortality rate in the mid-century, then possibly as many as 5,000 women's lives were 'saved' because they did not go through the dangers of pregnancy and child birth. Although this figure cannot account for all the female mortality advantage, it clearly could contribute.

The last biological explanation based on the immune response differences to infectious diseases between males and females is tempting. Unfortunately, cause of death is one of the least studied areas of famine mortality. The data we do have on this differential response to infectious diseases comes from multi-year, multi-country studies. Until more evidence from famines is available for analysis, disaggregated by gender, this explanation, while plausible, remains untested.

The same uncertainty may also be true of the socio-cultural explanations that theoretically point to specific survival strategies favouring women. Migration, for example, may be 'one of the most important survival strategies to which famine-struck populations have recourse' (Arnold 1988: 91), but does this translate into selective survival by gender? In many, but not all, famines, men seem to migrate earlier and at least in several historical famines probably came in contact with infectious diseases earlier than women. For example, Finnish men from regions where there was high migration appear to have died in greater numbers than their families who stayed at home. More recently in Malawi, Sudan, and Somalia, women left home later often after the support from their absent husbands had not been forthcoming, or they heard of their husband's death (Collins 1995; de Waal 1989; Vaughan 1987). In contrast, in Ethiopia, Lindtjørn et al. (1993) report that men in Wollo stayed behind in villages, hoping for rains so that they could plant the next harvest, while women sought help in the refugee camps. In Greece in the 1940s there was virtually no migration (due to the occupation of the islands), yet men still died in greater numbers (Hionidou 1999). It might seem from these examples that men are less likely to survive whether they migrate or not.

Sometimes several survival strategies are observed at the same time. Unusually, high female migration to Calcutta was reported in Bengal in 1943, and many of these women were thought to be turning to prostitution. In this city, 'rather than see their children die ... the women took up prostitution to survive' (Das 1949: 72). This was interpreted as 'the determination of young mothers *not* to remain in the villages where children would die from starvation, but to move to the city where food was available'. Das also mentioned that males may have decided to stay in the villages to care for property and because 'they felt that gruel kitchens in the city discriminated in favour of females and children who did not have as many options to earn food as did the males' (Das 1949: 72). Here one can see the possibility of multiple strategies and societal factors interacting together to favour women.

Intra-household issues—which includes the distribution of knowledge about survival foods, and access to food, and which may vary significantly between male and female members of the same household—are probably of some significance to female survival rates during famine. Once again, however, we are hampered by lack of data. Many researchers have analysed communities to understand their methods of coping during hard times or even economic crises, and have investigated gender differentials in consumption: whether related to a reduction of consumption (tightening the belt) or the seeking of 'famine' foods. Actual reports from field studies show availability of famine foods being a vital variable in determining the timing of migration in Ethiopia (Lindtjørn et al. 1993), Sudan (de Waal 1989), and Malawi (Vaughan 1987). Some research has argued that women are guardians of the knowledge of wild foods (Vaughan 1987) while at least one researcher argues that men—because they are more likely to be out in the fields with livestock or crops—are more knowledgeable about these foods (reported for Indian hill tribes in Agarwal (1990)). Obviously, more local-level analysis is needed, which needs to take into account multiple variables such as people's state of nourishment as well as gender differentials in knowledge of food. An eyewitness account from Ethiopia reported that although many people knew of famine foods they were often too weak to seek them out and prepare them, since the preparation required extra wood and water to cook the roots to reduce their toxicity when raw (M. Amin, personal communication, 1985).

Another survival strategy that may save women's lives is the stronger willingness to seek help, despite, or perhaps because of, a lower social status during normal times. In India and Bangladesh, where women's status is generally acknowledged as a proximate factor in high child mortality rates (Das Gupta 1987; Miller 1997) and higher than expected adult female mortality (Lopez and Ruzicka 1983), women have had higher survival rates during famines. This suggests that women's status may change radically during severe food crises, allowing women greater freedom to make decisions that influence theirs and their children's survival. Fitzpatrick (1997) discusses this phenomenon in the context of female entitlements that change during famine. Mehtabunisa (1984) suggests that 'women appeared not only to survive [the Bengal famine of 1943–4], but also to fight more tenaciously than men'. This supposition is reinforced by the following observation:

She was not more than 25, yet there was no womanly sign of breast. Only two nipples dangled from two parched sheets of skin from which everything else seemed to have dried up. Her hair had become matted: perhaps they (sic) were not attended since she left home. Her eyes had sunk in their sockets, but they had not lost their lustre as in the case of her husband. Indeed they had an unusual glow which was the outward indication of her great determination to survive this catastrophe, most probably for her children. (Das 1949: 79)

Finally, what of existing structural supports or policies that operate in favour of women during crises? It would seem that cultural ideas of female vulnerability, 'women and children first' and notions of the 'weaker' sex could hypothetically function to generate policies that protect these groups. Many non-governmental organizations (CARE, OXFAM, or Save the Children Fund) and international or multi-national humanitarian relief organizations (UNHCR or FAO), do have gender-specific policies that explicitly protect women and children in relief camps (Macrae and Zwi 1994). Of course, how well these policies work, and how much of the female mortality advantage these policies can explain is still questionable. Mokyr and Ó Gráda (1999), in their work on cause of death in Irish workhouses, imply that female patients exceeded males in fever hospitals, but that male deaths in these institutions exceeded female deaths. This could be interpreted as evidence that women were generally admitted to workhouses in greater numbers (though there is clearly a considerable range across the unions of Ireland), but one could also interpret this either as evidence that biological mechanisms provided women with a significant safety net, or that women may have reached the workhouses in a less worse state than men.

CONCLUSION

Given the consistency with which we see the female mortality advantage across time and across societies and across economies (in Table 12.1), it is reasonable to conclude that during famines over the past two or three centuries women have had lower excess mortality than men. This observation is not original since several nineteenth-century observers of famine appeared very comfortable stressing the female advantage, even if they could not explain it.

During the Indian famine of the 1870s, for example, it was noted that 'male deaths were nearly twice that of female deaths' (Eliot 1876). The report continues by saying, 'all authorities are agreed that women succumb to famine less easily than men'. In contrast, many modern demographers are evidently less sure of their opinion on the subject than were Eliot's authorities. While demographers have noted a female advantage during famine, few present adequate explanations. In fact, one commentator notes that the sex differential 'prompted perplexity, even embarrassment, on the part of analysts looking for further evidence of female victimhood' (Fitzpatrick 1997: 62). One advantage of cross-national research, as crude as it can be, is the exposure of phenomena that contradict assumptions (in this, the case of the *weaker* sex) based on cultural understandings and studies conducted in hard, but not crisis, times.

Such a cross-cultural phenomenon must have some biological foundation. But the theories and evidence of the biological links are weak, and largely based on empirical data from other mammals. The lowered fertility/lowered maternal mortality explanation is attractive, but insufficient to explain much of the differential. In addition, my analysis of these biological theses cannot satisfactorily explain the considerable within-famine mortality variation. Within certain famines, it has been noted that the gender-specific survival rates vary enormously from year to year. (See Ó Gráda (1999); data presenting gender differentials in survival during the Irish famine range from almost no advantage to 25 per cent greater chance of survival.) Even if one accepts the fundamental importance of the biological mechanisms to these differentials, explaining the temporal, internal variations within famines still requires social, political, and cultural explanations. In other words, even if one accepts that the biology of females gives them a certain advantage of body fat and immune responses, and, of course, the advantages of lowered fertility during famines, over men, one still needs to explain how in Ireland, for example, there is considerable variation in the gender mortality ratio across the unions and over time.

Another problem with the biological explanations is the lack of supporting data. In terms of the immune response to infectious diseases, we have the beginnings of some empirical work, but no studies from famines, so the conclusions are extrapolated from non-famine, non-crisis times. Of course, ethical demands mean that when people are dying it is unacceptable to merely conduct research upon them, and not feed them, and yet there are multiple questions that still need answers if we are to improve our understanding of the relationship between survival mechanisms and mortality.

The most likely explanations emerge from the combination of gender-specific survival strategies (migration, access to food, willingness to seek assistance, and thus to survive) and gender-biased institutional and political factors (relief or support programmes), with basic human physiology (body fat, immune responses, and reduced fertility) as an underlying cause of differential mortality. These factors may not only interact, but through their interaction they may generate synergistic effects beyond the additive effects one might expect.

Future research is needed in several areas. In general, more detailed analyses are needed to disentangle the sociological and cultural explanations from the biological ones. More data on cause (and timing) of death during famines are vital, as is a greater understanding of the role of the immune responses, hormones, and micronutrients in differential survival capacity. More detailed analyses are required of the severity and duration of starvation, the timing of epidemics, and how these factors influence the sex ratios of mortality. Also, more work is needed in the field during crises to determine, at the point of help (e.g. refugee camp), the impact of gender-biased policies, as well as a great need to differentiate between the long- and short-term effects of survival strategies. These analyses may help disentangle some of the political and cultural reasons for those who seek help, but what of those that do not? Investigations are needed using existing data to establish if there are consistent, cross-national patterns in the age-specific vulnerability across the sexes, since there appears to be evidence that the female advantage is much more pronounced at the middle ages (approximately 20–45) in many famines, but not so pronounced at other ages. This suggests the picture is not a simple gender advantage, but that there may be important age-sex interactions that effect group vulnerability.

If gender-based research has shown fairly convincingly that women are frequently the social and political inferiors to men in terms of their access to resources, their protection under law, their proportion of work within households, then how can we explain why they do better than men during extreme crises? If biology is not the only answer, then are women more adaptable or do they have more flexible survival skills, or are there societal impulses at work that discriminate against men during crises? Ultimately, I believe, we will find that the picture emerges of bundles of protective factors (both biological and sociological) for women, and aggressive or risk factors for men that work in a variety of ways to answer this question.

But in the meantime more local-level research is needed to identify and discriminate among these factors, and of course to do this we need a more comprehensive gender-sensitive approach for data collection and analysis. Finally, a more imaginative diversity of methods will be required to stretch our somewhat meagre data sources. For example, use of multiple methods to analyse existing data may produce more satisfying analyses—the combination of multi-level quantitative modelling methods and oral histories will surely allow more subtle interpretations of this interesting phenomenon of the female mortality advantage during famines.

References

Agarwal, B. (1990), 'Social Security and the Family: Coping with Seasonality and Calamity in Rural India', *Journal of Peasant Studies*.
—— (1992), 'The Gender and Environment Debate: Lessons from India', *Feminist Studies*, 18(1)(Spring): 119–57.
Alamgir, M. (1980), *Famine in South Asia: The Political Economy of Mass Starvation*, Cambridge, Mass.: Oelgeschlager, Gunn and Hain.
Arnold, D. (1988), *Famine, Social Crisis and Historical Change*, Oxford: Blackwell.
Ashton, B., Hill, K., Piazza, A., and Zeitz, R. (1984), 'Famine in China, 1958–61', *Population and Development Review*, 10(4): 613–45.
Boyle, P. B., and Ó Gráda, C. (1986), 'Fertility Trends, Excess Mortality and the Great Irish Famine', *Demography*, 23(4): 543–62.
Centers for Disease Control, (1992), 'Famine Affected, Refugee and Displaced Populations: Recommendations for Public Health Issues', MMWR, *Volume 41*/No. RR-13.

Chowdhury, A. K. M., and Chen, L. C. (1977), 'The Dynamics of Contemporary Famine', in *Proceedings of the International Population Conference, Mexico City, Volume 1*, Liège: International Union for the Scientific Study of Population.

Collins, S. (1995), 'The Limits of Human Adaptation to Starvation', *Nature Medicine*, 1(8): 810–14.

Das, T. K. (1949), *Bengal Famine (1943): As Revealed in a Survey of the Destitutes in Calcutta*, Calcutta: Calcutta University Press.

Das Gupta, M. (1987), 'Selective Discrimination against Female Children in Rural Punjab', *Population and Development Review*, 13: 77–100.

Deere, C. D. (1982), 'The Division of Labor by Sex in Agriculture: A Peruvian Case Study', *Economic Development and Cultural Change*, (30)4: 795–811.

de Waal, A. (1989), *Famine that Kills: Darfur, Sudan 1984–5*, Oxford: Clarendon Press.

Drèze, J., and Sen, A. (1989), *Hunger and Public Action*, Oxford: Clarendon Press.

Dyson, T. (1991), 'On the Demography of South Asian Famines, Parts 1 and 2', *Population Studies*, 45: 5–26 and 279–98.

—— (1999), 'Famine in Berar, 1896–7 and 1899–1900, Echoes and Chain Reactions', Paper presented at Fondation des Treilles, May 1999, and published in revised form in the present book.

El Bushra, J., and Piza-Lopez, E. (1994), 'Gender, War and Food', in J. Macrae and A. Zwi (eds.), *War and Hunger: Rethinking International Responses to Complex Emergencies*, London: Zed Books.

Eliot, C. (1876), *Report of the Indian Famine Commission*, in *Census of India*, Delhi, 1911.

Fitzpatrick, D. (1997), 'Gender and the Famine', in M. Kelleher and J. H. Murphy (eds.), *Gender Perspectives on Nineteenth-Century Ireland: Public and Private Spheres*, Dublin: Irish Academic Press.

Garenne, M., and Lafon, M. (1998), 'Sexist Diseases', *Perspectives in Biology and Medicine*, 41(2): 176–89.

Garenne, M., Waltisperger, D., Cantrelle, P., and Osée, R. (1999), 'Demographic Impact of a Mild Famine in an African City: The Case of Antananarivo, 1985–87', Paper presented at Fondation des Treilles, May 1999, and published in revised form in the present book.

Harrison, G. A. (ed.) (1988), *Famine*, Oxford: Oxford University Press.

Henry, C. J. K. (1990), 'Body Mass Index and the Limits to Human Survival', *European Journal of Clinical Nutrition*, 44: 329–35.

Hill, J. O., Talano, C. M., Nickel, M., and DiGirolamo, M. (1986), 'Energy Utilization in Food-restricted Female Rats', *Journal of Nutrition*, 116(10): 2000–11.

Hionidou, V. (1999), 'Send Us either Food or Coffins: The 1941–2 Famine on the Aegean Island of Syros', Paper presented at Fondation des Treilles, May 1999, and published in revised form in the present book.

Hoyenga, K. B., and Hoyenga, K. T. (1982), 'Theoretical Review: Gender and Energy Balance: Sex Differences in Adaptations for Feast or Famine', *Physiology and Behavior*, 28: 545–63.

Jannetta, A. B. (1992), 'Famine Mortality in Nineteenth Century Japan: The Evidence from a Temple Death Register', *Population Studies*, 46: 427–43.

Kane, P. (1988), *Famine in China: 1951–61: Demographic and Social Implications*, London: St Martins Press.

Kidane, A. (1989), 'Demographic Consequences of the 1984–5 Ethiopian Famine', *Demography*, 26: 515–22.

Lindtjørn, B., Alemu, T., and Bjorvatn, B. (1993), 'Population Growth, Fertility, Mortality and Migration in Drought Prone Areas in Ethiopia', *Transactions of the Royal Society of Tropical Medicine and Hygiene*, 87: 24–8.

Lindtjørn, B., and Alemu, T. (1997), 'Intra-household correlations of Nutritional Status in Rural Ethiopia', *International Journal of Epidemiology*, 26(91): 160–5.

Livi-Bacci, M. (1991), *Population and Nutrition, An Essay on European Demographic History*, Cambridge: Cambridge University Press.

—— (1993), 'On the Human Costs of Collectivization in the Soviet Union', *Population and Development Review*, 19(4): 743–66.

Lopez, A., and Ruzicka, L. (1983), *Sex Differentials in Mortality: Trends, Determinants and Consequences*, Canberra, Australia.

Macrae, J., and Zwi, A. (eds.) (1994), *War and Hunger: Rethinking International Responses to Complex Emergencies*, London: Zed Books.

McAlpin, M. B. (1983), *Subject to Famine: Food Crises and Economic Change in Western India, 1986–1920.* Princeton: Princeton University Press.

Mehtabunisa, A. (1984), 'Women in Famine', in W. Tietze (ed.), *Famine as a Geographical Phenomenon*, Holland: Reidel Publishing.

Miller, B. D. (1997), 'Social Class, Gender, and Intra-household Food Allocation to Children in South Asia', *Social Science and Medicine*, 4(11): 1685–95.

Mokyr, J., and Ó Gráda, C. (1999), 'Famine Disease and Famine Mortality: Lessons from the Irish Experience, 1845–50', Paper presented at Fondation des Treilles, May 1999, a different version of which is published in the present book.

Moser, C. (1989), 'Gender Planning in the Third World Meeting Practical and Strategic Gender Needs', *World Development*, 11(17): 1799–825.

Ó Gráda, C. (1999), *Black '47 and Beyond. The Great Irish Famine in History, Economy and Memory*, Princeton: Princeton University Press.

Pitkänen K. J. (1999), 'Famine Mortality in Nineteenth Century Finland: Is there a Sex Bias?', Paper presented at Fondation des Treilles, May 1999, and published in revised form in the present book.

—— and Mielke, J. H. (1993), 'Age and Sex Differentials in Mortality during Two Nineteenth Century Population Crises', *European Journal of Population*, 9: 1–32.

Razzaque, A. (1989), 'Socio-demographic Differentials in Mortality during the 1974–5 Famine in a Rural Area of Bangladesh', *Journal of Biosocial Science*, 21(13–22).

—— Alam, N., Wai, L., and Foster, A. (1990), 'Sustained Effects of the 1974–5 Famine on Infant and Child Mortality in a Rural Area of Bangladesh', *Population Studies*, 44: 145–54.

Rivers, J. P. W. (1982), 'Women and Children Last: An Essay on Sex Discrimination in Disasters', *Disasters*, 6: 259–63.

—— (1988), 'The Nutritional Biology of Famine', in G. A. Harrison (ed.), *Famine*, Oxford: Oxford University Press.

Sands, B., and Buelow, S. (1998), 'China's Great Leap Forward Population Disaster: New Insights and Explanations', Paper presented at Fondation des Treilles, May 1999.

Sen, A. (1981), *Poverty and Famines, An Essay on Entitlement and Deprivation*, Oxford: Oxford University Press.

United Nations (UN) Secretariat (1998), *Too Young to Die: Genes or Gender*, New York: United Nations Publications.

Valaoras, V. G. (1946), 'Some Effects of Famine on the Population of Greece', *Millbank Memorial Fund Quarterly*, 24(3): 215–34.

Vaughan, M. (1987), *The Story of an African Famine: Gender and Famine in Twentieth Century Malawi*, Cambridge: Cambridge University Press.

Watkins, S. C., and Menken, J. (1985), 'Famines in Historical Perspective', *Population and Development Review*, 11(4): 647–75.

Wheatcroft, S. (1983), 'Famine and Epidemic Crises in Russia 1918–22: The Case of Saratov', *Annales de Demographie Historique*, 329–52.

Wrigley, E. A., and Schofield, R. S. (1981), *The Population History of England 1541–1871. A Reconstruction*, Cambridge, Mass.: Harvard University Press.

Index

Africa 19, 39, 113, 135, 142–57, 204–17, 246
agency, *see* corruption
alveolitis of the jaws 209
Altenburg, G. 183
Ano Syros 185, 189, 191
Antananarivo 204–17
antibiotics 15, 38
Athens 183–5, 188–9, 194–5
averted famines 230, 237
Aykroyd, W. R. 22, 137

bang-bang famines 13, 111; *see also* repeated harvest failure
Bangladesh famine (1974–5) 37, 65, 243, 245, 253
Bengali famine (1943–4) 38, 65, 136, 170, 244, 254
Berar
  demographic history of 93
  famine in 38, 93–112
Biafra 37
birth rate
  decline in 4, 11, 99, 110, 192–4, 199, 206, 219, 224–5, 236, 252
  'rebound' 4, 101, 111
black market 183
body fat hypothesis 9, 173–4, 242–56; *see also* mortality and gender
Bombay, famine in 38, 115, 118–22, 131, 134
Boyle, P. P. 37, 65, 66, 242, 252
Braudel, F. 154
Bujumbura 148
Bukeye 149, 151–2
Burundi 14, 142–57
  embargo on food exports 147

cachexia 198, 200
calorific intake 155, 206; *see also* food availability decline
cardiovascular diseases 171, 212
CARE 254
cash crops 155, 181, 183

Catholic missions 145
cattle mortality 109, 116
causes of death
  in Antananarivo 214
  in Berar 107
  in Greece 197–9
  in India 107–9, 113–37
  in Ireland 2–3, 19–41, 51–3
  in the Soviet Union 171–7
  in the Warsaw ghetto 2
child mortality 77, 106, 148, 170–1, 208, 209, 211–12, 253
China 1, 204, 221, 241, 243, 245–6
Chinoy, A. D. 97, 99, 100
Chios 186
cholera 51, 98, 100, 121, 125–7, 133–4, 162–3, 169, 171, 216, 230
Christophers, S. R. 136
civil registration records 68, 165–9, 186, 187
climate 116–17, 136, 137, 146, 226–30; *see also* drought, weather
coitus interruptus 194
collective memory 142, 143, 145
colonial era famines 145–9
commandeering 147
common graves 188
communal tensions 147, 150
contraception 194
cooking facilities 34, 39, 250
corruption 19, 47–8, 58, 61–2, 215
Crawford, E. M. 21, 114
CUNCHU (Soviet-era Budget Directorate) 165–7, 169
Cyclades 191
cyclical models of famine 158–60

Darfur (Sudan) 37, 66, 246
Davis, M. 2
deaths, *see* mortality
defining famine 1, 19
delayed marriage 4, 103, 155
Devereux, S. 14

de Waal, A. 66, 113, 135, 241, 246
diarrhoea 24, 34, 98, 134, 205, 212
doctors 15, 35–6, 197
Drèze, J. 16, 21, 85, 115, 137, 245
dropsy 20, 31, 47, 48
drought 115, 121, 126, 134, 146, 225
Dublin 35, 51
Dupâquier, J. 149
Dutch Hunger Winter 2, 12, 39, 65, 114, 243, 246
dysentery 24, 98, 123, 125, 134; *see also* diarrhoea

Eiríksson, A. 47, 48
Ennistymon 48
entitlements 19, 137, 216, 241, 254
epidemics 10, 24, 111, 113–37, 213–14, 230–5
Ethiopia 15, 37, 81, 243, 246, 253
ethnic conflict 142, 146, 150

famine foods 21, 253
famine relief 44–5, 87, 110, 114, 126, 147, 177, 222, 254
    outdoor vs. indoor 46–7
FAO 254
female mortality advantage, *see* mortality and gender
fertility, *see* marital fertility
Finland
    famine in 3–4, 65–92, 173
    historical famines in 81
Fitzpatrick, D. 243, 248, 254
Fogel, R. W. 21
food availability decline (FAD) 13, 14, 16, 72, 100–1, 126, 146, 183, 206
food markets 5, 14, 40, 151, 183, 216
food prices 7, 98, 99, 117, 120, 128–32, 147, 183, 206

Great Leap Forward famine 1, 37, 204, 241
Greece 6–7, 39, 65, 114, 181–203
gender, *see* mortality and gender

Hayami, A. 219, 220
Hermoupolis (Syros) 185, 186, 189–90

Hyderabad 124, 125
hygiene 22, 36, 40, 62, 137, 198, 199

Illiffe, J. 14
immunosuppression 21, 83
India 93–143, 254
infant mortality 4, 105, 148, 169–71, 236
infanticide 243, 246
infectious disease 14
    absence of in Greece 199
    in Antananarivo 212
    in Finland 75–6
    in India 107, 108, 121, 123, 125
    in Ireland 21–2, 49–52
    in Japan 235
    in Russia 173
influenza 22, 98, 125, 230
International Classification of Diseases (ICD) 171, 207, 209
Ireland 19–64, 114
    famine of 1740–1 12
    poor law 45
    workhouses 3, 44–64

Japan
    famine in 218–39, 242
    temple death registers 65, 114
jaundice 125

Kaninya 148–9, 152
Keyfitz, N. 17
Kidane, N. 246
Kinoshita, F. 220
Koch, R. 39, 41

life expectancy
    in Antananarivo 207, 209–10, 219
    in India 4, 104–6, 109
    in Japan 224, 236, 237
    in Russia 162–3
life tables 104, 107, 162, 207
Livi-Bacci, M. 39, 164, 204, 243, 245
long-term effects of famine 9, 12–13, 19–20, 109–10, 219–20

McAlpine, M. B. 173, 243, 244
MacArthur, W. A. 23, 31, 35, 51
McKeown, T. 3, 18, 39

Madagascar 7, 214–17
Madras 115, 116, 133, 244
malaria 38, 116, 119, 126, 133–6, 205–6, 213–14, 216
Malawi 37, 243, 253
malnutrition 83, 154–5, 206
  synergy between infection and 10, 21–2, 113–14
Malthus, T. R. 14, 19, 142, 156, 218, 219
manori 6, 142, 146
marasmus 20, 47, 51, 200
marital fertility, decline in 84, 104, 237, 249
measles 10, 48, 73, 209
media coverage 16, 188, 216
medical care
  access to 15, 34, 114, 198
  quality of 35–6
Menken, J. 9, 96, 219, 220, 221, 235, 241, 245
Meuvret, J. 113
migration during famines 5, 13, 86, 87, 104, 105, 137, 147
  seasonal/cyclical 181
  sex-selective 68, 87, 89, 94–5, 236, 252–3
  absence of 200
miscarriages 84
monsoon 97, 100, 107, 110, 115
mortality
  and age 10, 33, 77, 78, 88–90, 101, 106–7, 195–7, 204, 210
  and class 14–15, 34–6, 109, 123, 135, 155
  difficulties in estimating 1, 23–4, 230
  and gender 4, 48, 65–92, 105–6, 172–7, 195–7, 240–60
  maternal 84, 212, 252
  neonatal 107
  seasonality of 26, 107, 115–16
Mykonos 5, 186, 191, 194–5, 197, 246

Netherlands, *see* Dutch Hunger Winter
NGOs 9, 189, 254
nosologies, *see* causes of death
North Korea 15
Nowlan, K. 37

oedema 20, 198, 252
opium 36
oral history 85, 145, 199
osteomalacia 205

Ostrobothnia 71–2, 80, 87
Oulu 72, 74, 77
Oxfam 254

Parsonstown workhouse 47
Pasteur, L. 39, 41
pellagra 41, 198
Phytophthora infestans 41
Piraeus 39, 188
plague 109, 119, 218
pneumonia 175
political famines 6, 14, 37, 166–9
Popov, P. I. 165
Porter, A. 133
Post, J. D. 114
post-colonial famines 14, 142–56, 204–15
process, famine as 111
prostitution 243, 250, 253
public action, *see* famine relief
public health 87, 98, 114, 137, 198, 199, 216
public works 87, 99–100, 119
Punjab 133, 136

rabi (spring) crop 98, 115
Ravallion, M. 5
refugees 22, 87, 155
rehydration 3
repeated harvest failure 70, 72, 74, 96–101
Roncalli, A. 184
Russia 6, 37–8, 158–80, 243, 245

Sahel 15, 37, 204
Sands, B. 245
Satakunta 72, 77
scarlet fever (scarlatina) 47, 51
scurvy 21, 34–5
Seaman, J. 204
Sen, A. K. 5, 16, 19, 21, 37, 85, 107, 216, 241, 244–5
smallpox 48, 108, 134, 147, 162
social disruption and contagion 15, 68–9, 114, 115, 116, 124, 146, 155
Somalia 204, 243, 252
soup kitchens 184, 186, 253
starvation 20, 26, 28, 31, 32, 99, 109, 124, 137, 151, 171–2, 236, 248
stillbirths 107
suicide 11, 109
Sudan 38, 204, 243, 246

Tokugawa period 8, 219, 221–4
trypanosomiasis 146
tsuyu (wet season) 228
tuberculosis 174, 199, 212, 214
typhoid fever 31, 34, 79
typhus 10, 34, 66, 79, 169, 171, 198, 199, 200

Ukraine 1, 37, 159–60, 175
underenumeration of deaths 23, 68, 163–9, 208
under-registration, *see* civil registration records
UNHCR 254
UNICEF 207
United Provinces (India) 117, 126–7, 132
urban areas and famine 5, 16, 35, 103–4, 186, 200, 204–17

Vaasa 72, 74, 77
vaccination 108, 109, 137, 147, 151, 198

Vaughan, M. 37, 243, 253
Viipuri 77
violent deaths 19, 25, 172, 174, 212
vital statistics 7, 95–6, 100, 101, 104, 160–1, 207–8
Volga region 159–60

war and famine 13, 14, 87–8, 147, 163, 181–5, 193, 246
Warsaw ghetto 2, 39, 204, 243, 246
Watkins, S. C. 9, 96, 219, 220, 221, 235, 241, 245
weather 97–8, 131–2, 136, 228; *see also* climate
Wheatcroft, S. G. 37, 38, 245
Wilde, W. 2, 23, 32, 34, 37, 51–2
workhouse deaths 44–63

ZAGS (Soviet-era civil registers) 165–9
Zurbrigg, S. H. 116–17, 134, 136, 141, 180